ENCOURAGING DIVERSITY

ENCOURAGING DIVERSITY

The conservation and development of plant genetic resources

CONNY ALMEKINDERS and WALTER DE BOEF

INTERMEDIATE TECHNOLOGY PUBLICATIONS 2000

Intermediate Technology Publications Ltd
103–105 Southampton Row, London WC1B 4HH, UK

© Intermediate Technology Publications 2000

A CIP catalogue record for this book is available
from the British Library

ISBN   1 85339 510 2

Typeset by Dorwyn Ltd, Rowlands Castle, Hants
Printed in the UK by SRP Exeter

4. Seed legislation and the use of local genetic resources   269
    NIELS LOUWAARS and ROBERT TRIPP

5. On-farm conservation: a matter of global concern or
    local survival?   275
    ROBIN PISTORIUS and JEROEN VAN WIJK

6. Intellectual property rights: patents or *sui generis* systems?   279
    NIELS LOUWAARS and JAN ENGELS

7. Institutional transformation to support diversity   284
    JANICE JIGGINS and HELLE MUNK RAVNBORG

8. Consuming diversity: a long way to go?   288
    JOOST JONGERDEN

9. Supporting the utilization and development of traditional
    leafy vegetables in Africa   294
    JAMES CHWEYA and CONNY ALMEKINDERS

10. Policies of The Netherlands on international co-operation
    and Agenda 21   299
    HENRI JORRITSMA

11. Agricultural biodiversity: a perspective of Dutch policy-makers 302
    PETER VERMEIJ, MARCEL VERNOOY and MARIO NAGTZAAM

12. Advocacy and lobbying in South-East Asia: experiences
    of SEARICE   306
    NETH DAÑO and RENE SALAZAR

13. Plant genetic resources in Europe: an NGO perspective   310
    PATRICK MULVANY

Synthesis: Towards integration of policy frameworks   317
    JAAP HARDON, JAN ENGELS and BERT VISSER

Section VII. Encouraging Diversity: a Synthesis of Crop Conservation and Development

1. Discouraging or encouraging diversity   323
    CONNY ALMEKINDERS and WALTER DE BOEF

2. Reversing the treadmill and restoring agro-ecosystem resilience 325
    WALTER DE BOEF, CONNY ALMEKINDERS and NIELS RÖLING

3. Synthesis between crop conservation and development   330
    CONNY ALMEKINDERS, WALTER DE BOEF and JAN ENGELS

4. Adaptive plant genetic resource management   339
    WALTER DE BOEF, CONNY ALMEKINDERS, JAN ENGELS
    and NIELS RÖLING

References   348

Foreword

M.S. Swaminathan and Gelia Castillo

Since the early 1980s, plant genetic resources have become a very hot global political issue and much has changed in the principle and concept of ownership of plant genetic resources. From the rather romantic ethos of genetic diversity as the heritage of humankind; it became an area of common concern, and now it is a matter of national sovereignty. Along with these changes came numerous meetings, plenty of words but not many deeds.

It has been our great privilege to know and work with Jaap Hardon, one of the leading authorities on issues relating to PGR. Jaap Hardon's distinctive contribution is achieving a synthesis between crop development and conservation. His inputs are unique because they come not only in thoughts, in words but also in actual deeds where advocacy is not a substitute for action. Long before the Convention on Biological Diversity (CBD) came into force in December, 1993, Jaap Hardon had been both advocating and practising the three major principles of CBD, namely, conservation, sustainable use and equitable sharing of benefits.

The current book and the associated workshop organized in 1997 in Baarlo, The Netherlands, provide us with a comprehensive and comprehensible array of experiences and insights on the science, ethics, economics, politics, dynamics and significance of plant genetic resources. Distinguishing features of the Baarlo get-together and the book *Encouraging Diversity* are that all participants and authors have actually done something about plant genetic resources, whether on the ground; in advocacy; in negotiations; in policy; in research; and in programmes on conservation and use. Although there are contentious issues and even conflicts, what emerge for us are many common threads pulling together and fewer divergences driving us apart. Even so-called predatory interests will need genetic diversity to sustain predatory activities.

Plant genetic resources are truly a human legacy whose reality comes through the sophistication of gene banks, the beauty of botanical gardens and arboreta, the commercial products of the formal seed system, and the literally down-to-earth existence of these resources in farmers' fields, in household gardens in tribal and rural communities, in forests, in diverse environments and in many nooks and corners of the world, some yet unknown and untapped. Plant genetic resources are truly a global resource on which all of us depend for our food and health security. It seems such a wonderful resource around which to build a One-World Community. Farm and rural families do not conserve plant genetic resources to serve the interests of humanity, in the abstract. It is also quite clear that cultural diversity will not endure without genetic diversity. What a boring world it would be if genetic uniformity became the norm, and diversity, the exception.

Above all, the 1997 workshop and present book will help us to articulate a community-centred Gene Management System. Tribal and rural farming communities have a long tradition of serving as custodians of genetic wealth, particularly landraces often carrying rare and valuable genes for traits like resistance to biotic and abiotic stresses, adaptability and nutritional quality. Several land types that carry valuable genes are preserved by farmers for religious functions and they constitute valuable material for conservation and sustainable use. Women in particular have been the principal seed selectors and savers. Local landraces are still being maintained largely by the rural and tribal poor. They thus serve public good at personal cost. Such poverty-ridden custodians of genetic wealth are increasingly confronted with severe socio-economic problems, which are rendering the maintenance of their traditional conservation ethics difficult. Steps are urgently needed to link their conservation efforts to the strengthening of their livelihoods.

While *in situ* and *ex situ* conservation efforts receive support from public funds, *in situ* on-farm conservation by rural and tribal women and men remains largely unrecognized and unrewarded. Yet, farmers addressed with this conservation strategy are responsible for the conservation of valuable intra-specific variability. High-yielding rice varieties developed at IRRI, for example each contain over 20 landraces in their pedigree.

No further time should be lost in giving operational content to the ethics and equity principles enshrined in CBD with reference to benefit sharing. Conservers and consumers should both derive benefit from genetic wealth. For in the final analysis, PGR issues are as much about people as they are about genetics. But in many ways, the technical specificities determine what the people's issues are and what can be done about them. In this regard, indigenous knowledge and modern science, social and biophysical environments, and breeders and farmers must meet for the common cause of plant genetic resources. We believe that these are the central messages of the workshop in Baarlo and of this book.

Acknowledgements

Based on their experiences in working for and with farmers in plant genetic resource conservation, various organizations and stakeholders, express a diversity of perspectives in the debate on how to link conservation and development objectives in agricultural development. *Encouraging Diversity* is a collection of experiences and perspectives of the people involved. In the summer of 1997, a diverse group of people discussed the link between plant genetic resource conservation and development in a workshop in Baarlo, The Netherlands. The workshop was followed by a process that shaped the present book, with the majority of the workshop participants acting as authors of the chapters. We should like to consider *Encouraging Diversity* as a subsequent step in the debate.

The authors were prepared to document and share with others their experiences and perspectives on local management of genetic diversity. We thank them for their participation in the discussions and for their inspiring papers. We also thank them for their patience during the long preparation and editing process. At times, this meant making or accepting dramatic changes in the length or flow of reasoning in their papers. We hope that the authors feel as we do: that the book's compilation and development has been a learning process.

We believe that *Encouraging Diversity* is loyal to its title as it presents and reflects a diversity of opinions and experiences, dialogues and debates. Each of these is relevant and forms a piece in a total picture forming a synthesis between crop conservation and development. We realize that some of our interpretations and reviews of contributions do not conform to authors' intentions. We have tried to maintain the original perspectives while positioning the papers in the book's overall structure in such a manner that the presentation of the diversity of perspectives becomes more distinct.

The book is the result of a three-year project of the Centre for Genetic Resources (CGN), The Netherlands in collaboration with the International Plant Genetic Resources Institute (IPGRI). A team consisting of the following people supported us in the process of organization of the workshop and development of the book: Jan Engels, Jaap Hardon, Niels Röling and Bert Visser. They were joined by Jürgen Hagmann, Gary Atlin, Gordon Prain and Trygve Berg in the editing process. We thank them for their vital contributions to the book in the form of ideas, guidance, critical reflections and support.

A range of people has been vital in realizing various aspects of the workshop and the book. Maurice Starren and Teatske de Vries provided administrative support to the Baarlo workshop and the start of the book, respectively. Jürgen Hagmann, Petra Künkel and Joshua Mushauri facilitated the process and debate during the workshop. Helga Verkerke-Berentschot supported us during the entire project. We thank her for professional support and for being our 'tower of strength' in various respects. Special thanks to Michel Pimbert. We thank Linda Sears, Ilonka Barsony and Anne Sweetmore for their support in editing and assisting the publication of the book. We particularly want to thank Neal Burton, because he always encouraged and inspired us.

The following organizations financially and institutionally supported the project that resulted in the workshop and this book: the German Enterprise for Technical Co-operation (GTZ), the International Development Research Centre (IDRC), The Netherlands Directorate General for International Co-operation (DGIS), The Netherlands Ministry of Agriculture, Nature Management and Fisheries (LNV), the Swedish International Development Authority (SIDA), the Swiss Development Co-operation (SDC), the Technical Centre for Agricultural and Rural Co-operation (CTA), the Centre for Plant Breeding and Reproduction Research (CPRO-DLO), the International Plant Genetic Resources Institute (IPGRI), the Royal Tropical Institute (KIT) and Intermediate Technology Publications (IT).

Finally, we want to express our appreciation to Jaap Hardon, the founding director of CGN. He has played an active role in the international PGR debate. Building on his role we were able to organize the workshop and develop the book. We consider the workshop and the book to be products of a period in Wageningen in which Jaap played an active role and contributed in a rather specific manner to the conservation and development discussion. We hope that the workshop and book are in line with his encouraging role.

Walter de Boef and Conny Almekinders
Wageningen, November 1999

Contributors

Conny Almekinders is an agro-ecologist; she addresses various fields in the management of agro-biodiversity (local seed supply and participatory plant breeding) and is involved in various international programmes. *Address: c/o Plant Research International – CGN, PO Box 16, 6700 AA Wageningen, The Netherlands.*

Woldeamlak Araia is agronomist and staff member at the University of Asmara, presently involved in studying mixed cropping systems in Eritrea. *Address: University of Asmara, PO Box 1220, Asmara, Eritrea.*

Gary Atlin is a professor in plant breeding. He worked as a plant breeder in Peru and is presently running a public wheat and barley breeding programme. *Address: Nova Scotia Agricultural College, Truro, NS, B2N 5E3, Canada.*

Carlos Basilio trained as a soil scientist; he has worked in IIRR and was ILEIA programme co-ordinator for the Philippines. He is presently a research fellow in UPWARD, addressing participatory R&D, sustainable agriculture and natural resource management. *Address: CIP-UPWARD, PCARRD Complex, Los Baños, 4030 Laguna, The Philippines.*

Frank Begemann is the head of the Information Centre for Genetic Resources (IGR) at the German Centre for Documentation and Information in Agriculture (ZADI). *Address: ZADI, Villichgasse 17, D-53177 Bonn, Germany.*

Trygve Berg is trained as a plant breeder, but is currently working on development issues on agricultural production with particular interest in the management of PGR. He is involved in a number of research programmes in Ethiopia. Berg is one of the founding members of the CBDC. *Address: NORAGRIC, PO Box 5001, 1432 Ås, Norway.*

Arma Bertuso is an agronomist working as SEARICE, addressing PGR, participatory research, plant breeding, gender and policy issues. She works in the CBDC programme. *Address: SEARICE, Unit 331 Eagle Court Condominium, 26 Matalino Street, Central District, Diliman, Quezon City, Philippines.*

Walter de Boef is trained as a plant breeder. He worked at CGN in PGR and international development (a.o. CBDC). He now works in the areas of agro-biodiversity, institutional development, and development of participatory approaches in research and planning. *Address: Royal Tropical Institute (KIT), PO Box 95001, 1090 HA Amsterdam, The Netherlands.*

Susan Bragdon is a lawyer by training, she works at IPGRI in Rome. She is an expert in the field of institutional, policy and legal aspects of plant genetic resources. She particularly supports national plant genetic resources programmes in this field. *Address: IPGRI, Via delle Sette Chiese 142, 00145, Rome, Italy.*

Rodrigo Catalán is a forester working at CET in the CBDC-project in Chile. He addresses in particular community strategies in the management and utilization of biodiversity in agriculture and in nature. *Address: CET, PO Box 200, Temuco, Chile.*

James Chweya was a crop scientist and professor at the University of Nairobi, specialized in African leafy vegetables. At the time of his death he was on sabbatical and worked full time with IPGRI as an honorary Fellow. He was also adviser to the African Programme of the CBDC. James Chweya died unexpectedly in May 1999.

Pompeyo Cosío is an agronomist working on root and tubercrops in Peru. *Address: University San Antonio Abad, Centro de Investigación de Cultivos Andinos (CICA), PO Box 973, Cuzco, Peru.*

Elizabeth Cromwell is an agricultural economist and a Research Fellow at the Overseas Development Institute, London, an independent non-governmental think-tank on development policy. Her particular interests lie in assessing policy for local-level crop genetic resources conservation and seed supply. *Address: ODI, Portland House, Stag Place, London SW1E 5DP, United Kingdom.*

Neth Daño is the Executive Director of SEARICE. She has degrees in development studies and community development from the University of the Philippines. She has initiated policy advocacy campaigns with SEA-RICE and joined the official Philippine delegation in several international negotiations on biodiversity and PGR. *Address: c/o SEARICE, Unit 331 Eagle Court Condominium, 26 Matalino Street, Central District, Diliman, Quezon City, Philippines.*

Arjan van Donk is a plant breeder at East-West Seed Company in the Philippines. He is in charge of the vegetable breeding programme. *Address: East-West Seed Company, PO Box 2384, MCPO, 1263 Makati, Metro Manila, The Philippines.*

Donald Duvick is a plant breeder by profession and was senior vice-president for research at Pioneer Hi-Bred International Inc., in the USA. At present he is an affiliate professor at Iowa State University, USA. He is involved in the international PGR debate, representing professional plant breeders. *Address: 6837 NW Beaver Drive, PO Box 446, Johnston, IA 50131, USA.*

Anne Elings is a plant breeder. He worked at ICARDA and CIMMYT. He has been working at CGN particularly addressing participatory plant breeding. He presently is with the Department of Crop and Production Ecology of AB-DLO. *Address: Plant Research International, PO Box 14, 6700 AA Wageningen, The Netherlands.*

Jan Engels is trained as a plant breeder. He has been involved in the development of PGR in various countries (Ethiopia, Costa Rica). He is Director of the Plant Genetic Resources Science and Technology Division of IPGRI. *Address: IPGRI, Via delle Sette Chiese 142, 00145, Rome, Italy.*

Miguel Esquivel has worked in the conservation of PGR in Cuba for a long time, as is clear from his many publications in that field. He is presently stationed at the Parque Natural Cristóbal Colón. *Address: Parque Natural Cristóbal Colón, Reparto Naútico, Cuidad de Havana, Cuba.*

Cary Fowler is a political scientist with experience in the field of PGR. He was in charge of the unit at FAO that led the process to Technical Conference in Liepzig, 1996, He now works at NORAGRIC addressing these issues in research and education. *Address: NORAGRIC, PO Box 5002, N 1532 Ås, Norway.*

Esbern Friis-Hansen is a social geographer at the Centre for Development Research, Denmark. He worked for a long time in Tanzania addressing issues related to PGR and seed supply. He has continued with this research work, being involved in a number of projects – particularly in Africa. *Address: CDR Gammel Kongevej 5, DK-1610 Copenhagen V, Denmark.*

Julio Gabriel is a plant breeder working at the PROINPA (Promotion and Investigation of Andean Products) Foundation. He has been collaborating with farmers in his potato breeding programme since 1990. *Address: Fundación PROINPA, PO Box 4285 Cochabamba, Bolivia.*

Gilda Ginogaling is a community trainer at CONSERVE (Philippines). She is involved in grass-roots work addressing on-farm conservation and supporting farmer breeding. *Address: CONSERVE, c/o Unit 331 Eagle Court Condominium, 26 Matalino Street, Central District, Diliman, Quezon City, Philippines.*

Cosmas Gonese is a conservationist, director of AZTREC, the Association of Zimbabwean Traditional Conservationists, a member of the COMPAS programme and networker for indigenous African knowledge in the Sadec area. *Address: c/o AZTREC, PO Box 9286, Masvingo, Zimbabwe.*

Jürgen Hagmann is working as a consultant, addressing the field of natural resources management, participatory approaches in planning and rural extension. He was involved for a long time in a project of the extension department in Zimbabwe. He acts as facilitator in meetings at various levels. *Address: Talstrasse 129, D-79194 Gundelfingen, Germany.*

Jaap Hardon is a plant breeder by profession; he was the founding director of the Centre for Genetic Resources, The Netherlands. In that capacity he was involved in the international debates on PGR. He fulfilled various functions in international programmes related to CG-institutes, but is also a founding member of the CBDC programme. *Address: Hartenseweg 18, 6705 BJ Wageningen, The Netherlands.*

Antine Hardon-Baars is a home-ecologist by training. Through her rich professional career she has gained extensive experience in fields that can be characterized as a combination of gender, participation, ecology, mediation and organizational aspects. She officially retired from the Wageningen University in 1999, but continues to function as the co-ordinator of the Dutch support group of UPWARD. *Address: Hartenseweg 18, 6705 BJ Wageningen, The Netherlands.*

Bertus Haverkort is an agronomist and social scientist. Presently he is programme manager of COMPAS, the programme for comparing and supporting endogenous development. *Address: ETC/Compas, PO Box 64, 3830 AB Leusden, The Netherlands.*

Theo van Hintum is a plant breeder by training and works at CGN. In his research, he addresses methodological issues related to genetic aspects, documentation and information related to PGR conservation. He has played a leading role in the development of the concept of core-collections. *Address: CGN, PO Box 16, 6700 AA Wageningen, The Netherlands.*

Devra Jarvis is an ecologist; she is the project co-ordinator of the IPGRI project on strengthening the scientific basis of *in situ* conservation on-farm. *Address: IPGRI, Via delle Sette Chiese 142, Rome, Italy.*

Janice Jiggins is a human ecologist, professor at the Swedish University of Agricultural Sciences. She has experience in the fields of rural service provision, agricultural research management and extension. Key areas are gender, participatory research and resource users' management of nature resources. *Address: Department of Rural Development Studies, Swedish University of Agricultural Sciences, PO Box 7005, 750 07 Upsala, Sweden.*

Joost Jongerden is a sociologist. He is involved in several special projects on the use of agrobiodiversity from the production chain perspective. *Address: Technology and Agrarian Development, Wageningen University, Nieuwe Kanaal 11, 6709 PA Wageningen, The Netherlands.*

Henri Jorritsma is the former Deputy Director of the Environment and Development Department in the Directorate General International Co-operation (DGIS). He is now Deputy Director of the Policy and Operations Development Department. *Address: Ministry of Foreign Affairs, PO Box 20061, 2500 EB The Hague.*

Krishna D. Joshi is a plant breeder, working with LI-BIRD in the field of participatory crop improvement. He has long experience in developing PCI approaches in Nepal. *Address: LI-BIRD Chitwan-office, c/o PO Box 324, Pokhara, Nepal.*

Dominique Louette is an agronomist who has been working for several years in a special project based in the Biosphere Reserve 'Sierra de Manantlan' of the University of Guadelajara. She studied maize seed production and exchange practices of the farmers in communities in the Biosphere. *Address: IMECBIO, 151 Avenida Independencia National, Autlan, Jalisco, Mexico.*

Niels Louwaars is a plant breeder by training. He has wide experience in seed programmes in developing countries. He is presently working at CPRO-DLO and focusing on seed sector programmes and related legislative frameworks. *Address: Plant Research International, PO Box 16, 6700 AA Wageningen, The Netherlands.*

Shawn McGuire is a biologist and social scientist working at Wageningen University. He is doing PhD research in Ethiopia addressing institutional and participatory aspects related to PGR and crop development. *Address: Technology and Agrarian Development, Nieuwe Kanaal 11, 6709 PA Wageningen, The Netherlands.*

Kristen Mercer studies weed ecology in the Department of Agronomy and Plant Genetics. *Address: University of Minnesota, Minneapolis, Minnesota, 55455, USA.*

Camila Montecinos is an agronomist. She is involved in the international PGR debate, but also works at the community level of PGR management. She is one founding members, and has fulfilled various functions in CBDC. *Address: CET, PO Box 200, Temuco, Chile.*

Stephen Morin is an anthropologist working in the social science division and involved in *in situ* activities at IRRI. *Address: IRRI, MCPO Box 3127, Makati City, The Philippines.*

Stephen Mugo is a plant breeder of the Kenyan Agricultural Research Institute (KARI), but has been working at CIMMYT in Mexico and is presently working at CIMMYT in Nairobi, Kenya. *Address: CIMMYT, PO Box 25171 Nairobi, Kenya.*

Patrick Mulvany is the Food Security Policy Adviser at Intermediate Technology Development Group (ITDG). He has wide experience in agricultural development activities and small-scale farmers. He is currently specializing on agrobiodiversity issues. Among his activities he is the NGO appointee on the Steering Group of the ECP/GR. *Address: ITDG, Schumacher Centre, Bourton Hall, Bourton-on-Dunsmore, Rugby, CV23 9QZ, United Kingdom.*

Helle Munk Ravnborg is a socio-technological and environmental planner and has worked at the Hillsides project at CIAT in Colombia. She has worked extensively on issues related to agricultural research and its relevance to poor farmers. She currently works on collective action in natural resource management. *Address: CDR, Gammel Kongevej 5, DK – 1610 Copenhagen, Denmark.*

Mario Nagtzaam is staff-officer in the Directorate Agriculture with specific tasks in the area of genetic resources. *Address: Ministry of Agriculture, Nature Management and Fisheries, PO Box 20401, 2500 EK Den Haag, The Netherlands.*

Jan-Peter Nap is molecular biologist at CPRO-DLO, working on the predictability of transgene expression in genetically modified plants and biosafety of transgenes in plants. *Address: CPRO-DLO, PO Box 16, 6700 AA Wageningen, The Netherlands.*

Julia Ndungú-Skilton is an agronomist/seed technologist. She is working at IPGRI within the project on strengthening the scientific basis of *in situ* conservation on-farm, supporting the projects in Sub-Saharan Africa, especially Ethiopia and Burkina Faso. *Address: IPGRI-SSA, c/o ICRAF, PO Box 30677 Nairobi, Kenya.*

Kahiu Ngugi is a biotechnologist of the Kenyan Agricultural Research Institute (KARI), stationed in Machakos. *Address: KARI, PO Box 340 Machakos, Kenya.*

Anja Oetmann is a plant scientist who works at the Information Centre for Genetic Resources (IGR) at the German Centre for Documentation and Information in Agriculture (ZADI). *Address: ZADI, Villichgasse 17, D-53177 Bonn, Germany.*

Isolde Peréz is a community trainer and research assistant in the field of PGR and seed supply at CET. She works in the CBDC-project in Chile. *Address: CET, PO Box 200, Temuco, Chile.*

Jean-Louis Pham is a geneticist seconded by the IRD (France) at IRRI. In his work, he addresses genetic aspects of *in situ* conservation of PGR. He is involved in a number of rice genetic resources projects in Asia. *Address: IRRI, MCPO Box 3127, Makati City, The Philippines.*

Robin Pistorius is a historian and political scientist. He was awarded the IPGRI Vavilov-Frankel fellowship for which he wrote *Scientists, Plants and Politics: A history of the plant genetic resources movement (1996).* He finished his PhD with *The Exploitation of Plant Genetic Information: Political Strategies in Crop Development* (co-author Jeroen van Wijk) in 1999. *Address: Plant Research International-CGN, Box 16, 6700 AA Wageningen, The Netherlands.*

Garrett Pittenger was president of the NGO, Seed of Diversity, Canada, a network of gardeners and farmers who are working to preserve the old crop varieties. He maintains old sweet corn and potato varieties on 20 hectares 50 km north of Toronto. *Address: 16812 Humber Station Road, R.R. #3, Caledon East, O LON 1EO, Ontario, Canada.*

Gordon Prain is a social anthropologist who has worked extensively in South America and Asia, especially on issues related to crop genetic diversity and seed systems. In Asia he was co-ordinator of a participatory R&D programme (UPWARD) with a strong genetic resources component. He now co-ordinates the CGIAR Global Strategic Initiative on Urban and Peri-Urban Agriculture. *Address: CIP, Avenida La Universidad 795, Apartado Postal 1558, Lima 12, Peru.*

Ram B. Rana is a socio-economist at LI-BIRD. He is currently involved in research on socio-economic, cultural and political contexts of farmer decision-making processes in PGR management on-farm. He is also

Acronyms

ACES	Agency for Community Education and Services, Philippines
AFLP	amplified fragment length polymorphism
BAZ	Federal Centre for Breeding Research on Cultivated Plants (Bundesanstalt für Züchtungsforschung an Kulturpflanzen)
BoANRD	Bureau of Agriculture and Natural Resource Development, Ethiopia
BSE	bovine spongiform encephalopathy
CAAS	Chinese Academy of Agricultural Science
CBD	Convention on Biological Diversity
CBDC	Community Biodiversity Development and Conservation
CET-CLADES	Centro Educacíon y Tecnología
CGIAR	Consultative Group on International Agricultural Research
CGN/CPRO-DLO	Centre for Genetic Resources, the Netherlands
CIAT	Centro Internacional de Agricultura Tropical (CGIAR)
CIMMYT	International Maize and Wheat Improvement Center (Centro Internacional de Mejoramiento de Maíz y Trigo) (CGIAR)
CIP	International Potato Center (Centro Internacional de la Papa) (CGIAR)
CPRO-DLO	Center for Plant Breeding and Reproduction Research, the Netherlands
DFID	Department for International Development, UK
DGIS	Directorate General of International Co-operation, the Netherlands
ECP/GR	European Co-operative Programme of Genetic Resource Networks
EMBRAPA	Empresa Brasileira de Pesquisa Agropecuaria
EPLF	Eritrean People's Liberation Front
EPRDF	Ethiopian People's Revolutionary Democratic Front
FAO	Food and Agriculture Organization of the United Nations
GEF	Global Environmental Facility
GRAIN	Genetic Resources Action International
GTZ	Gesellschaft für Technische Zusammenarbeit (German Development Agency)
HDRA	Henry Doubleday Research Association, UK

HYV	high-yielding varieties
IADP	Integrated Agricultural Development Programme, Ethiopia
IARC	International Agricultural Research Centre
IBPGR	International Board for Plant Genetic Resources (formerly IPGRI) (CGIAR)
ICA	Instituto Colombiano Agropecuario, Colombia
ICARDA	International Center for Agricultural Research in Dry Areas (CGIAR)
ICDA	International Coalition for Development
ICRISAT	International Crops Research Institute for the Semi-Arid Tropics (CGIAR)
IITA	International Institute of Tropical Agriculture (CGIAR)
INIAA	Peruvian Institute for Agricultural Research
INIFAT	Instituto de Investigaciones Fundamentales en Agricultura Tropical, Cuba
IPK	Institute of Crop Science and Plant Breeding (Institut für Pflanzenzüchtung und Kulturpflanzenforschung)
IPR	intellectual property rights
IRD	Research and Development, France (formerly ORSTOM)
IRG	International Rice Gene bank
IRRI	International Rice Research Institute (CGIAR)
ISTA	International Seed Testing Association
ITDG	Intermediate Technology Development Group
KADAMA	Confederation of Nationalist Peasants (Kaisahan ng Diwang Anakbukid na Makabayan), Philippines
KARI	Kenyan Agricultural Research Institute
MASIPAG	Farmer–Scientist Partnerships in Agricultural Development, Philippines
NGO	non-governmental organization
NORAGRIC	Norwegian Institute for International Agricultural Development
OECD	Organization for Economic Co-operation and Development
PBR	plant breeders' rights (legislation)
PCI	Participatory Crop Improvement
PCSD	Philippine Council for Sustainable Development
PGRC	Plant Gene Resources Canada
PGRFA	Plant Genetic Resources for Food and Agriculture
PPB	participatory plant breeding
PROINPA	Promotion and Investigation of Andean Products Foundation
PTA-net	Projeto Tecnologias Alternativas, Brazil
PVS	participatory varietal selection
R&D	research and development

RAFI	Rural Advancement Foundation International
RAPD	random amplified polymorphic DNA
REST	Relief Society of Tigre (Ethiopia)
SEARICE	South-East Asian Regional Institute for Community Education
SoDC	Seeds of Diversity Canada
SSE	Seed Savers Exchange, USA
STMS	sequence-tagged microsatellites
TPLF	Tigrean People's Liberation Front
TPS	technology protection system (Terminator gene)
TRIPS	Trade Related Aspects of Intellectual Property Rights
UNCED	United Nations Conference on Environment and Development
UNEP	United Nations Environmental Programme
UNHCR	UN High Commission for Refugees
UPLB	University of the Philippines at Los Baños
UPOV	Union Internationale pour la Protection des Obtentions Végétales
VCU	'value for cultivation and use' seed tests
WTO	World Trade Organization

international agreements, e.g. the Convention on Biological Diversity and the Agreements associated with the World Trade Organization, relate to conservation and development, and farmers' management and utilization of genetic diversity.

We conclude the book in Section 7 with four chapters that together outline the synthesis between crop conservation and development. This section brings together the diversity of perspectives as elaborated throughout the book. In the first chapter, we draw the conclusion that the synthesis can be achieved through encouraging diversity and learning in crop development. The second chapter proposes that a basic tenet of such a strategy is that crop development organizations approach farmers' PGR management in a context of farmers' dynamic livelihood systems. A way to move forward is elaborated in the third chapter. Actions that support and build upon farmers' collective action are emphasized as ways to reverse the treadmill of agricultural development and restore resilience in agro-ecosystems. In the subsequent chapter, the experiences reported in Sections 3, 4 and 5 are drawn together in one framework. The conclusion is that a diversity of activities of conservationists, breeders and seed technologists supporting farmers' management are reconciled in a common goal to support farmers' capacity to manage and utilize plant genetic resources. *In situ* conservation is seen as a goal that can be achieved by a multitude of activities and supported by a diversity of actors. The final chapter in Section 7 explores adaptive management as new framework that unites the perspectives of the actors involved. It further has the potential to guide a process that mainstreams and scales up individual experiences and efforts. In adaptive management, farmers, stakeholders, researchers and policy makers become engaged in a continuous process of experimentation and learning in PGR management. Practices in such an approach become responsive to dynamic agro-ecological and socio-economic conditions. We further elaborate on the synthesis between crop conservation and development, recognizing that 'encouraging diversity' is a common objective in defining action agendas. This section concludes by presenting some new options and perspectives that have the potential to contribute to developing an institutional framework that accommodates crop conservation and development by defining their common basis in PGR management. With this section, we do not attempt to arrive at a conclusion, but prepare a next step in the conservation and development debate. Above all, we place PGR management in a context of sustainable agricultural development and draw a new picture merging the local and institutional circles of crop conservation and development.

SECTION I
DIVERSITY, CROP CONSERVATION AND DEVELOPMENT

1.1. Genetic diversity, conservation and development

Jaap Hardon, Donald Duvick and Bert Visser

Overview

The scientific, social, political and legal environments surrounding agrobiodiversity have become complex and even contentious since the early 1980s. Agrobiodiversity has become recognized as a major strategic natural resource, unequally divided between regions but crucial to food security, poverty alleviation and sustainable development. At the same time, agrobiodiversity has become increasingly important to often-conflicting economic interests, providing the raw material for the increasingly privatized plant breeding and biotechnology industries. As such, biodiversity is now the focus of debate in multiple intergovernmental fora and is the subject of international conventions and laws and regulations in a growing number of countries. Developments are increasingly motivated by the economic interest of international industry in a globalizing market economy. These trends affect the livelihoods of farmers whose interests in agrobiodiversity are often poorly represented, and in general are not well understood.

International policy environment

In traditional agriculture genetic diversity is viewed as a common good freely exchanged among farmers and between communities. The FAO upheld that principle in the International Undertaking on Plant Genetic Resources (FAO, 1983), and referred to genetic diversity as a 'heritage of mankind', suggesting shared ownership and open access, and thus a shared responsibility for its conservation. The Undertaking represented an agricultural philosophy of mutual interdependence and shared interests. Plant breeders' rights (PBR) legislation, enacted in industrial countries since the 1930s to stimulate private investment in plant breeding, was considered not to be in conflict with the principles of the Undertaking as it does not restrict the use of protected varieties as a free source for further breeding. The concept of farmers' rights was introduced by the International Commission on Plant Genetic Resources to recognize the important role that farmers have played and are playing in conserving and managing genetic diversity.

However, the UN Conference on Environment and Development, the 1992 Convention on Biological Diversity, Agenda 21 as its Action Plan, and the negotiations of Trade-related Intellectual Property Rights (TRIPS) resulted in a fundamentally different situation. The previous modest agricultural philosophy of the FAO Undertaking was replaced by an industrial approach, viewing genetic resources as an economic commodity subject to national sovereignty and intellectual property rights. Owing to the unequal geographic distribution of genetic diversity, with major centres in the tropics and subtropics, control over genetic resources became an issue in global politics and the North–South dialogue. In addition, PBR protection was strengthened through negotiations of the Union Internationale pour la Protection des Obtentions Végétales (UPOV) agreement in 1991, limiting farmers in multiplying their own seeds of protected varieties and their use in further breeding. Hence all developments seem to conspire to reduce individual control, increase the dependency of farmers and promote the commercial interests of private industry.

The politicization of plant genetic resources has led to a reassessment of the value of genetic diversity as a basic resource for plant breeding and biotechnology. Biotechnology has opened the way (though still hotly debated) to patenting plants, animals and specific characters, suggesting opportunities for the commercial exploitation of original diversity. Large economic benefits are expected to be gained from employing biotechnology. Previously regarded as an abundant and free resource, biodiversity is now perceived in international policy dialogue as having economic value and scarcity through unequal distribution between countries and regions. This has introduced the issues of access and ownership.

Definitions of agrobiodiversity

Agrobiodiversity can be defined in different ways. The Convention on Biological Diversity adopted a very wide definition, which includes the genetic diversity among all living organisms associated with cultivating crops and rearing animals, and the ecological complexes of which they are part. This definition projects a holistic view of agriculture, and includes sustainability through interactions between crops and the total growing environment as an important consideration. FAO, in the International Undertaking on Plant Genetic Resources (FAO, 1983) and the 1996 (Leipzig) Global Plan of Action for the Conservation and Sustainable Utilization of Plant Genetic Resources, uses a more limited definition of agrobiodiversity which restricts it to the actual crops: the genetic diversity represented in (i) cultivated varieties (cultivars) in current use and newly developed varieties; (ii) obsolete cultivars; (iii) primitive (farmer-developed) cultivars (landraces); (iv) wild and weedy species, near relatives of cultivated varieties; and (v) special genetic stocks (including élite and current breeders' lines and mutants). To this should be added the animal genetic resources present in both modern and traditional breeds of farm animals, and the genetic diversity of forest species.

These definitions are not contradictory. The Convention on Biological Diversity's emphasis on the sustainability of agricultural production is concepts used to describe crop genetic diversity and its changes in agro-ecosystems. Any agro-ecosystem, whether 'modern' or 'traditional', can be described as a set of populations that compete or co-operate to occupy the land. To describe genetic diversity in an agro-ecosystem, this set of populations must be described.

Describing and estimating genetic diversity in agro-ecosystems

When studying genetic diversity, several levels can be recognized: diversity between crops and within crops, both spatial and temporal, and diversity at the system level, influenced by natural factors and human use. Here we discuss the diversity of crops and of varieties or landraces within crops.

Crops
In order to describe and estimate the genetic diversity of agro-ecosystems, it is necessary to understand the crops they contain and their spatial and temporal distribution. A common functional division is into food, fodder, industrial, medicinal and ornamental crops. Food crops can be further subdivided on the basis of their nutritional contribution into cereals (starch), pulses (proteins) and vegetables (minerals, vitamins). The main purpose of the system – primarily for household food supply, income generation (markets), or both – is critical to understanding.

Accounting for spatial or temporal distributions might require an analysis using weights, comparable to the calculation of effective population sizes in population genetics. If, for example, 10 crops are grown in an area, but one crop occupies 95 per cent of the total area, some weight factor could be included to differentiate between the 'actual' number and the 'relative' or 'effective' number of crops.

Varieties or landraces
Within each crop, genetic diversity in a system depends on the varieties or landraces grown. At this level we need to know the genetic diversity within and between these varieties or landraces, and their spatial and temporal distribution.

For quick descriptions of varietal diversity we could simply count the number of different populations, that is, varieties or landraces, grown in the system. The populations could be classified into functional groups according to farmers' or scientists' perceptions (late/early, home consumption/market, etc.). The population structure is also highly relevant. Are the populations highly homogeneous varieties of self-pollinating or clonal crops? Are they hybrid varieties? Or are they open-pollinated or highly polymorphic, selfing landraces? Finally, the presence in the agro-ecosystem of wild relatives should be taken into account if gene flow between wild and cultivated plant occurs.

Accounting for spatial or temporal distribution requires an approach similar to that described for diversity in crops.

Adaptive diversity

If we wish to go further and quantify within- and between-population diversity, a first obstacle is the definition of genetic diversity at this level. Is it the range of adaptive traits, or is it the number of alleles? If we use the last definition, do we consider neutral alleles or adaptive alleles, which are affected by selection? Again, the type of diversity considered will depend on the purpose of the analysis. The second problem is gathering data, because quantifying each type of diversity has its own problems.

To estimate adaptive diversity at the phenotypic level (the level at which it is expressed in the field) requires relatively large-scale field experiments in the area studied. Furthermore, the expression of adaptive traits such as agronomic characters (earliness, yield, disease resistance, etc.); aspects of plant habit (height, number of leaves, colour, etc.); and quality (taste, protein content, storability, etc.) is often strongly influenced by the environment in which the crop is grown. Therefore, to obtain a reliable estimate of genotypic expression we need to use replicated trials in different environments, if possible over several years. Because the environment does not have the same influence on expression in each genotype, estimates of diversity within and between populations will depend on the location where the testing is done. For example, if an experiment is carried out in an environment with a short growing period, all materials requiring a long growing period will show hardly any diversity for yield: they will all have poor yields. Only materials adapted to the environment will express their true diversity. A final complication of this type of diversity is that the expressed phenotype is usually based on large numbers of genes, each with a relatively small contribution to the actual expression. So what is being measured is not which genes are present, but the additive effect of all those present; a similar expression might be based on completely different genotypes.

Because of all these complications in measuring the diversity of adaptive phenotypes we may prefer to look at traits that are more closely linked to the actual genes, by studying DNA or looking at products derived directly from DNA.

Marker technology

The technology needed for this approach is generally referred to as marker technology. Many types of markers are available, such as storage proteins, isoenzymes and a large variety of DNA markers including RAPD (random amplified polymorphic DNA), AFLP (amplified fragment length polymorphism), STMS (sequence-tagged microsatellites), and other markers that are not discussed in detail here (see e.g. Bretting and Widrlechner, 1995). Factors to take into account when selecting a marker technology are the number of markers available of that type; the level of polymorphism per marker; the genetic behaviour of the marker (locus specificity, dominance, etc.); the reproducibility of results; technical demands; and (last but not least) development and operational costs (Karp et al., 1997). All these factors determine the choice of marker type. Once the investment has resulted in sufficiently good marker data for plants of each population to be

(Louette, 1994). Migrations from the outside world – local or modern varieties – make the metapopulation an open system.

Conclusions

Table 1.1 summarizes the questions addressed in this chapter. It also gives a few indications about the function of genetic diversity in agricultural ecosystems, a central topic that could not be discussed in this short chapter.

Table 1.1: Synthesis of the estimation, function and factors of changes in the genetic diversity of crops in agricultural ecosystems

Diversity	Estimation	Function	Factors of changes
Of species (cultivated, non-cultivated)	Functional groups Taxonomic groups Species richness Spatial/temporal distribution Biodiversity of associated flora and fauna	Risk aversion Diversity of use Compromise between farmers' objectives and opportunities/ constraints Biodiversity of associated fauna and flora	Changes in agricultural systems; changes in opportunities and constraints Changes in farmers' objectives
Of varieties within a species	Number of varieties Functional groups Estimation of diversity based on neutral and adaptive traits Spatial/temporal distribution Population structure Breeding system Polymorphism	Risk aversion Diversity of use Compromise between farmers' objectives and opportunities/ constraints Source of gene exchanges Source of evolutionary changes in varieties Relation to impact of pests/diseases Biodiversity of associated fauna and flora Role of wild relatives	Domestication Changes in agricultural systems: changes in opportunities and constraints Changes in farmers' objectives Variety loss, elimination, replacement Variety introduction by seed companies, public institutions, farmers Impact of farmers' practices on genetic drift, selection, gene flow from wild relatives, from other varieties Genetic recombination

We have emphasized the fact that agro-ecosystems are changing systems from a genetic point of view, either because of internal mechanisms of evolution, or because of the external input of new diversity. For thousands of years human migration and seed exchange have been major factors in the flow of genetic diversity between agro-ecosystems, nurturing the genetic diversity of crops by renewing the genetic base submitted to natural and human selection. Nowadays, in the increasingly important formal system, gene flow into agricultural systems originates mainly from gene banks which provide farmers, breeders and scientists with germplasm collected from farmers' fields. Therefore the gene bank should now be considered as part of an extended agro-ecosystem.

1.3. Diversity in different components and at different scales

Conny Almekinders and Paul Struik

Introduction

Variation in different components of the agro-ecosystem is complex and dynamic. An agro-ecosystem may be considered to consist of crops, livestock and environmental components: farmers manage these components and their interactions for the purpose of agricultural production. Each component of an agro-ecosystem shows variations, including genetic variation. Variation is complex: it shows itself in space and time, at different scales and in different forms. Scales and forms of genetic variation include, for instance, variation at the level of genes, species, landscapes, and related diversity of function (see Chapter 1.2). Genetic variation in agro-ecosystems interacts with variation in other components of the agro-ecosystem: soil, climate, and farmers' management practices. Management of genetic variation in crops and livestock is an aspect of the management of many forms of variation and their interactions, at different scales and in different dimensions.

Biotic diversity

Crops and livestock are the primary objects of farmers' attention – they are tended and favoured in order to yield agricultural produce. Agrobiodiversity, the genetic variation in crops and livestock, is only part of the overall genetic variation. A wealth of other organisms, each with genetic diversity, constitute the associated biodiversity. The most visible ones are wild animals, trees and plants, insects, and airborne fungi and bacteria. The wide range of soil organisms (earthworms, springtails, soil fungi and bacteria) are less tangible but represent a wealth of biodiversity in farmers' fields that interacts with crops and livestock. Some of these associated organisms, as weeds, insect pests and plant pathogens, directly interact with crops and

14

are harmful for their growth and development, e.g. locusts, tuber moths, *Striga* spp., *Phytophthora* and *Pseudomonas*. Others are beneficial, such as *Rhizobium*, earthworms and mycorrhiza. Organisms can interact with the crop and livestock by influencing the abiotic environment, such as N_2-fixing organisms. Many affect the biotic crop environment, such as organisms that may harm crops and livestock, or may be of benefit, e.g. ladybugs or insect-eating birds.

These interactions are the functions whereby relations between organisms are balanced and the stability of the agro-ecosystem is maintained. Predators of damaging insects (e.g. granulosis virus in potato tuber moth), and antagonists of destructive fungi and bacteria (e.g. springtails for *Rhizoctonia*), are examples of such interactions which function as feedback mechanisms in agro-ecosystems. The total construct of interactions represents the organization of the agro-ecosystem; the feedback mechanisms and balances between the organisms are regarded as the self-organizing capacity of the system.

Organisms each represent typical genetic variation which affects the genetic variation of other organisms, forming an intriguing complex of relationships which are the basic driving forces of co-evolution, influenced by farmers' management.

Abiotic diversity

The dynamics of interactions among organisms and their variation are shaped and driven by abiotic environmental variation. The principal abiotic factors are temperature, water and minerals; their variation is experienced in climate and soil. There is interaction among the abiotic factors, e.g. precipitation affects soil through decomposition of organic matter, splashing and mineralization; radiation affects temperature; temperature affects soil evaporation; and soil conditions influence the microclimate in a crop.

Variations in climate and soil conditions affect living organisms, including crops and animals, and thereby their interaction and genetic diversity. Water conditions in the soil influence the activity of N_2-fixing bacteria and the uptake of minerals by plant roots. Temperature influences the growth and development of organisms; radiation affects photosynthesis by plants.

The influence can also be the other way around. The use of green manure or windbreaks affects variation in day/night temperatures, and limits erosion. With mulching and the planting of windbreaks, for example, climatic variation on both micro- and intermediate scales can be modified. On a macro-scale, forest destruction affects the 'albino' factor of the earth and thereby climatic change.

Variations in time and space, and at different scales

The components of an agro-ecosystem show variations in space and time (Almekinders et al., 1995). The soil fertility of a particular field differs from that in another field, and from that in the same field later in the season or next year. Soil erosion by runoff, and the potential positive effect where the soil is newly deposited, is an example of variation in which time and space interact. The genetic diversity of a maize field is different from that of a neighbouring bean field, or from the same field in the previous year when it was planted with another variety or crop, or after harvest when the crop has been removed.

Variation also has an aspect of scale: variation in soil conditions exists within and between fields; temperature and radiation vary from hour to hour, from day to day and from season to season. Variation manifests itself over other timescales, for example in relation to climatic changes, silting of soils, temporal flooding or volcanic eruptions. As a consequence, assessment of variation requires definition of the scale involved.

Farmers' management of variation

Most ecosystems, both natural and agro-ecosystems, experience some form of human intervention. The principal distinction between a natural ecosystem and an agro-ecosystem is the character of the human intervention. In both systems the intervention can have the objective of obtaining a particular output. There are many natural ecosystems where a product is extracted, e.g. wood, fruit or wild plants, but where human intervention does not have the purpose of favouring the output-producing organism. In an agro-ecosystem, farmers favour the crop and animals over other organisms in order to obtain the output. Favouring the crop in an agro-ecosystem means management of all organisms, including the associated biodiversity and the interaction with the abiotic environment, at different scales in time and space.

Farmers can thus be seen as managing the totality of variation to achieve their objectives. These objectives are complex: within the farming system the level of investment in different crops and animals has to be balanced: straw versus grain, milk versus meat. Risk, labour availability, cultural considerations and market conditions also play an important role in the management decisions of farmers. In decisions on allocation of resources, farmers balance and weigh agro-ecological and socio-economic environmental factors.

Management decisions also vary from farmer to farmer. Rich and poor farmers have different access to resources and different risk considerations. Older farmers may have more knowledge than younger, men and women may have different interests, and cultural traditions can affect crop management or the planting of particular varieties to provide traditional food items. These aspects all contribute to different preferences and decisions on what crops and varieties or seeds to plant and how to deal with the associated genetic diversity.

Styles of managing variation and scales

Variation in the components of the agro-ecosystem can be managed in different ways: it can be ignored, eliminated, overruled, matched or even strengthened. The appropriate way of dealing with it depends, among other things, on the type of environmental variation. The relatively uniform and fertile Dutch polders demand a different style of management of variation than the rugged Peruvian Andes. This difference is reflected in the general differences in management of high- and low-input agricultural systems.

Farmers in systems such as the Dutch polders face relatively low season-al field variation and have inputs available at relatively low cost. They administer blanket applications of fertilizers, with the result that within-field variation of nitrogen produces hardly any between-plant variation. With such soil fertility the use of genetic variation is not advantageous, and the total effect is a reduction of variation both in soil and crop. In contrast, fields in marginal environments are normally much more heterogeneous, climate is more variable from season to season, and farmers have more limited access to fertilizer and other inputs. In such conditions the use of genetically heterogeneous varieties can be beneficial for yield stabilization.

In high-input systems, chemical crop protection largely eliminates the need for genetic variation which reduces pest and disease incidence. In low-input systems, where the use of chemicals is reduced, genetic variation is an important tool for farmers to control pest and disease incidence. This can be variation in genetic resistance within one variety; or variation in susceptibility among varieties or crops planted in a field rotation, within a farm or over a broader area. Pest and disease incidence may also be man-aged by making use of differences in maturity, insect-repelling leaf-hairs, etc.

With irrigation, variation in water availability in the season and over seasons is reduced, and the investment in fertilizer is more reliable: in such a situation the predictability of production conditions is relatively high and risk is reduced, favouring high input levels, monocropping and genetically uniform varieties. Remaining risks are dealt with through auctions and insurances rather than genetic diversification. Farmers in these settings tend to specialize in order to target the market better, take advantage of larger scales of operation, and maximize income; this changes the genetic diversity used on farms. Farmers concentrate on crops or livestock only, or on fewer crops or husbandry activities. Although it probably results in a reduced overall genetic diversity in agriculture, specialization can increase certain types of genetic variation. Differences between farms or regions may increase because of specialization in a specific species or variety; seen for example in the regional domination of particular potato varieties in the USA, or red roses grown on one farm and yellow on the neighbouring one. In vegetable production a relatively high number of varieties of one crop may be planted on one farm in order to be able to harvest and market over a longer period.

In rainfed agriculture, with erratic climatic conditions, limited access to markets and high transportation costs, the use of inputs is risky and less economic. Genetic diversity is a tool in such situations to match the en-vironmental variation or to exploit resource niches. Different crops and varieties can be used to match the different conditions in fields along the catena, with different soil conditions, at low and high altitude, at the same time also reducing risks from erratic climatic events and the multiple needs of household consumption and use. Planting a genetically heterogeneous landrace or mixed cropping in a field with wet and dry spots provides yield in high- and low-rainfall years. Accumulating fertilizer on the better spots and applying the available water to the most valuable crops are examples where farmers actually increase environmental variation to favour crop production.

Interaction between variation in different components

Only a part of the total variation is seen in farmers' objectives and management. While the farmer aims at reducing, eliminating or matching variation in the production system, there is other variation which is less visible, ignored or overlooked. Practices that aim at reducing and eliminating variation can reveal, generate, increase or dampen other types of variation, which may have positive or negative effects on the output or influence the genetic diversity in the system. Not acknowledging soil variation results in pollution of groundwater in high-input conditions. Where high doses of nitrogen applications are based on plot averages of nitrogen residues, ignoring the (relatively low) soil variation, relatively large quantities of nitrogen may leach to the groundwater, primarily from the high-fertility spots in the plots.

Effects on biodiversity
Mechanized crop cultivation, for example, associated with increased uniformity, causes soil compression on the wheel tracks due to the use of heavy equipment used for planting, spraying and harvesting. In these compressed areas conditions vary and soil life is affected. Narrowing of rotations and use of genetically homogeneous varieties and chemical biocides result in more erratic incidence of pathogens, e.g. when unhindered population build-up could take place or resistance is broken. Use of herbicides can result in a severe field infestation of escaping species, forming high-density patches in the field. More uniform seed-bed preparation favours uniform germination but may reduce diversity in seed germination characteristics in a landrace which was favourable under variable conditions. Similarly, irrigation or fertilization may affect the diversity of rooting characteristics in a landrace.

Effects at different scales of human intervention
The farmer's individual management practices intervene in interactions at the level of the plant, the crop or the farming system. The farmer's intervention or household activities can also affect other farming systems, for instance in water use or pollution. The farming community may manage water and land as a group, for example the traditional system of land allocation in the Andes which assigns land in different agro-ecological zones to each family, in order to cope with the complex environment and erratic climate.

The community is another level of intervention. Management of resources at watershed level, by stakeholders from various communities, is an

18

example of interventions which act at a different scale than the farmer's individual handling. However, these higher-level interventions do affect variation at the level of plant and field, including the genetic diversity. Irrigation schemes introduce the possibility for year-round production or specialization in high-input crops. Reduced variation in water availability can thus lead to intensification, introduction of modern varieties and more uniform cropping patterns, but also induces new variation of pests and diseases. The disappearance of wetlands affects bird populations, which may affect the occurrence of locusts or other agricultural pests and diseases.

Authorities regulate the prices of inputs, the use of pesticides and other chemicals in buffer zones of nature reserves, or regulate the presence of toxins on produce for consumption at a national or supra-national level, thereby affecting agricultural production technology and crop and lifestock activities at the farm and field level. Priorities in breeding programmes, seed and variety legislation, and importation of agricultural products are examples of decisions which affect the socio-economic environments of farmers, affecting the seed selection and variety choice of individual households or farmers. The decision to specialize in a particular crop or produce is also strongly influenced by the government's price policy. General national or regional economies also affect genetic diversity at the field level. For example, the offer of temporary jobs in the mining industry elsewhere leads to labour shortages and reduction of maize diversity in the Peruvian Andes (Zimmerer, 1991a). Rainfed terraces, and local sweet potato varieties adapted to cultivation on these terraces, are being abandoned in the northern Philippines due to urban migration (C. DeRaedt, pers. comm.).

On the other hand, variation at lower agro-ecosystem levels influences the effects of interventions at the higher level. Differences between ethnic groups and related differences in land use made policy measures in Cameroon, aimed at increasing cotton production, ineffective; the policy was based on village averages and did not take into account the differences within villages (de Steenhuysen Piters, 1995). Policy options to direct dairy production in the northern part of the Netherlands were reduced when studies revealed that farms have similar values for key production variables, but arrived at these values in very different ways (van der Ploeg, 1994).

The scale of human interventions (farmers, farming communities, local authorities or institutions, regional, national and supra-national authorities and policies) and the scale at which the variation is affected are not necessarily the same.

Conclusion

Crop genetic diversity is only one component of variation in the agro-ecosystem. Other components, the associated biotic and abiotic environments, also show variation and interact with the genetic diversity.

The different components show different scales of variation in time and in space, creating an organized construct of variation. Agricultural production can be considered as the management of a total construct of variation with the purpose of obtaining an output. The management of genetic variation should be understood in the context of this total construct of variation consisting of different components, managed by farmers and communities and influenced by higher levels of human intervention.

1.4. Use of genetic diversity in crop improvement

Anne Elings, John Witcombe and Piet Stam

A few definitions

The definition of genetic variation depends on the level at which it is studied. At the most basic level genetic variation is determined by the nucleotide sequences in the DNA molecule that encode for amino acids; at the level of hereditary factors that underlie biological characteristics, it is determined by the alleles (e.g. dominant A and recessive a) that form a gene (the gene pair A–a); and at the level of quantitatively inherited characters such as grain yield it can be statistically quantified using analysis of variance.

It is important to measure genetic variation rather than phenotypic, as phenotypic variation has an unstable environmental component. Molecular techniques that detect variation in DNA structures are probably the most unbiased methods for determining genetic variation as the environmental influence is minimized. Variation at the DNA level, for instance in quantitative trait loci, can be related to the phenotypic expression of particular characters. This is an improvement over traditional quantitative genetic analysis and electrophoretic techniques, where the influence of the environment is less precisely defined.

Sources of genetic variation

Genetic variation results from new (*de novo*) genetic variation, mutation or recombination. *De novo* genetic variation is the consequence of a change in nucleotide sequence that occurs, for instance, because of an error during DNA duplication; a mutation is an accidental change in the genetic constitution; and recombination represents the rearrangement of DNA at the level of chromosomes and genomes that takes place primarily during sexual reproduction. Most genetic variation is generated through recombination, which is characteristic for cross-fertilizing species, but which is limited in predominantly self-fertilizing species. Genetic variation allows selection through evolutionary processes of change and adaptation.

Plant breeding is in essence a modified and accelerated form of evolution by broadening access to genetic variation, mating between selected parents and directional selection pressure under carefully chosen growing conditions. Deliberate out-crossing between contrasting genotypes (hybridization) is the most important conventional breeding tool. Apart from within-species hybridization, most use has been made of crosses between related cultivated species (e.g. bread and durum wheat) and related wild species (e.g. between bread wheat and *Aegilops*, and cultivated and wild barley). Conventional breeding is limited by sterility barriers between species and genera. Inter-specific barriers can be broken by using a bridging cross where genes are transferred between incompatible species via an intermediate species with which they both cross, through embryo rescue or techniques such as anther culture to produce a fertile progeny. With the advance of biotechnology – recombinant DNA technology that enables gene transfer between distantly related plant species – the genetic variation of the entire plant kingdom is potentially accessible for crop improvement. For instance, genome mapping in the grass family shows extensive genetic co-linearity between oats, wheat, maize, sorghum, sugar cane, foxtail millet and rice, which should facilitate gene isolation and transfer (Devos and Gale, 1997).

Regions of origin and diversity

A small number of centres or regions of origin were originally proposed by Vavilov as the places of agricultural beginning. They have been adapted by other scholars, introducing terms such as non-centre, megacentre and complex, and have never really coincided with regions of diversity as initially hypothesized by Vavilov (1951). Harlan (1992) has suggested major climate or vegetation formations to explain the complex and diffuse pattern of agricultural origin and crop diversity. He distinguishes as origins the Near Eastern Complex; Africa; the Chinese Region; South-East Asia and the Pacific Islands; and the Americas, and remarks that actual domestication may have occurred elsewhere, or in more than one of those regions (see Figure 1.1). Murphy and Witcombe (1982) argue that Vavilov's theory holds only for qualitative characters with high heritability that are selected by farmers but are little influenced by natural selection. Quantitative characters follow a different pattern: their variation is determined by natural selection and adaptation to environmental diversity. For specific crops it may be best to determine regions of origin and diversity on a case-by-case basis.

Diversity during millennia of farmer-led crop improvement

As agriculture spread, germplasm moved with it into new environments. Accumulation of variation in so-called secondary centres of diversity appears to be influenced by a long history of continuous cultivation, ecological and human diversity, and introgression with wild or weedy relatives (Harlan, 1992). Accumulation of new characteristics is a slow process that requires long, continuous cultivation of crops. Spatial variation in environmental and crop management conditions leads to different selection pressures and therefore to different germplasm.

A good example of new genetic variation becoming available to a society are plant expeditions, that are known to have been conducted since 1495 BC in Egypt. Especially during recent centuries, European and Northern American botanists have collected and globally spread a large number of species, causing dramatic changes in agriculture. Well known examples are potatoes and maize from the Americas, coffee from Africa, and rice from Asia.

What has farmer-led breeding done to genetic variation? Sampling effects have played an important role during the domestication and spread of agriculture. It is likely that agriculture and the process of domestication started from small populations of wild plants. Hence the gene pools represented by the early domesticated crops were less diverse than those of their wild ancestors. (Preservation of species that are most closely related to cultivated species is therefore of great value.) In addition, crop populations have probably gone through various genetic bottlenecks during ages of agricultural evolution. Human selection pressure must also have had great effects on genetic diversity: selection in favour of desirable and against unwanted characteristics contributes to the loss of associated genetic variation. Genetic drift of isolated populations has led to loss of genes. On the other hand, mutation, introgression with wild relatives and *de novo* generation of genetic variation have increased heterogeneity. The integrated result of these processes resulted in landraces that were considerably less diverse than their wild ancestors, but more variable than current modern varieties.

How has crop improvement responded to environmental and management changes? Here we concentrate on grain and straw yield, as in most cases these are the dominant characters. There are indications that wheat grain yields in the better environments of the Near East in Biblical times may have exceeded 4t/ha, and that straw height may have been only about 45cm. Even if overestimated, these values are competitive with yields obtained in modern agriculture. Grain yields were much lower, at 0.6–1.8t/ha, from the Roman era until very recently, in farming systems that required large quantities of straw. It is argued that such changes are directly linked to soil nitrogen availability: great nitrogen uptake is associated with high harvest index and great grain yield (Sinclair, 1998). If such a scenario is correct, it would imply that crop improvement has not been a gradual process from domestication until the present time, but that changes in farming systems and environmental conditions demanded crops with specific characteristics. The other conclusion is that sufficient genetic variation to enable such changes has existed for a long time, and that modern breeding cannot claim to have brought together for the first time the genes necessary for great yields.

There is another element to this: total biomass production is remarkably stable over a wide range of cultivated species with different breeding histories (under good growing conditions, after correction for the duration of crop growth). Although physiological characters such as photosynthesis rate do show genetic variation, their integrated effect does not seem to lead to greater biomass because of negative correlations. This may explain why selection for greater biomass has offered only limited prospects (Elings et al., 1997). Throughout human history, breeding for a certain society with a particular farming system has favoured growth of plant organs that were of greatest value, at the cost of other plant organs. This occurred in addition to breeding for characters such as quality and disease resistance.

Diversity during a century of scientist-led breeding

For the greater part of human history, farmers have been society's breeders – and in many cases still are. It required a change in European conception of the world during the Enlightenment that paved the road for the evolutionary insights of Darwin and Wallace, and the laws of genetics of Mendel. These insights gave momentum to selection experiments that commenced from the end of the 18th century onwards, mainly in Europe. The first selection experiments were concentrated on selection and maintenance of the best plants, which suggests the notion of difference, and therefore variation, between plants. It was observed that careful selection would result in better varieties, and that characteristics were hereditary. Most genetic knowledge and understanding of environmental influences was still not available (understanding the interaction between genetic and environmental variation is still very much in progress). It was a Frenchman, Louis de Vilmorin, who discovered in the middle of the 19th century the difference between self- and cross-fertilizing species, by continuous selection of the best lines. For self-fertilizing wheat this did not lead to phenotypic changes, while the sugar content of cross-fertilizing sugar beet improved dramatically. Since then, the way that breeding has dealt with genetic variation in self- and cross-fertilizing species has differed considerably.

Modern plant breeding has affected genetic diversity at two levels that should be clearly distinguished. Firstly, high selection pressure imposed in cross-fertilizers and pure line selection in self-fertilizers has led to the high degree of uniformity found in modern varieties. Legislation concerning breeders' rights in many Western countries required varietal uniformity, which further stimulated the development of highly uniform varieties. However, it should be clear that this is, in itself, not equivalent to genetic erosion of gene pools. A collection of modern, uniform varieties may well represent a gene pool as diverse as a set of landraces, depending on how genetically different those varieties are from each other. The fact that modern varieties often share common genetic backgrounds is a different issue that must be dealt with separately. Secondly, in modern plant breeding improved selection methodology accelerated the narrowing of the genetic basis of many crops in the initial period. This narrowing was caused by mass selection of plants from genetically diverse landraces, and later by the repeated use of a restricted range of parental material without introduction of 'fresh blood'.

While in the first phase of modern breeding, genetic diversity within a variety was reduced, there are indications that it is increasing again. As

breeding continues, each new variety has an increasing number of ancestors; modern breeding utilizes more parental material in the search for the
best combination of genes; and participatory crop improvement has proven
to increase the number of accepted varieties (Witcombe et al., 1996). In
some instances genetic diversity in a particular region is already at a minimum and can only increase. For instance, only few potato genotypes were
brought from the New to the Old World, and continued utilization of
American landrace germplasm will increase genetic diversity in European
potatoes. In a few millennia, continents other than South America may
develop into secondary centres of diversity.

Although it is hard to generalize, modern breeders have utilized a limited
amount of wild and landrace germplasm to create favourable new gene and
trait combinations. For example, the resistance genes present in modern
tomato, potato and small cereal crops, and the dwarfing genes of wheat, trace
back to only a few wild relatives. Introgressive breeding has only partially
compensated the genetic erosion in cultivated crops. This is more so since wild
relatives and 'exotics' have mainly been utilized for transfer of monogenic
traits. Nonetheless, genome analysis in tomato has shown that introgression by
back-crossing can result in the introduction of large chromosome segments.

There appears to be general agreement on the view that sufficient genetic variation has existed, and still exists, somewhere in the plant kingdom
to develop crops that produce well. For example, Tanksley and McCouch
(1997) report that the amount of variation found in cultivated rice and
tomato is only a small fraction of the variation found in gene bank collections of wild relatives and 'exotics' of these crops. The real problem has
always been to find the proper genes and to bring them together. As
molecular technologies and understanding of the function of genes and
gene complexes improve, this will become easier.

Yield stability

Genetic diversity also has an agronomic function. Examples are horizontal
disease tolerance that is based on several genes (polygenic) and deployment of different resistance genes in the elements that form a multiline
variety. For economic reasons, most breeding companies still concentrate
on monogenic disease resistance and utilization over time of available
diversity. Molecular techniques may bring gene pyramiding and therefore
horizontal disease resistance within economic reach.

The presumed better ability of heterogeneous landraces and multilines
to cope with within-field soil heterogeneity, compared with uniform
modern varieties, has not been experimentally verified, nor has it attracted
much attention in modern breeding. Genetic heterogeneity of one variety
may improve yield stability on a heterogeneous piece of land. Aside from
the development of some multilines, this mechanism has not been deliberately used by the formal sector. The informal sector, on the other hand, is
to a great extent working with genetically heterogeneous landraces.

European organic farmers, who crop on more heterogeneous soils than
regular farmers, still prefer modern homogeneous varieties above old

heterogeneous landraces (new landraces do not exist). This is related to the landraces' unacceptably low yields. Even under high-input conditions in Western Europe, potato yields within a field can vary up to 50 per cent. Obviously there is a limit to within-field yield stability of modern varieties. In a different environmental setting the genetic gains made in open-pollinated maize varieties for low-input tropical agriculture may be associated with their heterogeneous nature.

Agriculture can be diversified in other ways: mixed cropping, intercropping, wide rotations, diversification of farming systems, etc. Indigenous systems provide many examples of such practices.

Future developments

Over a century of scientific breeding, breeders have made limited use of the available germplasm. For instance, USA maize hybrids contain on average less than 3 per cent foreign germplasm. Molecular techniques will further facilitate the tapping of genetic resources that are still available in *ex situ* or *in situ* germplasm collections (Tanksley and McCouch, 1997). Genetic diversity is hardly increased if one gene (complex) is simply replaced by another one. However, if molecular techniques are employed to create, for instance, polygenic disease resistance in one variety, or to develop a series of varieties with different rooting characteristics for different soils, genetic diversity will indeed be broadened.

The relations between yield level and stability and crop homogeneity/heterogeneity are still under debate. The increasing understanding of the genetic basis of crop physiological mechanisms that contribute to yield stability may establish an effective partnership between breeders and physiologists (Jackson et al., 1996). By linking genetics to crop physiological processes that underlie yield, its stability can, in principle, be estimated from DNA-fingerprinted genotypes. Approaches like this may in the future shed more light on the possibilities of breeding for yield stability.

Large breeding companies tend to concentrate on the development of broadly adapted varieties, as this on the whole increases the range of its market and therefore gives the largest returns on investments. Three observations can be made. Firstly, this approach leaves many niche environments outside the broad targeted environment for narrowly adapted varieties. Their deployment would add to genetic diversity. Secondly, even though a broadly adapted variety yields well in a range of environments around the 'average environment', it can be argued that it should be possible to develop a better variety for each particular environment if sufficient resources were available. In some crops at least, the existing variation among élite varieties is sufficient for farmers, when given the choice, to identify varieties for particular niches (see Witcombe et al., Chapter 4.11). Resources required to breed or identify niche-specific varieties form an important foundation for participatory plant breeding, which relies strongly on the human resources provided by farmers. A dominant key to the success of participatory plant breeding will be the extent to which successful locally adapted germplasm can be developed. Thirdly, as biophysical limits to crop productivity are approached in high-input agricultural systems (Loomis and Amthor, 1996), within- and between-variety genetic variation may be options to deal with within- and between-field variation in growing conditions, respectively. As long as actual and attainable (as determined by feasible management conditions) yields differ, scope remains simultaneously to optimize crop management and crop genotype towards the greatest-yielding phenotype. This applies especially to growing conditions that are limited by factors such as water and nutrient availability, and extreme temperatures (Loomis and Connor, 1992).

1.5. Strategies and methodologies in genetic diversity conservation

Jan Engels and Bert Visser

Introduction

This chapter presents various conservation strategies and methods and their advantages and disadvantages, and pays particular attention to the complementarity of the different strategies. The emphasis is on methods to maintain and store genetic diversity, whether for immediate or future use (Table 1.2). *In situ* conservation in protected areas, on-farm or in-garden, and *ex situ* conservation in the form of seed, pollen, *in vitro* stored material or in field banks is discussed. Complementary activities such as germplasm health inspection, characterization, evaluation, exchange and documentation are not dealt with.

Table 1.2: Characteristics of various conservation methods

Conservation method	Quantity of diversity	Direct utilization	Evolutionary process	Security	Accessibility	Characterization and evolution	Sovereignty	Cost-efficiency
in situ								
Protected areas	+	v	+	+	–	–	+	–
On-farm	+	+	+	–	+/–	–	+	+/–
In-garden	+/–	+	+	–	+/–	–	+	+/v
ex situ								
Seeds	+	–	–	+	+	+	–	+
Pollen	+	–	–	+	+	+	–	+
in vitro	–	–	–	+	+	+	–	–
Field banks	–	–	+/–	+	+	+	–	–

+ high; – low; v variable

26

In situ conservation

Traditionally, *in situ* conservation programmes have been developed primarily for the conservation of forests and sites valued for their wildlife or for ecological reasons. Limited experience exists with *in situ* conservation of agrobiodiversity. However, with the conclusion of the Convention on Biological Diversity and Agenda 21 in 1992, and more recently the adoption of the Global Plan of Action in Leipzig (FAO, 1996b), a significant impetus has been given to *in situ* conservation, both on-farm and in natural habitats. Due attention is paid to linkages between conservation and development. Also, increased attention is given to genetic resources of forestry species, minor crops of local importance, forages and medicinal plants. Both developments have promoted interest in *in situ* conservation strategies.

The conservation of agrobiodiversity in protected areas, which collectively cover a total of almost a billion ha worldwide (FAO, 1996b), is largely unplanned and is a result of nature protection. However, more and more conscious efforts are reported to include and monitor important agrobiodiversity in protected areas. This form of conservation has the great advantage that evolutionary processes continue to operate under the same or similar conditions under which the material developed its distinctive characteristics. In addition, if the protected area is properly managed considerable economic and environmental benefits can be derived from protected areas.

This strategy requires the location, designation and management of the site and monitoring of the genetic diversity. It is applicable to orthodox and non-orthodox seeded species and allows multiple taxa conservation in a single reserve. A disadvantage is that the conserved material is not instantly available for agricultural use and, in the absence of or because of limited management practices, only very limited characterization and evaluation might be done on the germplasm, hardly facilitating its use as a genetic resource.

The conservation of traditional crop varieties and cropping systems within traditional agricultural systems represents an alternative *in situ* conservation strategy (Maxted et al., 1997b). Farmers worldwide have been practising on-farm 'conservation' as long as agriculture has existed, although it can be questioned whether the objective of farmers has always been to conserve the genetic diversity of a given crop. For them, the most effective management practices are those which result in the highest yields and the highest food security. Usually these practices are based on significant amounts of species diversity as well as considerable intra-specific diversity, and have often survived in areas which are marginal from a modern agricultural production point of view. From a plant genetic resources management perspective, one can subdivide these into seed-producing crops, vegetatively propagated species and the wild and weedy or ruderal species. The great advantage of this 'conservation' method is the continuing maintenance and evolution of locally adapted traditional landraces and wild and weedy species which depend strongly on traditional agricultural practices.

27

Possible disadvantages of this method are limited access to the resources conserved, the lack of adequate characterization and evaluation, and the potential and continuous danger that farmers abandon the cultivation of traditional landraces because of their frequently disadvantaged competitive status. Careful monitoring practices and programmes to support on-farm conservation and development, such as the Community Biodiversity Development and Conservation (CBDC) programme and the IPGRI *in situ* conservation programme, will be needed. It has been suggested that the *ex situ* conservation method could be used as a back-up system to avoid possible loss of genetic diversity (Maxted et al., 1997b).

Several authors list the conservation of plant genetic diversity in home gardens as a separate 'method' (e.g. Maxted et al., 1997a). Although individual gardens might contain relatively little genetic diversity for a given species, especially in the case of perennials such as fruit trees and shrubs, home gardens collectively for a given community may indeed represent a high level of diversity. In many parts of the world home gardens are an important source of vegetable and spice production. Root and tuber crops, fruit trees and medicinal plants are other sources of food and medicine which can be frequently found in home gardens, both in rural areas and in the cities. The advantages of this 'method' are that it is as dynamic as on-farm conservation, plus it ensures the maintenance of many traditional landraces of minor crops, vegetables, etc. The inclusion of many gardens within a given community is necessary to provide for an appropriate coverage of ultra-specific diversity. Another potential disadvantage is the fact that accessibility to specific characteristics can be very restricted as characterization and evaluation efforts might be limited.

Ex situ conservation

The storage of seed is the most widely used and convenient method of *ex situ* conservation. It has received considerable research attention since the late 1960s, and much is known about the optimum treatment of the seed of most of the major food crops. Clear advantages of seed storage are its relative efficiency, reproducibility, and that it allows secure short-, medium- and long-term storage. Another advantage is the availability of detailed procedures to be followed, at least for most of the major food crops. Standards for seed storage in gene banks have been developed and recommended for international adoption (FAO/IPGRI, 1994).

However, it should be noted that many crop species, especially in the tropics, do not produce the so-called orthodox seeds which are amenable to the storage described above, but seeds which cannot be dried to lower seed moisture contents and, consequently, cannot be stored at low(er) temperatures. These so-called recalcitrant seeds therefore cannot be used for storage.

Another possible drawback of seed storage is its static nature while conserving the seeds, which are no longer exposed to the environment under which they developed. Over long periods one can even expect selection to take place for material which is more amenable to gene bank conditions, especially as several 'bottleneck' situations exist during the routine collecting and management of seed germplasm. One such bottleneck can be an unreliable electricity supply to the gene bank, a particular problem in developing countries. As a reaction to this, research was initiated on alternative approaches to low-temperature storage which resulted in the development of so-called ultra-dry seed technology, allowing storage under room-temperature conditions (Walters and Engels, 1998).

Pollen storage is comparable to seed storage, as pollen can be dried (less than 5 per cent moisture content on a dry weight basis) and subsequently stored at low temperature (below 0°C).

It is a common practice in breeding programmes to bridge the gap between male and female flowering time and to improve fruit setting in orchards. Because of the relatively short longevity of pollen grains compared with seeds (although this varies significantly among species), and since the viability testing is cumbersome and time-consuming, pollens have been used only to a limited extent in germplasm conservation. However, recent results show no decline in the viability of pollen after 10 years of cryopreservation storage. Disadvantages of pollen storage are that many species produce only a very small amount of pollen; that the transmission of organelle genomes via pollen is not effective; that sex-linked genes in species with separate male and female plants will be missed; and that pollen itself cannot be used to regenerate an accession (although initial indications exist that pollen can be regrown into whole plants). However, the fact that pollen storability is not correlated with seed storability opens possibilities for the conservation of species through pollen which produce recalcitrant seeds.

Field gene banks are commonly used for the conservation of germplasm that cannot be stored as seeds because of its recalcitrant nature or that does not produce seeds, or seeds that are sterile or that are preferably stored as clonal material because of the heterozygous nature of the genotype or the long generation cycle. Many of the temperate and tropical fruit trees fall into one or more of these categories, as do many of the commodity crops such as cacao, rubber, oil-palm, coffee, banana and coconut, as well as most of the root and tuber crops. The management procedures are similar to, or the same as, as those used during routine cultivation practices of those species, which makes the method relatively easy to adapt under local circumstances. Other advantages are easy access to the conserved material for research and use, and the fact that the conserved material can be characterized and evaluated while being conserved. Although restricted, the conserved germplasm is exposed to environmental conditions and thus some natural selection can take place, especially over a long period of time.

An accession usually consists of only one genotype, as in the case of *in vitro* conservation, and requires a considerable area of land, so the total intra-specific diversity which can be conserved is usually relatively small. Because of its exposure to prevailing cultural practices at the site of the gene bank, constraints can emerge that affect the germplasm. Also, natural hazards such as pests and diseases, drought, flood, cyclones, etc. form a permanent threat.

In vitro conservation involves the maintenance of explants in a sterile, pathogen-free environment and is widely used for the conservation of species which produce recalcitrant seeds or no seeds at all, or of material which is propagated vegetatively to maintain particular genotypes. Although research on *in vitro* techniques started only about 20 years ago, this technique has been applied for multiplication, storage and, more recently, for collecting germplasm material for more than 1000 species.

Different *in vitro* conservation methods are available. For short- and medium-term storage the aim is to increase the intervals between subcultures by reducing growth. This is achieved by modifying the environmental conditions and/or the culture medium: so-called slow-growth conservation.

Long-term storage of cultures can be achieved through storage at ultra-low temperature, usually achieved by using liquid nitrogen (–196°C). At this temperature all cellular divisions and metabolic processes are stopped, consequently plant material can be stored without alteration or modification for a theoretically unlimited period. Since such cultures are usually stored in small volumes and are protected from contamination, this method requires very limited maintenance (except for the regular filling of liquid nitrogen into the cryo tanks).

The advantages of *in vitro* techniques are that they allow the medium- to long-term conservation of germplasm (which so far has usually been conserved as whole plants in field gene banks), offer increased security, are reportedly more cost-efficient, and provide the curator with an option for the safe movement/exchange of germplasm. Disadvantages are the fact that each accession is (usually) represented by only one genotype, that only a limited number of accessions can be managed, that contamination of slow-growth cultures can occur, and that human errors can easily happen. The possibility of cultures losing their genetic integrity through somaclonal variation is an important drawback. The degree of somaclonal variation (aberrant phenotypes) varies greatly from one species to another and, in general, is not yet well understood.

The complementarity of conservation methods

From the advantages and disadvantages mentioned for each of the individual methods, it is easy to see how two or more such methods combined can lead to better conservation. The total genetic diversity included in the conservation efforts, its security and accessibility as well as actual feasibility and cost-efficiency, can be significantly improved by choosing the right conservation methods and combining them. In making such choices it is important to take a holistic view of the intended conservation effort and to place it in a wider context, whenever possible, as part of a development process in which genetic resources are being deployed for food production and income generation. It is also important to examine carefully the technical and human resources infrastructure, as well as the administrative and political environment of the conservation effort, in order to be able to avoid later constraints. It is important that all relevant biological information about the material to be conserved is available, essential in order to be able to decide on the strengths and weaknesses of the different options.

The most obvious combination of different methods is *in situ* and *ex situ* conservation, as this will allow the dynamic aspects of the *in situ* situation to be combined with the usually more secure and accessible approach of *ex situ*. However, the latter may cause severe ethical and political constraints to those who have been managing these resources and who would not like to lose their (sovereign) rights over the material. Besides the difference in conservation dynamism, there will also be significant differences in the quantity of genetic diversity that can be conserved. If the latter is an important constraint in *ex situ* activities, as would be the case for many of the minor crops and wild relatives, *in situ* conservation approaches will be indispensable. Furthermore, the consideration of integrating conservation and development is of critical importance to achieve sustainable conservation. Since the *in situ* approach would leave the genetic material with the people who actually use it, this method will obviously be a preferred option. On the other hand, 'conservation through use' might run the risk of losing specific alleles or genotypes and a back-up system through *ex situ* conservation may be required.

1.6. The role of agrobiodiversity in farm-household livelihood and food security: a conceptual analysis

Antine Hardon-Baars

Introduction

In the present international debate on Agrobiodiversity and Food Security (FAO, 1996a) the link between agrobiodiversity and farm-household livelihood has become a focus of interest (Thrupp, 1998). RAFI (1999) states that the tendency to look primarily at the major food crops masks the importance of plant species diversity to the world food supply. For example, the diversity encountered in home gardens is significant. Surveys carried out on home-garden diversity provide increasing support to their relevance for the 'womens's cooking pots', i.e. to household food security and especially its nutritional quality. In addition, they harbour and maintain important sources of genetic diversity (Chweya and Eyzaguirre, 1999).

In general, women's focus is mainly on the household subsistence economy. In the use of genetic diversity this balances the market pressures which tend to emphasize uniformity. In the farm-household system, biodiversity is used and conserved as a resource not just for production of crops but for multiple activities of the food/livelihood system such as storage, processing, preparation and consumption of food, and for housing, medicine, fodder and other purposes.

Hence it is obvious that major decisions on the use and management of agrobiodiversity are made at the household level, and as part of household livelihood strategies. There is, however, little insight into how farm-household practices and strategies on livelihood and food/nutrition quality relate to agrobiodiversity.There is some literature on the relevance of gender (for reviews see Swaminathan, 1997; Howard-Borjas, 1998), but these are based on only a few case studies. The main, and hardly surprising, conclusion is that women play a key role in the household as decision-makers on the use of resources, including genetic resources, to meet household needs.

Despite the lack of insight in this area, general recognition of the importance of household systems for improving livelihoods is growing, and increasingly influences the agenda for agricultural research and development. The lack of appropriate analytical frameworks and methodologies for examining interaction between local institutions and rural households is a recognized gap in R&D (FAO, 1998). The conceptual framework of agrobiodiversity recently presented by Ann Thrupp of the World Resources Institute (Thrupp, 1998) includes cultural and local knowledge as aspects of agrobiodiversity (Figure 1.2). Her study on agrobiodiversity and food security, however, misses the link with household livelihood resources, practices and strategies.

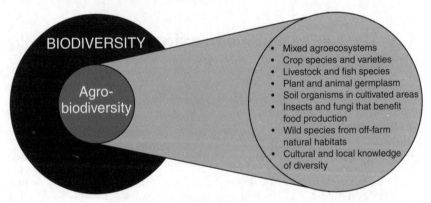

Figure 1.2: *Conceptual view of agrobiodiversity.* Source: L.A. Thrupp, World Resources Institute

A functional approach is the use of a household systems framework in agricultural R&D, as used by UPWARD projects (Hardon-Baars, 1996, 1997; Campilan, 1998).

The function of presenting a systems framework is to make visible how inputs to the system are transformed into outputs. A system is composed of five elements: components or clusters of factors, interaction between them, boundaries, inputs and outputs. Insight into components of factors and their interactions can help to systematize and organize data collection, and visualize the possible effects of external interventions as facilitating or constraining livelihood security. Figure 1.3 is a drawing of a household system, boundaries presented by dotted lines, open to the biophysical and socio-economic environment and to other household systems. The components of factors are bordered by drawn lines.

The household-system framework (Figure 1.3), recently also called a livelihood system framework (Campilan, 1999), can serve as a checklist in identifying factors and interactions to be studied.

The household is considered for our purpose as the smallest corporate unit where pooling and using resources takes place to satisfy the needs of its members. Members may share some goals, resources and benefits and be independent in others, and may also be in conflict in a wide variety of forms and functions.

The inputs to the system, as shown in Figure 1.3, are composed of factors including human and non-human resources (including agrobiodiversity) and the objectives of household members; the throughput consists of the practices and strategies of actors in the household (such as production, storage, processing and consumption of food, and other livelihood activities); and the output in this context is the livelihood/food/nutrition (in)security produced. Agrobiodiversity is thus a resource of the system; it also is an environmental factor belonging to the biophysical environment of the household. Human resources such as time, labour and knowledge (of members of the household, e.g. women) can be constraining factors for appropriate agrobiodiversity conservation activities to take place. The agrobiodiversity used is thus the result of different factors, and on the basis of the framework hypotheses can be formulated as to which factors are important in a specific environmental context. When women spend more time in paid work, this can result in a reduction of time available for conserving activities in their home gardens or on the farm. Male out-migration will probably result in less time and labour available for farm activities of the household. The demand of the market for certain crop varieties will influence the varieties being cultivated, etc.

External factors relating to agrobiodiversity use and conservation strategies of households include policies on *in situ* and *ex situ* conservation; access of farm households to planting material, including from gene banks; community strategies for conserving diversity; informal inter-household seed and variety exchange; informal and formal markets; local R&D activities such as participatory breeding, etc.

Figure 1.3 suggests the existence of a complex ecological system of interactions within livelihood systems that affect the management and use of agrobiodiversity. There are, however, few studies in which such factors and interactions have been studied. The household system has been treated as a 'black box' which urgently needs opening up.

Preliminary data from a PhD study by Almaz Negash on the diversity and conservation of enset (*Enset ventricosum*) and its relation to household food and livelihood security in south-western Ethiopia illustrate the relevance of such a conceptual framework in formulating hypotheses for

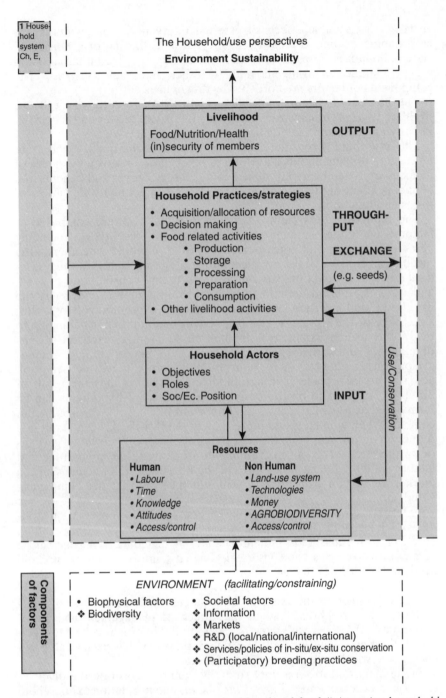

The Household/use perspectives
Environment Sustainability

Livelihood
Food/Nutrition/Health
(in)security of members

OUTPUT

Household Practices/strategies
• Acquisition/allocation of resources
• Decision making
• Food related activities
  • Production
  • Storage
  • Processing
  • Preparation
  • Consumption
• Other livelihood activities

**THROUGH-
PUT**

EXCHANGE

(e.g. seeds)

Use/Conservation

Household Actors
• Objectives
• Roles
• Soc/Ec. Position

INPUT

Resources

Human
• *Labour*
• *Time*
• *Knowledge*
• *Attitudes*
• *Access/control*

Non Human
• *Land-use system*
• *Technologies*
• *Money*
• *AGROBIODIVERSITY*
• *Access/control*

Components
of factors

ENVIRONMENT (facilitating/constraining)
• Biophysical factors   • Societal factors
❖ Biodiversity   ❖ Information
                          ❖ Markets
                          ❖ R&D (local/national/international)
                          ❖ Services/policies of in-situ/ex-situ conservation
                          ❖ (Participatory) breeding practices

Figure 1.3: *Linking agrobiodiversity to livelihood and food (in)security: household use perspectives*

relationships between factors of the household system and its environment, and for collecting data. This is summarized in Box 1.1, and includes some preliminary results (Negash, 1999).

Box 1.1

Almaz Negash formulates as a central hypothesis of her study that by maintaining genetic diversity of enset (household resources and practices/ strategies) a subsistence farmer can attain household food security (output of the system). She also tests the diversity at the genetic level in order to relate conservation strategies to use.

In situ conservation of the crop has been practised by farmers as part of their their livelihood system for centuries. *Ex situ* conservation is done by mandated institutes such as the Ethiopian Biodiversity Institute which maintains the germplasm and also reintroduces it to farmers when the need arises. Farmers maintain diverse genetic materials for different uses. Some clones are said to be for income, others for medicine, others for food. The different parts of this multipurpose crop are used for different objectives: leaves for baking bread, for wrapping, for shade, string and rope, for making mats and skirts, and as a brewing pot for preparation of the local beer. The pseudostem is very valuable, being the basal part where the starch used for food is stored. As the farmers express it: 'enset is our food, our cloth, our bed, our house, our plate; it is everything for us'.

Some preliminary findings are:

o farmers have certain criteria for classifying clones, and women farmers are said to be experts in selecting clones for different household uses, such as their appropriateness for medicine, for fibre etc.
o enset-growing households value genetic diversity and are interested to have more clones
o wealthier households in most cases retain greater clonal diversity than lower-income households; this is thought to be a status symbol.

Negash, 1999, ongoing PhD studies.

A case study from a project where the relationship between the use of agrobiodiversity in home gardens and the food/nutrition security of households is being investigated at the household level is presented in Box 1.2. (Campilan, 1998)

Methodological issues

The various interactions between factors of the livelihood system pertaining to agrobiodiversity are clearly complex. To gain insight into these interactions within and between households and their environments, and the actual and potential consequences, requires systematic studies. Participatory methododologies are important when exploring the possibilities of incorporating household members in R&D activities. The method chosen also depends on the objectives and the time available. Some of the recent publications in the field are listed in a literature review (Hardon-Baars, 1997). When the project is at the community level, participatory methods of joint learning are important. Focus group discussions involving interested members of households are a useful approach, taken from marketing studies, which are now widely used in locally specific agricultural R&D. The Focus Group Kit of Morgan and Krueger (1998) can help to develop tools.

1.7. Genetic resources and the policy environment

Cary Fowler and Janice Jiggins

Introduction

Charles Darwin begins the first chapter of *The Origin of Species*, 'Variation under domestication', by addressing that aspect of evolution and diversity with which people were most personally acquainted:

When we reflect on the vast diversity of the plants and animals which have been cultivated, and which have varied during all ages under the most different climates and treatment, I think we are driven to conclude that this greater variability is simply due to our domestic productions having been raised under conditions of life not so uniform as, and somewhat different from, those to which the parent-species have been exposed under nature.

(Darwin, 1859)

Some 10 000 years ago humanity began the slow yet inexorable transition from hunting and gathering to agriculture. For 10 millennia our farming ancestors have been the primary custodians and, more importantly, the principal developers of the crops which feed us today. Perhaps for Darwin in the 1850s it was easier to acknowledge – or more difficult to ignore – the contribution made by generations of farmers to the abundant diversity of crop varieties and domestic animal breeds. With the Mendelian revolution and the rise of organized, scientific plant breeding in the 20th century, awareness and appreciation of the role of farmers in conserving and improving plant genetic resources diminished considerably. Indeed, with Darwin collecting dust on the bookshelf, their achievements and capabilities were openly disparaged by those who might have known better – even by those who depended most directly on their legacy. Where Darwin saw human methodical selection at work, others saw accidents or inevitability. Where Darwin saw much improvement and modification (Darwin, 1859), many perceived nothing more substantial than Stone Age varieties, primitive cultivars and landraces. As late as 1985, the author of a review of the CGIAR's contribution to genetic resource conservation observed in a footnote that *in situ* preservation has not yet come under consideration by IBPGR (now IPGRI) or the International Agricultural Research Centre. Its potential impact is considerable for wild species, but it is perhaps of little or no importance for the cultigens (Hawkes, 1985).

Interestingly, the adaptation of agriculture to the myriad environments in the USA, as well as the rise of the commercial seed sector in that country, can be traced to farmer selection and breeding, using genetic materials imported and distributed by the government for just this purpose. From the early 1800s to the early 1900s, the government mailed small packets of seeds to farmers for testing and experimentation. At its height, the government was distributing over 20 million packets annually. Yet the impact of this undertaking became obscured with the rise of commercial plant breeding in the second half of the 20th century.

As political advocacy groups began to take up the plant genetic resources issue in the late 1970s, the attitudes of scientists and politicians alike came under more intense 'selection pressure'. For example, RAFI (1989) published its Community Seed Bank Kit (in English, French, Spanish and Portuguese) outlining methodologies and techniques for local-level conservation of genetic diversity, and followed this with work on community plant breeding. One of the most notable developments was the 'legitimization' of *in situ* or on-farm conservation, management and improvement efforts, particularly those taking place in developing countries.

Keystone International (1991) gave substance to this shift in thinking:

> Farmers have been found to: employ their own taxonomic systems; encourage introgression; use selection; occasionally hybridize; make efforts to see that varieties are adapted; multiply seeds; employ simple cell/tissue culture techniques to produce new plants; field test; record data; and name their varieties. In the course of this innovative activity (which is usually aimed at production, not conservation), they also conserve genetic diversity and encourage new genetic combinations and adaptions.

Keystone Dialogue participants – including, most interestingly, the heads of the world's largest government *ex situ* collections, as well as representatives of the private sector and NGOs – called for expansion and improvement of *in situ* 'on-farm community conservation and utilization' efforts. Following the close of the final plenary session of the Keystone Dialogue in Oslo in 1991, Jaap Hardon and Cary Fowler called a meeting to discuss the possibility of an initiative of scientists and farmers for the on-farm conservation and improvement of traditional crop varieties. This discussion eventually led to the establishment of the Community Biodiversity Development and Conservation (CBDC) programme. See Berg et al. (1991) for an early analysis of the history and potential of farmer selection and breeding.

Both the scientific and the political context for *in situ* and on-farm work were changing. There was active questioning of the roles and division of labour between plant breeders, gene banks and farmers. To what extent were farmers actually selecting and breeding their crops? What knowledge did they have of genetics, and how did they apply their understanding? Were they better able to select or breed for certain traits as opposed to others? How could on-farm projects scale-up and touch the lives of the 1.4 billion people living on farms who are largely self-reliant on their own farm-saved planting materials? (FAO, 1996a). What new forms of relationships are needed between farmers and scientists, if on-farm breeding and plant improvement is to be supported? Should gene banks step in and play a new role, seeing their constituency to be both scientific and farmer plant breeders?

Despite an upsurge in interest and activity over the past 10 years, many of these questions remain unanswered. The political and scientific climate, however, has changed dramatically in ways which are conducive to further research and action.

The Convention on Biological Diversity which came into force in 1993 places its primary emphasis on conservation *in situ*, although the focus of the relevant article (Article 8) is clearly on non-domesticated species. Nevertheless, the Convention also draws attention to the knowledge, innovation and practices of indigenous and local communities. A legally binding Convention with broad subscription and popular support, the Convention on Biological Diversity provides a political and legal context in which ignoring on-farm efforts is difficult.

The Convention's negotiating process, however, acknowledged the existence of several outstanding matters and delegated responsibility for dealing with these to the Food and Agriculture Organization of the United Nations (FAO). Among FAO's initiatives was the drafting and negotiating of the first Global Plan of Action for Plant Genetic Resources. The Plan was adopted at the Fourth International Technical Conference on Plant Genetic Resources, an inter-governmental meeting attended by 150 countries, held in Leipzig, Germany, in 1996 (FAO, 1996e).

The Global Plan of Action contains 20 priority activities, including one on Supporting On-Farm Management and Improvement of Plant Genetic Resources for Food and Agriculture. This section of the Plan specifies, in some detail, governments' commitments as well as responsibilities to be carried out by others, in order to better understand and improve the effectiveness of existing on-farm conservation, management, improvement and use of plant genetic resources. The Plan calls for changes in policy; for various capacity-building initiatives; and for considerable increases in research, including research on the questions identified above.

The Global Plan of Action has served to legitimize the subject of on-farm management and improvement of genetic resources, and to take the emphasis off the exclusive conservation-orientation of some previous work and literature. The Plan notes that:

Historically, farmer access to a broad range of germplasm in developed countries has contributed to yield increases and greater crop adaptability through farmer selection . . . Initiatives focusing on participatory, on-farm management and improvement of plant genetic resources for food and agriculture may offer the potential to reach large numbers of farmers and promote further agricultural development. It would, of necessity, depend on farmers themselves and their decisions and build upon and make use of their on-going efforts to improve their crops through mass selection and other breeding efforts.
(FAO, 1996e)

Over the past 10 years the context for research and action has clearly shifted. Once again, variation under domestication, as well as the agents of this historic and ongoing domestication process, have been recognized. There is, as Darwin might have put it, more grandeur in this view of life. The debate is no longer whether farmers engage in valuable crop improvement efforts, or whether support for such efforts is needed, worthwhile or legitimate. They do. It is. The most pressing questions to be answered now concerning *in situ* or on-farm management of agrobiodiversity are rather more scientific and practical than ideological.

Nevertheless, acknowledgement of the contribution of farmers to the conservation and improvement of plant genetic resources in certain political fora does not mean that all actors have adjusted their policies or programmes accordingly. The suggestion that the policy environment governing genetic diversity is driven by powerful bureaucratic and commercial interests, rather than technical necessity or a food security imperative, has been convincingly demonstrated for countries as seemingly different as China (Song, 1998), South Africa (Moss, 1996; Fakir, 1996a,b; Mayet, 1997), Sweden (Bengtsson and Thornstrom, 1998) and Switzerland (Hufny, 1998).

Further, country case studies such as these, as well as global analyses (Mooney, 1996; Softing et al., 1998), reveal that global conventions and agreements such as Union Internationale pour la Protection des Obtentions Végétales (UPOV), the World Trade Organization (WTO)/Trade Related Aspects of Intellectual Property Rights (TRIPS) and the Convention on Biological Diversity, co-exist with a complex of national laws, regulations and deeply entrenched standards and practices which contradict, ignore or serve as a basis for re-interpretation of the emerging global frameworks. This raises difficult issues of accountability and compliance which are far from being resolved and which are unlikley to be satisfactorily settled by either recourse to international law or threats to exercise commercial and political leverage.

Moreover, country case studies reveal that, at present, national policies governing genetic resources are neither uniform nor consistent. Sweden, for example, has more than 30 powerful institutional stakeholders working to a range of largely discordant and certainly uncoordinated policies, including six ministries (Bengtsson and Thornstrom, 1998). It is perhaps this more than any other factor which has permitted the (by now highly concentrated) commercial interests operating across the veterinary medicine, pharmaceuticals, agrochemicals, seed supply and biotechnology fields to secure a policy environment which is increasingly favourable to their interests.

While in theory it might be possible to identify mutuality of interest between commercial profit and the social good, there is convincing evidence that neither the UN system nor national governments have been able to maintain past levels of support for public-sector agricultural research and development activities, or to prevent companies from suppressing technologies of potentially greater social and environmental benefit in favour of those on which they can secure the most profit (Mooney, 1996; Softing et al., 1998). In default, the main check on the policy process is coming from civil society, on two fronts. Technically well informed and widely networked non-government organizations are securing a place at the key negotiating tables through advocacy and activism. Indeed, certain public-sector institutions such as the CGIAR are also playing an increasingly visible role in the struggle with expanding intellectual property rights regimes over which, if any, genetic resources should remain in the public domain. More unexpectedly, ordinary citizens are increasingly exerting their power as consumers in order to express a generalized unease, an amalgam of perceptions of unwarranted risk, well-founded mistrust of any undue concentration of power, and the assertion of deeply-felt values and motivations which constrain unbridled profit.

40

SECTION II
FARMERS' USE OF GENETIC DIVERSITY

Introduction

The cases in this section illustrate the factors influencing farmers' management of diversity, the details of those management practices, and the different ways in which diversity is utilized. The cases represent examples of
plant genetic resource management in the local system. It is a system in
which farmers maintain and use a wealth of crop diversity as part of the
local livelihood, but also harbours genetic resources with global significance. Because of this local and global resonance, maintenance and development of the local system is the main subject of this book. Most
authors in this section have taken this system as a starting point, aiming to
present farmers' holistic and integrated perspectives, without distinguishing between levels of biodiversity in agriculture and different management
components. The cases in this section illustrate integrated management by
farmers.

Many fascinating cases of farmers' use and management of genetic diversity are located in areas generally referred to as primary or secondary
centres of diversity, which are characterized by 'marginal and heterogeneous' conditions. Primary centres are located in the regions where crops
were originally domesticated, such as the Horn of Africa and the Andes.
Secondary centres, such as the island of New Guinea for sweet potato,
occur in areas where the crop has been introduced and then has experienced an explosion of genetic diversification linked to intensive and multi-
faceted use. Conservationists are interested in these centres because of the
wealth of genetic diversity still found there. The continued existence of
diversity is partly related to the fact that, in most cases, they have barely
been touched by official agricultural development in general, and crop
improvement in particular.

The first three chapters in this section are situated in such cradle areas of
diversity. Two chapters illustrate farmers' management of cereal diversity
in the Horn of Africa. McGuire (Chapter 2.1) describes farmers' seed
production practices in sorghum; he further analyses farmers' perceptions
of the variety of sorghum materials and their hybridization. The second
chapter focuses on a case from the northern part of this region, Abyssinia
(Eritrea). Woldeamlak, Araia and Struik (Chapter 2.2) describe *Hanfetz*,
the traditional intercropping system of wheat and barley landraces, and
analyse the logic of the use of this mixture. The analysis shows why this
intercropping system – and its associated genetic diversity – are likely to
disappear when input levels increase and market conditions change. The
third case looks at the maintenance of sweet potato diversity in Irian Jaya
(Indonesia), on the island of New Guinea. Use and management of the

crop have barely been influenced by outside interventions, and the study of this system provides an understanding of its potential to maintain genetic diversity in the future. Prain et al. (Chapter 2.3) describe the complexity of current management practices and demonstrate how the richness of diversity within one crop relates to various consumption and ritual objectives within the livelihood system.

A number of contributions throughout this book also relate to farmers' use and management of genetic diversity in these centres of crop diversity, and reflect the perspectives of conservationists, breeders and development workers and their approach to interventions. Examples include chapters by Sthapit and Subedi (Chapter 4.7) on rice in Nepal, Almekinders and Louette (Chapter 5.1.) on maize and beans in Meso-America; Sánchez and Cosío (Chapter 5.5) on potatoes in the Andes; Admasu Tsegaye and Struik (Chapter 5.7) on enset, and Teekens (Chapter 5.6) on cereals in Ethiopia.

The three subsequent chapters in this section are situated in areas outside centres of diversity and away from the keen attention of conservationists. Catalán and Pérez, describing a case in Chile (Chapter 2.4) and Friis-Hansen, writing about Tanzania (Chapter 2.5), discuss areas classified as less marginal in agro-ecological terms. The next chapter looks at a situation in Zimbabwe (Chapter 2.6) where farmers must deal with extremely marginal soils and face regular droughts. The Chile case illustrates how Mapuche communities maintain genetic diversity in a dynamic seed-supply system. Such an integrated system is also described by Sánchez and Cosío (Chapter 5.5) for management of native potato varieties in the Andes. Catalán and Pérez show how Mapuche perceive genetic and environmental variation as an integral part of their culture requiring specific management practices. The Tanzania case presents two contrasting experiences in the same country with two crops and various farmer categories. The cases show how the diversity of varieties fit farmers' needs; they illustrate how farmers' needs and, consequently, management of crop genetic diversity are influenced by the socio-economic context. The holistic perception of biodiversity of rural people in Zimbabwe is documented by Gonese and Haverkort (Chapter 2.6), who illustrate how world views differ and how these are reflected in the management and use of genetic diversity.

The final group of chapters in this section contains case studies of farmers' use of diversity in agricultural systems characterized by high fertilizer and chemical inputs, and by a dramatically reduced employment of crop genetic diversity. Cases from Luzon, the Philippines (Basilio and Razon, Chapter 2.10) and Minnesota, USA (Mercer and Wainwright, Chapter 2.7) illustrate how farmers in the North and in the South have run into problems as a result of high input levels and low levels of genetic diversity. Basilio presents experiences of Green Revolution rice farmers from Luzon, the Philippines. Mercer demonstrates how farmers in the Red River Valley in Minnesota, USA were forced to use short-term solutions which ultimately threatened the entire agricultural system with disintegration.

These chapters, and those by Wiskerke (Chapter 2.8) and Scott (Chapter 2.9), also demonstrate the activism of farmers in exploring alternative approaches involving greater use of crop genetic diversity. Wiskerke and Scott refer to experiences of farmers' groups in the Netherlands and Canada, respectively, of reintroducing genetic diversity; they are pioneer farmers trying to reverse a trend. Both cases also illustrate the problems these pioneer farmers encounter in their commercial and regulatory environments. Basilio's discussion of the use of rice genetic diversity in the Philippines shows that some farmers in the South share a similar desire for genetic diversification of their Green Revolution agriculture, and are meeting very similar institutional constraints.

2.1. Farmers' management of sorghum diversity in eastern Ethiopia

Shawn McGuire

Introduction

Although Ethiopia may not be a centre of origin, it is certainly a centre of diversity for sorghum: farmers manage an impressive variety of types throughout the country (Stemler et al., 1977). Sorghum is the second most important crop in Ethiopia, and has been the subject of formal breeding for 25 years; however, nearly all varieties planted are farmer varieties (CSA, 1997b). This chapter looks at farmer management of farmer varieties in eastern Ethiopia and is based on field work in Melkaa Horaa and Funyaandiimo Farmers' Associations in the lowlands and highlands, respectively, of Western Harerghe Zone.

Meeting a diversity of needs

Farmers use diversity to meet complex goals in the difficult farming systems of this region. They generally grow several sorghum varieties on their farms, planting these mixed together in their plots. Sorghum faces many stresses, including various pests, birds, soil infertility and drought. While farmers prefer varieties with good yield and marketing potential, they seek to lessen their risk with varieties that give stability. Moreover, grain yield is not their only concern: sorghum is also used for food, fodder, fuel and construction. Finally, environmental conditions such as soil type and texture, and social factors such as the level of market involvement, vary within the same community. These factors all affect variety choice. Thus farmers combine varieties to meet different needs (Table 2.1); varieties – and variety mixtures – planted can vary greatly between farms in the same community.

Table 2.1: Responses from 58 lowland and 83 highland farmers in Eastern Ethiopia for the traits they appreciate in the varieties they grow, with percentage of total farmers mentioning a given trait

Trait	No.	%
Lowland		
Food quality	30	51.7
Market price	23	39.7
Feed quality	14	24.1
Yield	11	19.0
Drought resistance	10	17.2
Stalkborer resistance	7	12.1
Everyone grows it	5	8.6
Fast maturity	5	8.6
Always had it/used to it	5	8.6
Locally adapted	4	6.9
Tillering	4	6.9
Timing of maturity	3	5.2
Like it	2	3.4
Sweet stalk	2	3.4
Colour	2	3.4
Bird resistance	2	3.4
Highland		
Food quality	40	48.2
Yield	37	44.6
Feed quality	32	38.6
Stalkborer resistance	24	28.9
Fast maturity	23	27.7
Market price	20	24.1
Locally adapted	20	24.1
Drought resistance	14	16.9
Everyone grows it	7	8.4
Always had it/used to it	5	6.0
Disease resistance	4	4.8
Storage ability	4	4.8
Fuel (capacity to burn)	3	3.6
Bird resistance	3	3.6
Strong seeds	2	2.4
Colour	2	2.4
Tillering	1	1.2
Large seed	1	1.2
Fermenting ability	1	1.2

Relationship of varieties with agro-ecology

Farmers note environmental variation in their own fields, but they generally mix varieties, and do not fine-tune variety planting in response to this. However, they do define environments at larger scales (a few hundred metres in the mountainous highlands, several kilometres in the flat lowlands) by topography, soil or rainfall patterns, and associate particular varieties with these. Farmers may thus distinguish between a cold, eroded hilltop, a poorly drained valley floor, or an area with peculiar rainfall patterns caused by the surrounding mountains. Local adaptation remains an important trait for farmers (Table 2.1).

Even though they generally work within their own agro-ecological zones, farmers still experiment with material from other zones. Generally, descending from the cool highlands temperature increases, rainfall is less secure and the growing season is shorter; highland farmers wanting faster-maturing sorghum may seek material from the lowlands that is adapted to the shorter rainfall periods there. Whether a variety is locally common or not, farmers often identify particular regions as preferred sources for seed of certain variety types. Such regions are generally areas where a given variety type dominates. This suggests that farmers recognize the areas where the variety is widely used as valuable seed source areas, for reasons of either seed quality or seed availability.

Ethiopian agricultural researchers define three broad environmental categories for the entire country: high-, mid-, and lowland, and formal sorghum breeding targets areas in these macrozones. Farmers' interpretations of agro-ecologies are more local, yet can cut across the macrozones defined by breeders.

Naming of varieties

Without detailed studies of diversity, through either genetics or direct characterization, our best indicator for diversity remains the variety names given by farmers. Farmers describe their varieties in eastern Ethiopia with a name composed of three terms: the first denotes a general variety type, the second usually refers to seed colour, and the third (when present) describes a subtype, which is generally a local term. In interviews in several highland villages, farmers mentioned over 30 different names for the sorghum in their fields, with an equal diversity of (different) names from interviews with lowland farmers. In northern Ethiopia, Teshome et al. (1997) found that farmers' naming systems for sorghum related well to scientific classifications.

Management of the same variety differs among farmers. Off-types arise from crossing between varieties: some farmers carefully avoid these when selecting seed to keep their varieties 'pure', though others do not, and mix them in. New and unfamiliar varieties, obtained through exchange or through accidental mixtures, are named and managed distinctly from known varieties by some farmers, who keep seed lots with different names separated, while others mix them into more familiar types. Furthermore, farmers give one name to all the modern varieties released, even though these can differ considerably. Thus the identity and diversity of a given variety may not always relate directly to variety names, but are also affected by farmers' management and criteria.

Seed sources and flows

Seed exchange among farmers is regular and extensive, especially in the lowland areas where risk of crop failure is high because of variable onset of the rains. One-third of the 250 farmers interviewed in 1998 mentioned giving or selling seed to others. Farmers who give seed tend to be better off than average (having more land or oxen); those who regularly need to borrow are often among the poorest, consuming their stocks before planting (the 'chronic seed insecure' of Cromwell, 1996). Farmers may retain seeds of their preferred varieties for many years (Table 2.2), often claiming they received no external inputs of seed to these lots. However, disasters occur, even to wealthier farmers, sometimes requiring complete replacement of seed stocks lost to poor harvests or to storage pests. For example, failure of early rains in the lowlands causes farmers to scramble for seed from fast-maturing varieties, as occurred in 1998. This partly explains the higher amount of off-farm seed that lowland farmers 'received' in that year (Table 2.2): for instance, 17kg is often enough to plant an average farm at standard seeding rates.

Table 2.2: Means (with standard deviations) of seed exchange parameters reported by 40 lowland and 55 highland farmers

Area	Parameter	Variety: first obtained*		Replaced seed stock†		Received 1998‡	Given/sold§
		No. years ago	Amount (kg)	No. years ago	Amount (kg)	Amount (kg)	Amount (kg)
Lowland	Mean	12.1 (10.9)	10.7 (8.7)	7.8 (6.4)	8.5 (7.2)	17.7 (22.9)	17.4 (20.3)
	No. varieties	54	30	10	10	7	11
	Percentage non-local¶	18		80		29	45
Highland	Mean	13.7 (10.9)	5.4 (3.8)	2.6 (2.2)	6.3 (3.6)	6.9 (8.2)	16.5 (18.8)
	No. varieties	76	42	9	8	7	24
	Percentage non-local¶	8		11		29	17

* The number of years ago each variety is first obtained and the starting amount (if known).
† Replaced seed stocks, and the number of years ago this last occurred, with amounts.
‡ Seed received from off-farm in current season (1998) only.
§ Seed given/sold in current season (1998) only.
¶ Percentage of exchanges from/to another locality.

Farmers store seed on-farm: those who can afford it store large amounts (>100kg) to enable several plantings if germination fails and to give to those in need, maintaining ties among neighbours. Much seed exchange is local, although a proportion extends beyond the local group of villages (farmers' associations), reflecting relationships among neighbours and kin in most cases. Merchants are also important, especially in the lowlands where they supply fast-maturing varieties from farms in other regions.

Seed sowing and hybridization

Sorghum usually self-pollinates, although a significant proportion of seed comes from crosses between plants (5 per cent, though some estimates are much higher). Farmers mix varieties, usually two or three, but sometimes up to 10 types in one plot. Most sorghum holdings are adjacent, with very few fields more than 100m from another. Farmers strive for fairly even maturity with their neighbours' fields in order to lessen exposure to bird attack: every one of 15 fields observed in 1998 had at least one variety that started to flower while another variety was in bloom in the same, or in an adjacent field. Furthermore, weedy sorghum is common in field margins, at least in the lowlands, and crosses readily with cultivated varieties (Arriola and Ellstrand, 1996; Pedersen et al., 1998). There is ample opportunity for pollen exchange within and between varieties, and even from weedy sorghum into cultivated types. Thus gene flow is dynamic within and among local varieties.

Different morphological types in a mixture can be considered as distinct varieties. Farmers generally choose seed from the distinct varieties that make up the crop in the field by mass selection, pooling seed for the coming year from individually selected heads. In general, they seek heads free from disease, with large and densely packed seeds and even maturity. Some farmers select a proportion of their seed before or during harvest, looking at the whole plant when deciding which heads to take. Most seed is selected after harvest from piles of heads left to dry. They select a quantity of seed of each variety roughly in proportion to their planting intentions the coming year. The total amount of seed saved varies greatly, with wealth an important factor. While mixture allows ample opportunity for crossing among varieties, many farmers select seed that is true to type for that variety, maintaining purity of colour and of traits they desire. Those selecting pre-harvest also consider other plant characters, especially for drought-resistant traits (e.g. juicy stalk, waxy bloom, flag leaf erect after mid-season drought). Varieties are pooled again when seed is threshed and stored. Such mechanical mixtures are an important means of introducing new diversity to farmers: in seed obtained from the market or neighbours, farmers often find unexpected (and sometimes unfamiliar) varieties mixed in.

Farmers' perceptions of hybridization

Farmers note off-types and other varieties in their fields. They commonly use the term *Dikala* to describe an unintended mixture. While this term can refer to crosses between plants or animals, the term is usually translated as 'bastard' when applied to humans. Although attitudes to mixtures are not entirely negative, most farmers seek purity in their variety selection, especially for colour. Farmers identify some crosses with particular names, and very actively avoid these. *Jengaa* can develop from crosses between white and red varieties: its vigorous growth and high yield seem impressive, but farmers find that its brown grain has poor food

47

quality. Crosses with wild types (*Qillee* in the lowlands, *Fechatee* in the highlands) have small, dark seeds that fall out before harvest – the highland name means 'shatter' in the Oromo language. Farmers actively remove the plants from these crosses from the field after flowering, when they can be identified. Popular descriptions of the origins of these types reflect farmers' dislike of these hybrid types. *Jengaa* is said to come from the urine of oxen (*ye beré shint*) that graze the stubble after harvest, while *Qillee* is thought to be transported in droppings of birds that nest in marshy areas. Though many younger farmers thought this was not literally true, such explanations for the occurrence of the hybrid types remain very common. Weedy sorghum is not obvious in the highlands, and curiously, highland farmers blame *Fechatee*'s presence on an act of deliberate contamination – they say that years ago one farmer collected it from the lowlands to secretly sow it in a rival's field as revenge, and it has remained in the area ever since.

Genetic diversity and change

Pollen flow and extensive seed exchange may blur genetic differences among different farmer holdings of the same variety. When asked if anyone had 'better seed', some farmers replied: 'nobody's seed is different because we all give to each other'. Seed viability after storage is an important trait in the quality of seed as it affects yield potential. Farmers also directly relate storage to seed performance: 'our seed is the same [as our neighbours'] because our storage systems are the same'. As mentioned above, farmers associate varieties with particular agro-ecological zones: continuous seed exchange (and gene flow) within these zones contributes to the development of wide adaptation, reducing genotype-by-environment interactions within these zones.

Extensive seed exchange and risk may also influence farmers' attitudes to mixtures and genetic change. In a hazardous environment varietal identity is important – farmers do not want to be surprised by a variety's grain quality, management requirements or maturity time. Because of past disastrous experiences with misidentified material from merchants, non-governmental organizations or even the government, many prefer neighbours as sources of seed. Certainty of identity is not just important for individual farmers, who depend for seed on others, it also has a social value. A dozen farmers in the lowlands (21 per cent) and highlands (14 per cent) gave reasons such as 'everyone grows it', 'always had it', 'used to it', or 'I like it' for growing their varieties, reflecting the value of having material whose performance is familiar to themselves and their neighbours. Although farmers in eastern Ethiopia plant variety mixtures and are always interested in trying new material, they remain cautious in the face of risk, and their practices serve to manage the degree of genetic mixture of their varieties.

2.2 Farmers' use of landraces in the *Hanfetz* mixed cropping system in Eritrea

Woldeamlak Araia and Paul Struik

Introduction

Mixed cropping is farmers' common practice in Africa, Asia and Latin America. It is defined as simultaneously growing two or more crops on the same land in the same growing season, broadcasting all component crops or mixing them within a row. The cropping system called *Hanfetz* is practised in the highlands of Eritrea and to a lesser extent in northern Ethiopia. *Hanfetz* is the Tigrigna word for mixed cropping of barley and bread wheat. Other types of mixed cropping practised by farmers in Eritrea include *Wahrer*, a mixture of sorghum and pearl millet or sorghum and beans, and *Sergen*, a mixture of white and red teff.

Most mixed cropping systems in the world contain a legume. This is not always the case, as demonstrated in Eritrea for *Hanfetz* and *Sergen*. In Eritrea, crops are exposed to many biotic and abiotic stresses, and under these conditions farmers opt for crop mixtures. In such stressful environments, benefits of mixed cropping may also be realized using mixtures of cereals without legumes. This chapter focuses on mixtures of barley and wheat (*Hanfetz*), using recent studies and surveys of Eritrean agriculture by the College of Agriculture of the University of Asmara, supported by Wageningen University, the Netherlands. This chapter is based on the authors' observations and expertise in *Hanfetz* through farming system surveys and research.

Farmers' practices

Sowing
From the end of June until the first week of July, a mixture of barley and wheat seeds is broadcast by hand. The amount of seed used per hectare ranges from 80 to 250kg. The amount of seed required for a mixed crop is lower than that of a barley monoculture crop, as farmers consider wheat to be stronger in tillering. The amount of seed provides a suitable ground cover for competing with weeds and produces an adequate number of spikes. Seed proportions of both crops used by the majority of farmers range from 67 per cent for barley and 33 per cent for wheat. Few farmers use a 50 : 50 seed mixture. The proportion used depends on the sources of seed available and the objectives for production.

Harvesting
Farmers harvest the crop mixture by cutting the stems close to ground level with a sickle. This practice is based on obtaining a maximum yield of straw. The period of harvest lasts from the end of October until mid-November. The barley crop is harvested when it has reached full maturity and when

49

wheat is starting to mature, changing its canopy colours to yellowish. To reduce losses through seed shattering, farmers usually harvest early in the morning when it is still humid. When the crop does not mature in a uniform fashion, farmers harvest patch-wise. Mature patches are harvested first, leaving the remainder to be harvested and threshed at a later stage.

Seed processing
If the crop is still humid, it is dried in a heap for 2 weeks. Oxen trample the harvest on a smoothed clay floor to thresh it. If the harvest is already dry after collection, the crop is threshed the first day after harvest. Subsequently it is winnowed by hand.

Seed and crop storage
Farmers store the harvest of the *Hanfetz* crop in bulk in traditional facilities made of earth mud. The seed for the next *Hanfetz* crop is separated from the bulk after harvesting. It is stored separately in bags for planting during the next season, and some farmers buy seed from the market and mix it in a proportion of 67 per cent barley to 33 per cent wheat. Environmental selection pressure affects the genetic composition of the mixture, with shifts between wheat and barley and between the various landraces within each of the crop components.

Crop rotation
Hanfetz is cultivated in various crop rotation cycles. The most commonly practised cycle concerns the 4-year cereal-based system (*Hanfetz* – teff – linseed – wheat or barley – *Hanfetz*). Another rotation cycle is the cereal/pulse-based system with a 4-year cycle (*Hanfetz* – wheat – fallow or pulses – pulses – *Hanfetz*) and with a 5-year cycle (*Hanfetz* – sorghum – teff – linseed – fallow or pulses – *Hanfetz*).

Use and consumption
Hanfetz is used for human consumption in the form of bread, locally known as *kitcha*; it is tasty and nutritious. The seed may also be roasted, and as a consumable product it is known as *kolo*. The seed is also used for preparing *sewa*, a local beverage. The straw is used for animal feed (cattle, sheep and goats).

Production of *Hanfetz*

The central highlands of Eritrea are the major production area for *Hanfetz*. In the period 1994–1999, the mean area under *Hanfetz* cultivation was 7160ha (see Table 2.3). The total area cultivated with *Hanfetz* depends on the onset of seasonal rains. If the rain starts early, farmers plant maize and sorghum. If it starts late, wheat, barley or mixed crops will be sown. In the period 1994–1999, *Hanfetz* production in Eritrea reached only 6200t. Owing to poor rainfall only 2300t were produced in 1995; the 1994 cropping season was better with a production of 7495t. In 1999 the production was 8500t. Especially in years with insufficient rainfall the production of

Table 2.3: *Hanfetz* total area of production, production volume and yield per ha in Eritrea in the period 1994–99

Production data	Hanfetz	Hanfetz *of wheat*	Hanfetz *of barley*
Area	7160ha	28% of total area	16% of total area
Production	6200t	30% of total production	14% of total production
Yield	0.84t/ha	20% > monoculture	11% > monoculture

mixtures is better than a single crop of wheat or barley. On average, yields of *Hanfetz* per ha are 20 and 11 per cent higher than yields of monocultures of wheat and barley, respectively.

Advantages of cultivating *Hanfetz*

In general, farmers indicate several advantages of mixed cropping in terms of yield, yield stability, quality of diet, animal feed from crop residues, and control of biotic stresses. In a number of surveys farmers have indicated the following advantages with respect to cultivating *Hanfetz*.

Yield advantage
The entire crop yield of *Hanfetz* is usually higher than for barley or wheat monocultures. In addition, the flour quantity per unit of harvested product is higher than for a sole barley crop. Factors contributing to this advantage in yield are:

○ better utilization of soil-borne resources by mixtures, due to niche differentiation
○ better lodging resistance of barley due to support provided by the sturdier wheat
○ prolonged yield ability – the early-maturing barley may be overgrown by the later and taller wheat thus lengthening the duration of a green crop in the field
○ better resistance of the mixture to drought.

Yield stability
Farmers grow *Hanfetz* as an insurance against drought. The basis of yield stability is that if one component crop fails or grows poorly, the other component makes use of the additional space and resources and may thus compensate for the potential loss in yield. This phenomenon depends on differences in either growth rate, duration of the growth cycle, resistance against drought or timing of sensitive developmental stages. For farmers, barley is the most favourable cereal under extreme conditions of drought, as it can be harvested earlier than other cereals. This earliness provides a drought-escape mechanism and guarantees a supply of food in years of drought. However, a monoculture of barley provides low-quality bread owing to its low gluten content. In years with adequate rains, the monoculture of barley does not make full use of the resources and potential offered

by the growing season, therefore it is mixed with wheat to produce a higher yield.

Food quality
Farmers indicate that bread made out of *Hanfetz* is preferred to that made of barley alone. It is tastier, and more palatable and digestible.

Animal feed
Crop residues are the major source of animal feed in Eritrea, and the total amount of straw is larger for *Hanfetz* than the amount for sole barley, even though barley straw is considered more palatable for animals.

Diseases, insects and weeds
Farmers in Eritrea reported that the severity of disease and insect problems in *Hanfetz* is lower than that in single crops. This requires confirmation through special field studies. The incidence of weeds (mainly wild oats) is also lower than in sole cropping, probably because mixed cropping provides a more competitive community of crop plants both in space and time.

Crop mixtures can have negative effects on yield and yield stability if the component species are not complementary, or if plant populations, and especially the proportions of component crops used, are not optimal. However, farmers in Eritrea do not consider that growing mixtures rather than monocultures is a disadvantage.

Hanfetz and genetic diversity

Farmers in Eritrea have, over time, evaluated and composed the most favourable crop and landrace combination in the *Hanfetz* cropping system. Farmers indicate that particular landraces of barley and wheat combine well, whereas others do not. A particular *Hanfetz* crop may be composed of, for instance, two barley landraces and two wheat landraces. The landraces used in the mixtures differ in maturity, drought and yield potential. The *Hanfetz* system is apparently a case in which the available cereal diversity in the area is utilized most optimally. Table 2.4 illustrates some of the landraces used in the cropping system. The production system in itself may be considered a contribution to the maintenance of this functional diversity.

Table 2.4: Landraces of barley and wheat used in the *Hanfetz* system

Crop	Landrace	Characteristics
Barley	Yeha	Early-maturing, drought tolerant, two rows, white seeds, frost tolerant
	Kuunto	Late-maturing, less drought-tolerant, six rows, high-yielding
Wheat	Itay/Kenya	Late-maturing, no awns, white seeds, high-yielding
	Mana	Early-maturing, white seeds, tall
	Russo	Late-maturing, long awns, flat heads, big seeds, high-yielding, susceptible to rust

Future trends

Farmers will continue the cultivation of the *Hanfetz* barley–wheat mixture in Eritrea as long as agriculture is characterized by low use of external inputs and by a high risk of drought. *Hanfetz* currently acts as an emergency and insurance crop. It is characterized by a relatively stable yield under potentially disastrous conditions. When irrigation and fertilizer become available, the advantages of the crop mixture in relation to yield and yield stability become less significant. The environment will be controlled to a higher degree and therefore will become more uniform. In addition, increased integration of production and market will favour monocropping over mixed cropping. The *Hanfetz* production is currently used for home consumption; *Hanfetz* is not sold on the markets. If production levels increased, surpluses would become available for commercialization and a surplus of monocrop production would fetch better prices. Mechanized harvesting would also favour monocropping: differences in plant height and differentiated maturity of wheat and barley are disadvantages in such a mechanized cropping system. It may be concluded that the *Hanfetz* mixed cropping system is well adapted to low-input agriculture in complex, diverse and risk-prone environments. The argument that mixtures are not easy to manage can be justified but mixed cropping should not be replaced by monocultures of one of its component crops even if the levels of inputs increases and the environmental variation is reduced. Mixtures should receive considerable attention due to various advantages that they provide to farmers, including the maintenance of biodiversity. *Hanfetz* can be managed almost as easily as barley or wheat monocrops, especially if planted in rows, even under high input and mechanization.

Opportunities for research

Since April 1996, the University of Asmara has conducted a study on the diversity, competition, yield advantages and yield levels of barley and wheat landraces in mixed cropping. This study had the following objectives.

○ To analyse optimal varietal composition in *Hanfetz* and identify compatible landrace combinations to obtain higher yields.
○ To study the effect of population densities and proportions of component crops to optimize productivity of mixtures.
○ To study the effect of moisture stress in *Hanfetz*, testing various genotype combinations and component crop proportions. In this manner the best crop component and genotype mixtures may be identified to maximize productivity under high-stress conditions.

The *Hanfetz* cropping system also provides a unique opportunity and model for testing other relevant research questions related to agrobiodiversity. Both authors are involved in studies to formulate answers to the following questions:

o how much variation do we need to obtain yield stability in an agro-ecosystem?
o how does abiotic stress affect the frequencies of component crops and the genotype frequencies within component crops?
o how do agricultural practices (sowing density, fertilizer application, etc.) affect the relative proportions of crops and genotypes?
o can we manipulate diversity to such an extent that it will serve as a tool to manage stress and abiotic variation in the agro-ecosystem?

Conclusions

Maintaining the biological diversity of crop species in Eritrea is being given much attention. In an effort to conserve plant genetic resources, *in situ* conservation has become a major strategy. Mixed cropping may play a major role in the *in situ* and on-farm conservation of landraces. Therefore much attention in research concerns the agronomic background of this cropping system, to support and strengthen farmers' management of land-races of barley and wheat under *Hanfetz* cultivation. An understanding of the basic mechanisms of the cropping system may enable farmers and scientists to develop crop improvements that combine increased productivity with the conservation of genetic diversity.

2.3. Farmers' maintenance of sweet potato diversity in Irian Jaya

Gordon Prain, Jürgen Schneider and Caecilia Widiyastuti

Introduction

Several studies have shown how small numbers of 'modern' or selected commercial varieties have come to dominate farming systems, contributing to fragmentation into pockets or islands of production and even causing the disappearance of indigenous cultivars (Fowler and Mooney, 1990; Brush, 1993). Although many studies tell us that this does occur, we still do not have a good view of crop variety maintenance and dominance in space and time. Without this kind of understanding 'from the inside', we cannot answer the following key question: is variety replacement and dominance of Green Revolution varieties something quite new and irreversible, specifically linked to 'modernization', or have there also been dynamic changes in variety areas and portfolios in so-called 'traditional' agricultural

54

replanted old beds. The former, which have higher fertility, are almost exclusively planted with original (*asli*) varieties, which they believe require better fertilization. The extreme case is the variety inin which is planted in a pile of ash from burnt branches of cleared garden to ensure good productivity. Thus, given the variability of the environment that exists in the uplands and especially in the mountains, we can expect to find considerable diversity, even where the cultural preferences seem to be very similar and very narrow.

In fact we find that household preferences are not at all narrow, and this is evident when we observe variety maintenance more comprehensively along the two dimensions described earlier: the frequency of planting in different beds as well as the more common measure of total plant number. While helalekue and musan are the most important sources of food and pig feed, respectively – the 'bulk' – several varieties are also maintained for more specialist but equally crucial needs, for example, infant food, sale to niche markets, and supplementary adult food. The most striking special need – an example, incidentally, which really questions the concept of 'basic needs' – is the role of particular varieties in rituals of first planting and consecration of land. Although less densely cultivated, these varieties appear to be no less essential than the bulk varieties. This vital contribution to the society is referred to as 'cultural saliency'.

Contrary to the Green Revolution type of varietal change, where high-yielding varieties tend to replace local cultivars and then replace each other (Prain et al., 1991), most of the dynamism of local maintenance in the case described here occurs among varieties that are planted in a few beds and with very few plants per bed. Women say they do not forget to plant any varieties, it is just that some get overwhelmed by other plants and die; it seems to be the ones in this third category that systematically disappear, as Figure 2.2 illustrates. This is in contrast to ritual varieties which also have very few plants per bed, but the many women who tend these few plants in most of the beds do not let them disappear. The dynamism of residual or experimental varieties does suggest the flow of a certain type of variety through local systems. There is reluctance among women to just discard or forget those varieties, but a hypothesis would also be that a residual variety has to show some specific valued characteristic to remain in the inventory as a more salient cultivar. Almost certainly these experimental varieties include the products of fortuitous seed germination, as well as the casually plucked vine cutting from a neighbour's garden, or those obtained from more exotic locations during travel. What is not known from the very brief period for which data are available is the way and extent to which farmers bestow greater cultural saliency on these experimental varieties so that they become more widely represented in gardens. The two introduced cultivars *Tinta* and *Wortel* may be a product of this process of experimentation and selection, ending up in a high proportion of beds in the 1998 survey, but barely present in 1994. Wagawaga women know this, but we don't. A lot more work with farmers will be needed to understand this process.

2.4. The conservation and use of biodiversity by Mapuche communities in Chile

Rodrigo Catalán and Isolde Pérez

Introduction

The Mapuche people are the largest group of indigenous peoples in Chile. The Mapuche have a tradition of thousands of years of gathering forest and garden products in the areas close to their homes. After the Chilean State occupied the Mapuche territory at the end of the 19th century, their economy underwent major changes that had an impact on their farming system. Since then, small-scale agriculture has replaced the old way of life of gathering, gardening and farming. A large number of crops now used were introduced from Europe, and in some cases these crops substituted for native crop species.

Information presented in this chapter is based on a survey conducted by the Centro de Educación y Tecnología (CET). The survey was part of the Chilean project of the Community Biodiversity Development and Conservation Programme (CBDC). Chapter 3.5 gives a general overview of this programme. The study area is located in the South Central Zone of Chile (38° latitude), 15km north-east of the city of Temuco. It comprises 3400ha and is inhabited by 208 Mapuche families belonging to the communities of Bochoco, Tromén Alto, Chanquin Alto and Juan Queupán.

The production system

The Mapuche production system establishes spaces within the farm. These spaces differ in their cultivation and use of products, as well as in the number and type of species cultivated, utilized and maintained. These subsystems are known as the *huerta*, *chacra*, *loma*, and forest area. They cover the following types of land use.

○ The *huerta* or home garden is the subsystem with the longest tradition within the Mapuche production system, and brings together a diversity of plants. In some cases this diversity covers more than 100 species in areas of less than half a hectare. A diversity of spatial arrangements of biodiversity has been observed in the *huerta*. Herbaceous, bushy and tree plants are found in three or more vertical layers, and plants are horizontally distributed according to local preferences. This subsystem has been described as 'living gene banks' (Qualset et al., 1997).
○ The *chacra* is a plot close to the homes of farmers where major crops such as legumes and potatoes are cultivated. This subsystem is rich in terms of biodiversity at the genetic level.
○ The area of extensive crop and pasture management, *loma*, constitutes a subsystem that was recently incorporated into the Mapuche production system. This area is used for cattle grazing and cultivation of cereal

crops. It is poor in biodiversity. Farmers generally use agrochemicals in this subsystem.

○ The remnants of natural forest cover areas around the farm that are rarely larger than 5ha. Forests contain high levels of biodiversity at the species level, providing a refuge for wild species. This subsystem is a starting point for any environmental restoration initiative seeking to expand the area of natural forests. Farmers use this space for gathering medicinal and edible plants. The area is strongly linked through farmers' management to the home garden.

These subsystems are interrelated through flows of plants, seeds, cuttings and organic material. Some of these interactions require human interventions, whereas for other flows the importance of human intervention is limited.

Genetic and species diversity

An inventory of the biodiversity made in the area demonstrated a greater richness in biodiversity at species than at generic level. Information gathered during the course of the inventory has been processed into a database. Knowledge of and information on the use of species or varieties is one of the components entered in the database.

Of the native species described, 96 per cent are wild or semi-domesticated. Nonetheless, Melnyck et al. (1995) point out that the word 'wild' does not necessarily imply the absence of human management of this species diversity. They have not been subjected to breeding processes, which could have generated greater intraspecific diversity. The genetic diversity of wild species within the area has barely been studied. However, at first appearance the genetic diversity within the encountered species does not demonstrate distinct ecotypes. In terms of cultivated plants, 95 per cent of the species included in the inventory are introduced (see Table 2.5).

Table 2.5: Origin of species diversity in four Mapuche communities, Temuco area

	Number of species	
	Wild	Cultivated
Native	144	5
Introduced	86	101

Table 2.6 shows that a limited genetic diversity of major crops was observed in the area during the inventory. Wheat and common beans are considered exceptions: wheat was introduced more than 300 years ago, common bean species (*Phaseolus lunatus* and *Phaseolus vulgaris*) were cultivated before the arrival of the Spaniards, and both crops play an important role as staple food in the diet of Mapuche families.

Table 2.6: Diversity of crop varieties encountered in four Mapuche communities, Temuco area

Crop	Number of varieties
Lentils, linseed, chickpea	1
Chilli peppers, faba beans, maize	2
Garlic, oats, lupin, quinoa, clover	3
Peas	5
Potatoes	6
Wheat	12
Common beans	35

Community conservation strategies

Despite the pressures of the Green Revolution, many bean varieties were encountered. Despite processes of deforestation, a great diversity of wild species used for many different purposes was observed. Maintenance of this biodiversity is largely owing to the existence of community strategies for biodiversity conservation. In the inventory, the following conservation strategies of the local people have been recognized.

Diversity of preferences and management of environmental heterogeneity

The existence of a large number of bean varieties in the study area has been determined by diversity in preferences at family and community levels. The type of exploitation and management of environmental heterogeneity is observed as an additional related factor. Figure 2.3 shows that in neighbouring communities various bean varieties are being cultivated. Significant differences were even detected in the varieties grown for sale. Bean varieties cultivated as cash crops are often common to families and communities. This diversity is explained by small variations in topography, microclimate and soil type among communities. These variations are responsible for a greater success of varieties that are better adapted to specific environments. On the other hand, some varieties grown for household consumption are found in only some communities, or in some cases among only one or two families within the community.

Community exchange networks

Another important conservation strategy concerns exchange networks for seeds, cuttings, plants and associated knowledge within and among communities. If a family or community loses a medicinal or forest species from their home garden or forest, or if they stop growing this species or variety, exchange with other members of the network who have not lost these materials or the associated knowledge facilitates the recovery of these species. In other words, each family or community has access to all the germplasm and knowledge possessed by members of the network for their needs. This phenomenon has been studied in small-scale farmer communities in other parts of the world. It is regarded a basis for introducing and

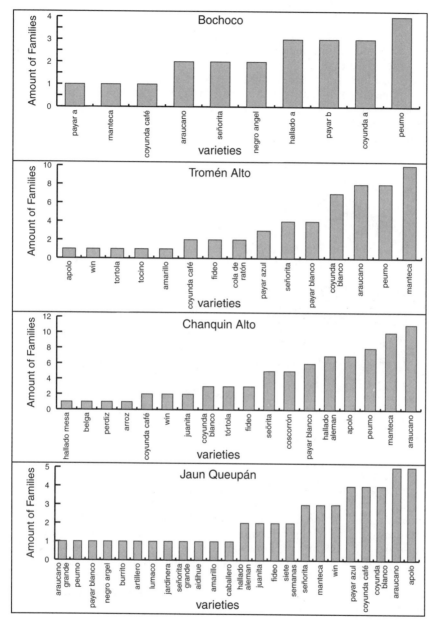

Figure 2.3: *Community exchange networks in four Mapuche communities*

recovering genetic material (Bellon et al., 1997), and is a form of de-centralized material supply system. Operation of this system is invisible to the rest of the society as it is not directly linked to the market. During a study of the structure and functions of these community exchange networks, we observed that not all families participated with the same intensity, nor did they have the same quantity of germplasm or knowledge to be shared among members. Families grow between one and 13 bean varieties. The number of varieties among communities varied from 10 to 24. Some families included only one or two neighbours in the exchange; others included the entire community and neighbouring communities. The group of farmers with an extensive network often maintains high levels of biodiversity. These families, and probably some communities, act as 'curators' of local genetic resources (see Figure 2.4).

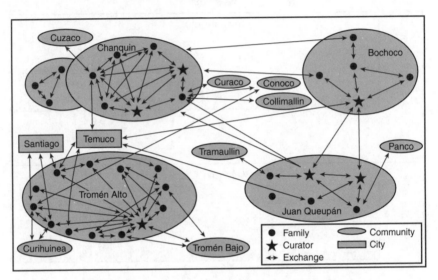

Figure 2.4: *Common bean varieties in four communities in the Temuco area*

Recovery of wild plants from the forest
Extinction of wild species that are given a high value by the communities has prompted women to recover samples threatened by overexploitation, or by the destruction of the wild habitat. These recovery activities involve the transplanting or reproduction of individual plants or species from their natural environment to a home garden where they are placed in similar soil, shade and moisture conditions. This strategy is of particular importance to wild medicinal plants, which were transferred from the forest to the family garden. At the same time, a process of domestication for these species has been started.

In vivo *conservation*
Another basic component of the community strategy is '*in vivo*' conservation of crops and wild plants. Many seeds of forest plants are recalcitrant. Conditions of high humidity make storage of seeds of these crops difficult. Maintenance of plants through yearly cultivation, or by letting them grow in gardens, forests and pastures, prevents such difficulties associated with

storage. In this manner the evolution of the species is continued in the face of a changing environment.

Strategies for the utilization of biodiversity

One of the major conclusions of the survey was that biodiversity is not distributed homogeneously throughout the landscape. Important differences have been observed with respect to the number and type of species and varieties among communities, and among farmers within each community. This diversity is directly correlated with environmental heterogeneity generated by biophysical factors such as topography and hydrography. However, it is also a product of the various ways in which soil fertility is managed.

This dynamic system of small-farmer production integrating conservation and use has been described more generally by Montecinos (1995). The system appears a constant characteristic of smallholder agriculture. The Mapuche people use and manage the biodiversity that surrounds them and has been cultivated by them.

To quantify and characterize strategies for the utilization of plants, the diversity, management and strategies for utilization have been processed and stored in a database. During the survey, 14 categories were identified as strategies for utilization. These include the production and utilization of biodiversity for food, construction wood, handicrafts, firewood, forage, rituals, fences and veterinary purposes. Information for this inventory of strategies for utilization has been gathered through individual interviews, group meetings, and walks through gardens and forests. Elderly women in the communities provided the most important contributions to this part of the research.

In 52 per cent of the cases relating to native plants, respondents indicated that they used these plants for medicinal purposes. For exotic species, 30 per cent of respondents indicated they used plants for food production. Eighty-seven per cent of all plants identified are used for at least one purpose, while this figure rose to 90 per cent for the native species. The average number of use products over all species was 1.5, though for some native tree species six products were used.

Conclusion

The use of biodiversity by the Mapuche communities is intimately connected to their culture. The diverse manners in which beans are prepared, the many remedies that make use of a large number of medicinal plants, and the ritual uses of alkaloid-containing plants are but a few examples that illustrate this relationship. The traditional knowledge that relates to these local plants is highly sophisticated. It has been gathered and transferred for centuries. Maintaining and recovering this wisdom is fundamental to the existence of a diversified system using local biodiversity.

Conservation, use and culture constitute an indivisible triangle in the Mapuche communities. Within this triangle women play a central role.

Biodiversity, and related knowledge and information, have been conserved through utilization. The diversity known is used, and people are aware that they conserve the diversity. This principle guides a number of strategies of Mapuche communities, which together constitute their system of integrated biodiversity management. This total of strategies has been efficient and has continued to persist over time, despite the numerous social and environmental changes of the 20th century.

2.5. Farmers' management and use of crop genetic diversity in Tanzania

Esbern Friis-Hansen

This chapter discusses farmers' plant genetic resource management and use of intra-species diversity of sorghum and rice in semi-arid areas of Tanzania. It will elaborate farmers' management and use of sorghum and rice genetic diversity, explore the social context of such management, and analyse the dynamics of plant genetic resource management. The information presented was obtained through a social science research project conducted between 1994 and 1997. The project worked with farmers in a sorghum-growing village (Mkulula) and a village dominated by traditional cultivation of irrigated rice (Nyelegete). A number of qualitative surveys were undertaken, including in-depth interviews of key informants, wealth ranking, and thematic interviews of farmer groups to identify and characterize local landraces and management practices. Qualitative information was combined with a quantitative survey covering 90 households.

Farmers' management and use of plant genetic resources

Farmers' management of plant genetic resources is based on local knowledge. Local capacities, skills and technical knowledge are linked to cultural, ecological and sociological factors. This knowledge base creates mutual understanding and a sense of identity among members of a farming community (Scoones and Thompson, 1994). Local knowledge is, in part, collective and embodied in socially accepted norms and practices for selection, treatment, storage, exchange, cultivation and end-use of local plant genetic resources. In addition, it is limited to specific innovative farmers. Plant genetic resource management is largely the product of collective social processes and institutions within a given community. It is dynamic, based on past experience and continuous processes of experimentation. Local plant genetic resource management is closely linked to the farming system and the social, cultural and economic context in which cultivation is practised (Friis-Hansen, 1996).

A high level of crop genetic diversity *in situ* may be beneficial to farmers under low external-input farming conditions, enabling crop varieties to adapt to changing environments and climates and to respond to the occurrence of new pests and diseases. It is difficult to judge whether or not a high level of crop diversity is positive for farmers' livelihoods. The same applies to judging the impact of genetic erosion on farmers' livelihoods (Wood, 1996). Genetic diversity is by far the most important element of crop diversity. This level of diversity enables farmers to satisfy multiple household production goals, optimize the use of household resources, and minimize the risk of crop failure. In Tanzania, characteristics of landraces relate to multiple production goals, such as:

○ combined use of both grain and non-grain products
○ palatability in relation to local preferences and cultural ceremonies
○ suitability for traditional methods of processing
○ specialized end-uses such as brewing of opaque beer.

For example, sorghum landraces in Mkulula village are tall and, in addition to grain yield, provide an important supply of supplementary fodder for livestock and building material. Through a process of continuous selection, landraces have become adapted to specific agro-ecological microniches, such as poor soil fertility (Graham and Welch, 1998). Table 2.7 illustrates specific adaptation of sorghum varieties to local microniches in Mkulula village. Farmers optimize their limited land resources by using a total of 16 sorghum varieties.

Table 2.7: Specific adaptation of local sorghum varieties in Mkulula village, Tanzania

Nature of local microniche	Sorghum varieties adapted to microniche
Fields continuously cultivated for years	Serena, PN3, Sandala, Tegemeo, Sanyagi
Fields cultivated for less than 2 years	Madzi, Hembahemba, Lugugu, Kasao
Loamy clay soils	PN3, Tegemeo, Sandala, Sanyagi, Msabe
Sandy soils	Serena, Madzi, Lugugu, Kasao

Data are based on 30 household interviews conducted in Mkulula village, Tanzania in the 1994/95 season.

Both modern varieties and landraces may be susceptible to pests and diseases. Many modern varieties have been developed based on the assumption that farmers use pesticides to control pests and diseases. This assumption ignores the reality of small-scale farmers in Tanzania who barely apply pesticides on crops that are used for consumption within the farmer household. Landraces are assumed to have some level of horizontal resistance to pathogens. The fact that in Mkulula village the sorghum disease loose smut is managed at a low and economically insignificant level is attributed to the existence of horizontal resistance to this pathogen in local sorghum landraces.

The social context of plant genetic resource management

In societies where a diversity of ethnic groups play an important role at community level, local plant genetic resource management is commonly closely integrated with the culture of each particular group. Significant differences have been observed in the use of sorghum varieties among ethnic groups in Mkulula village, and the history of the village offers an explanation for this diversity. A likely explanation for the difference in current use of sorghum varieties is the extent to which sorghum is a staple crop in the areas from which they originate. In the 1950s and 1960s, most families settled in what is today called Mkulula village. People from the Gogo tribe use 11 sorghum varieties, which is more than twice the number of varieties cultivated by farmers belonging to other ethnic groups. The cultural heritage of the Gogo tribe is linked to the traditional sorghum-growing area in central Tanzania. People from the Bena and Hehe tribes originate from areas with high rainfall, where there is a strong preference for maize. Masai people, on the other hand, are traditionally pastoralists and only recently took up the cultivation of crops such as sorghum.

Various social groups of farmers use a diversity of crop varieties. Varieties are adapted to optimize performance when cultivated under conditions constrained by a range of production factors and the availability of natural resources. Sorghum varieties cultivated by poor farmers in Mkulula village provide an excellent example. They use a significantly higher proportion of early-maturing sorghum varieties than the better-off farmers. An explanation for this difference is that poor farmers do not own a team of oxen and a plough, and therefore have to wait until the better-off farmers have completed ploughing their fields to rent an ox-team. This reduces the length of the already short growing season.

Another example describes the broader range of rice varieties cultivated by better-off farmers in Nyelegete village. These farmers cultivate and manage varieties which otherwise would be lost. Only the relatively better-off farmers cultivate the aromatic landrace called *Shingua ya mwali*, which may be translated as 'the neck of a virgin girl at pre-marrying age'. This landrace is low-yielding but has an excellent taste. It is primarily cultivated for subsistence consumption, although some is sold at high premium prices to the Indian community in Dar es Salaam.

Gender differentiation for rice management in Nyelegete village

Clear gender differences have been observed in local plant genetic resource management. Women play a dominant role in managing plant genetic resources as their responsibility includes crop production and seed multiplication. Traditionally, women are the seed selectors, who prefer to select for a range of criteria related to utilization of the product within the household. These criteria include household food requirements including palatability, taste, colour, aroma and cooking time. Women's focus on the household economy provides a balance for male-dominated market-oriented pressures that emphasize high yield and uniformity. In Nyelegete village, women are known to be more skilled than men in rice seed selection. Seed is selected in the field between the time of maturity and harvesting. Seeds are selected from fields with good levelling. Sufficient water is given to these fields, and they are considered to have a mature homogeneous plant population. The plants for seed are cut by hand with a small knife. Each household commonly selects sufficient seeds to meet the following season's requirements. Some farmers specialize in seed selection and seed production in Nyelegete village.

Replacement of sorghum landraces by one modern variety in Mkulula village

In response to the 1991/92 drought in Southern Africa, an international non-governmental organization (NGO) distributed 40t of an improved sorghum variety (PN3) as emergency seed to Ismani District, in which Mkulula village is located. The NGO had no knowledge of the performance of the modern variety. Seeds of PN3 had been purchased in Zimbabwe. The variety was developed by ICRISAT with farmers' involvement in the breeding process. PN3 has been very successful in Mkulula village: it matures early and its yield was similar to, or slightly higher than, the late-maturing landraces. As a result it was widely adopted among farmers. PN3 has white grains and farmers highly appreciate its palatability as a staple food; it is also a good source for brewing local beer. An additional advantage of PN3 over local landraces is that it is easy to process the grains for food preparation. Introduction of PN3 was highly successful; it resulted in widespread genetic erosion among local sorghum landraces. Following its small-scale introduction and cultivation in the 1992/93 season, the PN3 variety expanded to almost half the sorghum area in Mkulula in the 1993/94 season. PN3 is cultivated in 75–90 per cent of farmers' sorghum fields. Its widespread cultivation resulted in annihilation of five of the 16 sorghum landraces in the village. Several of the landraces that remained were observed to be cultivated in only such small quantities that they are threatened by loss. Farmers' adoption of PN3 has had an immediate positive impact on their household food production and security. The long-term effect of farmers' increased reliance on one variety is unclear. It is most likely that many remaining sorghum landraces will be abandoned. The community will be highly vulnerable in the event that PN3 becomes victim to a disease or pest. In 1995 some farmers in Mkulula reported that PN3 had begun to change some of its characters, and the time for maturity of PN3 had prolonged. This is caused by cross-pollination with local sorghum varieties. Absence of access to 'pure' PN3 seed causes this degeneration. Tanzanian seed companies do not produce PN3, therefore this situation is likely to create problems for farmers having to rely on this variety for their subsistence.

Replacement of rice varieties in Nyelegete village

Farmers in Nyelegete village have cultivated a large number of rice varieties over the past three decades. Rice varieties which once dominated the

area have frequently been replaced by new varieties. Some of the cultivated varieties are landraces from areas in Tanzania with long traditions of
rice cultivation; most varieties cultivated in the region are modern varieties. Variety selection criteria were inventoried during field work among
farmers in Nyelegete village. Major criteria included productivity, household requirements and market demand. Farmers seek to maximize their
total household rice production by using a range of varieties. The diversity
of varieties enables farmers to optimize the resources available. Farmers'
choices of varieties are based on a balance between access to land and
availability of labour. Large-scale farmers tend to sow late-maturing rice
varieties by broadcasting after early tractor ploughing; small-scale farmers
transplant early-maturing varieties following ox-ploughing or hand-hoeing.
Suitability of individual varieties to satisfy household preferences and
requirements is an important selection criterion. However, the importance
of this criterion has declined as rice production has become increasingly
commercial. Local landraces such as *Shinga ya mwali* are about to be lost
as they are replaced by modern, higher-yielding but less palatable varieties.
Market demand has increasingly become the most important variety selection criterion. During the 1980s the blanket price policy of the regional co-
operative union resulted in an increased use of high-yielding but relatively
poor-tasting varieties. Trade liberalization in 1988 had a dramatic impact
on farmers' selection and cultivation of rice varieties. Dar es Salaam consumer preferences began to determine market demand and resulted in a
price differentiation for rice varieties. An absolute or relative lack of seed
for most varieties reflects the fact that today the demand for previously
cultivated rice varieties has reduced dramatically. Three rice varieties are
dominant in the area: *Kilombero* (medium-maturing, medium yield potential, high price, good taste); *Fiya* (late-maturing, high yield potential, low
price, poor taste); and *Supa Mati* (early-maturing, medium yield potential,
medium price, poor taste). Today, farmers' choice of varieties is determined by the trade-off between price and volume.

Plant genetic resource management dynamics

Local plant genetic resource management is dynamic, as communities are
frequently exposed to changes in the external socio-economic context in
which they operate. Agricultural modernization policies have often had a
negative impact on local communities' capacity to manage plant genetic
resources, as they have attempted to replace traditional farming techniques
and crop varieties with modern varieties and to 'professionalize' the plant
genetic resource management system, often without considering the effects
on the overall farming system. Modernization policies in Tanzania in the
1970s and 1980s included a range of trends representative of many countries in the developing world. These trends included:

o government price subsidies for modern varieties and chemical inputs
o direct links between credit for small-scale farmers to purchase modern
  varieties and chemical inputs

70

o monopoly marketing institutions discriminating against the purchase of local varieties.

Such agricultural modernization policies were abolished or substantially reduced in the 1990s, following the economic crisis and structural adjustment programmes which instead have increased the influence of the private sector, donors and NGOs (Friis-Hansen, 1999a,b). The case of management and use of rice and sorghum genetic diversity in Tanzania demonstrates farmers' dynamic strategies to respond to the social, economic and natural environment. It shows that replacement of local varieties by other 'local' ones or modern varieties is part of farmers' response to changes in their environment. However, it is clear that genetic diversity of crops is crucial to keeping farmers' options open in order to respond to changes they may face in the future.

2.6. Cosmovision and natural resource management of the Shona people, Zimbabwe

Cosmas Gonese and Bertus Haverkort

Introduction

In this chapter we present a description of the cosmovision of the Shona people that illustrates its relevance for natural resource management and farming. Cosmovision, or world view, refers to the way a certain population perceives the world or cosmos (Gonese, 1999a). It includes the assumed relationships between people, nature and the spiritual world and can be considered as the philosophical and scientific premise of farmers' intervention in nature. It embraces all aspects of life: it does not limit itself to religion, to health or to farming. However, it has an impact on issues that are now receiving attention from the international community such as biodiversity and ecology. Cosmovisions have a great impact on the way farmers farm, and the values given to ecology and biodiversity.

Farmers have learned not to express their traditional belief systems and traditions to representatives of the outside world such as missionaries, teachers, government workers, extensionists and researchers. They have experienced that in order not to be ridiculed or suppressed, it is wiser to hide their knowledge about the natural world and to maintain their rituals and traditional institutions secretly.

Experience shows, however, that once the indigenous knowledge and cosmovision are taken seriously by outsiders, much traditional knowledge can be revealed and new partnerships can be developed.

71

The cosmovision of the Shona, or of any population, can be looked upon as an isolated and rare case, and its importance can be marginalized. This has happened consistently since modernization has begun to spread in developing countries. Yet the authors believe that it is exactly this attitude of outsiders that explains the large gap between indigenous farmers' knowledge and practices and the modern world. We feel that the time is ripe for a reversal of this situation, and to start from a respectful understanding of farmers' reality and a humble positioning of outside knowledge. In many cases it is traditional farmers who have been creating and managing the biodiversity of their environment. The reasons for this diversity management have barely been understood and frequently are not in line with the present (Western) concern for maintaining resources for future generations. Rather, they have to do with the concern of people with sacred nature, the ancestral world and the spiritual values represented by sacred places, plants and animals.

We feel that a strategy for enhancing agrobiodiversity should build on the dynamics of the real knowledge of the rural population. And a first step in this direction is understanding the dynamics in its proper context, that of its own culture.

The description of the Shona cosmovision is based on the results of a comprehensive study carried out by AZTREC. AZTREC promotes the rehabilitation of woods and wetlands, and land-use management systems which are based on African culture and knowledge systems. It is a member of the Compas network, the international platform for indigenous development (Gonese, 1999b).

The spiritual world

In the cosmovision of the Shona people the understanding is that there are three central pillars making up the living world: the spiritual world, the human world and the natural world.

Mwari, God, created the natural and human worlds. The spiritual world is composed of different spirits, they have different meeting places where they are delegated specific responsibilities. There are spirits that carry out different tasks and functions, for example spirits which specialize in war strategies, technology development, fertility, rain-making and human health (Figure 2.5).

The entire composition of the spiritual world inhabits the natural and human world. It can be in sacred places such as shrines, but it can also inhabit certain ecosystems, human bodies, or certain species of animals or plants within the natural world. In the animal kingdom there are selected sacred species such as lions, baboons, and certain birds and snakes. The human world to a large extent depends on special messages from the spiritual world transmitted via these sacred animals.

The sacred animals, to be able to perform their function as intermediary, need a dwelling place and thus require biological diversity. Once biological diversity is degraded, the valuable messengers between the spiritual world and humans would migrate to other places and could no longer serve the

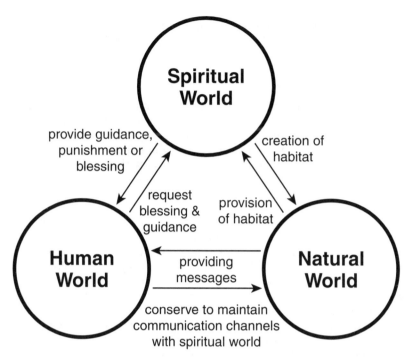

Figure 2.5: *The interaction of the Three Worlds based on traditional African cosmovision*

humans in the area. In the Shona concept, the rules and regulations for the management of natural resources are rooted in the belief of sustaining the communication channels between the spiritual and the human worlds.

The human world

Every human being has his or her own personal spirit. There are different categories and levels of spiritual authority. A special category of human beings is that of spirit mediums. These are people who are recipients of the spirit of a dead person. Important ancestors, such as the initiator of the clan, can take possession of a living human to communicate through him or her with the clan. In this way the ancestors appoint the chiefs and give them their guidance in important matters.

The approved chief is usually the highest authority within any one clan. Usually a chief is appointed by the spirit of the one who initiated the clan by having many children. Below him is a group of councillors or headmen of that clan, who may inherit the overall chieftainship when the current senior chief passes away.

Below this category are village or kraal heads. As descendants and representatives of ancestral spirits, they are responsible for land administration. Usually they are also advised by the ancestors through a spirit medium. According to traditional institutions, the spirits or ancestral spirits are the owners of humankind and are responsible for its social well-being.

The natural world

Because the spiritual world speaks through animals and habitats in certain places in the ecosystem, such animals and places are considered sacred. For example, all the vegetation, wildlife and many other natural resources surrounding sacred places such as Great Zimbabwe were made sacred because these were/are communication points within the spiritual world where the voice of God can be heard. In such places, people were/are no longer permitted to frequent the area for the purpose of hunting wild animals and birds.

Thus conservation of natural resources is understood as a by-law: if people violate taboos the voice of God will vacate the place. Such by-laws include unlawful cutting down of trees, hunting of certain animals and birds, collecting wild fruits for selling, not wearing certain clothes while entering the place, not performing rituals to show respect, violating the laws of totemic relationships by killing or eating your own totem, incest and adultery, etc.

At the shrines there are specific tree species such as *Muchakata* (*Parinari* spp.), where the actual ritual should be performed. It is the responsibility of the traditional institutions to make sure that these important tree species (believed to be habitats of various spirits) are not tampered with. The vegetation around a shrine, or any other place designated as a cultural site, should always be kept intact.

In the agricultural domain, people distinguish animals and crops that are used for rituals from animals and crops that are for consumption and commercial use. Commercial crops are frequently introduced from outside and lack a relationship with the ancestors. Rituals are associated with food crops and with ritual crops, but to a lesser extent with commercial crops.

Typically in Zimbabwe, *rapoka* or millet is used for brewing beer. The consumption of this beer is part of a ritual with an important spiritual significance, and it has to be brewed under certain conditions. Equally, tobacco is used as a snuff. This snuff and the alcohol in the *rapoko* beer help to put people in a trance to be able to communicate with the ancestral spirits. Maize, on the other hand, is generally grown as a cash crop. Here the application of mechanization, fertilizers and pesticides is not in conflict with the traditions, as the ancestors have not been living with these crops and have not set the rules for future generations.

Management of natural resources in the cosmovision perspective

The successful growth of crops depends on the good care of the spirits. Therefore, to please the spirits people have to perform rituals. In each chieftancy at least four different types of ceremonies are held each year:

before planting (for rain-making), for growing, at harvest, and during the winter period.

Further, each clan has a totemic relationship with a particular animal or plant. The members of the clans are not supposed to kill or to consume animals or plants with which they have a totemic relationship. There are clans who do not eat sorghum for that reason.

Farmers attach value to the traditional crops and varieties in the sense that they have received these crops and varieties from their ancestors. A decision to add a new crop or even a new variety therefore cannot be taken without asking the advice or the blessing of the ancestors. Here the spirit medium plays an important role.

Above all, the spiritual world owns both society and nature, because that is where all spirits live. When we talk about conserving natural resources and agriculture, we are talking about traditional institutions because they work together with the spirits. As far as natural resource management is concerned, the spirits would state the rules and regulations on how best the sacred natural species and places should be managed. Rules, such as no cutting of tree species without special permission, no hunting in sacred woodlands, no grazing around wetlands, no farming without sacrifices, no new crops or plant varieties to be grown without the permission of the ancestors, etc. are imparted to the chief who is the traditional administrator of the land.

The fundamental principle is that the habitat of those sacred natural species should be jealously preserved so as not to lose those valuable messages from the spiritual world. The conservation effort from an African perspective is not to enjoy the existence of a balanced biological diversity alone, but more importantly to sustain the interconnectedness and interdependency of the natural, human and spiritual worlds. Conservation in this respect is not a phenomenon on which traditional institutions need education. What they require are political, economic and social support mechanisms within which they can demonstrate their capacity to co-exist with nature, and where they are possibly supported in their efforts to address new issues emerging from recent developments such as population increase, commercialization, technology development and administrative reforms. Existing traditional institutions should be considered as prime partners for outsiders in agricultural development and nature conservation programmes, such as extension and research staff. Complementarity in roles can be used to the maximum only if a respectful dialogue is established that allows for challenging questions as well as for mutual learning.

2.7. (Dis)use of agricultural diversity in Minnesota, USA

Kristin Mercer and Joel Wainwright

Introduction

An agricultural crisis threatens the Red River Valley of northwestern Minnesota (USA). An epidemic of fusarium head blight has swept the region, causing the yields of the major grain crops, spring wheat and malting barley, to decline. A \$120 million tax relief package for farmers in the 1999 Minnesota legislative session comes too late for many; numerous farms have gone out of business in the past 6 years. In this chapter we examine some of the causes of these farm failures. Although various accounts have blamed the farm failures on different factors – farm mismanagement, loss of subsidies, and even bad weather – we argue that these failures must be understood within the context of decreased agro-ecosystem diversity. A decrease in diversity at several levels, when seen in conjunction with loss of financial support for wheat farming, has contributed to this new round of 'farm crisis'. In order to place these farm failures in a broader agro-ecological and historical context, we recount the decline in agro-ecosystem and economic diversity that has occurred in the area, especially since the 1970s. We then address limitations to diversification of the system and possible directions towards sustainability.

The Red River Valley: great land, bad location

The Red River Valley of northwest Minnesota is a unique environment. Situated in the lake bed of the glacial Lake Agassiz, the combination of silty deposition and prairie succession after glacial retreat developed the deep and rich soils. However, the arctic winters, cold springs and late snow melt provide climatic challenges to farming. In addition, its remote location makes transportation costs high.

There have been three main phases in the development of agricultural production in the area. Settlement of the area by European immigrants began in the late 19th century. The arrival of the railroad in the 1870s facilitated the first phase of agricultural development, which was characterized by large, corporate, spring wheat farms. The second phase of development started in the 1920s, after an economic scare, when these spring wheat farms were replaced by smaller family farms that produced a diversity of crops and livestock. Wheat production in Minnesota dropped from 3.6 million acres in 1915 to 1.4 million in 1930 (Minnesota Department of Agriculture). The third phase of development began in the 1960s, when there was a marked shift to reduced crop diversity due to economies of scale and specialization. Most farms emphasized either small grains or sugar beets, depending on whether farmers were growing small grains as the cash crop, or whether they were part of the American Crystal Sugar

Co-operative. This shift was encouraged by government subsidies for wheat, and import blockades placed on foreign sugar supplies. During this phase, tillage was reduced to save money and reduce erosion. These changes can be seen in the histories of multi-generational farms such as the one now owned by Jerry Kruger, a small grains farmer in the northern part of the Valley. 'In the 1950s we had livestock, alfalfa, oat, corn, a little wheat, barley. The farms were 160–320 acres. In the 1970s, subsidized wheat production increased and farm size increased to 1200 acres. Livestock decreased, wheat increased, and oats decreased. We started a wheat, barley, sunflower, and soybean rotation' (J. Kruger, pers. comm., 1998). By the early 1990s, grain farmers commonly planted 75 per cent of their acreage in wheat and barley, whereas sugar-beet farmers planted large acreages of small grains to lengthen the rotation between sugar-beet plantings.

Declining agro-ecological diversity

This decline of agro-ecosystem diversity in the Red River Valley created the conditions for a severe cereal disease outbreak in the 1990s. Starting in 1993, an epidemic of the cereal disease fusarium head blight or scab hit the wheat and barley fields of the Red River Valley. Fusarium head blight is caused by the fungal pathogen *Fusarium graminearum*. This pathogen is a saprophyte that feeds and overwinters on the dead tissues of grass hosts, including wheat, oat, barley, rye and maize. Wet weather in June and July are favourable for fungal reproduction. The numerous spores produced by the fungus are then plentiful during the time of heading, providing inoculum for kernel infection. This has two negative effects: (i) the pathogen stunts kernel development which decreases yields, and (ii) it produces a toxin that is difficult for non-ruminants to digest and spoils beer production. Thus farmers have reduced yields and lower prices for their grain.

In 1993, a year of disastrous flooding of the Red River, fusarium head blight had its first severe impact on the region. Localized yield losses due to fusarium head blight were as high as 33 per cent. In 1994, the disease decreased yields by 18 per cent. In 1995 and 1996 weather patterns kept inoculum levels low, but in 1997 yield losses increased again, to 12 per cent. Prior to the initial outbreak, yield losses due to scab were unimportant and infection was seen only in localized outbreaks. The severe yield losses seen during the 1990s beg the question: how did *F. graminearum* inoculum reach such high levels? And how did the cropping system of the Red River Valley suddenly become so susceptible to this disease? From an agro-ecological perspective, there are four main factors to consider.

○ Lack of diversity in crop type – there has been a long-term trend toward reducing the variety of types of crops grown, considerably increasing the proportion of grain crops in the rotation. Particularly after subsidies increased in the 1970s, grain farmers responded by increasing the acreage under production. Wheat production in Minnesota increased from 1 million to 3.6 million acres between 1970 and 1980 (Minnesota

Department of Agriculture). Sugar-beet farmers kept wheat in the rotation to decrease sugar-beet diseases associated with rotating with dicot crops such as sunflower. The abundance of grassy residue in these cropping systems created the perfect environment for the proliferation of fusarium head blight inoculum.

○ Lack of diversity in crop genetics – the diversity of the genetics of a given crop in a region is influenced by two factors: the number of varieties of the crop planted in the region, and the divergence of the genetics of each variety planted. Historically, within the Red River Valley there has always been a popular wheat variety that dominates the acreage. For example, in the mid to late 1980s Marshall, a variety with some scab tolerance, covered 70 per cent of the acreage. In the wheat- and barley-breeding programmes there was a strong push for bread- and beer-processing traits, respectively, which narrowed the genetic base of the varieties released.

○ Reduction in tillage – in the 1980s, throughout Minnesota and the midwest, farmers reduced tillage to decrease soil erosion and costs. In the Red River Valley increased residue left on the soil reduced wind and water erosion, but it also provided *F. graminearum* with plentiful residue on which to overwinter, thus building up inoculum levels.

○ Above-average rainfall – after the spring flood of 1993, the soils of the region remained wet long into the growing season. Additional rain during that year, and rain events around the time of heading during other years, provided the fungus with more than adequate moisture for infection.

These four factors increased the number of hosts for the fungal pathogen, and allowed the fungus repeatedly to complete its life cycle, resulting in the decline of yields and grain quality. While significant, these concerns represent only one part of the farm crisis as a whole. Fusarium head blight contributed to the crisis by coming at a time of increasing production costs, declining prices, loss of price supports, and tightening of credit. It is to these and other issues that we now turn.

Tightening political-economic diversity

Agro-ecological systems may lose genetic and crop diversity and not fall immediately into crisis. Some degree of stability, if not long-term sustainability, can exist if favourable economic and social structures surround and support the agrofood system. A crucial component of a healthy agrofood system is flexibility in financial, production and marketing options. A broad web of political and economic factors have affected the flexibility of the Red River Valley to react to the ecological crisis the farmers face. As a result there were 10 per cent fewer mid-size farms (500–999 acres) in 1997 than in 1987 (MISA, 1999). Here we briefly address two important, interrelated aspects of the loss of flexibility in the Valley.

Price subsidies for wheat production and the price protections on sugar beet (with consequent wheat rotations) led to an entire region dangerously dependent on large acreages of wheat. This steady expansion of small-grain production, in conjunction with reduced tillage, increased the susceptibility of the region to a fusarium head blight epidemic. Farmers suffered because yields have declined due to fusarium head blight, while real prices for spring wheat have been highly variable. From 1979 to 1984, farmers received favourable prices for spring wheat in Minnesota, roughly $4.71 per bushel (adjusted for inflation). However, with the exception of 1995 and 1996, prices have not reached these levels in the 1990s, averaging $3.51 per bushel (MISA, 1999). This decline in profitability has depressed land values and reduced financing options. Farmers who search for solutions have run into numerous constraints to change, namely a lack of support for alternatives. The lack of flexibility inherent in the financial, production and marketing systems has forced many farmers to expand or file for bankruptcy.

A second, related problem concerns the lack of diversity in agronomic support and research networks, or the limited variety of 'agro-ecological knowledge'. Historically, the state land-grant university system has been the major producer and provider of agricultural research and support for farmers in the American mid-west. This institutional network has emphasized research and breeding aimed at maximizing production and processing qualities for major crops, including spring wheat and barley. Most efforts within the system to confront the present crisis entail breeding for resistance to *F. graminearum*, a difficult task because of the complex genetics of the resistance and the genetic diversity of the fungal pathogen. The crisis has revealed the lack of breeding programmes and extension services that support the development of alternative agro-ecosystems. Many farmers desire a whole-system approach to change, but the existing institutional structures direct research and extension efforts toward large-scale, technological, commodity-driven 'solutions'.

The Red River Valley case shows that an entire agro-ecosystem system may fall into crisis when these economic and social structures limit solutions. While the 1999 legislative session yielded some support for Minnesota's rural areas, most financial aid comes in the form of one-time tax relief that is not tied to agro-ecosystem management. Thus it is unlikely to reverse underlying and unsustainable agro-ecological patterns, or the long-term trend toward fewer farms, of larger size, with fewer operators.

We have argued that the farm crisis in the Red River Valley should be seen as an agro-ecological crisis, and that any solution to the problems must begin by addressing the agro-ecological character of the crisis. However, there are significant political–economic barriers that make transition to a different system difficult for farmers faced with bankruptcy. From information obtained in farmer interviews, it is clear that many people want greater diversity in agro-ecosystem management. There are four immediate barriers to such change.

○ Because of the history of commodity-driven research in both public and private institutions, there is little mainstream information on alternatives for farmers if they want to change their systems. For instance, there is little state-subsidized research into alternative crop breeding or use of organic methods.

o There is a lack of capital to finance alternative cropping systems, or to bridge the 3–5-year transition period into a new or organic system. Insurance for alternative or new crops is prohibitively expensive.

o There are few agronomically attractive marketing and processing structures available for the region. For example, alfalfa would be an alternative crop for the region, but the lack of animal husbandry means that markets are limited. Alternatively, grass crops could be used for paper production, but processing facilities are not available in the area.

o High transportation costs from the Valley limit the profitability of alternatives. Recently 41 producers established a carrot co-operative; they were able to grow terrific carrots, but the distance to markets rendered the venture non-viable.

Any attempt to confront the problems in the Red River Valley must entail the use of scab-resistant varieties in conjunction with broader agro-ecosystem changes; support for production of a wider variety of crops and rotations; planning and breeding for alternative crops; financial and agronomic support for the conversion of individual systems; and concerted efforts to improve the value added in the region and captured through local economic structures (such as co-operatives). The overarching need is for more sustainable integration of functionally and genetically variable crops, genetic and system-level disease resistance, and pest, crop and soil management, to decrease the degree of risk in the system due to inflexibility. This is no small order. To develop such an integrated, diverse management capacity will require a heightened and refocused research leadership, a move away from commodity-based research and extension, subsidies that reflect sustainable agronomic practices and rational, diverse social goals, and the extension of crop insurance and operating loans for progressive farmers and local co-operatives.

Farm crises are not new to northwestern Minnesota. Although the unprecedented economic boom between World War II and the 1970s may have led some farmers to believe that growth would continue indefinitely, the massive number of farm closures in the 1980s indicated the fragility of rural economies in the mid-west. Although most economists praise the state of the rural economy in the 1990s, the difficulties of the Red River Valley raise questions of the long-term stability of agriculture in the USA. As the Red River Valley case indicates, without leadership for a comprehensive agrofood policy, we can only expect further crises.

2.8. The Netherlands: farmers' renewed interest in genetic diversity

Han Wiskerke

Major characteristics of agricultural development

Agriculture in the Netherlands has changed drastically over the past five decades. These changes are characterized by three simultaneous patterns of development.

○ Scale-enlargement – farm size and area per labour unit increased. This development was associated with a decrease in number of farms from 410 000 in 1950 to 111 000 in 1996, whereas the amount of land dedicated to agriculture decreased from 58 to 50 per cent (see Table 6.1).
○ Intensification: in this period yields of arable crops increased by 42 to 140 per cent, depending on the crop. For example, yields of winter wheat increased from 3900kg/ha in 1950 to 9100kg/ha in 1996. In the same period potato yields increased from 25 300 to 44 400kg/ha.
○ Specialization – mixed farming systems gradually disappeared and developed into arable or livestock farms. In arable farming, winter wheat, potatoes and sugar beet have became the predominant crops, and within each of these crops only a limited number of crop varieties have been cultivated at national level. Individual farmers used to cultivate only one or two varieties per crop.

Legal foundation of plant breeding

Yield improvement in arable farming has been the result of a combination of new and improved farming methods and technological innovations on the one hand, and the introduction of new and improved (higher-yielding) plant varieties on the other. This chapter focuses on the contribution of plant breeding to agricultural development in the Netherlands. Plant breeding has been a commercial activity in the Netherlands since the beginning of the 20th century. Commercialization of plant breeding was strengthened by legal protection after World War II: first by the 1941 Breeders' Decree, and subsequently by the Seeds and Planting Materials Act (SPMA) of 1967. The SPMA regulates breeders' rights and the trade of seeds and planting materials. Regulation of breeders' rights is based on regulations issued by the International Convention for the Protection of New Varieties of Plants, better known as the UPOV Convention, of 1961. In the context of the SPMA a plant breeder may obtain breeders' rights for a new plant variety once the variety meets the criteria of distinctiveness, uniformity and stability. After fulfilling these conditions, the new variety may be registered in the Netherlands Register of Varieties. This implies that for a period of 20–25 years (depending on the crop) no one but the owner (i.e. the breeder) is permitted to reproduce commercially and trade that variety (Wiskerke, 1995).

Measures taken in the 1920s were also intended to protect and reward breeders' labour. One of these measures concerns the Descriptive List of Varieties of Arable Crops, hereafter referred to as the List of Varieties. This list has been published annually since 1924. Initially its main objective was to provide guidelines for farmers in their choice of crop varieties. Upon the installation of the Breeders' Decree of 1941, the status of the list changed to take an obligatory and binding form. In other words, only seeds and planting materials of varieties that were on the List of Varieties were admitted for domestic trade. The Committee for the compilation of the List of Varieties (CLV) decides whether or not a new variety will be placed on the list. The decision of the CLV is based upon so-called 'agricultural value research' undertaken by a government research institute. The CLV uses two major criteria in the evaluation of a submitted new variety. Firstly, a new variety has to be of ample value to Dutch agriculture; secondly, it has to be better than existing varieties. For the past decades these criteria have been translated into a single goal for plant breeders, namely higher yields. Because of the export- and bulk-oriented character of Dutch agriculture, higher yields were considered a prerequisite for maintaining and enhancing the 'strong' Dutch position in the international agricultural market. 'Sufficient value' was thus perceived as sufficient yield potential, and 'better' as obtaining a higher yield potential than existing varieties (Wiskerke, 1997). The List of Varieties has, to a large extent, determined the shape and content of plant breeding activities in the Netherlands over a period of 50 years. This important role is based on its intermediary position between goals shared by the Netherlands government and the agricultural sector on the one hand, and the objectives of plant breeders on the other.

One of the major side effects of this exclusive focus on higher yields in plant breeding has been a loss of genetic diversity (Jongerden and Ruivenkamp, 1996). Genetic characteristics such as taste, resistance to pests and diseases, and quality aspects were considered of minor importance in breeding programmes. Pests, diseases and weeds could be controlled by chemical inputs; as a result there was no immediate need to incorporate genetic resistance in existing breeding materials. And because various quality aspects, for instance the baking quality of wheat, have a negative correlation with yield potential, these genetic characteristics were also excluded from breeding programmes (Wiskerke, 1997). Thus it may be argued that the contribution of plant breeding to the intensification and specialization of agriculture in the Netherlands has been successful in terms of its initial goals. At the same time it has resulted in loss of diversity in general, and in loss of genetic diversity in particular. Although not intentional, the specific organization of plant breeding with the List of Varieties as a steering element has guided this process of erosion of genetic diversity in the Netherlands (Jongerden and Ruivenkamp, 1996; Wiskerke, 1997).

Farmers' use of genetic diversity: arable farming in the province of Zeeland

A description of the development of agriculture in the Netherlands and the specific contribution to this development by plant breeding may lead to the conclusion that it is unnecessary to discuss farmers' use of genetic diversity. After all, genetic diversity within arable crops has become limited. However, recent research among arable farmers in the province of Zeeland (Wiskerke, 1997) demonstrated that, despite this limited genetic diversity, there is a demand for different crop varieties and specific genetic characteristics. This demand for genetic diversity is related to various farming styles, among other issues.

Before clarifying this diversity, the concept of a farming style needs explanation. A 'farming style' is a specific ordering of numerous farming-related aspects based on farmers' notions of the way farming should be practised. A farming style thus reflects a specific strategy with respect to farm management and development. Farmers themselves use folk concepts to classify themselves and others and to distinguish one style from another. Five farming styles are identified in arable farming in the province of Zeeland (see Table 2.8).

Table 2.8: Names and characteristics of farming styles in arable agriculture in Zeeland

Name	Characteristics
Yield farmer	Intensive land use, high yields, frequent use of pesticides and fertilizer, bulk production (wheat, potatoes, sugar beet, onions)
Machine farmer	Large scale, high level of mechanization and specialization, extensive crop rotation, bulk production (wheat, potatoes, sugar beet)
Saving farmer	Low costs, low input levels (pesticides and fertilizer), extensive land use
Plant grower	High technical efficiency (relatively low level of inputs and high yields), variety of arable crops, value added (e.g. seed potatoes)
Quality farmer	Small scale, labour intensive, special products and crops, value added, production for niche markets

Source: Wiskerke (1997).

Wheat cultivation is used as an example to illustrate the utilization of genetic diversity in Zeeland. No very clear relationship exists between farming styles and the choice of wheat varieties. Yield farmers and machine farmers tend to prefer high-yielding fodder wheat varieties such as Vivant, whereas the quality farmers prefer baking wheat varieties such as Hereward (lower-yielding) and various summer wheat varieties. The other two styles have an intermediate position. Clear relationships are observed at the level of genetic characteristics (see Table 2.9). Table 2.9 illustrates that resistance to diseases is an important characteristic for quality farmers. Yield is important to yield farmers and machine farmers, but not to saving

Table 2.9: Relationship between genetic characteristics of wheat and farming styles

	Genetic characteristics			
Farming style	Resistance to diseases	Yield versus baking quality	Straw sturdiness	Suitability as 'cover crop'
Yield farmer	−0.6 a	0.24 a	−0.15 a	−0.06 ab
Machine farmer	0.03 ab	0.24 a	−0.03 a	−0.24 a
Saving farmer	−0.13 a	−0.41 b	0.10 l	0.23 b
Plant grower	−0.15 a	−0.10 ab	0.27 a	0.29 b
Quality farmer	0.49 b	−0.37 b	−0.21 a	−0.05 ab

Calculated scores (i.e. indication of correlation) per column followed by dissimilar letters differ significantly (t test: $P<0.05$). Source: Wiskerke (1997).

farmers and quality farmers; instead they prefer good baking quality. For saving farmers and plant growers, it is important to grow wheat that is suitable as a 'cover crop'. This preference may be explained by the fact that good soil management is an important element of these two farming styles.

Similar relationships between genetic characteristics and farming styles are found for other arable crops (Wiskerke, 1997). This means that farmers themselves do not always share the same view as the CLV when it comes to defining criteria as 'sufficient agricultural value' and 'better than existing varieties'. The above also demonstrates a need among farmers for more diversity than the CLV has permitted for a long time.

Support to the utilization of genetic diversity

Although there seems to be a demand for more diversity on the List of Varieties, many arable farmers do not perceive the varieties currently available as a constraint on their practices and strategies. However, according to a small group of arable farmers in Zeeland, the List of Varieties limits their strategies. These farmers are united in an initiative called *Zeeuwse Vlegel*. In 1990 they founded a corporation, with the objective of realizing an ecologically sound and profitable cultivation of high-quality baking wheat and establishing close contacts between producers and consumers. Together the participating farmers produce 250t of wheat meal that is sold to 108 bakers. *Zeeuwse Vlegel* bread is sold in 265 bakeries and supermarkets (Wiskerke, 1997). To meet the corporation's objective, participating farmers decided to abandon the use of pesticides and chemical fertilizers.

The objective of the *Zeeuwse Vlegel* may be regarded as a critical reaction to mainstream agricultural development in the Netherlands. One farmer explained: 'You know where your wheat ends up and where and how it is milled. You have more insight into the producer–consumer chain. That's very important as far as I'm concerned. Most arable farmers just don't know where their wheat ends up or what is done with it.' Another farmer adds: 'I became convinced that conventional arable farming was a dead-end street. The increasing dependence on pesticides bothered me. I wanted to change that and the *Zeeuwse Vlegel* provided me with an opportunity to gain experience in environmentally sound wheat cultivation.'

The major problem confronting the *Zeeuwse Vlegel* was (and still is) how to obtain wheat varieties that suit its objective. The List of Varieties was of little help, as most registered varieties are high-yielding, non-baking wheat varieties. In addition, the few baking-wheat varieties on the List of Varieties are very susceptible to diseases and therefore of little use. Through international contacts the *Zeeuwse Vlegel* managed to obtain baking wheat varieties from various European countries (Belgium, France, Germany) that suited its objectives. As these varieties are registered on the European Union's List of Varieties, cultivation of these varieties is permitted in all member states. By growing a wide range of varieties that are not common to Dutch agriculture the *Zeeuwse Vlegel* contributes to creating genetic diversity at the regional level.

This brief description of the *Zeeuwse Vlegel* and its effort to support the utilization of a diversity of wheat varieties demonstrates that small groups of farmers succeed in increasing the use of genetic diversity in farming, instead of just using the few varieties recommended by the List of Varieties. Enhancing the use of diversity, however, demands considerable effort and innovation. Institutionalized economic and political networks can hamper such initiatives. It is hoped that the efforts of the *Zeeuwse Vlegel* will contribute to a thorough restructuring of this network, especially with respect to the legal system (UPOV, SPMA) and the criteria used in compiling the List of Varieties (see Chapter 6.3).

2.9. Wheat varieties for organic production and processing in New Brunswick, Canada

Jennifer Scott

Introduction

This chapter describes a wheat cultivar selection initiative that is a collaboration between farmers, a flour mill, government personnel, an informal network of seed savers, and a small collection of organic farmers throughout Canada and the USA. Our initial goal is to select a few wheat varieties that would be particularly suited to a humid climate, and to organic growing conditions. Our on-farm evaluation trials are unique and exciting because we have brought together seed from the Canadian Genebank, rare heritage varieties, varieties saved and selected over the years by organic farmers, as well as modern varieties.

Background

In New Brunswick in the late 1970s there were no mills for processing bread wheats, and all flour used in the province was imported. This represented a loss in local food self-reliance, given that 100 years earlier most grain for human consumption was grown and processed locally. The possibility for growing milling grains remained, so a group of enterprising people put together the Speerville Mill Co-operative and began to grind small amounts of wheat into flour.

Speerville Mill was created to encourage local growers to supply milling wheat, to create a market for organic wheat products, and to sell these products bio-regionally. Speerville's success in getting farmers to grow wheat, and selling the processed flour, gave them the credibility to ask for milling wheat variety trials (organic and conventional) to be done by the New Brunswick Department of Agriculture. Luckily there was a sympathetic grain specialist who carried these out for several years.

These variety trials confirmed that it is possible to grow high-protein (≥13.5 per cent) wheats with acceptable yields in New Brunswick under organic management. Farmers and researchers in the northeastern USA, seeking milling-quality wheats to supply the increasing demand for locally grown organic products, are looking to Speerville Mill to provide them with the leadership, experience and varieties needed to fill their markets.

Recently, demand for locally grown, organic grain products has been greater than the supply, causing Speerville Mill to think seriously about how to encourage organic farmers in the region to increase production. Farmers, on the other hand, are expressing dissatisfaction with the available popular milling wheat variety, *Roblin*. *Roblin* is a western-bred wheat with high protein content and good bread-making quality, but which yields poorly under humid eastern Canadian conditions. Despite the premium they would receive for growing the wheat organically, a higher-yielding variety would make it a more economically viable crop to grow. Also, other criteria were sought, such as ability to compete with weeds, ability to thrive in an organic production environment, and disease resistance in a humid climate. The Mill also had to make sure the varieties used had good quality characteristics such as adequate protein and bread-making potential. It was felt that wheat varieties bred and selected for western Canadian dry conditions, under conventional management (using herbicides, synthetic fertilizers, fungicides and other pest control products), were simply not meeting the farmers' or the Mill's needs.

One recent development that also makes organic farmers keen to have their own seed and varieties is the possible future introduction of genetically engineered wheat, which may be so popular that no other seeds will be easily available. Organic farmers are prohibited by standards from using genetically engineered crops (defined as crops with genetic material from another species).

Thus the Maritime Certified Organic Growers (MCOG) and Speerville Mill, in co-operation with the New Brunswick Department of Agriculture, initiated on-farm milling wheat variety trials at three MCOG-member organic farms in the province, in the spring of 1998. The growers in the group have a very practical orientation toward genetic diversity, in the sense that they would like to have a range of choices for producing wheat that thrives in the growing conditions on their farms. The growers who are particularly interested in maintaining genetic diversity feel that by growing out and maintaining different varieties they will have material to work with in terms of finding suitable varieties for organic production. They are interested in saving their own seeds and possibly nurturing their own variety.

Why is diversity important and what are its practical applications?

The first step to finding a good variety for our needs is to have a large selection of germplasm to select from. It was fortunate that we were able to tap into several diverse collections of wheat varieties. We were lucky to obtain very small samples (25 to 50 seeds) of various 'heritage' wheats from the Canadian Genebank, although in general these seeds did not germinate well. One wheat we were particularly interested in because it was actually bred and selected for Maritime conditions in the 1940s, before biocides were widely used, was *Acadia* – but out of our 50 seeds, only one germinated.

Seed of other heritage varieties was obtained from Seeds of Diversity Canada (see Pittenger, Chapter 3.4). They provided us with larger samples, but not enough seed to include in our replicated trial. In 1998 we therefore simply increased the seed of these cultivars and did some preliminary evaluation. This seed had been grown and saved by volunteers interested in preserving the old wheats. It was in good condition, and the grain yields were in the same range as the modern varieties.

We also obtained seed of four different varieties from organic farmers who are using and saving their own seed, year after year. These farmers were all saving older varieties, which were particularly interesting to us. Seeds of a variety such as Huron, selected and saved on a conventional farm for 10 years, may be quite different from seeds of the same variety selected and saved for 10 years on an organic farm. Although wheat varieties are homozygous and inbreeding, it is possible that populations from the two contrasting selection systems might show differences as a result of mutation and accidental crosses. A corresponding farmer in North Dakota tested that theory on his farm during 1998. Even within our own trials we found significant differences between populations of the same variety that came from different sources and were planted adjacent to each other.

We also obtained seed of modern varieties from seed dealers and conventional farmers who happened to have a supply. Even this was difficult, as varieties that were only a couple of years old were no longer being offered commercially.

Diversity among crop varieties is important, even without the intention of any selection or breeding project, for several reasons. Particularly in ecological agriculture, farmers need a choice of different varieties to suit their production schedules, farm equipment availability, natural features on the farm, production goals and markets. And it is important to have a variety of choices in case any of the above situations changes over time.

Also, with a crop such as wheat it is difficult to get all desired traits in one variety. For example, yield is often inversely related to protein content among varieties. Earlier-maturing wheats may not have such good disease resistance. Thus farmers wishing to take advantage of wheat with different characteristics to suit all their production environments and client needs will often plant more than one variety.

Varietal diversity can occur between farms, within farms, and even within fields. Different varieties are desirable because farmers further to the south might want to plant higher-quality wheats with a longer season, and those further north will want a variety that matures earlier. Livestock farmers may want longer-strawed varieties that in a good year could be a cash crop, and in a bad year could be used for livestock feed and bedding. A number of different varieties within farms could be useful for farmers with smaller equipment who want to spread the harvest time by starting with an early-maturing variety and later moving to longer-season types. They may also want to adopt a 'minimize risk' strategy in terms of disease by planting several varieties. Diversity of varieties within a field is not common, although it could prove beneficial in terms of over-yielding compared with each variety planted on its own. Farmers are clear, however, that they are not interested in mixing varieties that do not mature at the same time, as this would make harvesting the grain even more difficult than it already is.

Farmers are not only interested in having a range of varieties to choose from, they also want as much information with that variety as possible. Thus the diversity of varieties is useful only if a full package of information comes along with the seed. And the closer to home that information is compiled, the better. Farmers are certainly willing to try different varieties, and there are individual variety preferences even among neighbours. In 1998, all growers who supply Speerville Mill grew at least two varieties of wheat.

Our most rewarding connection has been with other organic wheat growers in Canada and the USA through volunteer seed-saving networks and organic growers' networks. The grower-to-grower connection is always the most important in terms of information exchange, and has proved fruitful in obtaining large amounts of seed from rare varieties. Like the farmers in Nepal who bring seeds as gifts when visiting, a package of seed from another grower who has been carefully selecting and improving their own variety for years is a truly profound gift.

Future plans and questions

We are only at the beginning of a multi-year effort. Already we see potential for expanding our original goals. It would be good to co-operate with farmers in neighbouring provinces. We would also like to experiment with mixing two or three varieties with similar maturity patterns, to see if that could increase the average yield and average quality of wheat stands.

There is also potential to cross some of the more promising wheats and then proceed with field selection using the F_2 generation of the cross. However, at this point we do not have the resources for this kind of work. Collaboration with public-sector wheat breeders in the region is being explored.

We should also like to find some way of assessing the nutritional quality of the wheat, with the objective of finding varieties with different gluten characteristics. Typically, high quality is associated with high protein and high gluten content, which creates fluffy bread, but as more people become gluten-intolerant, perhaps this is a misguided goal in the long run. In essence, we are seeking a balance between acceptable yields and high quality, and between practical farming considerations and optimum genetic diversity within the farm.

2.10. The use of rice genetic resources by farmers in Nueva Ejica, The Philippines

Carlos Basilio and Melencio Razon

Introduction

The *Kaisahan ng Diwang Anakbukid na Makabayan* (Confederation of Nationalist Peasants) or KADAMA is a confederation of four farmers' federations from five municipalities and one city of Nueva Ecija, Philippines. It has implemented programmes in community organizing, co-operative development, sustainable agriculture and development policy advocacy since its establishment in 1991. The members of KADAMA were the first farmers' groups that were involved with the Farmer–Scientist Partnerships in Agricultural Development (MASIPAG) Project.

KADAMA member federations are operating in the towns of Sta Rosa, Jaen and Zaragosa (DIWA), Cabiao (UGNAYAN), Carranglan (LIKHA) and Cabanatuan City (PMK). Nueva Ecija is considered as one of the rice bowls of the Philippines, supplying more than 20 per cent of the total national rice production since the 1930s. The province has acted as a laboratory for programmes in rice production and agrarian reform, including the Green as well as the Counter-Green Revolutions.

A heritage of diversity

Before the introduction of modern rice varieties, 3500 traditional varieties of rice were being grown by rice farmers in various parts of the Philippines (Mendoza et al., 1989). The country was richly endowed with rice cultivars of two major geographic races – indica and javanica. The maintenance of this diversity has been ensured by traditional systems of agriculture and land use.

In addition to the local landraces, there were also rice varieties coming from other countries such as Indonesia, India and Taiwan. In the late 1950s the Bureau of Plant Industry (BPI) tested 241 local varieties and 1326 varieties introduced from the US Department of Agriculture's world rice collection. Farmers drew from these varieties the genetic diversity required for their various needs. The pool of improved traditional rice varieties included those that came from nearby countries and those that were developed by Philippine institutions. Table 2.10 lists some of these varieties under specific categories.

Table 2.10: Some traditional and improved traditional rice varieties grown in the Philippines before the Green Revolution

| Traditional varieties | Improved traditional rice varieties | | | |
| | | Bred by national programmes | | |
	Introduced	BPI	UPCA	DANR/NSDB
Tadukan	Fortuna	BPI-76	C4-63	Milfor 44
Apostol	Bengawan	BPI-76 (NS)	C4-63(G)	Milfor 6(2)
Binangon	Seraup Kechil 36	BPI-121	C4-137	Milbuen 5(3)
Dose	Intan	BPI-3-2	C-12	Milketan 6-A
Guinangang	Peta	BPI 9-33 B	C-21	Buenketan 91
Kinumpol	Ramadja	Raminad	C-22	Buenketan 101
Buenavista	Tjeremas			
Milagrosa	Taichu-63			
Elon-elon	Ketan Koetoek			
Macan	Kra Suey			
Ramelon				
Pinursigue				
Kinawayan				

Disregarding diversity

The Green Revolution was ushered in by the search for high-nitrogen-responsive varieties and culminated in the development and massive promotion of an ideal rice plant type with the following characteristics: 110–140 days' maturity period, early vegetative vigour, high tillering ability, short and erect-growing leaves, short sturdy stems, and photoperiod insensitivity.

The use of these varieties and associated production techniques phenomenally increased rice yield. Modern rice varieties produced an average of 1 tonne or 61 per cent more per hectare than traditional rice varieties. Their early maturity and photoperiod insensitivity also provided opportunities to plant a second wet-season crop or a dry-season rice crop. Masagana 99, the country's Green Revolution programme, enabled the Philippines to become a rice exporter in the 1970s. Until 1980, rice output increased at an average of 3 per cent per annum. The average yield per hectare also increased from 1.3t in 1966 to 2.8t during the 1990s.

From a mere 2.4 per cent in 1966, the share of modern rice varieties of the total area harvested and production steadily increased through the years (Figure 2.6). Just a year after the release of IR8, 22.5 per cent of the total area cultivated for rice was planted to Green Revolution varieties. It rose to 50 per cent after 5 years, and almost 90 per cent after 25 years. In Central Luzon, the rate and extent of adoption is much faster and more extensive: as early as 1990, 99 per cent of the harvested area was already planted to modern rice varieties.

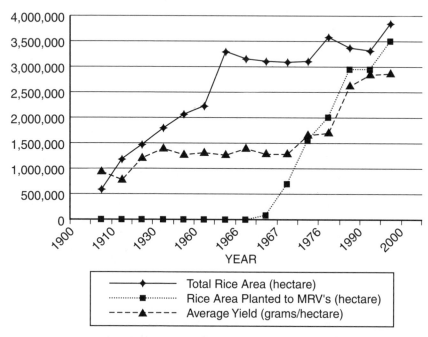

Figure 2.6: *Total land area planted to rice, area planted to modern rice varieties and average rice yield in the Philippines (1903–98)*

The promise of increased yields, coupled with the active promotion of the government and the provision of irrigation, credit and other key support services, enticed KADAMA farmers to grow modern varieties. Government programmes encouraged the use of modern varieties as part of a technology package which included the use of chemical fertilizers and pesticides. Farmers who adopted the recommended technology package were given priority for extension, credit, crop insurance and other government support services.

Promoting genetic vulnerability

A few years later, despite increases in production, farmers began to express their dissatisfaction with modern varieties. They observed that varietal performance declined with time, and that they needed to buy new seeds after three cropping seasons in order to avoid steep declines in yield. There are several explanations for the decreased performance of the modern varieties.

The rapid decrease of the cultivars' performance in relation to pest and diseases can be attributed to the practice of crossing élite lines to develop new varieties. This practice results in a narrow genetic base (see Pham and van Hintum, Chapter 1.2 and Elings et al., Chapter 1.4). Genetic uniformity leads to genetic vulnerability to pests. The consequences are increased incidence of severe crop failure directly due to pests, and/or increased use of pesticides to shield the crops from undue crop failure due to pests. Variety IR8 was wiped out by tungro (an insect-transmitted virus) in the 1970s. A few years later IR20 was severely attacked by brown planthoppers. It was replaced by rice varieties with single gene resistance for brown planthoppers, but four cropping seasons later these varieties (IR26, IR28, IR29 and IR30) succumbed to a new biotype of brown planthopper. In the 1980s, rice fields in the southern Philippines were infested by Malayan black bug in epidemic proportions.

Farmers noted the disappearance of fish, crabs, frogs, mole crickets and other edible flora and fauna that are usually associated with paddy fields. They also learned that populations of beneficial insects, spiders, parasitic wasps and helpful fungi and bacteria, that keep the balance between pests and rice crop under control, were decimated by unnecessary use of chemicals.

Modern rice varieties require high inputs of water, fertilizers and chemical pesticides. Instead of getting seeds from their fields or from their neighbours, farmers were also enjoined to buy certified seeds from authorized dealers every cropping season. The farmers wanted to go back to their old system of farming, but they could not, as they did not have their old seeds.

Breaking free

In 1982, the Agency for Community Education and Services (ACES) Foundation facilitated participatory research on the effects of modern rice varieties on the environment and livelihood of farmers in the four villages of Jaen, Nueva Ecija. The results of the research showed that the introduction of modern rice varieties and associated technology packages caused problems for farmers instead of helping them. They acknowledged that the programmes were able to help them to increase yield and income, but these effects did not last long. High interest rates for credit, high prices of farm inputs and irrigation fees provide the farmers with high yields, but low income.

The results of the study were also found valid by ACES in other villages of Nueva Ecija and by other groups working with farmers in other parts of the country. The research results were discussed in regional consultations and later on at a nationwide conference on rice issues where farmers presented their findings and demands to policy-makers and government officials, as well as to the Director General of the International Rice Research Institute. However, the farmers received no support to address these demands. After the conference, representatives of farmer organizations, non-governmental organizations and the scientists' group from the

University of the Philippines at Los Baños (UPLB) decided to jointly develop and implement the Farmer–Scientist Partnerships in Agricultural Development (MASIPAG) project.

Recovering the lost heritage

MASIPAG started with a national call for the retrieval and collection of traditional rice varieties, with several key national farmers' organizations spearheading the activity. The project was able to access 140 farmers' collected rice cultivars and 21 advanced lines from the Department of Agronomy of UPLB College of Agriculture.

KADAMA members established community seed banks in farms managed by each federation, and at the same time each tried to maintain at least five varieties in their own farms. Under this set-up the varieties were not only characterized and multiplied, but were also subjected to variety adaptability trials. These trials enabled farmers to observe closely the cultivars and select the best ones to constitute locally adapted varieties. The criteria for local adaptability are defined individually by each farmer or, as in the case of federation-managed farms, collaboratively. Selection was done for each crop cycle, but all varieties were observed over several seasons.

Observations are shared with other members during their meetings. Cross-farm visits and field days are conducted for more systematic evaluation of rice cultivars. During field days, other farmers and staff of government and non-government organizations are also invited to farms. These field days are usually held some days before harvest.

Dealing with realities

The early success of KADAMA's programme on plant genetic resources and conservation was hampered by existing realities of rice production, trading and marketing in the province. Much of the good harvests that they got from locally adapted varieties were not bought by traders nor by the government-sanctioned rice-procurement agency because their varieties are not recommended by the Philippine Seed Board. For the same reason, farmers planting locally adapted varieties are not eligible to receive support services from government rice-production programmes, nor can their farms be covered by crop insurance.

On top of an unsupportive policy environment, the programme was also affected by KADAMA's inability to respond to increased demand for seeds. Without financial support, KADAMA is finding it hard to maintain federation-managed farms for testing, evaluating and multiplying seeds they have accessed. Although members are willing to provide labour, very few members can afford to forgo income that could be generated to allow land to be used by the federation.

Reliance on farmers' seed production and exchange was found to be vulnerable to a number of biophysical threats. The regular occurrence of natural calamities such as floods, typhoons and drought, that usually destroy crops and drastically reduce yields, prevented farmers from reserving enough seeds for the next cropping season. Low yields or total loss of the crop due to weeds, golden snails and other pests also contribute to the problem of limited seed availability. KADAMA has found it increasingly necessary to rent or buy lands to maintain trial farms.

The extent of KADAMA's rice genetic resources campaign is still limited to members of the confederation. DIWA has 170 members from six villages, UGNAYAN 69 members from five villages, LIKHA 369 members from eight villages, and PMK 109 members from two villages. However, a number of farmers including some KADAMA members are still not fully convinced of the practicality of farm diversification and integration. Others are just not willing to take the risks associated with the shift in farming techniques.

Sowing seeds of sustainability

The shift to the use of modern varieties from traditional ones radically altered KADAMA farmers' systems of rice growing, from one crop a year to two or more per year, from animal-drawn implements to hand tractors, from waiting for rain to come to coaxing irrigation personnel to release water into their farms. Government programmes promoting modern rice varieties transformed biodiverse fields into genetically uniform tracts of land. These programmes also pushed farmers to move from a self-reliant to a highly dependent system of production.

KADAMA believes that farmers must have access to and control over resources for rice production. They would like to have access and control over a range of rice cultivars and varieties with different characteristics. If necessary, they will explore opportunities to experiment on and develop their own varieties. Their main rationale for shifting into more genetically diverse farming is at present economic: to decrease costs and distribute the risks of production. However, they are aware that genetic diversity is necessary if they want to adapt to changing ecological, economic, socio-cultural and political conditions. KADAMA's call was not only for the conservation of genetic diversity – they are advocating more sustainable agricultural systems.

Synthesis: Farmers' management of diversity in local systems

Gordon Prain and Jürgen Hagmann

Introduction

The story told in this section is about the way farmers seek to balance the twin needs of 'managing' nature on the one hand, and satisfying a range of

prioritizing yield as the dominant criterion for accepting new varieties on to the official Descriptive List of Varieties. Yet this policy rationalization failed to take account of the diversity of Dutch farming styles, which generates different varietal requirements. The most encouraging element reported in these two cases is the way farmers have taken the initiative to try to rebuild greater resilience in their farming through genetic diversification. Activist farmers in both countries have found ways to access sources of crop genetic diversity which had been squeezed out of their own systems. A group of Dutch farmers exploited the membership of their country in the European Union to access baking wheat varieties in other member countries which were not available on the Dutch Descriptive List. New Brunswick farmers accessed bread wheat varieties held in gene banks in other parts of Canada.

There appear to have been multiple driving forces behind this farmer activism. Environmental concerns weighed heavily with certain Dutch farmers who refused to accept the dependence of modern farming on the use of pesticides to combat disease, seeking instead host-plant resistance in varieties coming from sources outside the Netherlands. Self-sufficiency in production of bread wheat was a factor in the actions of Canadian farmers. Among Philippine farmers various factors have led to attempts to recover rice genetic diversity. These include the rescuing of an indigenous heritage; a wider range of needs than can be satisfied by one or two modern, high-yielding varieties; the reduction of risk through mixtures; and the availability of varieties requiring lower levels of fertilizers and pesticides. Farmers were also concerned about the consequences of highly pesticide-dependent modern varieties: the loss of flora and fauna normally sharing the paddy with the rice crop and providing protein supplements and other needs to local communities.

An important factor in the Philippines case is the role of outsider activists in helping farmers develop a public culture of concern about diversity loss, documenting the effects and then lobbying for changes. Activists have also been involved in attempts by farmers' groups to reverse genetic erosion through setting up seed banks and accessing collections. One reason for the apparently greater role played by activists in the Philippines compared with the Netherlands and Canada may be the difference in the politico-economic context, particularly the degree to which smallholder farming families are marginalized from decision-making processes in the Philippines. The institutional and financial environment in the Philippines appears to be fully opposed to the kinds of reversals being proposed by farmers and their activist supporters. Of course, the institutional context is also negative for increased diversity in the Netherlands, Canada and the Red River Valley of Minnesota, and this is one of the main challenges facing farmers and their supporters in these countries.

Looking to the future

The combination of dynamic management of crop genetic diversity in resilient systems such as Irian Jaya and Chile, and the evidence of a return to resilience by farmers in highly commercial farming areas such as the Netherlands, Canada and northern Philippines, should offer some grounds for cautious optimism. Yet the narrowing of production goals described in Tanzania and the resultant dependence on a single variety is a pattern that is increasingly common. A diversity of production goals contributing in multiple ways to income generation and to cultural cohesion is likely to be the best hope for continued farmer management of crop genetic diversity. In this regard it is noteworthy that the role of consumers in biodiversity conservation, which has been shown to be important, for example, in the recovery of indigenous grain crops in the Andes of Peru, is not addressed directly in any of these chapters. The issue of genetic diversity conservation tends to be viewed almost exclusively from the farm and farmer perspective. We certainly need to bring consumers more into the picture. There needs to be an economic as well as an ecological demand for diversity. Cultural and spiritual factors can also continue to motivate farmers to maintain biodiversity not only as a short-term solution, but as a long-term goal which exists alongside economic objectives. This of course depends on the conservation of belief systems such as those held by the Dani of Irian Jaya, within which sweet potato diversity is fully embedded. Respect for and support of cultural diversity is thus a crucial component of biodiversity conservation.

In conclusion, farmers' management of biodiversity has always been a dynamic process responding to varying ecological, economic, social and cultural conditions. Maintenance of diversity by farming families is a function of the multiple users of crops and varieties to satisfy a complex set of local needs.

Farmers need genetic variation, but not necessarily the same genetic variation all the time and in every place. Access to potentially useful genetic variation is as important for the resilience of the system as the genetic diversity that is most useful at a particular point in time.

Farmers' management of biodiversity has been most closely associated with small-scale, subsistence-oriented agriculture, with collective natural resource management systems (e.g. seed-exchange networks) and with optimization of benefits (e.g. risk aversion, using multiple niches) rather than with economic profit maximization. The challenge is to build upon such indigenous diversity-management systems as economic returns become an increasingly vital consideration for rural households – to build on them, not replace them with an agro-industrial model.

However, the maintenance of biodiversity goes beyond conserving crop diversity on-farm. Ultimately it depends on the continued existence of heterogeneous social and cultural systems within the production environment, and a diversity of demand for agricultural products by consumers.

CONSERVATION OF CROP DIVERSITY

Introduction

The need for conservation of crop genetic diversity to curb genetic erosion was first recognized and formulated by breeders in the formal sector, and this influenced the strategies that were adopted to conserve diversity. The concept of gene banks, already in operation in some countries to manage seed stocks collected from elsewhere in the world for breeding purposes, matured, now focusing on the comprehensive conservation of genetic diversity in a large number of food crops.

In the late 1960s a debate was started on conservation strategies, and leading scientists argued that conservation of crop genetic diversity should take place not preferentially in gene banks, but in the farming systems that harboured this genetic diversity, and in the natural ecosystems containing wild relatives. In the early 1990s *in situ* and on-farm conservation regained attention from the conservationists and development-oriented research. It was realized by all major stakeholders that these strategies should be employed in a complementary way, combining the advantages of both. This section deals with aspects of on-farm conservation and support to the use of crop diversity, but from the perspective of the conservation of genetic diversity.

The contributions to this section highlight several of these efforts. The contribution of Begemann et al. (Chapter 3.1) deals with national genetic resources programmes in Cuba and Germany. It shows how the degree of industrialization of agriculture determines to a considerable extent the choice between *in situ* and *ex situ* conservation strategies, and how this relates to the role of gene banks. The contribution of Pham et al. (Chapter 3.2) on the activities of IRRI's International Rice Gene Bank clearly demonstrates how CGIAR perspectives on the relevance of local management of crop diversity, and on the support the public sector can offer, have changed. From a unidirectional relationship (farmers and national programmes supplying the landraces for *ex situ* conservation) linkages are becoming bidirectional.

Bertuso et al. (Chapter 3.3) highlight some features of on-farm conservation of genetic diversity on the basis of their experiences with the Philippines CONSERVE project. They describe how the activities also relate to the conservation of indigenous knowledge about crops: the focus is on conservation of the entire farming system with all its interdependencies. Interesting differences exist between the roles of non-governmental organizations (NGOs) such as CONSERVE in the South, and Seeds of Diversity Canada in the North. Pittenger (Chapter 3.4), describing the latter, illustrates that the objective is much more on conserving traditional varieties than on their development, and often there is a focus on vegetable and fruit crops. But there are also clear similarities. The control of genes is an issue for NGOs in both North and South, and the value of associated indigenous knowledge is recognized.

The NGO-driven Community Biodiversity Development and Conservation (CBDC) Programme is presented by Montecinos and Salazar (Chapter 3.5). The CBDC programme is an attempt to join forces at the global level, and by doing so to improve results of local on-farm management of genetic diversity: the programme links partners from the South and North, NGOs and governmental institutions, field-oriented and policy-oriented organizations. A related but different activity is the IPGRI *in situ* project presented by Jarvis and Ndungú-Skilton (Chapter 3.6). This is also a global effort, but focuses more on the scientific aspects of *in situ* conservation on-farm, in line with its origin in international agricultural research. Both CBDC and the IPGRI *in situ* project stress the local nature of *in situ* plant genetic resources conservation on-farm.

This element is addressed from a different perspective in the final contribution to this section. Visser and Jarvis in Chapter 3.7 deal with the issue of upscaling: how to enlarge the impact of on-farm conservation activities, or in other words, how to move on from a more-or-less anecdotal phase and produce a sustainable conservation strategy. Several options are discussed, the central theme being ways to 'mainstream' (or popularize) the concept of on-farm conservation and integrate it with other activities in the agricultural sector.

3.1. Linking conservation and utilization of plant genetic resources in Germany and Cuba

Frank Begemann, Anja Oetmann and Miguel Esquivel

For 10 000 years, with the domestication and subsequent cultivation of plants, farmers have continuously selected plants to improve their livelihood. Through these practices and through environmental influences, the diversity of plants has been considerably increased. The genetic diversity of crops provides farmers with opportunities to optimize economic returns in highly variable environments, and offers some level of insurance against uncertain environmental and biotic conditions.

Small-scale farmers attach considerable importance to genetically diverse crops as they are often deprived of easy access to external inputs. They maintain and use genetic diversity, and are actually the key players in

○ Participatory methods are used to evaluate new sugar cane varieties in 23 co-operative farms in Las Tunas Province.
○ Traditional cassava varieties have been rescued in Granma Province; local seed banks have been created in close collaboration with farmers' groups.
○ A system for participatory sweet potato evaluation has been developed. Farmers evaluated a collection of 13 promising CIP clones and local varieties in various localities in Holguín Province. The clones best meeting the requirements of participating farmers have been selected and disseminated.
○ In 1989 the golden mosaic virus (GMV) destroyed almost all the bean fields in Holguín, the country's most important bean-producing area. In 1990, the Horticultural Research Institute introduced various GMV-tolerant accessions from the Regional Bean Programme (PROFRIJOL). In 1992 and 1993, field days were organized at experimental fields, where hundreds of farmers evaluated the collections. Seeds of promising materials were distributed through extensionists and farmer leaders. These people further evaluated and disseminated the materials in their respective agro-ecological zones. In subsequent years, farmers selected and disseminated the material in their localities. By 1995, tolerant varieties covered Holguín Province.

Conclusions

Two parallel approaches have been developed for genetic crop resource management, *ex situ* and on-farm management. The approaches are complementary not only in their conservation objectives, but when implemented in an integrated manner they also link the conservation and utilization of plant genetic resources. In both Germany and Cuba on-farm management cannot be separated from utilization: maintenance is realized through continued cultivation and utilization by farmers. However, the strategy for implementation of on-farm management in agriculture, and the role of gene banks within this strategy, are different in the two countries.

The opportunities for maintenance of plant genetic resources on-farm and the roles that gene banks play in supporting the use of plant genetic resources are limited in countries and farming systems characterized by a high availability of modern varieties and a formally organized and commercially oriented seed sector. On-farm management is realized by the continued cultivation of locally adapted varieties by specific groups of farmers and gardeners.

Hammer (1998) pointed out the comparative advantage of on-farm management, especially in areas where genetic diversity is still high, where subsistence farming is based on intercropping systems of diverse numbers of crops and landraces and in home gardens. He mentioned the particular importance of on-farm situations to facilitate introgression. There is a decreasing South–North gradient of the potential for on-farm management.

In general, it could be concluded that on-farm management of genetic resources can complement the *ex situ* conservation efforts in gene banks, preferably where no strong specialized breeding sector exists. This seems to be the case for many neglected or commercially less important crops in developing or developed countries alike, as well as even for some major crops in developing countries, for example in Cuba. Consequently, gene bank services clearly depend on the users: in a very industrialized country such as Germany the gene bank has a clear service function for research and plant breeders (commercial and non-commercial), and perhaps a lesser role in providing a direct germplasm service to farmers for the major crops. Nevertheless, the latter service needs to be clarified.

3.2. Approach to *in situ* conservation on-farm by the International Rice Genebank

Jean-Louis Pham, Jane Toll and Stephen Morin

The 16 Centres of the CGIAR share a mission to contribute, through research, to the promotion of sustainable agriculture for food security in developing countries. The Centres' research efforts are targeted at increasing productivity and protecting the natural resource base. These are commitments to the conservation and sustainable use of agricultural biodiversity. In this chapter we present a brief overview of the CGIAR centres' approach to the conservation of plant biodiversity and *in situ*/on-farm conservation. Experiences of the International Rice Genebank (IRG) as part of the International Rice Research Institute (IRRI), a CGIAR centre, are used as illustrations.

CGIAR's approach to the conservation of plant diversity

The CGIAR is well known for its contribution to the *ex situ* conservation of plant genetic resources and their use in crop improvement. The increasing attention over recent years to *in situ* approaches for the conservation by CGIAR gene banks is a response to global recognition of *in situ* strategies. Gene banks of 11 CGIAR Centres together hold more than half a million accessions of crop, forage and agro-forestry species. According to the Report on the State of the World's Plant Genetic Resources for Food and Agriculture (FAO, 1996b), CGIAR Centres hold the largest collections of many major crops of importance to developing countries and approximately 10 per cent of the entire world holdings of plant genetic resources. These collections possibly constitute a much greater proportion of unique accessions under long-term conservation. The collections have been assembled over the past 25 years through collecting missions undertaken with national partners, donations from institutes and plant breeders around the world. Recognizing the global importance of these collections, the CGIAR Centres signed agreements in 1994 placing them in trust for the benefit of the international community, as part of the FAO International Network of *Ex Situ* Collections.

Material in the CGIAR gene banks is especially rich in wild crop relatives, farmers' varieties, landraces and old crop cultivars that provide an abundant reserve of genetic diversity. The collections represent an insurance against genetic erosion and a source of genes and gene complexes conferring tolerances to diseases and pests, climatic and other environmental stresses, improved quality, and yield traits for plant improvement.

CGIAR has supported the development of national programmes for the conservation and use of genetic resources. Support activities include the restoration of national collections, supply of genetic material, collaboration in research, and strengthening human and institutional capacity. These activities have been directed to assist *ex situ* conservation, study and use of the species and genetic diversity of concern to the formal sector of crop development. More recently the CGIAR and national programmes have developed new relationships among conservationists, breeders, farmers and local-level institutions (e.g. community-based organizations and NGOs). These relationships are being developed in response to growing attention to *in situ* approaches and, in the case of cultivated species, to on-farm management of genetic resources.

CGIAR activities addressing *in situ*/on-farm conservation

The CG Centres, with national partners from the formal sector and community-based organizations, are working with farmers to better understand the dynamics of on-farm conservation and farmers' breeding systems. Research activities concern the following issues:

○ environmental, biological, cultural and socio-economic factors that influence farmers' decision-making on the maintenance and selection of cultivars
○ population structures of local cultivars and geneflow with wild and weedy relatives
○ factors contributing to environmental and human selection
○ seed and varietal supply systems
○ breeding, market and policy constraints.

This research pursues participatory approaches and involves multidisciplinary work in the areas of population genetics, ecology, agronomy and social sciences.

The Centres are currently developing research activities and programmes within their mandate areas that relate to the conservation and use of genetic resources *in situ*. Farmers' practices in managing diversity and their implications for *in situ* conservation of maize and rice have focused on research conducted at the International Maize and Wheat Improvement

Center (CIMMYT) and IRRI, respectively (Louette and Smale, 1996; Pham et al., 1998). IPGRI is carrying out a project that aims to strengthen the scientific basis of *in situ* conservation and support to the development of knowledge required in national programmes. This project also aims to determine where, when and how on-farm conservation will be effective. The research targets key crops in various agro-ecosystems within the nine participating countries (Chapter 3.6). The International Potato Center (CIP) is investigating factors influencing the management and use of Andean root and tuber crops by farmers in this region (Valdivia et al., 1998). This work also involves the study of rational strategies for both *ex situ* and *in situ* conservation of crops, including the role of community gene banks. The wild and weedy species related to crops have also become a focus of the Centres' activities with respect to *in situ* conservation. Centro Internacional de Agricultura Tropical (CIAT) is studying the gene flow between wild, weedy and cultivated beans and its exploitation by farmers. The International Center for Agricultural Research in Dry Areas (ICARDA), in collaboration with the Syrian national programme, is currently identifying and monitoring sites for *in situ* conservation of wild relatives of cereals and food legumes. These examples, although by no means exhaustive, provide an overview of the range of activities currently being undertaken by the CG-Centres and their national programme partners in this field.

The integration of formal-sector breeding efforts and those of farming communities is stimulated through participatory breeding, seed networks and diversity fairs. This integration is stimulating the flow of genetic resources and information between the formal and informal sectors. The Systems-Wide Initiative on Participatory Research and Gender Analysis for Technology Development and Institutional Innovation promotes farmer–scientist collaboration in plant breeding and natural resource management. The Programme operates under the umbrella of CGIAR and includes national agricultural research systems, NGOs, independent research organizations, grassroots organizations and CGIAR Centres.

Linking the gene banks to on-farm management of diversity by farmers may guarantee long-term conservation of landraces of primary importance to farmers. This linkage may provide farmers with a wider range of adapted materials and improved germplasm. It will also facilitate a more comprehensive conservation of crop gene pools through the integration of *ex situ* and *in situ* approaches. By further integrating its work on *ex situ* conservation in activities with respect to farmer conservation and improvement of genetic resources, CGIAR will strengthen its contribution to the conservation and use of genetic resources for the benefit of farmers and the world community.

The International Rice Genebank and local management of rice diversity

IRRI has been involved in the conservation of rice genetic resources since 1962. The International Rice Genebank (IRG) of IRRI undertakes actual collection and storage of germplasm. The IRG's activities relate to the conservation and distribution of rice germplasm and associated information, and in particular address the description and analysis of rice diversity. *Ex situ* conservation has been IRG's core activity. IRG is the world's largest rice gene bank. It holds more than 80 000 accessions of cultivated and wild rice, and between 1991 and 1995 it distributed more than 43 000 samples to users. The importance of *ex situ* conservation of rice plant genetic resources is only for historical reasons. Cultivated rice is a highly selfing crop with orthodox seeds. Its *ex situ* conservation does not pose major biological problems; therefore it is a pragmatic answer to genetic erosion.

IRG recently expanded its research activities to on-farm conservation, within the project 'Safeguarding and conserving the biodiversity of the rice gene pool'. Before being able to conceptualize, design or implement on-farm conservation, IRRI scientists decided that a research phase was needed to gather empirical data on farmers' management of rice diversity and its genetic consequences. Three study sites in Asian countries have been selected and research has been conducted since 1995 in partnership with national research institutions. Partner organizations include the Huê University of Agriculture and Forestry and the Vietnam Agricultural Science Institute (Vietnam), the Indira Gandhi Agricultural University and the National Bureau of Plant Genetic Resources (India), and the Philippines Rice Research Institute (Philippines). The project is also supported by IRD (Research and Development, France, formerly ORSTOM). Two distinct aspects of the perspective of an international gene bank such as IRG on local management of rice diversity have been elaborated: the first concerns local management as a means of conservation, and the second addresses local management as a source of information for researchers and conservationists.

Local management and the formal system of conservation

The rationale behind IRRI's commitment to on-farm conservation research is that on-farm conservation must be beneficial to the overall system of rice genetic conservation. On-farm conservation is seen not as a competitor to *ex situ* conservation, but rather as a necessary complement. To complement the static nature of *ex situ* conservation, on-farm conservation is expected to play a complementary role. On-farm conservation is expected to address the dynamic components of genetic resources in terms of evolution. IRRI scientists have been attempting to answer the question: 'What is the role of farmers in rice genetic conservation?' They use the following instruments: socio-economic surveys, anthropological studies, seed collection and genetic studies. Results from the Cagayan Valley, the Philippines strongly suggest that genetic changes occur in farmers' fields (Pham et al., 1998). This is an important result as it shows that under certain conditions farmers' management practices still contribute to evolutionary processes.

Local management as a source of information to the institutional sector

Brush (1995) suggested that people involved in on-farm conservation may have other objectives than those directly involved in dynamic conservation, such as through the maintenance of diversity in *in situ* crop biology 'laboratories'. It is obvious to the IRRI team and its partners that their research results in very detailed knowledge of *in situ* diversity. The picture of diversity obtained from the study sites in Vietnam, India and the Philippines is far more accurate than that obtained from any seed collection undertaken for the purpose of *ex situ* conservation. This is due to the inclusion of both geneticists' and farmers' viewpoints in the collection work. The latter part is covered by involved social scientists. To understand the linkage between social and genetic aspects and the manner in which farmers' decision-making, policy, and agro-ecological conditions are related is a challenge.

This better understanding of actual on-farm diversity and its management by farmers, and the transfer of local knowledge among farmers, will find applications in the design of seed collection strategies for *ex situ* conservation. In addition, it will provide valuable information for participatory rice breeding projects. Farmers understand better than anyone else the varieties they maintain. This information on farmers' preferences is valuable to breeders in their quest for improving the adaptation of varieties to local conditions, which will become more useful to farmers. Most importantly, the information is an indication of how to promote on-farm diversity, especially considering whether or not it is a dynamic process. Clearly, making such information available and supporting the use of genetic diversity on-farm are also part of the mission of a gene bank within the context of *in situ* conservation.

On-farm management: linking gene banks and farmers

Continuity exists between the *ex situ* and *in situ* activities of the IRG. A flow of genetic material has emerged from on-farm conservation study sites to national gene banks held by IRRI's national partners in India, the Philippines and Vietnam. An ongoing operation in the Cagayan Valley (the Philippines) has provided farmers who contributed to the surveys with seeds of local and modern varieties. Farmers were pleased to receive the seeds, in part because drought in 1997, flooding in 1998, and inadequate seed storage facilities had decimated their seed stock. Farmers' enthusiasm for these seeds indicated significant value of the germplasm located in gene banks, and of the technical expertise of plant genetic resources officers (e.g. seed drying and storage technology). Linking farmers and gene banks is considered an important element of the projects.

As stated by IRRI scientists, on-farm conservation is something that farmers do, rather than something that is imposed on them by institutions (Bellon et al., 1997). This does not mean that institutions should be passive about on-farm conservation. It means that farmers are the main actors who take decisions according to their own goals, aspirations and assessments of risk and benefit. The role of IRRI and the other CGIAR Centres is to co-operate with national research and extension organizations in order to identify strategies to make management and use of diversity a viable alternative for farmers.

3.3. Community gene banks: the experience of CONSERVE in the Philippines

Arma Bertuso, Gilda Ginogaling and Rene Salazar

The introduction of genetically uniform varieties in farmers' fields has changed the rice landscape in the Philippines from the use of an estimated 3000 varieties to only six to eight modern varieties that are widely grown in irrigated rice fields. The improved varieties are developed by the institutional system; this has reduced the role of farmers as plant breeders and seed selectors in particular, and as actors in the generation of agricultural technology in general. It has also created a dependency of farmers upon the formal breeding system for innovation of their planting material. This chapter presents the experience and lessons of CONSERVE, an NGO in the southern Philippines, working at the grassroots level to establish community gene banks and support farmers' plant breeding. The work of CONSERVE addresses conservation and plant breeding through the creation of capacity and awareness at the grassroots level, reducing the emerged dependency of the formal sector. This chapter focuses on the rice crop and the lowland irrigated rice production system only, and therefore does not give a complete overview of the activities of CONSERVE.

Plant genetic resources are important to farming communities not only for food production, but also because of their role in people's culture and traditions. When plant genetic resource diversity is lost, it is not only the genetic base of agriculture that is eroded, but also rural peoples' cultural identity and knowledge system. The varieties used by farmers for production and for other uses go beyond being an agricultural technology: varieties have their purpose in the culture and knowledge system, and are needed for social activities of farming communities. In the case of the Philippines, the link between rice varieties and rural people's culture is indisputable.

An example of the loss of cultural identity associated with the loss of local varieties is related to changes in local systems of shared work, called *Bayanihan*. In traditional systems, farmers used to help each other in many aspects of rural life. *Bayanihan* is the local system for exchange of labour in farming (as in transplanting or maintenance of irrigation systems), but also

117

in social and cultural activities (weddings, construction of houses). This system has gradually disappeared in the rice Green Revolution areas in the Philippines because of the commoditization of rice production. Cultural activities such as traditional dances associated with rice farming are changing or lost. An example is the traditional dances based on single-panicle harvesting of rice; they have become meaningless in areas dominated by dwarf rice varieties that are harvested by sickles. The tradition and knowledge base of women as seed selectors is gradually lost when varieties and seeds become a purchased, external input. In South-East Asia, access to new external inputs such as agricultural chemicals and seeds is transacted by the male population, resulting in social, cultural and economic changes.

The link between culture and varieties, and access to genetic diversity as resource of the community, provide the main rationale for the establishment of CONSERVE. The guiding principles of CONSERVE are to retrieve farmers' central role in agricultural research, to empower farmers to take part and decide in plant genetic resources management, and to develop technologies appropriate to their specific conditions.

CONSERVE: establishment of a grassroots plant genetic resources-oriented NGO

CONSERVE was established in 1992 in the municipality of Roxas, Cotabato Province in the southern Philippines. The establishment of CONSERVE was part of the Seeds of Survival programme of the (SEARICE) in Manila, the Philippines. The area addressed by CONSERVE covers 3500ha of irrigated rice lands, tilled by around 3500 families. In addition, CONSERVE works with five communities in upland rice-based farming systems in the surrounding hills and mountains. The main guiding premises of CONSERVE's work on plant genetic resources are as follows:

o plant genetic resources conservation and development by farmers is not a static but a continuous and dynamic process
o on-farm plant genetic resources management is linked to increasing farmers' access to diverse genetic materials
o farmers' plant genetic resources options and materials to work on should be broadened
o farmers conserve by utilizing plant genetic resources; conservation should therefore be linked to farmers' needs, criteria and conditions
o losses and/or changes of plant genetic resources and the generation of diversity in farmers' fields are part of this dynamic process.

On-farm conservation and establishing a community gene bank

One of the first activities of CONSERVE was to conduct a survey within an area approximately 100km radius around the CONSERVE farm. The objective of the survey was to determine the amount of existing genetic diversity and level of genetic erosion. As expected, farmers' diverse rice varieties were found in the upland farming systems while the irrigated lowland is dominated by modern cultivars. A total of 113 lowland rice, 235 upland rice, 14 maize and 53 germplasm samples of other crops were collected during the 1992 survey (Magnifico, 1996). The collected samples were regenerated, characterized, documented and evaluated on the 1.5-ha CONSERVE farm.

The survey also aimed to collect local varieties that could be disseminated to farmers in the region and thus to contribute to the realization of on-farm conservation. To realize this objective, CONSERVE distributed 169 local varieties to 45 farmer curators in lowland areas in the initial year. For the lowland irrigated area, approximately 10 different varieties were provided to each farmer. Over 2 years seeds were also given to 400 farmers in upland areas. After some growing seasons, discarded materials or germplasm that farmers considered not to be useful were returned to CONSERVE for storage.

In addition to maintenance by farmer curators through utilization, CONSERVE stored seeds of the accessions in small quantities at its farm. The seeds were stored in bottles with silica gel as desiccator. These samples were intended to serve as duplicates of the varieties that were maintained by farmers. After a few years CONSERVE and its farmer partners realized that the objective had to be shifted to dissemination for use rather than for on-farm conservation in the strict sense. As a result of this shift, the status of the collection at the CONSERVE farm was modified in 1995 to become a kind of community working collection, instead of a duplicate collection. CONSERVE learnt that the redistribution of local varieties had been very instrumental in enhancing access of farmers to local genetic diversity and their awareness of the importance of this access. In cases of farmers' revived interest in stored materials, the collection was easily available for redistribution.

A minimum amount of seeds is currently maintained at CONSERVE. Storage for the long term (community base collection) is organized through a black-box arrangement with the gene bank of the Philippine Rice Research Institute (PhilRice). In the black-box arrangement, seed samples of the varieties of the community are stored in a closed box in the national gene bank. The key to the box remains with the representatives of the community, as does the information on the seed samples. CONSERVE, with the assistance of SEARICE, has played a facilitation role in establishing this black-box arrangement between the communities and PhilRice.

Shift to dissemination and varietal selection and breeding of local varieties

In 1995, CONSERVE shifted its emphasis and began to concentrate more on the improvement than on-farm conservation of rice varieties. Through its dissemination of local varieties to farmers, CONSERVE had already become involved in a kind of participatory varietal selection. Since CONSERVE was launched it has distributed a total of 169 lowland and 400 upland local varieties to farmers. Some high-performing, well-adapted and suitable varieties were identified, further propagated by farmers and disseminated to other community members. In 1996, six local varieties had gained good acceptance and were distributed and utilized on a large scale.

Adding another step to the participatory varietal selection work, project staff started to provide short training courses to farmers on rice breeding and making crosses. The farmers who were trained in turn shared these techniques with their neighbours. Plant genetic resources conservation and breeding were added to the ecological pest management curriculum in CONSERVE's farmer field schools. CONSERVE has adapted the approach of integrated pest management as developed and disseminated by FAO, and has added components addressing plant genetic resources and soil management. The ecological pest management farmer field schools are part of the ongoing education programme of CONSERVE. In 1995, 31 farmers received training in plant breeding, but only four are enjoying and continuing the hybridization and breeding work. These farmers are selecting and testing their own parental lines, producing and testing their breeding lines, and have started pure-line selection. More than 10 farmers take pleasure from and have proven capable of handling segregating lines (F_4 and F_5) and selecting from populations. More than 20 farmers had been trained in further improving their selection techniques. The potential farmer-breeders were selected from those who participated in the farmer field schools because they were known in the community as good sources of farmers' seeds of local varieties. As well as supporting farmer breeding, the CONSERVE project staff started a small breeding programme at their farm. They selected and subsequently distributed six F_7 lines to farmer-partners. In 1995, CONSERVE assisted the distribution of eight bulk-bred varieties from the Farmer–Scientist Partnerships in Agricultural Development (MASIPAG).

In 1995 a survey was implemented to assess the impact of the programme. After 2 years of CONSERVE disseminating local varieties and supporting farmer breeding in the lowland project area, the number of farmer-respondents cultivating modern varieties reduced from 36 to 18 per cent, whereas the number of farmer-respondents cultivating local and traditional varieties increased from 64 to 82 per cent fields (Magnifico, 1996).

Rice farmers at the CONSERVE project areas were in general highly interested in receiving seeds of new varieties. However, few farmers proved to be interested and skilled in more detailed management of and selection within genetically heterogeneous and segregating populations. Farmers who apply more intensive mass selection for the next season's seeds tend to be able to handle later-generation lines and populations. The same trend is observed by SEARICE in its other projects in the Philippines and South-East Asia. In their selection work, farmers use both local and modern varieties from the government. Some skilled farmers in the project area of CONSERVE have started to produce and disseminate their own varieties and begun to share their seeds with many other NGOs and farmer organizations in the country.

Lessons from a community plant genetic resources and breeding project

Biodiversity conservation has many different aspects and is an enormous and complex task. Several NGOs in the different regions are doing work on these issues at the grassroots or community levels (Cooper et al., 1992). The work at CONSERVE is one of many grassroots-level initiatives contributing to the global effort to conserve agrobiodiversity.

The activities of CONSERVE in community plant genetic resources management and crop development provide an interesting sequence of lessons supporting farmers' use and development of plant genetic resources. In its initial activities, CONSERVE aimed to contribute to on-farm conservation in a strict sense, disseminating local varieties to farmer curators for maintenance through continued cultivation. This approach was not successful from a conservation perspective: farmers did not maintain all the varieties disseminated. The activity was, however, very successful from a crop development perspective, as farmers selected adapted and high-performance varieties from the material distributed. In that sense the dissemination became a kind of participatory varietal selection exercise, disseminating and testing local varieties. The result was exciting and increased the use of local varieties by farmers.

In response to moving into this kind of participatory varietal selection, CONSERVE started to support plant-breeding activities by farmers by including selection and crossing methods in the curricula of farmer field schools. An important lesson from teaching plant-breeding techniques to farmers was that only few farmers are interested and have the capacity to become really involved in farmer breeding. The use of the techniques by a few farmer-breeders has, however, resulted in a number of interesting local varieties being adopted by neighbouring farmers. In that sense, the activities of CONSERVE contribute to the development of approaches to participatory plant breeding which take farmer-breeding as a starting point. This starting point appears quite unique in participatory plant breeding, which is usually developed from a strong researcher or breeder perspective (Berg, 1996).

The experience at CONSERVE showed that on-farm plant genetic resources conservation and development cannot be restricted to saving and preserving specific varieties on-farm in the strict sense. Farmers use and maintain only those varieties that fulfil their needs and requirements. The experience of involving and training farmers in plant breeding showed that rice genetic diversity can be increased, and that on-farm plant genetic resources development contributes to the maintenance of diversity within a genetic pool rather than the conservation of specific local varieties. Another important lesson was that farmers' knowledge and skills regarding crop development and the maintenance of local varieties is conserved and strengthened more than the genetic diversity itself.

The experience of CONSERVE demonstrates that access of farmers to knowledge and germplasm is crucial in on-farm management work of local organizations. For on-farm conservation, community gene banks can be established. The community gene bank is developed as a system of an active working collection with the local NGO (in the vicinity of the community) and a base collection through black-box arrangements with a national gene bank. The control over access to germplasm and associated knowledge remains entirely in the hands of the community. Its establishment, however, depends on the facilitation of grassroots-oriented NGOs such as CONSERVE. The experience with the formal gene bank made CONSERVE and SEARICE realize that for particular tasks and responsibilities the formal sector is much better equipped, and that the work of farmers and NGOs at the community level should be complemented by the formal research institutions (see Chapter 3.5). At the same time CONSERVE is exploring ways to sustain the community gene bank and reduce its own role.

With respect to the policy framework, the link of the communities with CONSERVE, and through this organization with SEARICE, has proven very important to raising awareness at the local level on policy issues at the national, regional and global levels (Salazar, 1992). The link of SEARICE with the community, through CONSERVE, has been important to enhance the recognition of farmers' roles in conservation and crop development (Salazar, 1992; see Chapters 3.6 and 6.12).

We wish to emphasize that on-farm plant genetic resources conservation and development is only one aspect of CONSERVE's approach contributing to sustainable agriculture. We consider the maintenance and use of plant genetic resources one of the most important components of ecological pest management. At the end of 1997 it was estimated that the use of insecticides had been reduced by 50 per cent. The use of local varieties and the enhanced capacity of farmers in pest management have proven successful in reducing the incidence of pests and the use of pesticides. At the grassroots level, plant genetic resource activities go hand in hand with many other elements contributing to building sustainability in agriculture.

3.4. Seeds of Diversity: a living gene bank in Canada

Garrett Pittenger

Historic background

For much of the twentieth century, and at an accelerating pace since World War II, Canadian gardeners and farmers have relied on commercial sources for the majority of their seeds. There have been many good reasons for this: convenience, access to new and truly improved varieties, increased agricultural specialization, and the difficulty of producing high-quality seed due to wet harvest weather in some parts of the country.

Before World War II, private firms and the government experiment stations did much plant breeding for small-scale farmers and home gardeners. Since that time there has been increasing divergence between the products of plant breeding and the needs of organic farmers and gardeners. Much of the new breeding turned its focus on the requirements of larger-scale agriculture, itself often oriented to high inputs of chemical fertilizers and the use of chemical pest control measures. Large commercial seed and breeding companies needed wider markets to support their infrastructure. Government agencies, increasingly under funding pressure, looked to corporate sources for funding and targeted corporate needs to keep their programmes politically justifiable. This has been the story of agricultural research in Canada.

Before the early 20th century, most of the improved varieties originated from farmers and market gardeners through selection from their production crops. Superior varieties of both food crops and ornamental plants were selected and perfected as an adjunct to good farming and horticultural practice. Locally adapted varieties came out of the same process. Famous Canadian melon and sweet corn (maize) varieties of the 19th and early 20th centuries are notable examples, as evidenced by their chronicle in 'The Vegetables of New York', published in the late 1920s (Hedrick et al., 1928–37). The importance of these varieties to our agriculture can be illustrated by the story of Red Fife spring wheat, an accidental introduction from Scotland grown and selected by Ontario farmer David Fife in 1842. Selected by Fife as an individual plant, then multiplied over several years, it was earlier and more disease-tolerant than any other available spring wheats, and permitted the establishment of wheat production on the Canadian Prairies.

Crop genetic diversity in Canada: heritage varieties

In contrast to the situation in countries within Vavilov's centres of origin for cultivated crop plants, Canada's agricultural biodiversity rests on the varieties originating from the aboriginal peoples and from the imported 'folk' varieties brought by immigrants to our shores. In addition to the pool of varieties from these two streams of origin, we can add the improved varieties based on them, both those developed by farmer-breeders and those created in the government-sponsored experiment stations. This complex constitutes the bulk of what we call 'heritage' varieties. We certainly do not perceive these varieties as obsolete.

The origin of a part of the heritage varieties goes back even further to the aboriginal varieties. Bean, squash and corn varieties developed in native American agriculture and have provided the foundations for commercial agriculture in some North American species. Many remain relevant even under modern farming conditions, surviving as favourites to this day.

As a grassroots membership organization, the primary focus of Seeds of Diversity Canada (SoDC) is on discovering and conserving the heritage varieties for vegetable crops of Canada. The great majority of these are the result of farmer-based plant breeding, both by aboriginal and later immigrant settler farmers. Our efforts to date have concentrated on conservation because of the urgent need to save varieties at risk of extinction. We see the return of seed saving and plant breeding among farmers as an integral part of conserving agricultural biodiversity. In the Canadian context it should be noted that the aboriginal varieties contain important adaptations for our generally short growing season. Some immigrant varieties may be conserved only in Canada, having to a large extent disappeared in their homelands. The carrot cultivars Topweight and Red Elephant may be examples of this phenomenon. They are still maintained by grassroots seed exchanges and some small commercial seed companies in Canada, but have been excluded from the European Union's Common Catalogue and are thus not permitted in the European seed trade.

One of the often-overlooked consequences associated with the loss of our older crop varieties is the fading and disappearance of knowledge and awareness of them as one generation of farmers is succeeded by another. What was commonplace to one generation is rare, unusual or unknown to another. A possible consequence of this generational loss of knowledge is that breeders may seek out and try to develop characteristics that may already exist in now obscure varieties that live, literally, in Canadian backyards.

Plant breeders, too, have for a long time tacitly assumed the availability of previously collected material and have not worried extensively if the material would be available in the future. Only when we think of the immense amount of time, effort and money that was expended by generations of farmers, plant collectors and breeders in the past can we imagine the wealth of the cultural capital that comprises our current inventory of plant varieties.

As Canadians we need the locally adapted varieties that meet our demanding climatic conditions at a time when many seed merchants feel the market necessity of selling varieties that can be marketed to many localities. With this target, merchant's seeds perhaps do not really respond to farmers' special needs in the same way that the old, local, aboriginal and farmer-developed varieties once did. These varieties are not museum pieces, to be maintained as curiosities in isolation from the farming systems in which they originated. The varieties and a sustainable farming system form an integral and evolving ecosystem. The varieties are as dynamic as the farming system, gradually adjusting to environmental changes and challenges. The farming itself also changes gradually in response to the development of the variety, its characteristics and the markets for which it is grown.

Heritage varieties: responsibilities and opportunities

A significant benefit of maintaining and improving farmers' own varieties is the security of supply and independence. Favourite open-pollinated varieties have disappeared from many commercial sources without notice.

Often catalogues will note the sudden disappearance of hybrids that farmers or gardeners have become accustomed to, or the crop failure of a variety they have come to rely upon. Within SoDC we aim to encourage farmers and gardeners, but also plant breeders and researchers, to take direct responsibility for conserving our crop genetic heritage, not just to take and use it.

As growers concerned about sustainable agriculture we need to take care and control of the destiny of the genetic resources that make our choices possible. Farmers and gardeners will be contributing to food security at a time when there are increasing concerns in the markets about genetically modified plant materials. Opportunities and alternatives are expanding the horizon of choice in varieties, increasing the knowledge of the specific performance and suitability of these varieties, maintaining and selecting them under local conditions. Perhaps within our lifetimes we may see a resurgence of interest in the value of the old crop varieties, as new growers become familiar with them once again and make their own judgements based on their own experience.

Seeds of Diversity Canada

Seeds of Diversity Canada began as the Heritage Seed Programme of Canadian Organic Growers in the late 1980s. We started with roots firmly in the organic movement. SoDC is a membership-based organization with a network of over 1300 members. Our members are gardeners and farmers who are dedicated to discovering and perpetuating the biodiversity of our cultivated plants. SoDC concentrates in particular, but not exclusively, on crops we grow for food. The foundation of SoDC is that someone, somewhere, is always growing these endangered varieties; the varieties will not become extinct. We work as a 'living gene bank'.

The heart of SoDC is a network of growers – our members grow endangered varieties in their gardens. About 140 growers, 10 per cent of our total membership, maintain old varieties for their own use and to supply other members. Seed samples are provided only to other members. The members practice proper seed-saving techniques to keep the varieties pure, save seeds, and make these seeds freely available to other members. An illustrated booklet, *How to Save Your Own Vegetable Seeds*, has been published to enhance the members' capacity in seed production.

In January of every year we publish a seed listing of the varieties which we share amongst ourselves (www.seeds.ca). This listing is different from a seed catalogue as we ask the growers who take seeds from it to grow the seeds, practice proper seed-saving techniques, and save seed to share with other members. In that sense the growers can utilize our varieties for production, but they are obliged to produce seeds of these varieties in a proper manner at the same time. Table 3.6 presents an overview of the varieties grown in 1998.

In addition to seed and variety exchange and conservation, we offer informative articles in our magazine which is published three times a year. The magazine covers such subjects as heritage gardens and heritage

Table 3.6: Number of varieties cultivated by SoDC members in 1998

Crop	Number
Tomatoes	675
Beans	275
Peppers	76
Potatoes	45
Eggplant	37
Squash	37
Peas	37
Garlic	21
Other vegetables, fruits, flowers and herbs	300

Source: www.seeds.ca.

varieties, and provides information about seed companies that sell heritage and regionally adapted non-hybrid varieties. The magazine also provides information on other projects in Canada and around the world which work to preserve the horticultural and agricultural heritage.

We network and co-operate with other organizations involved with plant genetic conservation. Because we do not have a centralized collection, we co-operate with Seed Savers Exchange (SSE) in the USA, a kind of sister organization to SoDC. We supply them with seeds of Canadian heritage varieties that are not in their permanent central seed bank. SoDC and SSE share the policy of open access to plant genetic resources; this policy is firmly established in our traditions. All of the varieties that the members offer to others remain in the public domain. Our co-operative and non-confrontational approach is founded on the belief that free thinking and free exchange are fundamental to all scientific and cultural improvement. Restriction is believed to bring with it a climate of narrow thinking and retrogression.

Collaboration with the Canadian Gene bank

In 1991 SoDC signed a memorandum of understanding with Plant Gene Resources Canada (PGRC), the national Plant Genetic Resources Programme. SoDC is represented on the Expert Committee of Plant Gene Resources, a committee of scientists and other experts from across the country which advises on national conservation policies. PGRC focuses on plant material which has current commercial value and which is of interest to plant breeders. Since there is very little vegetable breeding being done in Canada, the PGRC vegetable collection is poorly developed. SoDC specializes in vegetables and also preserves varieties which are of interest to backyard gardeners, small-scale farmers and speciality growers. These are not featured in the collection at PGRC. We play an important role in increasing public awareness about the importance of genetic conservation. There have been several direct collaborations between SoDC and PGRC. In the past, SoDC members have rejuvenated vegetable variety accessions for the gene bank. This programme ceased during the restructuring of PGRC in the mid-1990s, but we hope to re-establish it.

SoDC's largest and most successful collaboration with PGRC and Agriculture and Agri-Food Canada has been in the preservation of heritage potato varieties. The preservation of clonal crops is a special challenge for individual growers because of their susceptibility to the accumulation of virus that ultimately threatens their existence. Clean-up of tissue cultures from these clones and the subsequent propagation of healthy planting stock is the first step in getting them back into the wider cultivation needed to ensure their continuation. In 1997 SoDC sent samples of 24 heritage varieties of potatoes for virus clean-up and tissue culture by the PGRC Potato Node at Fredericton, New Brunswick. As a result of our close co-operation with the Potato Node and provision of articles for their newsletter, the Potato Node will completely fund this clean-up and maintain tissue cultures at Fredericton, ensuring the preservation of these varieties. In addition, the PGRC Potato Node at Fredericton has curatorship of seven historic potato varieties imported into Canada by SoDC from the Scottish National Collection, bringing the total of heritage varieties in tissue culture preservation to 31. SoDC is also co-operating with SSE in their efforts to clean up their potato collection.

Conclusion

SoDC is both a working conservation organization and a constituency of support for the work done by PGRC, the international gene bank network, other NGOs, and farmers involved in the preservation of crop genetic diversity. SoDC and similar organizations differ from the formal gene banks in that we focus on conservation through evaluation, re-introduction and use. Collaboration between formal gene banks and grassroots organizations of growers interested in conserving genetic diversity in use has been demonstrated to be fruitful and effective in North America. Some of the varieties in the network of both SoDC and its US counterpart SSE are varieties from gene banks that have once again become part of the living genetic diversity in our farms and gardens. We are committed to preserving, *in situ* and in active use, both heritage varieties and the knowledge needed to use them, on living farms and in the minds of farmers.

3.5. The CBDC Programme: an experiment in strengthening community management of agrobiodiversity

Camila Montecinos and Rene Salazar

Background

Recognition of farmers' innovation in plant genetic resources management has increased over the past decade. The Convention on Biological Diversity (CBD) and the International Undertaking for Plant Genetic Resources for Food and Agriculture (PGRFA), incorporated in the FAO Global Plan of Action, have enshrined farmers' plant genetic resources management as a major programme area. However, a major gap exists with respect to information on farmers' plant genetic resource systems. Tools and research instruments to study, assess and strengthen these systems are lacking. And more importantly, a framework for collaboration is required combining the expertise of civil organizations such as NGOs with scientific research institutions. These needs have led to the building of the Community Biodiversity Development and Conservation (CBDC) programme. Founders of the programme originate from NGOs and research institutions, who started planning the CBDC as they found common ground in an international dialogue on plant genetic resources, organized by the Keystone Center between 1989 and 1992. These founders consider the community plant genetic resources management system to be an innovative system of research and development which functions in parallel to the more formal and institutional system.

CBDC is a programme that addresses two different types of goals. Firstly, it aims to develop tools and provide data that facilitate assessment of and support to the community plant genetic resources management system. This goal addresses the community system as a system of innovation, i.e. research and development. Secondly, CBDC aims at developing a framework for collaboration among formal and informal institutions that permit effective support to the community plant genetic resources system.

The hypotheses

To assess the community plant genetic resources system, the CBDC programme formulated hypotheses that cover various aspects of local conservation of genetic resources (see Box 3.1). As the programme approaches the completion of its first 4-year phase, CBDC members have gathered evidence which indicates the enormous potential of local community systems as well as the serious weaknesses and threats they are facing. Local innovation systems will not continue to develop and will not survive if some important policy, technical, methodological and economic changes do not take place, and if these changes are not supported by a large number of

Box 3.1: Hypotheses of the CBDC programme

○ Local crop development (management and conservation) implies the *in situ* survival of genetic variation and may therefore complement the *ex situ* approach to conservation of crop genetic resources. Local crop development and conservation also generate and conserve local knowledge of genetic resources

○ Local crop development and conservation maintain varieties/landraces and secure local seed supply

○ Local crop development and conservation expose crops to natural and artificial selection, which ensure reasonable adaptation to growing conditions and local needs

○ Local crop innovators are capable of providing high-quality seeds with respect to some of the technical criteria of seed quality, but not all

○ In many areas local crop development is limited by lack of genetic diversity. Supply of appropriate genetic materials may enhance local crop development

○ Landraces tend to be specific, expressing a substantial level of phenotype–environment interaction

○ Landraces under specific conditions satisfy farmers' requirements better than modern varieties

○ In many cases local crop development is limited by methodological constraints. Scientific knowledge and methods may contribute to enhancement of local crop development

people and a wide range of institutions. One of the biggest challenges of the CBDC programme in the future is to become an effective actor and facilitator of co-ordinated efforts of the large number of actors involved in these changes.

Organization

For a programme that aims to develop new structures for collaboration between farmers, informal and formal institutions, the organizational aspects of its own functioning are important. NGO leaders and scientists from research institutions participating in an international dialogue called the Keystone International Dialogue on Plant Genetic Resources (1989–1991) initiated the CBDC programme. These founders included Dr Jaap Hardon of the Centre for Genetic Resources, the Netherlands (CGN/CPRO-DLO); Dr Trygve Berg from the Norwegian Institute for International Agricultural Development (NORAGRIC); Pat Roy Mooney from Rural Advancement Foundation International (RAFI); Henk Hobbelink from Genetic Resources Action International (GRAIN); Camila Montecinos from the Centro Educacíon y Tecnología (CET-CLADES); Dr Melaku Worede of the Ethiopian Biodiversity Institute and the African

Seeds of Survival Programme; and Rene Salazar of the South-East Asian Regional Institute for Community Education, based in the Philippines. The Programme Co-ordinating Committee is its highest policy-making body. It is composed of the founding members – three of these people are in charge of the Regional Co-ordination Units for Latin America, Africa and South-East Asia. The Programme Co-ordinating Committee, in between meetings, operates through its chairman. The Global Co-ordinating Unit is situated at CET-CLADES in Chile. The Regional Co-ordination Units lead the regional programmes and are directly responsible to the Programme Co-ordinating Committee. The three units are assisted by the Regional Co-ordinating Committees composed of representatives from national project partners and their technical advisers; and by the Regional Advisory Body. The national partners, most of them NGOs, implement the national projects.

The International Technical Programme was co-ordinated by the CGN/CPRO-DLO in collaboration with NORAGRIC. This programme provided technical advice and information for projects in the regions, and assisted regional and national partners in developing and implementing research approaches through visiting communities co-operating with the projects. Technical Programme staff participated in technical meetings in the regions, where research results were presented and critically analysed. RAFI and GRAIN have led the International Policy Programme. The objective of this programme was to ensure that policy implications derived from projects are analysed and fed into policy work at national and global levels.

The fact that decisions must be made at local level as much as possible is a basic organizational principle of the CBDC programme. Therefore, a bottom-up approach has been pursued. CBDC has another fundamental principle, that local communities must retain control of and full freedom to decide on the use of genetic resources and knowledge they possess or require. Therefore a set of guidelines on transfer of information, genetic resources, and relationships in general between communities and partners as well as among partners has been defined in a Programme Protocol. After 4 years of operation and use, the Protocol will be reviewed and adapted if necessary. A logical aspect of a bottom-up approach and the defined relationships between partners in the CBDC is a large degree of autonomy of the national projects, while sharing the common objectives of the programme.

The projects

Most national CBDC projects started with assessments of the community plant genetic resources system, including an inventory of the diversity available and an estimation of the level of genetic erosion. Lessons have been learned and methods have been developed. Based on the inventories, activities supporting the community systems were designed.

The focus of the diversity studies in the projects depends on local systems and the importance of various crop components in these systems. The project in Peru has been extensively involved in an assessment of the local system of management of genetic diversity, in particular addressing potato species. In their diversity assessments, projects in South-East Asia paid much attention to rice diversity and two or four additional crops. In Africa, the project in Sierra Leone also focused on rice, whereas that in Kenya focused on the diversity of local vegetables. Sorghum, wheat and barley were among the crops covered in Ethiopia, whereas Burkina Faso worked with sorghum. The project in Zimbabwe was less focused, but maize and small-grain cereals were major study crops. Maize was also addressed by the project in Brazil, in combination with beans. The projects in Chile and Colombia have worked with a farming systems perspective, encompassing all components of local plant biodiversity; and their work has put emphasis on medicinal plants, forest species and food crops. Communities working with the CBDC projects are situated in marginal areas or in favourable conditions with fertile soils and access to irrigation systems.

Activities to support the community plant genetic resources systems involved re-introduction of traditional varieties to local communities. Community variety trials have been the major instrument for reintroduction. From these trials, methods for plant varietal selection were refined. In addition to the reintroduction of traditional and local varieties, the projects were also involved in the introduction of modern cultivars from research institutions. This was particularly the case for major crops. In some of the projects participatory plant breeding (PPB) was developed based on these plant varietal selection activities. The projects in South-East Asia focus on PPB in rice. Elements of PPB and plant varietal selection are integrated in the farmer field school modules developed by FAO Integrated Pest Management (see Bertuso et al., Chapter 3.3).

CBDC projects have developed activities in the area of crops considered minor from a global perspective but locally thought to be of major importance. The focus of the project in Kenya has been on the reintroduction and re-popularization of local vegetables. Projects in Thailand, Vietnam, Sabah, Burkina Faso and Zimbabwe worked with (semi-)domesticated indigenous vegetables. The Chile project worked on home gardens. The Peru and Colombia project worked with quinoa and fruit species; the Philippines and Vietnam concentrated on sweet potato, yams and taro. After making an inventory and detailed studies of their importance and uses, reintroduction efforts to increase the diversity of these crops have also been made. These efforts involved comparative trials, seed production and selection by farmers of local and reintroduced cultivars.

Interactions between partner projects

Methodological contributions have been made from one project to another. A clear example of such an interaction has resulted in the organization's seed diversity fairs and development of elements of plant varietal selection and PPB in the three continents. Seed diversity fairs started in Peru, but are currently successfully implemented by the project in Zimbabwe. Plant varietal selection and PPB have been implemented in South-

East Asia and Brazil. Elements of PPB will be part of the future work of various other projects. Such cross-project use of approaches and methods provides opportunities for comparison, and will increase the understanding of similarities and differences among crops and communities in various parts of the world. Interactions also facilitate the common learning of lessons and the development of research approaches and appropriate participatory research instruments for major as well as local crops.

The International Technical Programme co-ordinated by CPRO-DLO has worked with projects in the Philippines and Vietnam. CPRO-DLO is implementing molecular studies. The genetic analysis of the various types of the Tai nguyen rice variety popular in the Mekong Delta is an example of this type of co-operation. RAFI and GRAIN, the regional partners and some national partners are active in policy discussions. RAFI and GRAIN have developed policy documents which were extensively used by CBDC partners and other organizations. These documents have been instrumental to partners when participating in policy discussions in their own countries and when present during international negotiations. RAFI and GRAIN have produced important briefing papers in advance of international meetings: the Conference of Parties to the Convention on Biological Diversity, the FAO Commission on Plant Genetic Resources for Food and Agriculture, the Fourth International Technical Conference and the International Undertaking on Plant Genetic Resources. RAFI and GRAIN have also monitored developments in the seed industry that will have an impact on farmers' plant genetic resource systems. An example of issues addressed by these organizations is the research and campaign against the 'terminator technology', research on cases of bio-piracy, and intellectual property of farmers' germplasm.

CBDC programme: an institutional experiment

With its goal to develop new structures of collaboration, the CBDC programme draws from its experience four novel types of association among partner organizations. The first concerns co-operation between civil society organizations (represented by NGOs) and formal scientific research institutions. This combination of informal and formal organizations ensures that the perspective of those outside the state power, i.e. those who regard plant genetic resources as an issue of power relations, is given paramount importance. At the same time, collaboration with scientific institutions will ensure that the socio-political and development agendas of civil society organizations are backed up by research data and results. Furthermore, the collaboration provides opportunities for influencing formal research agendas and including community perspectives and priorities in setting these agendas.

The second form of institutional association in the CBDC concerns Northern and Southern organizations. Partner organizations based in the North include two civil society organizations and two public (government) research institutions. The same holds true for organizations based in the South: this group includes both NGOs and government research institutions. As a consequence, various partners in the programme represent a diversity of perspectives. This institutional diversity contributes to the lively development of the programme.

A third combination of collaboration in the CBDC programme concerns that between NGOs working at local grassroots level and those working at national and international policy levels. Skills and traditions of local organizations are based on concrete partnership with local communities. As a result they face concerns that are specific and practical. Activities of NGOs at the grassroots level are thereby constantly checked and validated by their partner farmers. Organizations that work at policy level, no matter how hard they try, are at some distance from the reality of farmer communities. However, local community concerns and interests need to be raised at policy level. The linking of local, national and global levels depends on formal and informal networks. CBDC is a programme that tries to combine all these levels into one programme.

A fourth, and important, level of association is the combination of various disciplines. Social issues and participatory approaches, which pay much attention to power relations and address issues such as access to and control over plant genetic resources, are combined with natural science research on gene flow and conservation of genetic combinations in crops.

Lessons and opportunities

The CBDC programme is regarded as an experiment on validating and strengthening farmers' plant genetic resource management. CBDC is also developing a new mode of operation in research and development that combines civil society organizations, with their socio-political bias, and scientific institutions, with their technical–statistical bias. The experiment is envisaged to produce two types of programme output. One will address the concerns of local farmers and directly benefit farmers in their management of plant genetic resources. Examples of these outputs concern a farmers' field manual on PPB, and models for material transfer agreements for farmer germplasm exchange. These outputs will contribute directly to re-strengthening farmers' plant genetic resource management and broadening the genetic base of crops. Replication of these programme approaches by other farming communities will augment the impact of the programme in other areas; the outputs are also foreseen to have an impact on or contribute to policy and institutional reforms. The second type of result will be those that are directed toward the scientific community and policy-makers; these outputs will be scientific publications and policy recommendations. The objectives of the CBDC programme are complex. Organizations that decided to embark on this experiment have positioned themselves in a situation which easily yields criticisms. However, the collaborative learning process of the partners in the programme is unique and provides an excellent basis for further collaboration.

3.6. IPGRI *in situ* project: research and institutions supporting local management of agrobiodiversity

Devra Jarvis and Julia Ndungú-Skilton

The Convention on Biological Diversity (CBD), the Agenda 21 and the FAO Global Plan of Action (GPA) for Plant Genetic Resources for Food and Agriculture have put *in situ* conservation for crop genetic diversity on the global and national policy agendas for biodiversity conservation and utilization. The urgent need was raised at national and international fora to develop *in situ* conservation approaches, to establish such approaches within national plant genetic resources programmes (NPGRPs) and to link *in situ* and *ex situ* conservation. The International Plant Genetic Resources Institute (IPGRI) recognized that the science and practice of *in situ* conservation lagged behind these policy commitments. This institute realized that a global framework of scientific methods for testing conservation practices and tools, as well as a system for disseminating useful experiences and tools between countries and across agro-ecosystems, was required. The need for such a global framework was a starting point for IPGRI to initiate a global project with the objective of strengthening the scientific basis of *in situ* conservation of agrobiodiversity.

The project

To understand and support the mechanisms of *in situ* conservation on-farm IPGRI, together with national partners in nine countries, has formulated a global project entitled 'Strengthening the scientific basis of *in situ* conservation of agricultural biodiversity'. The project was established in 1995. It involves NPGRPs in Burkina Faso, Ethiopia, Hungary, Mexico, Morocco, Nepal, Peru, Turkey and Vietnam. It supports research on the biological and social bases of *in situ* conservation, including the following elements:

○ collecting a data set that links farmers' decision-making on the selection and maintenance of crop cultivars with measurable indices of genetic diversity
○ training of national scientists, extension workers and development workers in *in situ* conservation research
○ identifying target areas for *in situ* conservation programmes
○ building bridges among conservationists, farmers, agricultural development agencies and policy-makers.

The project strategy is to promote on-farm conservation by strengthening the relationships of formal institutions with farmers and local level institutions. Examples of formal institutions include universities, conservation and agricultural research, extension and rural development organizations within the ministries of agriculture, natural resource management, science and technology. Examples of organizations operating at the local level are community-based organizations, farmers' groups and non-governmental organizations. Although working through national and therefore formal programmes may be considered as a centralized approach, the *in situ* conservation strategies that result from the approach developed in the project are based on information from and requirements of farmers (Jarvis and Hodgkin, 1999).

A range of partners

IPGRI's traditional partners for plant genetic resources conservation include national gene banks, public plant breeding and agricultural research organizations. An *in situ* conservation project is a multi-actor and multi-objective activity. The range of stakeholders and institutions involved renders the implementation of *in situ* conservation a complex institutional process. Partners in such a project are identified beyond those traditionally involved in NPGRPs or gene banks. To implement the project, NPGRPs must develop a more integrated framework covering various conservation strategies, and to build coalitions with other organizations and stakeholders. The boundaries of the plant genetic resources arena are changing, increasing the participation of actors in society in the conservation effort. In principle such an integrated framework needs to be in place before the project can be implemented. Therefore the first step to initiation of country components has been the elaboration of an integrated framework. The instrument for this has been the formation of multi-disciplinary and multi-institutional research teams and project committees (Jarvis et al., 2000).

Farmers and conservation organizations

National programmes interested in *in situ* and on-farm conservation of crop diversity must achieve the objectives of both conserving processes which promote crop genetic diversity and ensuring that these resources are competitive enough to improve farmers' living standards (Jarvis and Hodgkin, 1999). To formulate an on-farm conservation strategy, knowledge is needed on how farmer selection practices affect crop genetic diversity. The study of such processes requires scientific expertise from a variety of sources. To ensure the sustainability of an on-farm conservation programme, partners in the NPGRP must understand how, when and where a farmer continues to maintain genetic variation. The NPGRP must also be able to promote strategies that make the conservation of local crop diversity a competitive option to other choices a farmer might have (Jarvis et al., 1998).

Implementation of an on-farm conservation programme conditions the existence of integrated frameworks linking central and local levels. Another precondition is that effective teams for project implementation are already in place. In many countries, this is not the case. In the IPGRI-supported global *in situ* project, the first step has been to support or enhance the formation of such an integrated framework and form multi-disciplinary teams in a 'planning for project implementation' phase.

Diversity of projects

At first glance the country components within the IPGRI-supported global *in situ* project appear similar. Most country components concentrate on major staple food crops, including some minor or under-utilized crops. All projects concentrate on annual crops so that changes in population structures within the timeframe of the project (5 years) may be measured. However, each country component has its own characteristics. These are founded on the diversity of agro-ecological and farming systems, crops, institutional frameworks and type of partners. Another difference among country components is that the partners vary in focus on research, conservation and development. Table 3.7 presents a matrix providing a brief characterization of ongoing country components in the *in situ* project. As an illustration, we describe three country components.

The project in Mexico is situated in the centre-north of the Yucatan peninsula, an area where almost 50 000 families still practise the *millpa* system of shifting cultivation with maize, lima bean, cassava, yam, squash and other crops. These crops are cultivated in a multi-cropping system in tropical sub-humid lowland. The crops show a considerable degree of genetic diversity. The farming system is currently threatened. Modification of the farming system will have serious implications for the crop genetic diversity encountered. A group of agricultural research organizations and universities participate in the project; they work at local level through an NGO and through the government extension service.

A unique array of agro-ecosystems with an equal range of genetic diversity for a number of crops is encountered in Morocco. The project in this country is situated at three distinct sites, one in the mountains of the high Atlas, one in an oasis area and one in the Rif Mountain area. This country component focuses on barley, durum wheat, faba bean, alfalfa and bread wheat. The genetic diversity of these crops is highly valued among farmers, although it is under threat. Preliminary genetic diversity surveys have been carried out. The country component is co-ordinated by and implemented within the institutional framework of the NPGRP. Through this framework, various institutions of the NARS are involved in the research and conservation activities. At the local level, the project is conducted in collaboration with extension and rural development branches of the Ministry of Agriculture and a number of NGOs.

Nepal is a rich centre of crop genetic diversity reflecting extreme ranges in altitude, ecological variation, antiquity of agriculture, and numerous ethnic and cultural groups. Three regions have been selected for the project on the basis of the level of genetic diversity present and the status of farmers' management of agrobiodiversity. The regions represent high-, medium- and low-altitude crop production ecosystems. Upland, rainfed and irrigated production systems have been included. The project takes a farming-systems approach and thus does not take single crops as a starting point. Major crops addressed in the project include rice, finger millet, barley, buckwheat, taro, sponge gourd and pigeon pea. Diagnostic surveys covering various aspects of genetic diversity and farmers' management

Table 3.7: Characterization of IPGRI *in situ* country components

Country	Agro-ecology	Farming system	Crops	Geographic scope	Type of partners	Strength and focus within the global perspective
Mexico	Tropical lowland	Shifting cultivation	Maize, beans, squash, chilli peppers	Yucatan	National agricultural research organization, universities and community organizations	Participatory plant breeding agro-ecosurveys, farming systems research
Nepal	Mountain, mid-hills and lowland	Irrigated and rainfed agriculture	Rice, barley, buckwheat, finger millet, taro, sponge gourd, pigeon pea	Three eco-regions countrywide	National agricultural research organization, NGOs and community organizations	Participatory approaches; research on genotype × environment interaction
Vietnam	Tropical lowland, medium elevation	Irrigated and rainfed, upland agriculture	Rice, beans, millet, taro	Four eco-regions countrywide	National agricultural research organization, universities and NGOs	Agromorphology characterization and farming systems research
Morocco	Mountain, semi-arid and oasis	Irrigated, rainfed and oasis systems	Durum and bread wheat, barley, alfalfa, faba bean	Three eco-regions countrywide	National agricultural research organization, universities, community organizations and NGOs	Institutional development and linking research levels
Burkina Faso	Arid and semi-arid	Rainfed	Sorghum, cowpea, millet, okra, Solenostemon	Three delineated eco-regions countrywide	National agricultural research organization, universities and NGOs	GXE interactions in stress environments
Ethiopia	Tropical highland	Rainfed, dryland	Sorghum	North Shewa and south Welo	National agricultural research organizations and universities	Time series on farmers' management of landraces

(Source: Jarvis et al., 2000)

137

have been conducted. The project focuses on participatory approaches to research, conservation and plant breeding. The partners in Nepal aim to find an institutional and professional balance among national agricultural research service and NGO researchers in implementing the project. In that sense, the Nepal country component is an institutional example to the other components of the *In situ* Project.

Research: strengthening a scientific basis

As indicated in its title, the project has been set up to strengthen the scientific basis for *in situ* conservation on-farm. It has been developed as a global research effort, addressing farmers' management and the specific characteristics of locally managed genetic diversity (landraces). This research objective is primarily based on a global and general research and conservation interest in farmers' management of agrobiodiversity.

Creating a framework of knowledge to support on-farm conservation requires expertise from a variety of disciplines (population genetics, biology, ecology, and economics) and the ability to work with farmers' groups. An agricultural research organization may lack expertise in social sciences, while social science departments of research organizations or universities may lack expertise in working directly with farmers' groups. In contrast, agricultural extension workers and community-based organizations may possess expertise in working with farmers' groups but lack skills in systematic sampling and farmers' management practices related to population genetics. An integrated team of disciplines from formal and informal organizations and farmers is needed for a meaningful investigation aiming to answer questions concerning farmers' decision-making related to the management and use of genetic diversity.

Identification of research sites
A first step in the project has been to develop a method for selecting regions for *in situ* and research work. Initial agro-ecological identification is followed by a natural and social science baseline survey conducted by a multidisciplinary team. The teams evaluate the initial agro-ecological zones with mutually agreed criteria, such as the availability of genetic diversity, desired agro-ecological variation, accessibility to the locality, links to agricultural extension work and, most importantly, local communities' interest and willingness to co-operate. Actual selection of sites and participant-farmers has taken place using an interactive process approach involving researchers, agricultural extension workers, NGO partners and farmer communities. Following consultations with national thematic and local teams, a national committee decides on the site selection.

Data collection
In 1997 IPGRI organized a global workshop for the project to discuss and agree on the type of information needed and the methodologies to be used to understand the effects of farmers' decision-making on genetic diversity. This standardization is necessary to create a foundation for the required

global synthesis across countries, crops and farming systems (Jarvis and Hodgkin, 1998). The following issues were addressed:

o defining basic units or strata of measurement
o timing of data collection
o aggregation over space and time.

Decisions were also taken on how to measure and analyse these units or strata based on information collected from farmers and from researchers' data obtained in the field. These issues have been elaborated during the development of project plans. The plans indicate whether data or information are being collected as part of a research survey (understanding local management and local genetic diversity), or as part of an effort to strengthen local and farmers' management and conservation of genetic diversity (local capacity-building). Tools for research design and basic data sets were elaborated for the following fields:

o socio-economic, cultural and biological influences
o population structure, factors relevant in the breeding process, selection criteria
o environmental selection factors (natural and human managed areas)
o agro-morphological characteristics – description and selection criteria
o seed/germplasm exchange and storage systems.

With respect to information on farmers' perceptions of management and genetic diversity, the workshop elaborated a set of data to be collected. Surveys and research activities are primarily targeted at obtaining better understanding of farmers' management and the genetic diversity being maintained at local level.

Balanced and integrated research, conservation and development work

With its strong focus on research and conservation, and operating through the NPGRP, the project has a broader focus supporting *in situ* conservation on-farm at the operational and local level. Research is targeted at understanding farmers' management. Research outputs will provide conservationists with tools and instruments to link their mandate in conservation to farmers' activities in the utilization and management of genetic diversity. Research is therefore directly integrated in the establishment of local platforms for genetic resource management. These local platforms are crucial and integral parts of country components developing local capacity for *in situ* conservation. The link between local capacity-building on the one hand and research implementation on the other is enforced when more interactive approaches are used. At the same time rural people and conservationists become better linked. Strengthening capacity at local level is important; more participatory and development-oriented research approaches are preconditions to the implementation of any *in situ* conservation.

A project linking local, national and global dimensions

Country components are developed within the frameworks of the NPGRPs. However in most countries, people involved in *ex situ* conservation, research and plant breeding run these programmes. More social actors have a stake in the conservation and utilization of agrobiodiversity than those initially involved in conservation, research and breeding. In the context of the project, the NPGRPs gradually develop into national platforms, involving more social actors and entering into processes of institutional learning and development. Clear variations exist among the country components. The projects aim to create the opportunities for learning among the national and local partners participating in these platforms. At the same time, involvement of the broad range of social actors operating in the informal sector (NGOs, farmers' organizations) is stimulated by IPGRI. Through the project, the national platforms for genetic resources management and conservation are opening for their participation. The involvement of these local organizations is crucial to the successful implementation of *in situ* conservation on-farm at national and local level (Jarvis et al., 2000).

Taking into account the various levels at which the project is operational, a balance has to be found to direct the research and scientific efforts addressing research questions formulated at global, national and local levels. Thus a balance should be found in trying to answer global research questions and those emerging and relevant at local levels. The science in the project is clearly directed at creating an understanding of the nature of genetic diversity and its management at local levels. The knowledge and information gained will constitute a basis for the further development of *in situ* conservation approaches. In this manner, the various outcomes of the research process may be compared and may contribute to a synthesis on a more global level. The country components differ with respect to their scientific basis; in some countries projects are primarily built on a research programme with people from involved universities, whereas in others they are much more part of a conservation programme. It is clear that a balance must be established between research, conservation and development objectives. The differences among the projects provide opportunities to develop a diversity of perspectives and obtain a range of insights into the development of institutional frameworks and methods for the implementation of *in situ* conservation on-farm (Jarvis et al., 2000).

Involvement of more local organizations (NGOs) in the country components and in the related plant genetic resources work has added a development orientation to the overall project. Taking into account the local nature of *in situ* conservation, bridges between conservation and development work emerge; a direct link between conservation and utilization of agrobiodiversity in unavoidable in this work. Interactive and participatory research methodologies need to be used in the implementation of local research activities. The various country components vary in particular for this point. The degree of organization at local level and links between the institutional and local systems of crop development are essential.

The diversity of locations where the IPGRI *in situ* country components are being implemented constitute a basis for a range of experiments for developing methods for *in situ* conservation on-farm. IPGRI realizes that one country component may be stronger in addressing global research issues than another, which may be stronger in developing links between conservation and development elements in their activities. IPGRI co-ordinates the project in such a manner that it directs country components supporting the partners in that location developing their own assets, while contributing to the overall lessons learnt about *in situ* conservation. In this sense, the diversity of projects provides opportunities for exchanging ideas and experiences. The global nature of the project is reflected in the synthesis of these elements and makes them accessible to a broader audience involved in conservation, research and development.

3.7. Upscaling approaches to support on-farm conservation

Bert Visser and Devra Jarvis

Upscaling poses a challenge

In situ conservation of crops and their relatives may have two important advantages over complementary *ex situ* approaches: a much larger diversity is conserved, and this diversity co-evolves with changing conditions, whether biological or abiological, natural or imposed by humans. However, currently we have limited experience with *in situ* conservation in general and on-farm conservation in particular. Hardly any of the involved conservation activities have exceeded a local scale, and few attempts have been made to increase the impact of local activities to benefit larger communities. This means that advantage of scale mentioned above refers to a potential only, and ways to realize this potential have to be explored.

Elements of external support to on-farm conservation of diversity

Before embarking on a discussion of approaches to upscaling on-farm conservation-directed activities, two important characteristics of on-farm conservation should be stressed. The first characteristic is that, in contrast to *ex situ* conservation, the farmer is the central actor. The second characteristic of on-farm conservation is that the farmer's focus is on livelihood security and income generation through utilization of diversity. In other words, for most farmers conservation is an instrument rather than a goal in itself. From a genetic perspective, farmers manage their crop germplasm, conserving some and developing other characteristics, and in the process acquiring and maintaining some and losing other genes.

External support to farmers' communities to maintain their farming systems and the diversity involved is endorsed by fast and irreversible changes in global agriculture which pose a threat to traditional farming systems in which diversity is maintained and utilized. These changes include growing population pressure, habitat destruction, opening of markets, and government policies favouring the introduction of commercial varieties. Such external support may include the following elements:

○ monitoring existing (and changing) crop diversity
○ documenting variation in properties of varieties
○ documenting indigenous knowledge of crops and farmers' varieties
○ improving farmers' breeding and selection skills
○ introducing exogenous germplasm for selection and cross-breeding
○ documenting and improving seed selection
○ documenting and improving harvesting and storage methods.

Facilitating farmer-to-farmer training in the above elements may become part of support activities. In addition, empowerment must be recognized as an essential element of these support activities.

Non-governmental organizations, as well as extension services, universities and research institutes, provide external support. Furthermore, local or national government itself is involved in setting conditions which can either positively or negatively influence opportunities for success and sustainability in support to on-farm conservation. Various actors are involved, and each of these may play a role in attempts to broaden the impact of activities.

Upscaling

What may definitely be excluded as a viable strategy for upscaling on-farm conservation support activities is a simple multiplication of current efforts – such an approach would not be financially sustainable. New approaches will have to be developed and combined to accomplish upscaling of on-farm conservation of crop diversity. Some strategies for upscaling support to on-farm conservation are elaborated below.

Farmer field schools

Much can be learned from integrated pest management (IPM) programmes. In IPM a broad experience exists with respect to upscaling learning processes at local levels. IPM programmes aim to support and empower local communities in their ability to control pests and diseases. They were confronted with upscaling challenges similar to that currently faced in supporting on-farm conservation. Part of the upscaling process in IPM has been the development of the concept of farmer field schools. In this approach, farmers replace professionals in teaching other farmers about the tools and instruments utilized in IPM. The upscaling takes place through demonstration and farmers teaching their fellow farmers the benefits of changing from the use of chemical pesticides to IPM. This approach may be adopted to facilitate upscaling and qualitative improvement of on-farm conservation activities. Model farmers could be involved in teaching methodologies and informing fellow farmers in other communities about their experiences. This strategy should be placed centrally in upscaling support to on-farm conservation. An exchange of ideas and experiences between people working in the field of IPM and on-farm conservation may be instrumental in using farmer field schools to upscale support for on-farm conservation.

Seed fairs
Transfer or exchange of crop material, e.g. through seed fairs, becomes a key element in networking and collaboration among farming communities. Seeds may be used for comparison among and direct selection within varieties, but may also contribute to participatory plant breeding. To exploit these options fully, ways should be explored to turn local diversity fairs into regular events leading to some sort of county-, municipality- or nation-wide events. Eventually, these fairs might become an important link with, or even the basis for, diversified product markets. In this approach, informal systems may remain or again become the main source of good quality seed in some areas or even countries. NGOs will have a vital role to play in organizing these activities.

NGO networks
In relation to the strategies discussed above, NGOs active in the area of on-farm management could build networks, offering a platform through which accumulated knowledge of various communities may be used more widely. The Community Biodiversity Development and Conservation Programme (Montecinos and Salazar, Chapter 3.5) has developed as such a network. NGOs could link with other NGOs active in rural and agricultural development (e.g. IPM, soil management, small-scale enterprise development and marketing local products) to convince them to integrate crop diversity aspects into their programmes. NGOs may raise awareness among consumers as a means of influencing local and national governments. Although farmers may be the first consumers of crop products, the produce is frequently sold in local or urban markets. This means that consumers should be aware of the value of agrobiodiversity and the need to conserve genetic diversity (Jongerden, Chapter 6.8).

The role of the public sector
Government organizations are needed for formal support. Through their involvement, local approaches and techniques may become components of an official approach to research, development and extension. The public R&D sector is indispensible in this process of upscaling support to on-farm conservation. Government institutions may be bypassed because they are weak or domineering, and all energy may be directed to creating parallel

143

structures through NGOs. The approach of developing such 'informal' parallel structures is probably not sustainable. The objective should be to foster change from within, to put pressure on the system and to support innovative individuals (Daño and Salazar, Chapter 6.12). NGOs are successful in taking small-scale initiatives, and provide a defence for rural people against repressive states. An opportunity emerges under the current conditions of increased decentralization and participation in planning R&D. Innovative work may be a catalyst and contribute to change in government policies.

Extension services and groups at universities or research institutions may complement the activities of farmers and NGOs. Extension services may adopt, institutionalize and disseminate effective approaches and methodologies. University and research groups may contribute through analysis of situations and approaches, through offering documentation and information facilities, and by providing back-up facilities to local seed storage capacity. Information on existing experiences must be gathered, documented and analysed to facilitate implementation of on-farm conservation support activities on a larger scale. Also, concepts of participatory selection and breeding require much attention and professional input covering a wide field of disciplines. Extension services and university groups might collaborate with NGOs and complement their activities and expertise. Of major importance for university groups is the possibility of integrating local approaches towards on-farm conservation into curricula at undergraduate level. In some countries, involving major farmers' unions may result in their support for local approaches. An objective of their involvement may concern integration of approaches and techniques into their policies and activities.

Linkages between institutional and informal organizations should not be taken for granted, not even when all partners have adopted the same objectives and working principles. These linkages are not established automatically, but involve considerable attention to prevent both groups simply co-existing peacefully in similar programmes without real integration. The ambition is to adapt and enrich both institutional and informal systems in order to face the challenges.

Government policies

Involvement of organizations and groups which (unlike farmers, extension services and NGOs) are not locally based may also help to influence government policies. Policy makers should not respond with attempts to control diversity (seed laws), but on the contrary should support these attempts and create an institutional environment that increases their sustainability. A strong national base might be important to resist international pressure to focus on global staple crops or Western consumer markets, and to opt for uniformity in production and intellectual property protection of commercial germplasm.

Critical policy areas where change could help on-farm conservation are:

○ seed legislation and pricing
○ co-ordination of various seed policies

○ adapted public plant breeding programmes
○ seed technology research for the informal sector
○ attention to improving institutional linkages.

Relaxing national seed quality standards, retaining emphasis only on those aspects that are of real relevance to small-farmer seed users, is an example of such policy issues. Adaptive seed quality regulation facilitates seed trading by small-scale farmers. Another relevant issue concerns official seed prices frequently not reflecting the full cost of seed production. Agricultural subsidies and credit programmes are tied to the use of modern varieties. Questions emerge such as 'Why are farmers' varieties not subsidized as well?'. Adaptive seed policies should be designed through national seed boards or seed policy units to prevent counter-effects and stimulate diversity. This is in line with the Convention on Biological Diversity (Bragdon, Chapter 6.1).

From the formal breeding sector, the demands of farmers are not so much for finished varieties but for advanced material for selection at farm level. The formal breeding sector should strengthen the participation of farmers in the breeding process, include farmers' preferences in the selection, and breed for diversity within varieties. Improvement of local seed storage techniques may remove another bottleneck in maintaining the use of farmers' varieties. The improvement of linkages between the actors in the institutional and informal systems of crop development poses an important challenge.

Diversity in crops linked to diversity in approaches

Upscaling will be effective only if these activities are set up and undertaken from a perspective that attempts to offer options (a basket of opportunities) rather than to impose solutions. This issue is particularly important given the fact that farming communities and agro-ecosystems often demonstrate a high level of variation. Upscaling support for on-farm conservation of diversity is only in its infancy, but poses a challenge to reach a long-term, sustainable impact on the struggle for maintenance of diversity on-farm.

Synthesis: The common goal of conservation of genetic resources

Bert Visser and Jan Engels

Conservation of crop genetic resources is on the agenda of many stakeholders. This is reflected in the diversity of the contributors to this section. Not surprisingly, different stakeholder groups take different socio-economic positions and operate from different perspectives. Consequently, the motives for and objectives behind their conservation efforts differ, in general reflected in the policy frameworks and institutional mandates which influence the direction of their efforts. The resulting conservation efforts have long taken divergent directions. However, most stakeholders have gradually become aware that a considerable interdependence and complementarity exists among them. Although such an observation should not result in a simple plea to start collaboration and forget about dichotomies and differing interests, the sense of mutual interdependency and complementarity should be followed by an appreciation and acceptance of the different positions and should be used to maximize the significance and impact of conservation efforts. The contributions to this section have shown ways in which this value of conservation efforts can be augmented.

Conservation efforts can be treated from several angles, and different criteria can be applied to categorize them. Some issues are elaborated below in order to highlight some of the contrasting views apparent from the various contributions to this section, in an attempt to better understand them.

A range of conservation concepts

Conservation means very different things to different stakeholders, and is often not recognized or conceptualized as a separate activity, but is undertaken implicitly. Different conservation efforts may be distinguished.

In situ conservation of wild relatives may take place within and outside agro-ecosystems. In the former case, farmers may consciously maintain or tolerate wild relatives, possibly to allow for introgression of traits into their varieties. In the latter case, it is either unmanaged or managed by public authorities within the boundaries of nature reserves, frequently without the knowledge of the existence of wild relatives.

Genetic diversity in farmers' varieties or landraces is managed by farmers or farming communities and takes place at the individual farm level. Community seed banks (Bertuso et al., Chapter 3.3) have been established to increase access to and exchange of farmers' genetic diversity. They frequently involve centralized seed management combined with an organized attempt to maintain diversity, in order to promote exchange of germplasm and contribute to the improvement of crops at the community level. These efforts can be regarded as an integral part of on-farm management of diversity.

The formal sector, in its efforts to conserve plant genetic resources, has resorted to seed and field gene banks. Field gene banks are often established in the area of origin of conserved crops, especially for vegetatively propagated crops and species which produce recalcitrant seeds. Seed gene banks are mostly specialized institutions which may be located far from the areas where the genetic diversity originated. Since field and seed gene banks are managed by professional staff, and are are no longer an integral part of the production system, one can regard them as true *ex situ* conservation efforts. In such cases conservation has been externalized from the agro-ecosystem.

In all the cases involving gene banks listed above, the facilities and technology needed are, in principle, limited to drying facilities and cold storage rooms. These low thresholds for seed and field gene banks have allowed several organizations in the informal sector (NGOs) to embark independently on *ex situ* conservation efforts by establishing field or seed gene banks, with the intention of complementing on-farm management activities which they support. In the case of *in vitro* storage of vegetatively propagated crops which cannot be maintained in the form of seeds, more sophisticated technology is required. Cryopreservation is increasingly practised for *in vitro* stored germplasm to reduce labour requirements of *in vitro* storage and to allow long-term conservation. Such technology is currently almost exclusively practised by the formal sector.

The most reductionist method of preserving genetic diversity is in the form of DNA. DNA functions only as a source of genes, as the original genotype of the individual in question cannot be reconstituted from DNA. Therefore storage of DNA serves only biotechnological applications for crop improvement, as it allows introduction of a character into an existing genotype.

In this context another concept is relevant: a focus on the genetic distances between germplasm accessions. The primary gene pool consists of the crop germplasm itself and other related species which freely intercross with the crop species, whereas the secondary and tertiary gene pools increasingly represent more distantly related species which can, with some or great difficulty, be intercrossed with varieties of the crop species. Biotechnology adds an imaginary fourth gene pool which encompasses all other genetic material that can be transferred into the given crop species. Applying the concept of gene pools to conservation, we can conclude that on-farm management is largely confined to the first gene pool, whereas *ex situ* as well as *in situ* conservation cover potentially all gene pools. The foregoing highlights the difference in scope of the various conservation approaches, as well as in the potential utilization of the conserved germplasm.

Various conservation strategies and concepts have been developed by different stakeholders, each from their own perspectives, and each having its own advantages and disadvantages. Stakeholders may increasingly seek to adopt complementary approaches and thus widen their options.

Conservation and utilization

In all cases, conservation of genetic resources is linked to utilization. Sometimes this linkage is very strong and direct, or even inseparable, as with on-farm management of diversity. In the case of *ex situ* conservation, the linkage between conservation and utilization is much more indirect, but (future) use is still both motive and objective. Although very different actors are involved, on-farm management and *ex situ* conservation do not differ fundamentally with respect to use; it might be only the time factor of the use which varies. However, the two approaches differ in other aspects, as outlined below.

On-farm management and *ex situ* conservation have mutual comparative advantages and limitations. On-farm management takes place in the wide diversity of existing farming systems, including genetic diversity which occurs in backyards or home gardens worldwide, whereas *ex situ* conservation is usually concerned with selected gene pools. *Ex situ* conservation is static whereas on-farm management is dynamic, which implies that genetic diversity could be lost in on-farm conservation situations since it is no longer selected for, and simultaneously new diversity might develop (Pham et al., Chapter 3.2 and Bertuso et al., Chapter 3.3). Although *ex situ* conservation may cover only a limited part of the gene pool, it is comparatively secure. However, the aspect of security may also be attractive to farming communities and NGOs, for instance to establish a safety back-up for their preferred germplasm. Therefore the informal sector may wish to collaborate with the formal sector or adopt part of the *ex situ* conservation approach to add more security to their conservation efforts.

Finally, the scale at which *ex situ* and on-farm conservation efforts have been organized shows clear differences. *Ex situ* conservation often represents a national effort, and regional or global collaboration in setting up collection missions, characterizing the germplasm and establishing central databases has become a dominant feature. On-farm conservation focuses on the farming community and its interests, and on local adaptation rather than global coverage of crop diversity.

Gene banks have been established mainly to provide germplasm for the formal breeding and research sector. However, gene banks may also provide germplasm to local communities for selection, introgression and breeding (Pham et al., Chapter 3.2). Gene banks may be motivated to do so because they regard local communities as one of their user groups, but also because they realize that farming communities do play a major role in maintaining, utilizing and developing crop genetic diversity, some of which will also find its way to gene banks and their traditional users in formal breeding (Begemann et al., Chapter 3.1). In doing so, gene banks may recognize and underpin the activities of the informal sector and play a wider role in the development of national plant genetic resources programmes. Different stakeholders stand to benefit from each other in both their conservation and utilization efforts, if they co-operate with each other and thus take advantage of the complementarity of the *ex situ* and *in situ* conservation approaches.

The formal and the informal system

In analysing agroproduction systems in general, and conservation practices in particular, formal and informal systems can be distinguished. However, reality does not fit such a simple model, and many different intermediate forms exist: farming communities might be part of both systems, and many interactions between the two systems occur. In general terms, the formal system can be typified as relying on specialization of production; making use of external inputs such as seeds, fertilizers and pesticides; and often producing for far-away markets. The informal system can be described as relying on its own seed supply system; being less dependent on external inputs; and often producing for local and sometimes nearby urban markets. In developed countries the informal sector has almost disappeared from the mainstream agricultural production and survives only in the hands of hobbyists (Pittenger, Chapter 3.4).

In the formal sector we can distinguish the public and private sectors. In many developed countries the public plant-breeding sector has been decreased to a large extent and, simultaneously, private breeding has become the domain of a small number of international companies with a strong focus on a relatively small number of major crops. In many developing countries public breeding has been reduced to those crops which are of national importance, whereas other industrial crops are being left to the private sector. At the same time neglected or under-utilized crops, as well as crops of local importance, are the domain of the informal sector, i.e. the farming communities (Begemann et al., Chapter 3.1).

Conservation efforts largely follow this division between the systems. Few gene banks maintain substantial collections of neglected crops, thus the conservation of these crops has remained almost the exclusive responsibility of the farmer. Gene banks largely maintain collections of crops which are produced for the market, and often also form a source of variation for those crops for which only private breeding programmes have remained. Nevertheless, there is interaction and exchange of germplasm between the two systems: gene banks are involved in collecting farmers' varieties, studying them and supporting on-farm conservation efforts, while NGOs and farming communities make use of gene bank-maintained germplasm (Chapter 3.1).

Conservation efforts not only cross the 'classical divide' between the formal and informal system of agricultural production and breeding, but also provide a special opportunity for linking with organic production. Organic production is dependent on alternative and new germplasm sources which allow selection for specific traits, thus promoting a wider use of genetic diversity in highly industrialized agricultural systems as well as in low-external-input agriculture. The latter allows us to make a link with on-farm management of plant genetic resources, as many on-farm conservation efforts are related to organic production (Bertuso et al., Chapter 3.3). Integration of IPM and ecological pest management approaches with efforts of on-farm management of genetic diversity is thus a logical outcome. Lessons from IPM programmes are rapidly absorbed by traditional high-external-input agriculture, and recognition of the value of genetic diversity for sustainable production may follow in a similar manner.

A picture emerges in which historic dichotomies are superseded by an era in which a set of complementary approaches are being used and increased interactions become the norm.

Germplasm, indigenous knowledge and cultural patterns

The maintenance of indigenous knowledge is closely linked to on-farm management of crop diversity. Its coverage in gene bank documentation databases, associated with *ex situ* conserved germplasm, is very limited or non-existent. Therefore the maintenance of indigenous knowledge is heavily dependent on sustainable on-farm management of crop diversity. However, given the threats to local farming systems, documenting this knowledge needs urgent attention, in particular by the informal sector. Where possible and necessary, support by the formal sector, in particular by gene banks, should be provided.

The maintenance of crop diversity is also closely linked with local culture. Farming systems determine gender roles. Whereas women play a more pronounced role in those systems that maintain their own diversity, men will be more involved in industrialized systems (Bertuso et al., Chapter 3.3 and Pittenger, Chapter 3.4). Furthermore, increased attention to on-farm conservation activities usually contributes to social and political empowerment of the communities involved (Montecinos and Salazar, Chapter 3.5).

Such issues are foreign to *ex situ* conservation programmes, and the technical experts involved in these programmes often have difficulty in recognizing and managing aspects related to the complementarity of the on-farm conservation approach. Nevertheless, the socio-economic, cultural and political aspects are tightly linked with the utilization of germplasm, an area which deserves increased attention from traditional gene banks.

Ownership and access

Farmers all over the world have traditionally adhered to the idea that genetic resources were a common good, at best 'owned' by the community, and thus exchanged freely. Farmers allowing others to use their landrace material or varieties could expect access to someone else's germplasm in return. This concept, that germplasm is a 'common heritage of mankind', was the basis for the FAO International Undertaking on Plant Genetic Resources.

Two more recent developments have seriously challenged the concept of common heritage. Through the Convention on Biological Diversity, governments agreed that genetic resources which occur within the borders of a given state fall under the sovereign right of that state, thus allowing for negotiations on the conditions for the export of germplasm as well as for its use by third parties for commercial purposes. In this concept governments have to provide for the necessary legislation and might opt to represent the local communities which developed the genetic diversity at stake.

Another recent development, the application of biotechnologies to crop improvement and plant breeding, allowed for the introduction of the industrial patent system which has already resulted in full privatization of breeding products through the application of patents. This leads to restricted use of the protected variety for breeding (Louwaars and Engels, Chapter 6.4).

These developments have raised the issue of access to and ownership of genetic resources, which in turn influenced conservation strategies. In the on-farm management scenario, germplasm and the related indigenous knowledge remain with the farmers who developed the material and

150

knowledge. In contrast, the principles of national sovereignty and the recognition of farmers' rights when applied to farmers' varieties maintained in *ex situ* collections are by no means secured. On the one hand, the introduction of so called Material Transfer Agreements by a number of gene banks, including those of the CGIAR and CGN should prevent the subsequent appropriation of the conserved germplasm accessions through an intellectual property rights. On the other hand, Material Transfer Agreements have not provided a mechanism for benefit-sharing on revenues accrued from the commercialization of breeding products based on farmers' varieties. These and other issues are currently being negotiated between countries in the process of revising the International Undertaking.

It is probably fair to say that the Convention on Biological Diversity, as well as the recent emergence of patents on plant materials, have already hampered the free exchange of germplasm and will continue to do so. These developments might also interfere with on-farm development efforts and *ex situ* conservation activities. As a consequence, it certainly negatively influences conservation efforts, as it renders exchange of germplasm and collaboration between different stakeholders more complex and insecure.

Development and research

For some stakeholders, in particular NGOs, development (food security, income generation) is the primary objective of on-farm management; for others, such as IPGRI, the study of farmers' management of genetic diversity is most important, to better understand the value and contribution of this conservation approach to conservation in general (Montecinos and Salazar, Chapter 3.5 and Jarvis and Ndungú-Skilton, Chapter 3.6).

Proponents of the first objective hold that development can be the only sustainable driving force of on-farm management of genetic diversity, and consequently focus heavily on the integration of conservation efforts in wider development activities. Learning by doing is often a feature of this approach. In the *ex situ* conservation approach, the focus is primarily on the scientific quality of the efforts themselves, aiming at long-term conservation without changing the genetic integrity of accessions.

Some spokesmen from the formal sector question the actual contribution of on-farm management as a conservation strategy, by pointing at the difficulty of maintaining specific varieties (in local systems varieties change continuously) and the risks of losing valuable genes or genotypes through biological problems (pests and diseases) or non-biological interference (climatic conditions, political unrest). Although such risks are undeniable, they apply to *in situ* as well as *ex situ* approaches, and can be contained to a considerable extent by increasing the scale and quality of on-farm conservation efforts. Moreover, these risks do not outweigh the advantages of on-farm strategies, in particular with respect to the wide coverage of genetic diversity under these strategies and the direct link between conservation and use. The discussion on the significance of on-farm management of genetic diversity as a conservation method can be resolved only by studying

151

the dynamics of genetic diversity in local farming systems and the ways farmers handle this diversity over a longer period of time.

NGOs and local organizations are primarily concerned with development when discussing and implementing on-farm conservation activities, whereas the formal sector is more interested in the research issues which underlie the actual management of genetic diversity. However, many NGOs recognize the need to increase their impact and, consequently, have started to establish links with the formal sector and to familiarize this sector and the general public with their development-oriented approach (Visser and Engels, Chapter 3.7). The different perspectives meet when development-oriented conservation efforts become part of university courses and training for other professionals such as extensionists.

Conservation and development

The different conservation efforts result in diverging utilization of the germplasm concerned, and have diverging effects on the genetic make-up of the crop. *Ex situ* conserved germplasm collections have traditionally served the formal breeding sector with starting materials (Begemann et al., Chapter 3.1), and this sector has realized high yield gains, as well as causing a major reduction in the field of agrobiodiversity in general and genetic diversity in particular. On-farm management of genetic diversity has been closely linked with the diversity of seed supply, and focuses increasingly on participatory variety selection and participatory plant breeding (Bertuso et al., Chapter 3.3, Montecinos and Salazar, Chapter 3.5 and Jarvis and Ndungú-Skilton, Chapter 3.6). Most of these latter efforts have resulted, or aim to result, in development of crop genetic diversity resulting in the socio-economic development of the communities concerned. Whereas in the formal sector conservation and development have been separated, in on-farm management of diversity these two are closely interlinked. Again, the picture has become more complex lately.

Traditional gene banks in the formal sector have recognized farmers and farming communities as legitimate users of their germplasm collections, in addition to breeders and researchers (Begemann et al., Chapter 3.1 and Pham et al., Chapter 3.2). Germplasm conserved by gene banks is now increasingly used in the framework of re-introduction programmes to make up for losses of genetic diversity due to calamities, to revive interest in locally adapted germplasm, and to improve local germplasm to yield better crops. And NGOs and local organizations increasingly value the contributions to crop improvement from external sources, partly maintained in *ex situ* collections.

Conservation efforts a continuum

Classical barriers between various conservation approaches and the stakeholders involved are gradually fading, and the realization that an increased exchange of ideas and growing collaboration between stakeholders should occur is becoming more widespread.

A continuum becomes apparent in conservation strategies where organizations operating gene banks become involved in support for on-farm management of diversity, and NGOs adopt *ex situ* approaches to complement community development efforts. A continuum has also developed in the objectives of stakeholders, on-farm management of agrobiodiversity being accepted by the formal sector as intrinsically linked with development goals, and long-term conservation of local genetic resources increasingly valued by the informal sector. Stakeholders from different backgrounds have begun to exchange experiences and to collaborate, and programmes involving formal- and informal-sector organizations have emerged. Organizations involved in on-farm management have realized the need to increase impact by enlarging the scale of their operations, whereas organizations involved in *ex situ* conservation have come to realize the need for local adaptation of germplasm.

But whereas old conflicts gradually seem to dissolve, a novel threat of dynamic on-farm management and conservation of diversity has emerged in the growth of privatization and decreasing access to germplasm. To withstand that threat it might be essential that the different conservation approaches become integrated in overall national programmes which are duly participative in their operation, thus allowing the various stakeholders to participate actively in the decision-making processes and in the responsibilities to be distributed, as well as in sharing the benefits which will undoubtedly arise from conservation efforts now and in the future.

SECTION IV
PLANT BREEDING AND GENETIC DIVERSITY

Introduction

This section presents a wide range of perspectives on and experiences in crop development by plant breeders. Formal plant breeding is typically characterized as a process of generating diversity with an output that consists of the introduction of a few genetically uniform varieties to farmers. Where successful, introduced breeders' products have replaced local materials, resulting in many cases in the complete disappearance of local varieties from farmers' fields. Thus plant breeding is considered an activity that conflicts with the maintenance of genetic diversity in farmers' fields. However, in this section authors present viewpoints and experiences to show that this conflict is not as straightforward as it may sound.

The first group of chapters presents a range of experiences and perspectives of breeders in the formal public and commercial sectors. The cases of public breeding in Kenya (Ngugi and Mugo, Chapter 4.1), and Canada (Atlin, Chapter 4.3) illustrate in different ways the limitations of public breeding activities. They also address the effect of public breeding on the genetic diversity available to and employed by farmers. Van der Werff and van Donk (Chapter 4.4) present the breeding approach of the commercial seed and breeding company East-West Seeds in South-East Asia. They demonstrate how crop development – even when building on local germplasm – inevitably narrows the genetic basis in farmers' fields. However, from the same case it is clear that introduction of new materials contributes importantly to widening the genetic base of the varieties deployed. Ngugi and Mugo (Chapter 4.1) and Smith (Chapter 4.5) also address this point. Stephen Smith of Pioneer Hi-Bred presents a different viewpoint on the effect of plant breeding on genetic diversity in farmers' fields. Nap (Chapter 4.6) adds a further dimension to the discussion: the effect of crop improvement on the use of genetic diversity. He describes the development of biotechnology, transforming crop improvement into a quest of searching for and using fragments of DNA in the most effective manner.

One aspect of formal plant breeding remains clear: it has been less succesful in addressing the needs of farmers in marginal environments than in producing gains in more productive environments. Despite the successes and contributions of modern plant breeding and biotechnology, traditional seed selection and seed supply persist in both marginal and high-potential areas. Explanations for this persistence are found in the economic constraints and limitations within the conventional system, and specific needs of farmers in diverse target areas. This is described by Hardon et al. (Chapter 1.1), and illustrated by cases in Section 2. Some reasons for the poor performance of modern varieties in some cropping systems are described in various contributions in Section 4. The mismatch of formal breeding objectives and farmers' needs is well illustrated by the case of public breeding in China (Chapter 4.2). Song's contribution also describes the development of local crop improvement activities by women in response to the ineffectiveness of the public system. The case presented by Machado (Chapter 4.10) also results from farmers' initiatives in reaction to the need for maize varieties adapted to harsh conditions.

To improve outcomes in marginal environments, some breeders are adopting approaches and activities that involve farmers more deeply in the breeding process. The way farmers can or should be involved, and the effectiveness and up-scaling of this involvement, are still being explored. The activities of Sthapit and Subedi (Chapter 4.7) and Weltzien (Chapter 4.8) are among the first experiences showing the potential of involving farmers in breeding programmes. Sthapit and Subedi present the experiences of LI-BIRD, a Nepalese NGO, with participatory rice breeding. Weltzien reports on her experiences as a breeder in ICRISAT in developing pearl millet varieties with farmers and various local organizations in Rajasthan. Sthapit and Subedi, Weltzien, and Witcombe (Chapter 4.11) were among the first to conceptualize participatory breeding and document participatory varietal selection (PVS) and participatory plant breeding (PPB). Sthapit and Subedi's contribution presents definitions and concepts of PPB and elaborates on the reasoning behind these approaches.

Gabriel et al. (Chapter 4.9) present the experiences of the PROINPA potato programme in Bolivia. They show that the problems in Participatory Crop Improvement (PCI) relate not only to collaboration between breeders and farmers, but also to the necessary interdisciplinarity among participating researchers. They show how lessons from these experiences are used to further shape PCI activities of the organization. Machado (Chapter 4.10) presents collaborative breeding activities in the marginal agricultural production environment of the State of Rio de Janeiro, Brazil. The experience of Machado and his collaborators shows that the opportunities of PCI go beyond the stage of PVS. The experience proves that more complicated designs of selection and collaboration are possible and can be successful.

It is clear from the contribution of Witcombe and collegues (Chapter 4.11) that the opportunities of PCI are restricted not only to marginal agroecological environments. They show that farmers need diversity everywhere, and demonstrate the potential link between PPB and the maintenance of diversity in farmers' fields, estimating in a quantitative manner the effect of PVS in high-potential areas on the deployment of crop genetic diversity. The final contribution to this section, by Smith and Weltzien (Chapter 4.12), presents thoughts on the possibilities and limitations of up-scaling the location-, farmer- and crop-specific experiences that have been discussed.

4.1. The use of genetic diversity in maize breeding in Kenya

Kahiu Ngugi and Stephen Mugo

Background

Kenya is self-sufficient in food production in normal years. When national maize production is substantially reduced by stresses such as drought, maize must be imported. National agricultural and crop improvement policies emphasize the need for increased food production to meet the ever-increasing demand, which is estimated to increase at about 2 per cent per year due to population growth.

In total there are approximately 100 breeders active in Kenya in a range of food crops (cereals, legumes, horticultural crops and oil crops) and cash crops (coffee, tea, pyrethrum and cotton), among private and public organizations. About 20, the largest group, are involved in maize improvement. The Kenyan Agricultural Research Institute (KARI) is responsible for crop improvement in Kenya, and addresses food crops including cereals (maize, sorghum, millets and wheat), grain legumes (pigeon pea, cowpea, dry beans, dolichos and greengrams), oil crops (sunflower and safflower), horticultural crops and tree fruits. For sorghum, sweet potato, cassava and wheat, most parental breeding lines have been derived from germplasm from the CGIAR institutions CIMMYT, ICRISAT, IITA and CIP. A number of CG institutions, including CIMMYT, have regional programmes with a headquarters in Nairobi; these form a basis for interaction with the national agricultural research services in the region. KARI is the principal contact institution responsible for agricultural research and development in Kenya.

Use of genetic diversity in Kenyan breeding programmes

Roughly half of the Kenyan breeding effort goes into crossing parental materials and selecting progenies with desirable traits. The other half involves selection of potential varieties from the international trials of the CG centres. Cultivars in these trials are generally not adapted to the Kenyan environments in terms of flowering time and growing period. They may nevertheless have greater yield potential and other improved traits as compared to the local cultivars. Considerable resources and effort are therefore devoted to improving adaptation of these exotic materials, by crossing them with local germplasm and by recurrent selection.

Particularly in wheat, sorghum and millets, which have had stable regional programmes with international technical support and funding and have been accorded priority in national food policies, Kenyan breeders have relied (and were expected to rely) heavily on materials provided from international programmes, and tended to use less and less of the local genetic diversity for improvement. However, this is not so clearly the case for maize.

Maize breeding

Maize improvement in Kenya is carried out at five locations, each targeting a particular agro-ecological zone defined by elevation and the length of the growing season (Table 4.1). Maize improvement in Kenya started in the 1950s at Njoro in the Rift valley, but quickly shifted in 1955 to Kitale where there were large areas with commercial maize farms (Gerhart, 1975). Early releases were synthetic varieties from local landraces such as the Kitale Synthetic II (KSII) which was developed from farmers' material known as Kenya flat white maize, a mixture of landraces from the USA, South Africa and the West Indies (Harrison, 1970). Later, reciprocal recurrent selection was initiated using exotic materials in combination with KSII (Table 4.1). Maize breeding was decentralized and breeding programmes were initiated in Katumani (1956), Mtwapa (1962), Embu (1965) and Kakamega (1988) in response to recognition that the soil and climatic variation within Kenya could not be covered by a breeding programme in one location.

Table 4.1: Characteristics of the major maize agro-ecological zones and major local and exotic maize germplasm in Kenya

Characteristics	Highland	Mid-altitude	Mid-altitude	Mid-altitude	Lowland humid
Maize type	Late maturity	Late maturity	Intermediate maturity	Early maturity	Coastal
KARI Centre	Kitale	Embu	Kakamega	Katumani	Mtwapa
Elevation (m a.s.l.)	>1800	1400–1800	1400–1800	900–1800	<900
Annual rainfall (mm)	>1800	100–1800	800–1200	400–800	400–1400
Growing season (days)	120	180	170	120	120
National maize area (%)	30	42	16	8	4
National production (%)	35	25	25	10	5
Potential yield (t/ha)	6.7	5.2	3.7	2.7	3.3
Farmer yield (t/ha)	2.0	0.7	1.1	0.5	1.0
Yield gap (t/ha)	4.7	4.5	2.6	2.2	2.3
Major local germplasm	KSII*	Ex-Kitale†	KSII/Local‡	MLW	Ex-Embu/Katumani
Major exotic germplasm	Ec573	Embu II	Ec573	Taboran	Ex-Embu/Katumani

KSII = Kitale synthetic II; *Ec573* = Equador 573; MLW = *Machakos* local White.
* Githigu (Cuzco maize).
† Bunyore and Rarienda 88.
‡ Other locals were Muratha and Ena.

Because recurrent selection cycles take a minimum of 2 years, and several cycles are usually needed to produce populations that show consistent improvement over parents, improvement of exotic materials through introgression of characteristics from local landraces (i.e. crossing followed by recurrent selection) is a breeding strategy which requires long-term commitment (approximately 10 years). This strategy is being continued to the present. For example, Mugo and Njoroge (1997) used local germplasm from Katumani and drought-tolerant materials from CIMMYT to develop two heterotic, drought-tolerant populations. Local landraces Bunyore and Rarienda 88 were crossed to exotic materials in the Kakamega programme (Njoroge et al., 1992), although results are not available. At all of these stations, to varying degrees, the breeding strategy has been to produce synthetic varieties including both indigenous and introduced germplasm, and to develop hybrids between local varieties and Latin American populations introduced by CIMMYT.

Development and use of local maize varieties

Maize was probably introduced to Kenya around 1800, but was restricted to the coastal region for many years until it spread up-country and was used as food. True landraces, as exist in Central America, may not have developed in Kenya during this period, but the maize has been cultivated in Kenya long enough for specific adaptation to develop and for populations to acquire tolerances to pests and diseases common in Kenya. Local landraces prior to the initiation of maize improvement tended to be coloured and low-yielding, and were overlooked by early European farmers who preferred white varieties brought in from South Africa.

While in the 1980s CIMMYT concentrated on the development of open-pollinated varieties, as this was considered to generate more useful products for farmers in developing countries, breeders in Kenya focused on the development of hybrids. The tradition of an important colonial agriculture is the explanation for this focus. The production of maize was initially not important for small-scale subsistence farmers; they traditionally grew sorghum. However, maize improvement in Kenya has been relatively successful, although there have been drawbacks related to this success. Firstly, many local varieties of sorghum and maize have been replaced by the more drought-sensitive modern maize varieties. In many cases this replacement was stimulated by subsidies for seeds and fertilizer with the objective of boosting national food production, especially early in the century. After subsidies were lifted, the results of this switch were not always favourable for the farmers.

Lately the use of local materials in the breeding programme has improved due to global attention given to the advantages offered by indigenous germplasm. However, there is still less use of local germplasm than would be desired. As an example, the strategic plan for cereals in Kenya (1993–2013) is silent about the use of local germplasm for maize improvement (KARI, 1994), which shows a low priority of use of local landraces. The transfer of enhanced germplasm (for yield potential and stress tolerance) from international centres such as CIMMYT to Kenya has contributed considerably to Kenya's maize crop improvement, particularly through the incorporation of resistances to various biotic and abiotic stresses which were lacking in the local materials. This has probably been at the expense of local material and 'local genes'.

The fact that KARI's maize hybrid programme relies on only a few inbred lines, and that fewer than five open-pollinated varieties are marketed for an area covering 80 per cent of Kenya's agricultural area, is of serious concern (Hassan et al., 1998). This represents a narrow genetic base for Kenya's most important food crop and could be a threat to food security.

Breeding in other cereal and pulse crops

This picture of the use of genetic diversity in maize breeding contrasts with crops such as cowpea and pigeon pea. These crops are traditionally grown in the dry and marginal areas of Kenya. However, in these crops genetic erosion is also creeping in, due to efforts to introduce exotic traits such as earliness and short stature in pigeon pea, and tolerance of diseases and pests in cowpea. One factor in the genetic erosion in these crops is also the promotion by the public breeders of improved varieties derived from international, exotic germplasm originating from CGIAR breeding programmes. For instance, farmers in the semi-arid areas of Machakos and Kitui prefer and continue to grow tall, long-duration and large-seeded pigeon pea landraces. However ICRISAT, which has a regional headquarters in Kenya, has supported a major campaign to promote multi-coloured, small-seeded, short and early-maturing types developed specifically for farmers in the Indian subcontinent. Many local landraces of sorghum with desirable traits are still grown in western Kenya. However, 4 years ago KARI and ICRISAT introduced cultivars such as KARI-Mtama I, with many exotic genes from the Indian subcontinent, without having exploited the potential of the local genes in sorghum improvement.

Conserving and promoting the use of diversity

KARI has not been able to organize regular collecting missions to collect threatened local varieties of the different field crops. Organized germplasm collections were infrequent, regional, and rarely national in coverage. One germplasm collection mission in 1984 covered the semi-arid regions of Kenya. About 150 landraces were collected, some of which have been used at Katumani and Muguga as sources of drought tolerance (K. Njoroge, pers. comm.). KARI also lacks the financial capacity to document, characterize and rejuvenate the old accessions stored in the central gene bank at Muguga for *ex situ* conservation. The cold stores constructed a few years ago by the Gesellschaft für Technische Zusammenarbeit (GTZ) in various KARI centres to hold duplicate accessions of the central gene bank have collapsed and are no longer functional. There are no, or very few, activities aiming at *in situ* conservation for most of these crops. Traditionally, *in situ* conservation takes place with farmers, most often unconsciously. There is, however, a threat of genetic erosion here too, due to replacement with modern varieties as well as seed depletion during the frequent famines caused by drought (Muhammed et al., 1985). Considerable genetic diversity may already have been lost.

New approaches in breeding

In Kenya, as in other countries, breeders are adopting new approaches to address more effectively the needs of the poorest farmers, who are often women. In the years before 1980, the breeder on the research station set priorities for selection individually; now he or she consults agronomists, entomologists, socio-economists and, most importantly, key farmers. Recently, breeders and researchers have also started to use participatory approaches to involve small-scale farmers in criteria definition and priority setting. This process is time- and resource-intensive, and thus is a more expensive way of breeding than before. Paradoxically, because a country such as Kenya does not have many resources, this may be the only way to develop materials with specific adaptation that meet farmers' preferences. Communication lines with the farmer-client are poor and complex as compared to those in developed countries, and thus efforts to capture the needs of the farmers are more cumbersome. However, because resources are scarce it is important to minimize the risk of failure. Furthermore, because of the variable agro-ecological environment it is difficult to develop a variety which is adapted to all conditions and preferences. Decentralization of the breeding programme allows the breeding of genotypes with good yield stability for specific local conditions, such as the dry areas. Further decentralization with more and earlier on-farm testing in Kenya requires the involvement of the stakeholders in the breeding process. These are not only the farmers, but also the extension officers, local NGOs, churches and women's groups. The transformation of a centralized breeding programme into a decentralized, participatory programme also requires considerable resources for training, resources the breeding programmes at present do not have. However, first of all such a transformation requires a change of attitude from breeders and extensionists, but probably also from the informal sector and the farmers themselves, in order to result in concerted action. With limited resources from the formal sector, farmers may have to get used to the fact that the state will not take care of agricultural research and development, and they may have to look for means to finance the research and development activities which aim to improve their agricultural production. This may work quite well for cash crops such as coffee or export vegetables, but it is not clear what such an approach would mean for the subsistence crops of the most marginalized.

4.2. A mismatch: the case of government and community maize-breeding strategies in China

Song Yiching

Introduction

The great famine in China in the late 1950s to early 1960s, and the poor socio-economic situation of agriculture at the time, stimulated the construction of a modern technology-oriented approach. Since then, in agriculture the number one goal of the central government has been national food security via self-sufficiency. Government policy began to emphasize modern technology and inputs in the form of modern varieties, fertilizers and irrigation schemes. The most noteworthy development was the establishment of agricultural research and extension systems for variety development and distribution (Lin, 1998). The development and distribution of modern varieties of the three main staples, rice, wheat and maize, has been the core task and the first priority for these systems from the beginning. Modern technology has become a kind of universal tool for policy-makers for the achievement of the overall goal of food self-sufficiency, and hybrid breeding has become almost the only method of formal plant breeding in China.

Impact of the government breeding strategy (1960s–1980s)

This modern variety strategy, together with a top-down hierarchical public agricultural knowledge system, made the Green Revolution in China possible. It is widely accepted that it has been a successful formula for increasing food production and productivity. The central power and the collective production system through People's Communes in Mao's period helped to prevent extreme poverty, not by abolishing it, but rather by its equal distribution. However, the situation changed after the rural reforms and the introduction of a market economy at the beginning of 1980s. Farmers began to cultivate their own crops at the individual household level, and had more freedom to make their own decisions. Simultaneously, the public agricultural research and extension systems experienced privatization and commercialization as part of the reform.

In this time frame the Chinese Academy of Agricultural Science (CAAS), in collaboration with CIMMYT, initiated a maize-breeding programme in the late 1970s in southwest China, with the general objective of poverty alleviation. An impact study on this collaborative programme has been carried out by the author (Song, 1998) and some of the research results are presented below. The study revealed a large and growing gap between farmers' needs and formal breeders' interests, and identified farmers' initiatives and efforts to meet their own needs.

Maize breeding and the real needs of farmers in diversified farming systems

In the southwest of China there are about 25 million poor farmers in remote upland areas who depend basically on maize as their staple. Both the agro-ecological and socio-economic conditions of these areas are quite different from the northern corn belt. An important difference is the variation in farming systems. However, the regional variations are more or less neglected by the generalized and centralized 'hybrid-policy' and high-yield priority of the public breeders.

CIMMYT's breeding material in China

Unlike the normal situation in other developing countries, breeding material is distributed entirely through the dominant public systems (Figure 4.1). The programme followed a top-down, linear technology transfer process through which CIMMYT's breeding materials made their way to farmers. With the single purpose of increasing productivity, almost all public efforts go into the development and diffusion of several uniform, high-yielding hybrids, especially single-cross F_1 hybrids. The focus on hybrid variety development has been further stimulated by the reform of agricultural

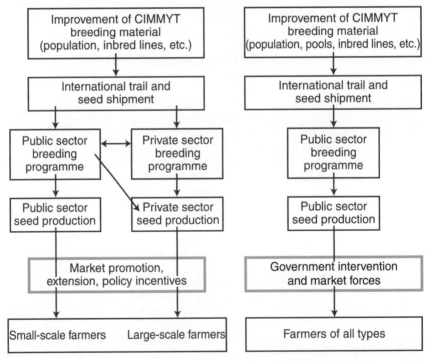

Figure 4.1: *Flow of CIMMYT breeding material in most countries (left) and in China (right)*. Sources: Lopez-Pereira and Morris, 1994; Song, 1998

162

research funding in 1990, when the government reduced the funding of agricultural research with public money.

This reform has shifted funding to competitive grants, and encouraged research institutes to commercialize their technologies, using part of the proceeds to subsidize their research (Lin, 1998). The agricultural research institutes have had to become more profit-driven, through either their research or other activities. This has resulted in a strong public-sector focus on several profitable hybrids, and neglect of unprofitable open-pollinated varieties needed by farmers in unfavourable marginal areas. As a result, the formal seed system supplied fewer and more limited options for farmers (Table 4.2).

Table 4.2: Trend in public maize breeding in southwestern China, 1980–96

Types	Period			
	1980–96	1980–85	1986–90	1991–96
Total release	48	23	18	7
Hybrid	39	18	14	7
Open-pollinating	9	5	4	0

Source: Song (1998).

Meanwhile, the regional variation in farming system and user differentiation are resulting from changes which emerged after the recent reforms, e.g. development of a rural industry, commercialization of agriculture, feminization of agriculture, etc. This generates a quite different and heterogeneous need for technology and genetic diversity.

The impact study found a clear discrepancy between the multiple needs of farmers, especially the poor and women in marginal, harsh areas, and the public seed system's single interest of yield increment through hybrid breeding and distribution. This has resulted in a large gap between the breeders' limited supply and farmers' diverse needs. This situation led to the development and active function of indigenous knowledge systems through which farmers work on the neglected improved open-pollinated varieties and landraces to meet their own needs.

Impact through the informal system

The impact of CIMMYT's breeding material in China is achieved through both the public and informal systems. The macro-level impact is gained mainly through public breeding efforts, and reflected in the adoption of CIMMYT-related hybrids and yield increment with limited benefit for resource-poor farmers in marginal, rain-fed areas. Nevertheless, CIMMYT's great impact on household food security and poverty alleviation for poor and women farmers continues in an informal way through the wide distribution of CIMMYT's improved varieties via the farmers' own systems. For instance, three improved populations from CIMMYT, Tuxpeño

163

1, Tuxpeño PB C15 and Suwan 1, have had an annual adoption of 310 000ha, covering about 15 per cent of the total maize area in the provinces where the programme has been active since the early 1980s. They are mainly cultivated by poor farmers in the marginal and environmentally less-favoured areas where maize farming systems are complex (Song, 1998). There has been little public effort to maintain, improve and distribute these varieties due to the low interest of the public seed system in open-pollinated varieties.

Local management: farmers' response and strategies to meet their needs

In response to the failure of the formal breeding to meet their diverse needs, farmers are making efforts to maintain and develop their preferred improved open-pollinated varieties and landraces. Because of the feminization of agriculture and other socio-economic factors, local seed selection and breeding are mainly done by women. The Wenteng case study is an illustration of this situation.

Tuxpeño 1 (local name 'Mexican 1') is an improved population that was developed by CIMMYT from a landrace that originated from Tuxpe, Mexico. Tuxpeño 1 was introduced in southwest China in 1978, originally as constituent for variety improvement and hybrid combination. However, Tuxpeño 1 was rapidly disseminated through the three provinces, principally through informal seed exchange. Due to its broad adaptability, stability and strong stress tolerance (especially lodging resistance), Tuxpeño 1 became popular with farmers in the remote mountainous areas. It has contributed significantly to household food security and poverty alleviation in the past 2 decades. However, since maize is an out-breeding crop, with no maintenance breeding Tuxpeño 1 has degenerated by outcrossing, resulting in a decrease of yield, increase in plant height and a partial loss of stress resistance.

Farmers requested the government to assist them to improve the material, but no government attention was received. Due to lack of institutional support, and the popularity of Tuxpeño 1, women in Wenteng village organized themselves in the late 1980s to maintain and improve Tuxpeño 1. This activity was initiated by an innovative woman who had tried to maintain Tuxpeño 1 since its adoption. The crop development methods used by the women include: spatial separation through use of plots at different locations, temporal isolation and seed selection. The women explained that due to the popularity of Tuxpeño 1 and the impact of the women's initiative, it is easy to organize women to grow Tuxpeño 1 in adjoining fields, isolated from other varieties. The selection method used by women farmers is mass selection. The three steps in seed selection are (i) to select the best plants (good plants with large ears in the middle of the field), then (ii) the best ears (based on cob size, length and number of seed rows), and then (iii) the best grains (from the middle part of the ear seeds are selected for kernel size, shape, quality and colour). They claim that their skills have been passed on for generations, as they have also used similar techniques for the maintenance of landraces.

As a result of the womens' production and selection practices, the quality of Tuxpeño 1 in Wenteng village has been maintained and even improved in the sense that it is better adapted to the local conditions than before. It is not surprising that the locally improved Tuxpeño 1 has spread rapidly to neighbouring areas through farmers' informal seed-exchange systems. Now Wenteng has become a source for quality Tuxpeño 1 seed for a large surrounding area.

Responsive and adaptive management

The case of Wenteng is one piece of evidence found in the impact study suggesting the failure of the formal breeding system to meet farmers' needs, the initiatives and capabilities of farmers, and the functioning of farmers' informal knowledge networks. This case also shows that farmers were trying to meet their own needs through their own efforts. If they could have had help from scientists and more institutional support from the formal sector, they would have had greater impact in addressing the issues of food security, poverty alleviation and natural resource conservation in China.

The formal system, which has a top-down and non-interactive institutional framework, tends to use one-way communication only, hence there is little feedback and interaction with farmers. There have been difficulties in responding and adapting to farmers' interests and needs. More flexible and responsive seed systems, with an adaptive rather than a centralized management, are urgently needed in China for greater response to farmers' needs.

4.3. Influences on the use of genetic diversity in Canada's public breeding of grain crops

Gary Atlin

Introduction

Genetic diversity in the fields of Canadian grain farmers is affected by government policy and regulations, plant breeder's rights (PBR) legislation, marketing systems for grain and seed, the organization of plant breeding programmes, and the attitudes of farmers and breeders. The purpose of this chapter is to explore the effects of these factors, with emphasis on the role of public sector research and regulation.

Plant introduction and breeding programmes were among the earliest publicly funded research enterprises in both Canada and the USA, and had the objective of identifying crops and varieties adapted to the interior of the continent. Although this research increased the number of plant species under cultivation and broadened the genetic base deployed, this was not a conscious goal of agronomists, but a by-product of their efforts to develop or introduce adapted cultivars and establish new crops. Since the early 1960s the development of new crops has accelerated, with the introduction of brassicas, field peas and lentils in western Canada, and the expansion of maize and soybean production in the east. Public breeding and introduction programmes have thus increased the genetic diversity of Canadian cropping systems.

The effects of variety registration and breeders' rights

Until the 1970s, most cultivars released in Canada were developed or introduced though public-sector breeding. Government research therefore contributed greatly to genetic diversity in grain crops. However, government activities also acted as a brake on the evolution of more genetically diverse cropping systems, because regulations and policies tended to promote the deployment of a few cultivars over large areas. Among these were the regulations on cultivar registration. The Canada Seeds Act states that '. . . no person shall . . . sell or advertise for sale or import into Canada seed that is not registered in the prescribed manner'. Certified seed may not be sold under a cultivar name unless that cultivar has been registered by the Variety Registration Office of the federal Ministry of Agriculture. In most crops registration is based on the criteria of 'distinctiveness' and 'merit'. Cultivar merit is determined by recommending committees, through field testing programmes organized on a provincial or regional basis. The committees, which include public- and private-sector breeders, pathologists, agronomists, farmer representatives and industrial end-users, determine the extent of testing and establish merit criteria. Cultivars meeting the criteria are recommended to the Variety Registration Office for registration. The system was originally designed to protect farmers from unadapted varieties. Merit requirements were rigorous until the late 1980s; cultivars were not usually registered unless they were superior to the standard in at least one characteristic. Committees limited the number of registered cultivars on the grounds that it was not in the interest of farmers to release many varieties of similar performance. Committees also felt responsible for ensuring that overall productivity was not reduced through the accidental release of inferior cultivars. Although the system was effective in delivering adapted cultivars, it did not promote diversity.

In recent years, following the adoption of PBR legislation in 1990, the registration system has undergone changes that have nearly eliminated its hampering effect on the deployment of new cultivars. Pressure from seed companies wishing to market their varieties has led to a reduction in the testing requirements for most crops, and the merit standard has been relaxed by most committees, who now generally recommend registration of any cultivar that is equal in performance to the current standard. The merit requirement has even been eliminated in maize with no apparent ill effects, and cultivar registration committees in Ontario accept data from private in-house trials for registration purposes. The weakening of the merit requirement has contributed to an increase in the rate of cultivar registration in most grain crops.

The introduction of PBR has probably contributed to an increase in private-sector plant breeding in Canada, but its effect is difficult to separate from that of downsizing of public programmes (which has made them less competitive with the private sector) and the advent of new genetic technologies that encourage annual seed purchase. There are several forces that have affected the rate of cultivar deployment, as outlined below.

○ PBR encourages direct private-sector investment in plant breeding. Private-sector investment in cultivar development and introduction has increased since the mid-1980s, when it became apparent that PBR would be instituted. This increase has been modest, however, in crops where returns to breeding investments are difficult to capture due to the continuing practice of Canadian farmers, particularly in the main western grain-producing areas, to replant their own seed. Investment is concentrated in commodities where genetic technologies encourage annual seed purchase, e.g. herbicide-tolerant canola varieties which are marketed by Monsanto under agreements that prohibit replanting by the farmer.

○ Increased private-sector breeding forces regulators to weaken registration requirements. Through their participation on committees overseeing variety registration, private-sector plant breeders have exerted intense pressure to reduce or eliminate field-testing requirements for registration. For example, until 1993 data from testing in 18 official co-operative trials was required for a new barley cultivar to be considered for registration in Ontario. Now data from only eight in-house trials is required. This reduced testing requirement, and the acceptance of in-house data for registration purposes, has significantly reduced the cost of bringing new cultivars to market. Pressure from private-sector breeders has also resulted in a relaxation of the merit standard from 'better than' to 'equal to' the standard variety. Reduced testing requirements and relaxed merit standards have resulted in an increased rate of new cultivar registration.

○ PBR encourages the release of more cultivars. Before the advent of PBR, most Canadian public-sector breeding programmes released new cultivars on a non-exclusive basis, providing breeder seed to any interested party. Royalties were rarely collected on public releases, and breeders had no incentive to release anything other than their best lines. Now exclusive-release agreements, in which the right to market a variety is granted on an exclusive basis to one seed company in return for a royalty on sales, are encouraged by research managers in the hope of recovering some of the costs of variety development. Seed companies without in-house breeding programmes want proprietary varieties, and are even willing to pay for the exclusive right to market 'second-best' public-sector lines if the best line has been released to another company. This increased demand for proprietary germplasm, coupled with a relaxed merit requirement and the ever-increasing emphasis on cost recovery, has given public breeders a strong incentive to release more cultivars from their pool of advanced lines.

These changes have been associated with rapid growth in the number of new cultivars registered annually. In 1972, 79 new cultivars were registered in all crops subject to the merit requirement, including small grains, oilseeds, maize and potatoes. In 1992, 204 new varieties were registered (L. Duke, pers. comm.). It is not clear to what extent the increased rate of registration has affected genetic diversity actually deployed on-farm, because the registration of a new cultivar does not guarantee that it will be adopted, and there are no statistics on Canadian crop production areas broken down by cultivar. However, it is reasonable to assume that more cultivars are grown now than before 1990. Even if registered varieties are not immediately deployed, they constitute a reserve of adapted germplasm that could be deployed on short notice in the event that current cultivars become vulnerable to a pest or pathogen.

The effects of marketing systems on deployment of genetic diversity

Seed and grain marketing systems have a great impact on the deployment of genetic diversity. Evidence for this is seen in Table 4.3, which summarizes cultivar registrations in eastern and western Canada for the 15-month period ending December 31 1998 (Canadian Food Inspection Agency, 1998). Over this period in western Canada, three times more canola than wheat varieties were registered. Expressed on a cultivar per 10^6ha basis, the rate of canola variety release was six times that of wheat. Barley variety release rates, on the same basis, are intermediate to wheat and canola. The low rate of cultivar release in wheat is probably due to the extremely restrictive quality and kernel visual distinguishability requirements of the centralized western Canadian bread-wheat marketing system. Canadian wheat cultivars registered for use in western Canada must conform to strict quality standards imposed by the Canadian Wheat Board (the centralized wheat marketing agency for western Canada), and must have a kernel phenotype that permits them to be assigned to one of the Wheat Board quality classes on the basis of visual inspection. These standards, which support a marketing system designed to deliver a bulk commodity with uniform characteristics, greatly reduce the rate of new cultivar registration. This impact of quality requirements was noted by van Beuningen and Busch (1997a,b). They reported that Canadian hard red spring wheat cultivars have become more interrelated since the 1950s, while US wheats in a similar quality class, which are not subject to a centralized marketing system, showed decreasing interrelatedness. Feed barley and canola cultivars are registered mainly on the basis of agronomic performance, permitting a greater range of phenotypes of registered cultivars. The greater rate of new cultivar development in canola is probably mainly due to private-sector involvement in hybrid breeding and the development of herbicide-tolerant transgenic lines.

Table 4.3: Production area and number of registered cultivars for five major Canadian crops

Crop	Seeded area in 1997 ($\times$ 10^6ha)	Number of registered cultivars	Registered cultivars per 10^6ha
Western Canada			
Wheat (*Tribicum aestivum* and *T. durum*)	11.14	12	1.1
Barley	4.37	10	2.3
Canola (*Brassica napus* and *B. rapa*)	4.76	31	6.5
Eastern Canada			
Wheat (*T. aestivum*)	0.27	11	40.7
Barley	0.35	10	28.6
Soybean	1.06	57	53.8

On a cultivar per 10^6ha basis, the higher rate of cultivar release in eastern relative to western Canada results in part from the greater tendency of eastern farmers to purchase certified seed each year (due to the more humid, less favourable climate for seed production), and to a disproportionate investment in public-sector agricultural research in the east, considering that approximately 80 per cent of arable land in Canada is located in the western Prairie provinces. However, differences in marketing systems also play a role, particularly in wheat. Because eastern Canadian wheat is not marketed through the Canadian Wheat Board, kernel visual distinguishability and quality standards are less rigid, and end-users are left to decide on the acceptability of particular varieties. As a result of this more open registration and marketing system, nearly as many wheat cultivars were registered in eastern as in western Canada in the period from October 1997 to December 31 1998, a 40-fold difference on a cultivars per 10^6ha basis. Differences among eastern Canadian crops in the deployment of diversity are also related to grain and seed marketing differences. The extremely high rate of soybean cultivar release is related to the large number of (export) niche markets available for special food types, and to the fact that farmers tend to purchase soybean seed annually, rather than replant saved seed.

Farmers' attitudes to the deployment of genetic diversity

Canadian producers value cultivar diversity primarily as a crop-management tool. Producers with extensive areas planted to a single crop may wish to seed cultivars with a range of maturities, to spread their harvest workload. They use herbicide-tolerant cultivars to diversify their weed-control options. There is little evidence, however, to indicate that they place great value on the availability of a large number of cultivars *per se*. On the contrary, informal discussions with farmers and reading of the farm press indicate that farmers are confused by the great proliferation of maize, soybean and canola cultivars, and often have difficulty in deciding which they should grow. Like highly mechanized farmers everywhere, they value within-cultivar uniformity in height and maturity. Lack of uniformity in these traits tends to make crop management more complex and expensive in mechanized systems.

Attitudes of public-sector plant breeders: impact on the deployment of diversity

Public-sector plant breeders have, until recently, produced the majority of Canadian cultivars in crop species other than maize, and breeders' nurseries are the main working repositories of crop genetic diversity. Breeders generally consider this diversity as one of the determinants of selection response, and as a factor in the stability of agricultural systems, rather than as a good thing *per se*. Although the position of public-sector plant breeders is slowly changing as private breeding investment expands, the mandate of most government and university-based breeders is still to develop finished cultivars. This role limits the extent to which they can contribute to the diversification of the deployed genetic base. Many public breeding programmes are now at least partly dependent on royalties from the cultivars they release, and increasingly these cultivars must compete for market share, on the basis of agronomic performance, with private-sector lines. Under these circumstances, both public- and private-sector breeders focus on the crossing of parents that are agronomically élite, and are highly constrained in their ability to use exotic or unadapted parents.

Unless the mandate of public breeders shifts from 'downstream' cultivar development to 'upstream' germplasm mobilization, the impact of public-sector research on the genetic diversification of crops will continue to be limited. There is evidence that this shift may be occurring. For example, due to private-sector competition, the emphasis in federally funded canola research has shifted from cultivar development to biotechnology and germplasm enhancement. This is likely to occur in other species in which private breeding activity intensifies.

Conclusions

Public-sector plant breeding has had a major impact on the diversity of Canadian agriculture through the development and introduction of new crop species, but its effect on intraspecific genetic diversity has been more limited because of the focus of most public programmes on cultivar development. Breeders who must produce market-ready cultivars restrict parent choice to élite, adapted materials. This situation is likely to continue if public-sector breeding programmes are forced to increase their reliance on royalties.

The regulatory environment, new genetic technologies, crop-marketing systems and seed industry structure are the prime determinants of crop genetic diversity in Canada. Increased private-sector breeding investment, in response to the introduction of new genetic technologies that reduce the use of farm-grown seed, appears to have increased the rate of release of new cultivars in some crops, presumably increasing deployed genetic diversity. More flexible registration standards in some species have also increased release rates. In crops with rigid quality standards and marketing systems, little private sector involvement, and a low frequency of certified seed purchase by farmers, deployed genetic diversity remains low. Increased genetic diversity in these species can probably be achieved only through a redirection of public-sector research effort away from cultivar development and towards germplasm mobilization.

4.4. Use of genetic diversity in the breeding programme of the East-West Seed Company in South-East Asia

Marietta van der Werff and Arjan van Donk

Introduction

The East-West Seed Company (EWSC) is a vegetable seed company specializing in tropical lowland crops of South-East Asia. EWSC is presently active in five South-East Asian countries: the Philippines, Thailand, Indonesia, Vietnam and Bangladesh. Each of the five EWSC sister companies operates independently and targets the local market by way of its own research and development, production and marketing programmes. The company's philosophy can be phrased as: 'East-West Seed Company works to support the vegetable industry through the supply of high quality vegetable seed in sufficient quantity and at reasonable prices. It intends to promote efficient vegetable production, thereby increasing farmer income and facilitating an improved supply of quality vegetables at affordable prices.' The company operates in the belief that local market demands will continue to sustain this approach as a viable enterprise.

EWSC learned early that each country in Asia has its own very specific horticultural sector. This refers to crops, agricultural history, farming style, farmers' attitudes and product characteristics. It was soon understood that a local focus of plant breeding activities is the only way to provide farmers and the market with truly improved varieties. A location-specific plant-breeding approach, making use of local germplasm, ensures adaptation to local farming conditions as well as acceptability of the product to local tastes and market requirements.

With 'farmer-added value' to the end product being the highest priority, EWSC has utilized local genetic variation to develop the local horticultural sector. The path to this development is highly locality-specific, as illustrated by the situation in the Philippines and Thailand.

The traditional use of seed in Philippine vegetable production

At the start of EWSC operations in the Philippines in 1982 there was hardly any activity, government or other, on plant breeding or distribution of improved varieties of widely grown vegetables such as bitter gourd, pumpkin, eggplant, etc. Farmers relied for seed on the collection of seed from their own crops, exchange of seed among fellow farmers, small agricultural dealers who would collect and sell excess seed from local farmers, and imported seed. The imported seed would typically be distributed by small enterprises who purchased seed lots of unknown origin and quality through traders in Hong Kong or elsewhere. Similarly, branded seed of (American) varieties did not necessarily give any guarantee as to the exact identity of these seed lots. As a result, farmers traditionally regarded seed as an inconsistent and unreliable product. This initially complicated the establishment of EWSC as a reliable source of improved seed.

Traditionally, Philippine lowland farmers are not professional vegetable farmers. Vegetables were usually grown as a second priority crop, while staple crops such as rice and corn had first priority; vegetables were not considered a major source of farm income and therefore did not get much attention. This perception of vegetable crops is reflected in farmers' seed practices. In maintaining seed from their crops, Philippine farmers do not engage in selection of more desirable types. In general, farmers sell the bulk of their crop and keep only the last, non-marketable fruits for seed. Due to this unintentional selection pressure, typical Philippine farmers' varieties, in contrast to other Asian germplasm, is late-maturing, but 'strong', i.e. disease-resistant.

Specialized vegetable production and backyard gardening

The Philippine climate has a pronounced rainy season with occasional destructive typhoons. Vegetable farming during the rainy season is considered risky and is not widely practised. Vegetable supplies drop dramatically during the off-season and prices of fresh vegetables are consequently high. Most commercial vegetable production in the Philippines takes place in concentrated areas. Villages, towns or even complete provinces specialize in production of a certain vegetable (e.g. eggplant from Pangasinan, onion from Nueva Ecija), which is then traded country-wide, but particularly to urban centres. Philippine farmers are to a large extent

172

financially dependent on traders and financiers, who often dictate what they should grow. Before improved varieties were introduced, these specialized areas would usually have their 'own' variety, which would be the type accepted by the traders.

Another important source of vegetables for a large part of the Philippine population is backyard farming. Many households, especially in rural areas, keep a small plot of vegetables for home consumption. Most towns have an open market day during which households can sell their excess produce.

In the Philippines these are the two major 'niches' of genetic diversity, each with its own utilization characteristics and requirements for crop development and conservation.

The success of variety improvement

EWSC plant-breeding activities in the Philippines started with the collection of farmers' varieties country-wide, followed by evaluation and selection from the local genetic material. To ensure the performance of improved varieties under local conditions, EWSC adopted typical farmers' practices, such as planting distances, fertilizer rates or trellising practices, for its evaluation and selection trials. Breeding goals initially focused on yield increase, improved off-season adaptation, improved disease resistance, improved product quality such as shelf-life and shipping quality, and a variety of minor goals.

While local material would always be the cornerstone of the breeding programme, some characteristics absent from local material (such as earliness) were incorporated from foreign genetic resources. Presently EWSC supplies a wide selection of improved varieties, both hybrids and open-pollinated varieties. The impact of improved varieties on the Philippine horticultural sector has been large. Some farmers, having recognized the potential of vegetable production, have turned from rice and corn farming to full-time vegetable farming; off-season vegetable production has increased, with more farmers planting confidently during this season, and the total acreage under vegetable farming has increased; the supply of vegetables has improved and become more stable through the year.

Improved varieties have so far principally benefited commercial vegetable growers. These growers increasingly turn to improved varieties, which supply a base for improved production and income. Research, through collection, selection and combination within local genetic variation, as well as introduction of invaluable foreign genetic variation, has created substantial 'added value' for farmers who traditionally regarded the horticultural sector as being of minor economic importance. Commercial plant breeders will need actively to conserve traditional genetic variation as it is rapidly being replaced by a relatively narrow collection of improved varieties.

Backyard growers still mainly use their own landraces. Their needs and preferences represent a very localized and specialized niche, with its own requirements for variety improvement. These growers are likely to continue to use their own material to a certain extent. It is foreseen, however, that even the non-commercial and semi-commercial sectors will gradually adopt improved varieties. Active conservation of the genetic material is thus needed to secure the specific requirements of this sector.

The traditional use of seed in vegetable production in Thailand

In Thailand there have always been farmers specializing in vegetable production, as well as many who combine growing vegetables with planting staple crops such as rice or corn. Important vegetable crops in Thailand are, for example, cucumber, ridge gourd, eggplant, leafy vegetables and herbs such as kangkong, chaisim, coriander and basil. The vegetable varieties traditionally used were partly imported (particularly crops of temperate origin and hybrid varieties), and partly local farmers' selections. There has always been some trading in seed alongside farmer-saved seed.

The first seed companies in Thailand focused on seed trading, importing seed as well as collecting and selling locally produced seed. The purity and genetic consistency of these varieties was questionable, and varied between brands and over the years. As the economic and political situation in Thailand improved, the demand for higher and more consistent quality vegetables and seed increased. EWSC was one of the first companies to recognize this need and started activities in Thailand in the mid-1980s. As in the Philippines, local breeding, seed production and marketing activities were combined in one local company.

The market soon recognized the advantage of high-quality seed suitable for Thai conditions. The extra cost of seed was easily made up for by higher yields and better product quality. Farmers had to get used to buying seed that they had previously saved themselves, but many became convinced of the advantages of using hybrid seed, including better and consistent germination, improved yield levels, disease tolerance and earliness. Many commercial farmers shifted to reliance on improved seed instead of saving seed themselves, although this varies among crops.

Use and conservation of genetic variation

As a result of the introduction and widespread adoption of improved vegetable varieties around South-East Asia, the genetic diversity in many 'success' crops is dramatically diminished. Although the improved varieties, in the case of EWSC products, are direct selections from or combinations of local germplasm, they do represent a narrower range of local genetic diversity as compared with the sum of all landraces. As landraces, local selections and varieties become obsolete, a large part of the market is dominated by just a few varieties which may even share the same genetic background.

There has been no government initiative so far in the Philippines or Thailand to preserve the genetic diversity of vegetables. There are only a few scattered collections at various universities and institutions held by people interested in a particular crop. The private sector has a wide genetic base at its disposal, built up during years of collecting local material, but this is not accessible to outsiders. Standard documentation, evaluation or a database on available germplasm are non-existent.

Not all is negative though. Thanks to the introduction of foreign material into local breeding programmes, the genetic potential of materials at farmers' disposal has increased and genetic diversity has widened. Planting foreign material under local conditions is not usually a viable option, but the use of foreign material in breeding programmes introduces new genes into locally adapted varieties. In vegetables, this could never have been achieved on such a large scale and in the same time as is done by (mostly) the private sector.

However, this does not eliminate concern about the loss of genetic diversity. This should certainly be an issue for commercial seed companies. In the case of 'success' crops, where improved varieties have replaced local varieties to a large extent, we are left with relatively small and inaccessible collections at various places and institutions, and significantly reduced diversity in farmers' fields. For some crops, such as winged beans or lima beans in the Philippines, there is still a relatively large backyard production for which farmers rely on their own varieties. Many of these backyard crops do not receive high priority from seed companies, but this situation is slowly changing and it seems that these crops are heading in the same direction as the commercial crops.

Conclusion

There is a consensus in the private sector that concerted action in the conservation of genetic resources is necessary. It is also recognized that participation of communities, community gene banks and the private sector do have a role to play in this conservation, alongside the public sector. It is a challenge to all parties to look for collaboration and complementarity in the conservation of genes for the future. Practical obstacles, such as limited budgets and manpower/responsibility issues, have until now barred implementation. National initiatives tend to be too scattered, while conflicting interests complicate co-ordination. International efforts may be the only viable option to overcome the national obstacles.

4.5. Perspectives on diversity from an international commercial plant breeding organization

Stephen Smith

Genetic gain increases food production, saves land and reduces inputs of chemicals, fuel and water. If yields of five major US crops had increased

175

since 1930 due to improved husbandry, but no genetic gain had been achieved, then an additional 158 761 000 acres (248 064 square miles) would need to be cultivated to meet current production. Genetic gain will become more important as agricultural management practices change, including to more ecologically based systems (Matson et al., 1997). For example, nitrogen usage in Iowa has declined since 1975, while genetic inputs have caused a 20 per cent yield increase. The attribute of diversity *per se* does not provide more yield. For example, genetically heterogeneous US maize landraces were highly susceptible to insects (Holbert et al., 1934; Patch et al., 1941) and failed under drought stress (Baker, 1984). Successful crop improvement depends upon access to technologies, skills, knowledge and finance to adapt and utilize genetic resources from a range of élite and exotic sources, including transgenics.

The world's population of 6 billion will reach at least 8 billion by 2050 (Klug, 1998). The average yield of all cereals must be increased by 80 per cent between 1990 and 2025 (Borlaug and Downwell, 1994). But opportunities to cultivate new land sustainably remain only for sub-Saharan Africa and South America. Changes in the structures of rural communities will probably continue a global shift toward urbanization and production agriculture, affecting how genetic resources are conserved and improved. In the USA and Europe only 2–7 per cent of the population remains active in farming. Nearly 70 per cent of Latin Americans live in cities. Urban areas are growing by 6–8 per cent per year in sub-Saharan Africa. 'Soon, more people will live in towns and cities than in the countryside in developing countries as a whole. The young and more vigorous people tend to migrate leaving women, children and the old to carry the burden of work' (FAO, 1995).

Changes in genetic diversity are complex and inadequately understood (Tripp, 1996). The introduction of new varieties has reduced diversity (Cummings, 1978), changed diversity (Brush, 1993), or increased diversity (Dennis, 1987). Bretting and Duvick (1997) cite the rapid disappearance of landraces from farms in North America and Europe and the disappearance of old varieties of barley and finger millet in Nepal. Perrino (1994) estimates that 90 per cent of traditional Italian wheat varieties have disappeared recently because rural agrarian societies have themselves disappeared. It is advisable to prepare for the eventuality that *in situ* conservation of plant genetic resource diversity for agriculture will become unfeasible as farmers increasingly use the currently most productive varieties.

A commercially funded breeding organization serves a constituency of stakeholders comprising farmers and industrial customers, shareholders and employees. Significant risks and investments are required to utilize exotic germplasm that is unadapted, unimproved, uncharacterized and unevaluated. Practically all investments in conservation and most investments in genetic enrichment utilizing exotic germplasm, therefore, require government funds. Additional private funds may be forthcoming for pre-breeding, utilizing a broader germplasm base as new information and technologies reduce risks and cut timelines to product introduction, and as strong intellectual property protection is available for varieties *per se*. But many farmers, especially in developing countries, cannot purchase seed from commercial companies due to poverty or the lack of infrastructure and business opportunities. The totality of needs for agriculture and environmental security means that both public and private funds, partitioned according to commercial viability of investments and the need for long-term public funding of basic infrastructure, are required.

There are myths and misconceptions about genetic diversity. US maize yields were in decline prior to the 1930s. This unsustainable trend was reversed due to changes in husbandry and the cultivation of hybrids. A review of pedigrees for US maize hybrids shows dynamic change in germplasm used on farms in the central corn belt during every decade of hybrid production. For example, by the 1960s one pedigree component (Leaming), that was the second largest contributor in the 1930s had disappeared, while contributions had been added from 10 other pedigree backgrounds. By the 1990s only one of the components that was new during the 1960s remained (Minnesota 13), while 12 fresh components had appeared. Reid Yellow Dent was the predominant germplasm of pre-hybrid landraces and contributed 80 per cent of the pedigree of hybrids during the 1940s. Corn breeding has broadened genetic diversity and raised productivity by introgression of new germplasm into the central US corn belt.

Research by the International Wheat and Maize Improvement Centre (CIMMYT) in Mexico shows multinational dependencies for germplasm. The simplistic and politically convenient notion that germplasm has flowed from 'Southern' developing nations to 'Northern' industrially developed nations is inaccurate and misleading. The most productive wheat varieties have germplasm from a diversity of locations, South and North, developing and industrialized. For example, CIMMYT cite seven landraces used before 1900 that are important in the pedigrees of today's wheat varieties. The variety Sonalika, a bread-wheat variety that was grown across the largest area of the world in 1990, has a pedigree involving landraces that originate in 17 countries, and breeders' selections made in 14 countries from six continents.

For most of the history of agriculture, cultivated genetic diversity has exotic origins compared to farm sites. Crop varieties have migrated around the globe. Incomplete sampling of wild germplasm prior to domestication, partial sampling of crop diversity prior to migration, the continued evolution of wild and cultivated germplasm under different selection regimes, and changing pests and pathogens mean that no single region or accession provides the ideal germplasm. Significantly increased on-farm productivity is dependent on successive, new genetic combinations that raise yield potential. Yield advances require infusions of new and exotic germplasm. New capabilities from genomics research enhance the importance of accessing a broader germplasm base (Tanksley and McCouch, 1997). However, exotic germplasm will not be used in variety improvement unless it is conserved, evaluated, adapted and enhanced with élite varieties. Financial, technical and intellectual resources are required to accomplish these tasks.

Professional plant breeders have greater access to a broader base of genetic diversity through international networking than is the case for locally based farmer-breeders. By the 1950s, farmers in the US corn belt were utilizing a range of genetic diversity that had not been available to an earlier generation. At least four changes occur when farmers specialize in production and professional breeders specialize in crop improvement. Firstly, breeders create more diversity by making many controlled crosses and by importing new exotic diversity. Secondly, diversity is sequestered in breeding programmes and is arrayed in time (Duvick, 1984) as a succession of new varieties appear in farmers' fields. Thirdly, full-time plant breeders can devote more time and call upon more resources. Fourthly, farmers concentrate on maximizing productivity. The most effective conduct of plant breeding combines genetic diversity and increased productivity. Multi-national companies have the ability to move germplasm globally between breeding programmes and thus dramatically increase both the diversity and productivity of germplasm in a local area.

Agriculture is not sustainable unless it is also productive. Genetic diversity will not be conserved unless it can be utilized to improve productivity or unless there is sufficient belief that it harbours potentially useful germplasm. Germplasm conservation is an insurance policy, protecting those resources for future use. These prospects are unpredictable due to lack of knowledge of the agronomic attributes of conserved germplasm, and unforeseen changes in the environment, husbandry or consumer demands. Loss of genetic diversity would curtail future options and would elevate our dependence on combinatorial chemistry to levels beyond which our knowledge of genomic function has reached, or may ever reach, especially with regard to quantitative traits. It is in the best long-term interest of society as a whole to conserve germplasm resources for food and agriculture.

Additional investments are needed in plant genetic resource conservation and utilization (Mann, 1997). Private investments are increasing due to new genetic information, new technological capabilities, and abilities to obtain strong intellectual property protection. But there are global deficiencies that require remedy. Commercially funded plant breeders will not invest in exploring and utilizing exotic genetic resources when the end-products from those risky, expensive and time-consuming activities are immediately and freely available to competitors. A lack of strong intellectual property protection on plant varieties removes incentives to source and to introduce new germplasm diversity. Worse still, a relative lack of intellectual property protection for innovations in crop germplasm, compared to the strong protection that is available for genes and technologies (i.e. the current intellectual property protection situation in Europe), could encourage a narrowing of the existing germplasm base by directing plant-breeding activities toward making relatively minor genetic changes to a small cadre of the most élite and currently available varieties. It is important to establish intellectual property protection regimes that can encourage further private investments in the whole spectrum of plant breeding, including the utilization of exotic germplasm.

There are also gross inadequacies regarding public funding of germplasm conservation and utilization. Investments by governments in genetic resource conservation and utilization for food and agriculture are diminishing. The FAO Global Plan of Action (FAO, 1996e) has not been funded. The US National Plant Germplasm System is underfunded (GAO, 1997). Additional effort must be directed globally toward germplasm enhancement to build a stronger foundation of genetic resources (Simmonds, 1993; Frey, 1998). But additional government funds have not been forthcoming because a sufficient constituency of support has not been engaged from industry and the public at large. It is important to correct this situation immediately.

4.6. Plant biotechnology: the quest for useful pieces of DNA

Jan-Peter Nap

Introduction

Over the past 20 years advances in plant biotechnology have had a significant impact on plant breeding. Notably over the past 3 years this has resulted in numerous marketed products that use some form of biotechnology in either production or processing. Plant biotechnology comprises at least three technologies that are currently used in plant breeding and production: (i) *in vitro* technology; (ii) marker technology; and (iii) gene technology.

In vitro technology is the rapid and large-scale propagation of genetically identical plant material in glass jars that takes place in specialized laboratories. This technology is used for rapid multiplication of material as well as for obtaining disease-free starting material. It has developed to such an extent that *in vitro* technology is now considered to be relatively 'low-tech' and routine.

Marker technology has been successfully implemented in current breeding strategies. A marker is a protein or, more often, a short sequence of DNA, the presence of which is linked to a desired trait. Using the marker as a flag, complex or difficult-to-assay traits can more easily be evaluated and selected for. This speeds up and improves the accuracy of breeding. A considerable part of current plant biotechnology research is aimed at identifying such markers in breeding material.

Most of the attention and discussions about plant biotechnology are focused on gene technology. Genetic engineering techniques allow introduction of any piece of genetic material (DNA) into a host organism. This chapter concentrates on this aspect of plant biotechnology and focuses on its relationships with diversity and the conservation and use of plant genetic resources.

Biotechnology and plant breeding

The final outcome of the application of genetic engineering in plant breeding is the introduction of genetically modified or transgenic plants in farmers' fields and products on the consumer markets. Notably in the USA, transgenic crops are nowadays planted on a large scale and have taken root in the economy. The crops now marketed generally contain a single added gene that confers a single desired trait, such as resistance to specific insect or viral pests, longer shelf-life, or tolerance to a specific type of herbicide. Aim and outcome are not so very different from what is achieved in breeding through hybridization, but genetic engineering widens the scope of plant breeding and (potentially) the speed of achieving desired results. Developments are moving quickly, and there are already various examples of multiple agronomically relevant transgenes in a single variety.

For some time breeders have pointed out that the agronomically really important traits, such as yield, quality and other quantitative traits, are determined by complex polygenic networks that would never be amenable to genetic engineering. Results from quantitative trait mapping, however, suggest that also in complex quantitative traits relatively few genes exert the largest part of the effect. If so, this opens up the possibility of also improving quantitative traits with genetic engineering. Other goals of plant biotechnology in the not-too-distant-future go far beyond the aims of classical breeding, and may turn plants into chemical factories. By modifying metabolic pathways, common crops will be redesigned into units that produce virtually anything on demand, from commodity chemicals to pharmaceuticals and cosmetics. It is to be expected that, when realized, such trends and developments will further influence and change the way the plant-breeding industry is organized.

Biotechnology thrives on genetic diversity

In order to improve or change a crop by genetic engineering, a biotechnologist requires genes to do the job. Biotechnology has a continuous need for well characterized genes, preferably available as pieces of DNA or cDNA (cloned RNA). Characteristic for biotechnology is that the origin of the gene of interest is not important. DNA is virtually independent of the organism from which it originates. The organism may be a plant, but can also be a bacterium or a whale: the concept of 'wild relative' is of no relevance for genetic engineering. The added value of biotechnology to plant breeding is not the further exploitation of farmers' varieties, but the use of genetic material from unrelated species.

The attitude of plant biotechnology to breeding is as straightforward as it is ambitious: for any trait desired, somewhere there will be an organism that is able to do the job. The challenge is to find that organism, identify the gene or genes involved, and transfer those genes into a suitable crop. Bioprospecting, the identification and evaluation of properties in organisms for potential application, is currently becoming a major input in (plant) biotechnology. In plant biotechnology there is huge interest in diversity useful for making speciality chemicals, pharmaceuticals or crops with improved pest resistance. Continuing development of techniques will further speed up the identification of novel genes and their function. The rapidly growing databases of genes and further development of the techniques of so-called functional genomics give a new dimension to the concept of genetic diversity.

In the conservation of plant genetic resources, people distinguish between the primary, secondary and tertiary gene pool, based on the ease of crossability between plants. In the framework of this terminology, biotechnology mainly focuses on what could be considered the 'quaternary gene pool', i.e. all genetic material that occurs in nature but cannot be introduced into a crop by any sexual means. In the future, biotechnology may also be responsible for a creation of diversity that could be considered a 'fifth-level gene pool'. There are some examples of novel diversity created in the laboratory. By DNA shuffling, new genes that encode improved proteins emerge out of random recombination of existing genes. The created gene can result in a protein that has an activity far exceeding the specifications of the parental proteins. This laboratory-based accelerated evolution can be considered as the molecular equivalent of heterosis in plant breeding. It could create genetic material in the laboratory that does not necessarily have a counterpart in nature.

Biotechnology and the management of diversity

Biotechnology clearly has a resource-centred view on diversity; organisms contain genes that can and should be exploited, for example for crop improvement or crop design. Such a resource-centred view on diversity does determine the perspective of biotechnology on genetic resources and the management of genetic diversity. The interest of biotechnology in genetic diversity is more broad than a typical gene bank collection or populations being conserved through on-farm management. Botanical gardens, national parks or virgin nature may be as useful, hence as valuable, as the diversity in local farming communities. Any organism in any ecosystem may contain genes that are or may become of use for any application. Such an organism should therefore be conserved. Biotechnologists are thus in the forefront to realize the importance of genetic resources. The key issue is documentation: what genes/properties/compounds are present in what organism; what are these genes/compounds doing; where can the organism or the relevant DNA or cDNA be found?

As long as gene banks limit themselves to the primary, secondary and tertiary gene pool of plants, they will have a fairly limited function for biotechnology. To comply with the wishes and requirements of current biotechnology in plant breeding, gene banks should consider storing DNA and cDNA from a much wider range of species. For biotechnology, local management of crops has no added value by definition, it depends on what is managed and how unique that material is. Especially local indigenous knowledge, for example on the use of plants for herbal medicines or pest control, is likely to be an important source of hints at properties of organisms (plants, fungi, insects and others) that may result in an application for biotechnology.

The organization of plant biotechnology and the ownership of diversity

A novel and controversial issue introduced to plant breeding by biotechnology is 'ownership'. Biotechnology is a costly approach, and in order to survive biotech companies feel they should make a return on their investments. The old proverb of science, 'publish or perish', has in current plant biotechnology changed to 'patent or perish'. Nowadays the field is suffering from an unparalleled patent frenzy that is mainly in the interest of patent lawyers and patent offices. Patents attempt to protect genes and crops carrying the genes, as well as methods to obtain the genes from any other source. The old situation under plant breeders' rights was that the commercial use of varieties could be protected, but such varieties were free for further breeding. Patent rights put an end to this situation. An accompanying global trend is a continued concentration of biotech companies. This has transformed plant breeding and seed production from a more rural activity to an important part of the agrochemical (pharmaceutical) complex. Current plant biotechnology is dominated by a six-pack of giant international corporations (Monsanto, DuPont, Novartis, AgrEvo, Zeneca, Dow Chemical) that set goals and aim to define markets and market shares. Local farming communities are not generally considered to be interesting markets for plant biotechnology products. It is unlikely that commercial plant biotechnology will make plants adjusted to the requirements of small- and medium-sized farming communities. This implies that such communities will not receive much new input for breeding and improvement. The current organization of plant biotechnology may therefore result in the situation that too few control too much.

An important, but difficult, issue in the discussion about ownership is how to balance or capitalize the contributions in biotech products of local farmers, indigenous knowledge and the maintenance of natural areas and ecotypes on the one hand, with the knowledge and expertise developed by biotechnologists on the other. Although this is a valid and necessary discussion, most biotechnologists will consider such issues beyond their horizon, i.e. issues for lawyers, politicians and decision-makers. A notable example of how issues are looked upon in different ways is the recent patent describing a method to obtain inviable seed (the 'terminator' technology). Biotechnologists generally marvel at the scientific elegance, the potential applications (e.g. for biosafety) and the commercial implications. NGOs stress the undesired consequences and call for a ban on the technology.

Conclusion

It is unrealistic to assume that transgenic plants, or any related technology that is perceived to have a market, will not be put into practice. Proper rules and regulations are needed to control their application in a manner that satisfies the interests and concerns of all parties involved. This requires more dialogue between stakeholders focusing on consensus, rather than what is currently going on between industry, regulators, NGOs and other interest groups.

4.7. Participatory approaches in plant breeding: experiences and insights of an NGO in Nepal

Bhuwon Sthapit and Anil Subedi

Introduction

Crop varieties generated through formal breeding have largely been suitable for resource-rich and high-production environments. Their benefits have not always been realized in the marginal environments where typically a vast number of landraces are being grown and maintained by farmers. The main reasons for maintaining high biodiversity by farmers are mostly to ensure food security and to meet various qualitative preferences and household requirements (see Chapter 1.1 and Section 2). The crop varieties bred by the national research system in most developing countries, including Nepal, must pass through a highly centralized process of varietal testing, release and certification. By the time materials reach farmers, choice of seed for farmers is already restricted to acceptance or rejection of a few finished cultivars. The needs and problems of the farmers in marginal conditions, the process of local crop development and the value of landraces in crop improvement are not adequately addressed by the conventional, centralized breeding system (Chapter 1.1). The challenge therefore is to address these concerns by involving farmers in the breeding process. This chapter deals with examples of innovative participatory approaches adequately to address the needs and problems of farmers in marginal conditions in Nepal.

In Nepal, more than 2500 landraces of rice can be found in different production systems, counting different seasons and conditions. Over time, 43 improved varieties have been released in Nepal, and more than 500 varieties in India. However, their adoption by farmers in marginal environments has been poor (Sthapit et al., 1996). Participatory research on rice conducted in Nepal presents various experiences which have contributed importantly to the conceptualization of participatory variety selection (PVS) and participatory plant breeding (PPB) approaches (see Box 4.1). One such experience is the case of *Ghaiya* upland rice in Tars, Nepal. This type of rice crop covers 10 per cent of the total rice area in the country. However, Ghaiya rice is not a priority research crop as it is grown in marginalized areas. Its rice culture is very traditional and unique to socially and economically disadvantaged ethnic communities (Subedi et al., 1992). The Ghayia crop is labour-demanding and has a low market value, but is adapted to the *tar* conditions where other crops provide no food security. Of the 43 released rice varieties in Nepal, only one has been recommended for upland conditions; its adoption was very poor and its breeder seed is difficult to obtain. In exploratory fieldwork LI-BIRD staff noted that the available varieties lack farmers' preferred quality traits and high harvest index, and therefore a PPB programme is needed to add value to the local Ghaiya landraces (LI-BIRD, 1998).

Chaite rice in the low hills of Nepal

Early-season, irrigated, low-hill rice cultivation, *Chaite*, is new to Nepal, and 98 per cent of this production area is planted with the variety CH-45. It is grown under assured irrigation and high-production potential systems. Lumle Agricultural Research Centre achieved diversification by using one of the simplest forms of PVS. In 1992, seeds of five pre-released and one recently released variety of *Chaite* rice type were distributed to 1802 farmers in 20 villages in the area. In 1993 a survey of a sub-sample of 192 farming households showed that one-third of the farming households made use of the introduced varieties (Joshi et al., 1997, see also Witcombe et al., Chapter 4.11). This approach involved minimal external inputs and proved to be highly cost effective in identifying farmer-preferred cultivars.

High-altitude rice of western Nepal

Rice grown at elevations ranging from 1500 to 2000m a.s.l. in irrigated and transplanted conditions is generally known as high-altitude rice; in Nepal it covers about 26 per cent of the 1.5 million ha rice land. The limitations of rice culture in these domains are chilling injury and sheath brown rot disease (caused by *Pseudomonas fuscovagainae*). This combination of characters is not important elsewhere in the world and thus is not ad- dressed by formal breeding. Of the 43 cultivars released, only two have been recommended for the high hills. To address farmers' varietal needs, a total of 528 exotic cold-tolerant lines from the International and National Rice Cold Tolerance Nursery were screened by Lumle Agricultural Re- search Centre at high-altitude testing sites (1500–2000m a.s.l.). The major- ity of exotic cold-tolerant varieties failed to set grain at Lumle (1675m) and Chhomrong (2000–2200m a.s.l.) because of low temperature at anthesis (Sthapit, 1991) and cold-associated diseases (Sthapit, 1992, Sthapit et al., 1995). In these on-station environments local landraces collected from the western hills of Nepal were found to be the best among the tested

Box 4.1: Definitions and steps in participatory varietal selection (PVS) and participatory plant breeding (PPB)*

PVS is the selection of fixed lines (released, advanced lines or landraces) by farmers in their target environments using their own selection criteria.
  A successful PVS involves the following four steps:

○ identification of farmers' needs in a cultivar
○ a search for suitable materials
○ experimentation on its acceptability in farmers' field
○ wider dissemination of farmer-preferred cultivars.

PPB, in which farmers select cultivars from segregating materials in the target environment, is a logical extension of PVS. PPB needs to be used when the possibilities of PVS have been exhausted, or when the search process in PVS fails to identify any suitable cultivars for testing. Prior to parent selection and crossing in PPB, the research programme should have a clear breeding goal based on farmers' needs and preferences.
  A successful PPB programme usually has the following features:

○ setting of goals jointly to meet farmers' needs
○ decentralized testing in farmers' fields
○ use of farmers' observations and opinions
○ use of local parental materials
○ selection of site and management decisions by farmers
○ selection of cultivar by farmers
○ skills/knowledge transfer between breeder and farmer
○ use of multiple selection traits by farmers, including women
○ monitoring of varietal spread by scientists
○ use of informal seed supply systems for wider dissemination.

According to Witcombe et al. (1996) and Ceccarelli et al. (1996), PPB is more likely to be successful in producing farmer-acceptable varieties than a conventional breeding programme because:

○ genotype × environment interaction is greatly reduced since selection is always done in the target environment and under farmers' actual management conditions
○ at least one parent is well adapted to the target environment
○ the impact of genotype × year interactions is reduced
○ farmer participation at early stages of breeding process.

* Based on Witcombe et al. (1996, 1998); Joshi and Witcombe (1996); Sthapit et al., 1996.

materials. In comparison to most exotic cold-tolerant materials, a population from Chhomrong showed good cold tolerance with blast- and sheath brown rot-resistance (Sthapit et al., 1996). It can adapt to aquatic as well as rainfed upland conditions. The landrace population was further developed and selected for better cold tolerance, sheath brown rot and blast resistance; the best panicles were bulked for testing in multi-locational trials (Sthapit et al., 1996). In 1991 the Nepal Agricultural Research Council released this variety under the name of Chhomrong Dhan for over 1500–2200m a.s.l. This variety has since spread to new high-altitude areas of Nepal, stretching from Dhankuta in the eastern region to Bajura in the far western region.

In 1992, during focus group discussions women farmers requested breeders to improve the grain colour and quality of *Chhomrong Dhan* rice. This rice has a coarse grain with a red colour, but white-grained rice is socially preferred and saves women time in milling. This was probably the first time that Nepali breeders realized the importance of setting breeding goals with the farming community, and signified a radical departure from conventional practice. Sthapit et al. (1996) found that the degree of farmer participation increased when farmers were involved in setting breeding goals. The level of women's participation increased particularly after the inital step of developing cold tolerance and disease resistance, i.e. when selection for the elimination of the red pericarp began.

For this purpose *Chhomrong Dhan*, known for cold tolerance and resistance to sheath brown rot and blast, was crossed with Fuji 102, a Japanese cold-tolerant variety with favourable grain-quality characteristics. Farmers were given F_5 bulk families (i.e. still segregating), harvested from the most promising F_4 rows, for evaluation in their fields. Decentralized selection ensured selection for local adaptation, including resistance to sheath brown rot which has never been a priority disease in the national or international context. The best selections developed thus jointly with farmers were superior and outperformed the best entries from the conventional breeding programme (Sthapit et al., 1996). The new variety developed through PPB, Machhapuchhre-3, was released in 1997 by the Nepal Agricultural Research Council (Joshi et al., 1997). This case is an example of adding value to local materials by incorporating preferred traits from exotic cultivars.

The products of PPB have occupied about 34 per cent of the total area in villages participating in the PPB programme, and do not totally replace the landrace gene pool (Joshi et al., 1998). In the process of up-scaling the use of PPB varieties, particularly M-3 and M-9, a problem of shattering was identified by farmers and a mutation breeding of the M-3 population has now been initiated by LI-BIRD in collaboration with the University of Wales, UK.

Up-scaling the LI-BIRD experiences

In Nepal, LI-BIRD has taken the initiative to up-scale PPB. Knowledge and expertise in such approaches can be mobilized to strengthen the capacity of other organizations, and can also be scaled-up at national level and beyond. LI-BIRD has institutionalized the innovative approach of PVS and PPB in cereals and vegetable crops, under different agro-climatic conditions in various institutional settings. CARE-Nepal, an international NGO, in partnership with LI-BIRD and farming communities, launched a PVS programme in another part of Nepal in 1997, and has plans for other parts of the country in the future. With the expertise of LI-BIRD, PLAN International has also launched a PVS programme in the Terai district of Sunsari, where adoption of modern rice is limited despite its potential. The European Union-funded Gulmi Arghakhanchi Rural Development Project commissioned LI-BIRD to assess the problems and needs of farming communities and to formulate a suitable strategy for implementing a PVS programme in Gulmi and Arghakhanchi Districts. The Gulmi Arghakhanchi Project, district line agencies and local government have decided to integrate PVS as an important component in their agricultural development programme. LI-BIRD uses its network projects, the national system, and Indian agricultural universities to search for suitable genetic materials.

In order to analyse the cost-effectiveness of PPB, LI-BIRD has provided access to a wide range of fixed as well as segregating lines of rice to the community in Maranche village (1400–1700m a.s.l.) and is now monitoring the spread of cultivars and documenting reasons for adoption and rejection so that future parent selection and PPB can be refined. The village is near a research station and shows a minimal adoption of rice varieties through the formal system. The village has no staff and made no formal effort to mobilize the community. Within 2 years of intervention in Marangche, the adoption of M-9, M-3 and *Chhomrong Dhan* was significant, covering 13, 8 and 1 per cent of the area, respectively (LI-BIRD, 1998). Within 5 years, considering the different entries as a single varieties, the diversity of rice gene pool increased from one to seven varieties. This situation suggests that PPB does not necessarily replace all landraces, as some of the conventional *in situ* conservationists argue.

In order to test the hypothesis that PVS and PPB approaches are also functional in high-potential production systems, LI-BIRD, with the support of the UK Department for International Development, has worked with PVS and PPB in 18 villages of the Chitwan and Nawalparasi Districts of Nepal. Initial results show that the PVS approach has increased yield by 20–25 per cent over existing *Chaite* and main-season rice, with increased varietal diversity (Chapter 4.11).

PPB is also linked to strategies for the *in situ* conservation of crop biodiversity, in which farmers' management is recognized as an important source of genetic variation (Friis-Hansen and Sthapit, 1999). Currently the Nepal Agricultural Research Council and LI-BIRD are collaborating with IPGRI to strengthen the scientific basis of *in situ* conservation of agrobiodiversity in Nepal (Jarvis et al., 1998). PPB is a major component of the project and is envisioned to play a role in adding value to local diversity, thereby increasing the chance of their being maintained by farmers where they originated. Similarly, a farmer-led PPB on maize has been initiated, with support from system-wide programme participatory

187

research and gender analysis, to capitalize on farmers' knowledge and breeders' expertise in skill transfer and empowerment.

Contribution of PPB

In the experiences of PVS and PPB in Nepal, the impacts are seen.

○ Local adaptation: selection under local conditions generates materials which are stress-tolerant and well liked by farmers.
○ On-farm conservation: especially in the cases where landraces crossed with modern cultivars are employed, the breeding strategy gives added value to landraces which makes them more attractive to farmers (Sthapit et al., 1996).
○ Empowerment of farmers through involvement in defining breeding goals, selection of materials and transfer of skills.
○ Cultural and equity considerations: through PPB the needs of those living in the most marginal environments can be addressed. These people are often ethnic minorities, and the use of varieties or crops often relates to socio-cultural identity.

Limitations and constraints of participatory methods

Despite the encouraging response of farmer participation in plant breeding and selection, a number of constraints, both institutional and technical, limit the participatory approaches. A serious problem is the fact that the majority of breeders have still not been exposed to PPB approaches and still work in centralized conventional breeding programmes. Those very few breeders who are exposed to and practising participatory approaches (Eyzaguirre and Iwanaga, 1996; Sperling and Loevinsohn, 1996) have basically taken initiatives to develop approaches through learning and employ them in the field without clear support from their own institutions (Hardon, 1995). A lack of critical mass of researchers, and institutional rigidity in both international and national systems, are probably the major constraints to institutionalizing the PPB approach in the formal system.

Conclusion

Participatory approaches to plant breeding offer a tremendous opportunity to develop farmer-preferred cultivars, enhance on-farm conservation and empower farming communities. Such an outcome is difficult to match for complex, diverse and risk-prone environments by formal breeding. Participatory approaches in breeding are, at present, being initiated by a small group of innovative breeders and are employed in a small area and a limited number of crops. There is a need for their wider testing and application in both marginal and high-potential production environments of the developing countries by involving informal as well as formal institutions and transferring skills and knowledge to farmers. So far, plant genetic resource specialists, plant explorers, ethnobotanists, social scientists and plant breeders have enriched their knowledge and gene banks from the farming community. The time has now come to reverse the process through equitable benefit sharing of on-farm conservation. Linking local seed systems with other on-farm activities such as diversity fairs, community gene banks and farmer breeding will further strengthen the process of on-farm conservation of local genetic resource base, PPB and formal breeding alike.

4.8. Supporting farmers' genetic resource management: experiences with pearl millet in India

Eva Weltzien

Introduction

Farmers' decision-making regarding the choice and diversity of crop varieties, the production and selection of seeds, seed storage and exchange of information, as well as seed materials, affects the the composition and make-up of this germplasm. Concrete actions to support genetic resource management by farmers can be successfully planned and carried out only when farmers' practices and objectives for seed management are adequately understood. The case of ICRISAT's pearl millet (*Pennisetum glaucum*) improvement work for the marginal desert region of Rajasthan in India offers an example of how more detailed understanding of farmers' genetic resource management influenced the orientation of a breeding programme. This understanding helped to obtain a more coherent interpretation of previously obtained results from on-farm trials, and enabled the further development of participatory plant breeding activities for pearl millet in this region (Weltzien et al., 1998).

Arriving at a better understanding of farmers' plant genetic resource management

Formal crop improvement for Rajasthan is co-ordinated through the All India Co-ordinated Pearl Millet Improvement Project (Witcombe et al., 1998). Regular survey results indicated that the uptake of improved varieties in this region is low, and that the available modern varieties do not meet farmers' needs and expectations (Kelly et al., 1996). There are few experiences of approaches to achieving a better understanding of farmers' needs. The ICRISAT team for Rajasthan, with its partners, took an approach that included understanding farmers' production objectives, their strategies to cope with the large seasonal variations in rainfall, social conditions in the villages, and gender differentiated responsibilities,

189

especially regarding seed-related activities, in addition to understanding in detail farmers' strategies for managing seed of pearl millet. The team used largely semi-structured interviews with members of different social groups, experts in seed production and experts in pearl millet. For specific issues we developed new communication tools, or adapted the tools of participatory rural appraisal to the local situation. A village-level workshop proved to be a very effective approach for enhancing farmer–scientist interactions. Details on the methodology, information collection and primary results are outlined by Dhamotharan et al. (1997).

Some of the key insights the team gained from this series of interviews, visits and observations were as follows.

- Farmers in the drier parts of this pearl millet-growing region (below 400mm annual rainfall) differentiate not between different varieties of pearl millet, but between different plant types, based on combinations of a range of plant characteristics. They associate different adaptations to specific growing conditions, and different grain and straw qualities with these different plant types.
- As farmers use seed lots in which the different plant types are mixed, they do not have specific names for different local varieties, and do not differentiate between local varieties within western Rajasthan, a region with a dry, hot and highly unpredictable climate. Some farmers know of other local varieties from eastern Rajasthan, where many local varieties are differentiated (Christinck et al., 1999).
- Farmers owning good/more land produce and store their own seed, usually for more than one season. This is a region with frequent droughts: a bad droughts hits in 3 years out of 10, thus seeds need to be stored for more than a year if a family wants to preserve their particular seed stock.
- These farmers select panicles after harvest if time permits, and if they perceive that such selection warrants the effort. Not all farmers consider panicle selection worth the effort.
- Farmers who practise selection among harvested panicles usually select panicles that fulfil minimum criteria for maturity and ripeness.
- Farmers who practise panicle selection include panicles representing a very wide range of diverse plant types. Farmers' explanation for selecting very different plant types as components of their pearl millet seed lot was in all cases related to improving the chance of coping with the large seasonal and spatial variation on their farms.
- Women do most of the work at harvest, including selection of panicles for use as seed. Women are also responsible for storing grain for food and seed.
- They also prepare the seed mixtures at the time of sowing by combining seed from different species in specific combinations for specific fields – pearl millet is mostly intercropped with legumes, sesame and cucurbits.
- On farms where seed is stored separately from food grain, usually only one seed lot is maintained, i.e. the seed from threshed ears of the different plant types are not separated but are kept in a mixture. However, they sometimes maintain different seed lots harvested in different years.

190

- Poor farmers commonly own only land of poor soil quality, which in this region means very sandy soil, often on steep-sloping sand dunes highly deficient in nitrogen and phosphorus, at pH 8–9.
- Farmers generally perceive that the local landrace type of pearl millet is better adapted to those poor soil conditions than the plant type of modern varieties (hybrid and open-pollinated varieties) that are for sale in parts of the region.
- Poor farmers rarely produce sufficient for their food needs, and rarely maintain their own seeds. At the time of sowing they depend for their seed supply on relatives, better-off farmers or purchases of commercial seed. Farmers who produce their own seed are very well respected in the village.
- Farmers interested in obtaining seed from another farmer usually request a certain quantity of seed before harvest (booking system). The seed is given at a slight surcharge over regular food grain.
- Farmers who are in need of seed at the time of sowing are given food grain by those who have surplus stocks. It is expected that farmers who received such seed grain will return the same quantity of grain after harvest.
- Most farmers who regularly produce their own seed, i.e. the better-off farmers, are interested in diversifying their seed lots by introducing new plant types into the seed lots. This is often related to the farmers' efforts to deliberately diversify the growing conditions within their own farms through use of manure, soil and water conservation measures and the management of trees and shrubs in their fields.
- In areas where modern varieties are sold, better-off farmers use small quantities of this seed, normally in mixture with their own seed, to diversify the range of plant types grown in their fields.
- In contrast, poor farmers in these areas (who often have to purchase or 'borrow' seed for the next planting), especially women, expressed concern about the increasing difficulty of obtaining pure seed of the local-variety plant type that is best adapted to their poor soils.

How this information changed the activities of the ICRISAT breeding programme

Earlier results from the field study had shown that individual farmers are interested in a wide range of plant traits and types. Individual farmers were interested to have 'a variety' that is high-tillering, early and tall with large panicles (Weltzien et al., 1996). But different members of a family expressed different preferences, e.g. women were much more interested than men in early-maturing plant types with a higher stability of grain yield. Farmers from the same village also expressed different preferences. Thus a picture emerged of a very broad range of varietal trait preferences that could not be combined into any single variety. For instance, high tillering is a characteristic which conflicts with large panicle size, and also shows a trade-off with stem thickness and tall plant height. The understanding that

191

farmers grow mixtures of plant types and actively select for these types within their harvest lot provides a solution to this dilemma: even the most incompatible plant traits and types can be combined in a physical mixture of seeds. It thus became more relevant for the breeding programme to identify potential components of mixtures which would be of most benefit to the local system of using and disseminating seeds.

On several occasions farmers expressed very clearly the need for plant types with adaptation to poor soil, which is the predominant soil condition in western Rajasthan. Poor farmers were keen because they own only poor soils and lack reliable sources of appropriate seeds; better-off farmers were interested because for them also production on their poorer fields and in poor years is essential for food security.

ICRISAT's pearl millet-breeding efforts for Rajasthan – the main pearl millet-production zone in India – thus started to focus its activities on developing breeding populations with the plant type best suited to these poor conditions, i.e. high basal and nodal tillering, early flowering and thin stems combined with traits that assure good grain yields: disease resistance, good set and grain filling under a wide range of poor growing conditions. These populations were largely composed of superior landrace populations from the gene bank collections held at ICRISAT's headquarters, originating from Rajasthan. The parentage and selection procedures for each of these populations are described in detail by Yadav and Weltzien (1998). Progeny testing for population improvement was done only in locations in Rajasthan. Fertility management at the research stations was changed so that only minimal application of mineral fertilizer was used, primarily to reduce within-field variation and control the experimental error. Efforts are under way to develop uniform fields for selection, that are depleted of nitrogen and phosphorus to represent the growing conditions in farmers' fields. Selection indices were used to identify superior progenies, capitalizing on the traits with relatively higher heritability at each location and favouring the traits of the preferred plant type as described above.

Farmers evaluating these populations in the same villages where the interviews and discussions had been held indicated that the new populations were getting closer to farmers' needs, but more specific effort to improve adaptation to poor fertility conditions seemed necessary (E. Weltzien and P. Jaiswal, pers. comm.). Thus plans for farmers' involvement in further improving these populations, specifically for adaptation to poor soil conditions, were made in co-operation with the national pearl millet improvement programme for Rajasthan.

Additional initiatives as a result of increased understanding

In addition to changes in the breeding programme, the better understanding of farmers' management of seeds also led to some other initiatives. The testing and release procedures for pearl millet varieties were examined together with the appropriate authorities, to allow for releases of a wider range of plant types and of material with specific adaptations to harsh growing conditions.

The local NGO, Grameen Vikas Vigyan Samiti, interested in assisting poor farmers through appropriate seed supplies in emergency conditions, started a programme with the assistance of ICRISAT to identify the most appropriate source of seed of the local variety plant type for these villages. In farmer-managed trials they compared local varieties from nearby areas and breeding populations based entirely on local germplasm. They would then multiply the seed of the preferred material in the village and use the seed for distribution to those in need at the time of sowing.

Based on the information from the field study, ICRISAT also initiated a detailed study of farmers' management of pearl millet genetic resources across a wider area in Rajasthan, and a more detailed assessment of farmers' utilization of modern germplasm in the development of their seed lots. These results aim at identification of potential strategies for *in situ*/on-farm conservation of local pearl millet germplasm in Rajasthan that are compatible with crop improvement (Christinck and vom Brocke, 1998; Christinck et al., 1999).

Acknowledgement of the roles of collaborators

The experiences described with pearl millet show that the participation of a range of partners was needed to arrive at improvements in the breeding and seed supply in Rajasthan. The breeders have learned from the women and men farmers of Aagolaie, Kichiyasar and Digadi villages in western Rajasthan. These farmers spent effort and time in explaining often trivial things to people who were strangers to them. Mohan Dhamotharan, extensionist in the Pearl Millet Improvement Project, and his keen interest in bridging differences between vastly different knowledge systems through effective communication, provided many key insights and tools to enhance the interaction between scientists and farmers. The staff of partner NGOs (GVVS, Jodhpur; URMUL Trust, Bikaner, Nokha; and SWRC–Tilonia, Ajmer) spent much of their time introducing the breeders to their programmes and to the villages they were working in; and discussed findings and ideas from their ongoing work. The co-ordinator and breeders of AICPMIP working in Rajasthan, and their openness and willingness to experiment with changes in breeding and release procedures, were also important to the implementation of improvements in pearl millet breeding for farmers in the drier parts of Rajasthan.

4.9. Participatory approaches in potato improvement: experiences of PROINPA in Bolivia

Julio Gabriel, Rudy Torrez and Graham Thiele

Introduction

Potatoes are the most important smallholder crop in Bolivia (De Franco and Godoy, 1993). Farmers grow approximately 800 landraces, principally of *Solanum tuberosum* ssp. *andigena, S. × curtilobium, S. × juzepczukii, S. × ajanhuiri, S. phureja, S. stenotonum* and *S. goniocalyx,* in highly diverse and geographically dispersed agro-ecosystems. Landraces are estimated to cover 85 per cent of the area planted with potato. The PROINPA (Promotion and Investigation of Andean Products) Foundation, formerly part of the Bolivian national agricultural research system, is now a non-profit-making private institution recognized by the Ministry of Agriculture as having the national mandate for potato research. It holds many landraces in its germplasm bank and is exploring ways to use them better. PROINPA breeds for durable resistance to late blight (*Phytophthora infestans*), which causes large yield losses on-farm, and for other biotic and abiotic constraints. Conventional breeding programmes which seek broad adaptation could lead to the disappearance of landraces that have lower yields and are less resistant to pests and climatic stresses. Breeding programmes based on landraces and participatory plant breeding (PPB) are an alternative; they aim to incorporate resistance from other sources into the local materials.

The project described here focuses on participatory varietal selection (PVS) and PPB for resistance to late blight. Much of the on-farm selection was carried out in Cochabamba in two areas (Chulchunqani and Morochata) where late blight is endemic, at altitudes between 2900 and 3300m. Three phases are distinguished in this work: for each we describe how farmers were involved, what use was made of local genetic resources, and the achievements and difficulties. Thiele et al. (1997) provide a more detailed description of the PVS phases. Most of this chapter centres on the PPB phase, which seeks new varieties with improved yield and resistance for specific niches. Finally, future directions for this work are discussed and some general conclusions are drawn.

Participatory varietal selection, 1990–94

In the first year of PVS farmers evaluated 138 clones and controls on a researcher-managed field trial. No use was made of local genetic materials because there was no advanced locally bred material available, and existing local varieties were all susceptible to late blight; all of the clones evaluated came from outside Bolivia, from the International Potato Centre (CIP), Peru and Instituto Colombiano Agropecuario (ICA), Colombia.

Clones preferred by farmers from the first year's trial were retained for trials in the next year, together with the promising clones selected by breeders. Over the four growing seasons the number of clones evaluated reduced from 135 to 10, and farmers' role in the management of the trials progressively increased. Techniques for evaluating with farmers changed as knowledge of farmers' criteria increased and as understanding of how to involve farmers improved.

A range of different methods for evaluating clones were tested, and much was learned about farmers' criteria for selecting new varieties. Breeders assimilated the results of farmers' evaluations and paid more attention to colour, form and size of tubers when selecting germplasm.

Communication between social scientists and breeders was a crucial issue in the PVS activities. Initially, in 1990–91, not all the breeders agreed with involving farmers in selection with such a large number of clones. Subsequently there were problems with farmers' management of seed of some of the clones. These problems were exacerbated and affected the quality of collected data when the objectives of breeders and social scientists diverged and social scientists' interest shifted from evaluating materials as such, to understanding processes by which new materials diffused amongst farmers. Because of these difficulties breeders' involvement in the participatory on-farm trials progressively declined, and as a result the direct impact of PVS on varietal release was limited.

Parallel to the PVS led by social scientists, more formal non-participatory trials were run by breeders. Breeders were influenced by the PVS but made independent decisions about which clones to select, so when they released six varieties with late blight resistance these did not coincide at all with those preferred by farmers (Carrasco et al., 1997).

Participatory varietal selection, 1995–98

When social scientists and breeders had overcome their communication difficulties, they analysed and built on their earlier experiences with different evaluation techniques and different ways of involving farmers. They jointly developed a protocol for involving farmers at different stages of varietal selection, ensuring that results of farmers' evaluations could be compared across sites and over time. Social scientists still led evaluations, but on the understanding that breeders would progressively take responsibility. Following the protocol, fixed groups of around 10 farmer-evaluators were established including both men and women, who evaluate separately.

In partnership with the Investigación Participativa en Agricultura Project of the Centro Internacional de Agricultura Tropical (CIAT), Colombia, PROINPA became a centre for training in participatory methods and establishing committees of farmer-experimenters. As a result, methods promoted by the CIAT project have become standard practice for PROINPA's scientists. Individual preference ranking is the main technique used when evaluating 10–30 clones for morphological characteristics (Ashby, 1990). Clones that rank highest for morphological criteria, such as skin colour and tuber shape, are all cooked and tasted by farmers who score them using absolute evaluation. Researchers are mainly responsible for managing this material in on-farm plots. Farmers take home tubers of the clones they prefer (maybe 5–7 clones) to plant out and test performance on their own farms.

Production of planting material

Tuber seed has very low multiplication ratios compared to cereals. Involving farmers in seed production of selected materials is one way around this bottleneck. Farmers at higher altitudes – where late blight is less of a problem – can produce good quality seed of potentially resistant varieties, but are less interested in using it because they can manage the disease with their existing varieties. Farmers at lower altitudes are more interested in using resistant materials – because late blight pressure is greater there – but they lack access to suitable conditions for producing good quality, healthy seed (at lower altitudes viruses are more of a problem and affect seed quality). To get round this problem, PROINPA is working in PVS with both groups. Farmers involved at high-altitude sites are multiplying up the most promising potential varieties for sale as seed to farmers at lower altitudes. Linking PVS and seed use through the informal seed system in this fashion is helping to overcome the multiplication bottleneck (Thiele, 1999).

PROINPA breeders are aiming to develop varieties that are intermediate between native landraces and European varieties. For this purpose, native cultivars from our germplasm collection are evaluated and used in crossings, including *Qoyllus* from the species *S. stenotonum*, *S. andigenas* (such as *Sakampayas*, *Las Wilas*, *Palis*, *Palas* and *Imillas*), *S. phureja* (such as *yema de huevo*, 'egg yolk'), as well as a number of wild species such as *S. avilesii* and *S. chacoense* as sources of genetic resistance for late blight.

The protocol for involving farmers in evaluating clones is now used for all breeding work, and most scientists in PROINPA realize that farmer participation needs to be permanent and institutionalized. Discussions hinge on when farmer participation should begin and how farmers' and scientists' evaluations should be integrated. Whilst breeders and social scientists have learned to work much more closely together, this has still not been properly reflected in research reports, partly because of an institutional format which tends to separate research findings by discipline.

Participatory plant breeding, 1997–98

The PROINPA team has initiated PPB as a pilot experience. The breeders in PROINPA were encouraged to try PPB by the success of a family of farmer-breeders in releasing new potato varieties in Ecuador (Bastidas, 1991). Social scientists played a supporting role.

The aim of the PPB activity was to see whether PPB was effective and develop training methodologies so that farmers themselves could breed improved varieties with higher yield potential and resistance and adapted to specific niches, using local genetic resources. Morochata was picked as a test site because of the good relationships between farmers and PROINPA staff, a history of farmer involvement in PVS, and the presence of a committee of local farmer experimenters who were interested in taking part in PPB.

The team began by explaining to farmers as clearly as possible some fundamental genetic concepts such as variability and its manipulation. They used elements that the farmers already understood. They explained to farmers that the brothers in a family are all different, that each one has its own phenotype and genotype, which means they respond differently to different problems. The team showed farmers that plants could be divided into males and females, just as amongst people and animals. Farmers were able to distinguish the anthers (male) and stigmas (female) of the potato flower.

Farmers identified late blight and false root-knot nematode (*Nacobbus aberrans*) as the problems for which they would like new varieties. Farmers selected three varieties which could be used in a local breeding programme: *Waych'a*, a landrace (*S. andigena*), which is their main commercial variety and has excellent cooking properties; *Gendarme* (*S. andigena*) which also has good culinary quality and is resistant to the false root-knot nematode; and *Runa Toralapa (Perricholi)* which is a locally popular hybrid grown for its resistance to late blight and for its high yields.

From the breeders' perspective this was interesting material to work with. *Waych'a* has minor genes for resistance to late blight, and *Runa Toralapa* has residual resistance to late blight which derives from defeated major genes. Combining these varieties should lead to higher yield through hybrid vigour. It is possible that good resistance to late blight and nematodes could be obtained in the first generation of crosses without the need for back-crossing.

Five farmers from the committee of local farmer experimenters, who have been active in PVS and who were interested in joining us in this new experience, were given specific training in making crosses. We told farmers that Waych'a should be used as a male because its pollen is more fertile. Farmers used the caps of toothpaste tubes to collect pollen from flowers of *Waych'a* in the field. They cut the inflorescences of *Gendarme* and *Runa Toralapa*, fertilized their stigma using the pollen from *Waych'a*, and put them in plastic bottles filled with water. They labelled the crosses using cardboard labels. A month later the farmers collected the fruits and extracted the botanical seed. The seed was dried and left for a month to break dormancy, then planted in rustic wooden nursery boxes in farmers' houses. At the time of writing, seeds have germinated and will be planted out shortly.

Future perspectives

Although we have learned a lot about farmers' preferences, we have not systematized all the information. We are planning a national mapping exercise of farmers' local potato ideotypes to help target breeding work more effectively.

We hope to involve a local NGO in our PPB work. Our plan is to develop a trainers' guide that NGOs and other development institutions could use to give training courses in PPB to farmers. Our hypothesis is that increased involvement of farmers and other institutions should mean that new genetic materials can be developed at lower cost in areas where PRO-INPA does not work, perhaps due to constraints not addressed here.

Furthermore, PPB should contribute to maintaining genetic diversity in farmers' fields. Using landraces as parental material and selecting from amongst their progenies should lead to a large number of the genes they contain being maintained. It is likely that progenies selected by farmers will not be genetically uniform, which should be advantageous for the durability of resistance and for the maintenance of *in situ* diversity.

However, so far this is a pilot experience. PROINPA will continue to do conventional breeding, complemented by PVS, for durable resistance to late blight and for other constraints. We hope to document our experiences in PPB and compare costs and benefits with conventional breeding. If experience shows that PPB is advantageous, at least under some circumstances, then we shall begin to promote it more widely. Even if PPB proves not to be advantageous it will help us learn more about farmers' decision-making in varietal selection.

Lessons learned so far

We have learned that by involving farmers earlier in the selection of materials, they begin to regard them as their own and feel part of the breeding process. For PVS the best moment to involve farmers is when there are around 30 advanced clones. We have also learned that it is best to have a fixed group of farmers, including both men and women, who are involved over a number of years in the selection process.

Farmers have been fascinated by the crosses they have made in the PPB work and are keen to continue with it. We have begun to develop training materials based on the talks and training sessions with farmers.

Although there were difficulties in bringing together the work of social scientists and breeders at the start, this experience helped us to identify bottlenecks and search for better ways of integrating disciplinary experiences. Breeders are now managing participatory methods with the active and integrated participation of the social scientists.

Because of our experiences with PVS, we are generating materials which better fit farmers' needs with regard to skin colour, flesh type, tuber shape, blight resistance and culinary quality. Since 1996 most clones being evaluated have emerged from PROINPA's own breeding programme that has included local progenitors including *S. stenotonum*, *S. andigena*, *S. goniocalyx* and *S. phureja*.

PPB should be a way of making better use of germplasm collections *in situ* and maintaining more genetic diversity. Involving farmers in breeding should ensure that their specific needs are addressed, leading to more rapid deployment and uptake of resistant materials. However, we need to avoid rushing into PPB before we really understand the pros and cons. PRO-INPA, has made a large investment in conventional breeding, enriched by PVS, and we are just learning how to do PPB. Our pilot experience should help us learn which is more appropriate under which circumstances. Success will depend upon breeders, social scientists and farmers working closely together.

4.10. The collaborative development of stress-tolerant maize varieties in Rio de Janeiro, Brazil

Altair Toledo Machado

Maize breeding in Brazil

The public research organizations in Brazil initiated their breeding programmes in the 1930s with local varieties that had mostly been collected from small farmers. With the dissemination of improved materials among farmers, natural crossing between the different types of materials took place. From the crosses between indigenous and exotic, and new and old commercial varieties, and their use and maintenance by farmers in the different agro-ecosystems, a large diversity of local varieties and adaptation developed.

Between the 1960s and the 1980s, the public maize-breeding sector was always focused on seed marketing and therefore on hybrid development. The link with the commercial seed sector and with commercial agricultural production by large landowners was successful because of the access of these producers to the necessary technology package in maize. Due to the lack of a strategy to make the technology package available to small farmers who have different reasons to produce their maize (for home consumption and on-farm use), there was an estrangement of the small-farmer sector from the breeding and seed sectors. The adverse conditions of many of these farms and their lack of financial resources made the application of improved varieties and technology packages extremely inefficient and expensive.

In the 1990s rising concern for environmental sustainablility stimulated a rethinking of the strategies of agricultural development in general, and breeding in particular. Sustainable agriculture is characterized by a more holistic approach in which there is more attention for the incorporation of variables that reflect the efficiency inputs, less dependency on external inputs, more reliance on ecological mechanisms (use of mixed cropping, rotation, soil conservation, biological control, etc.). To support sustainable agricultural development and bridge the distance between maize breeding and the small farmers' community, a re-orientation of concepts and strategies is required. In order to address the needs of small farmers, centralized approaches have to be modified and will need to include participatory and

199

integrated actions, along with attention to nutrient efficiency and tolerance to biotic and abiotic stresses and other agronomic crop features.

Collection and evaluation of local maize diversity

At the end of the 1980s and beginning of the 1990s, small farmers from the south and southeast of Brazil expressed concern about the disappearance of the local maize varieties, which were being increasingly replaced by bred varieties and hybrids. These concerns stimulated the organization of a meeting involving farmers, the staff of the extension service of the Rede Projeto Tecnologias Alternativas (PTA-network), and a researcher-breeder of Empresa Brasileira de Pesquisa Agropecuaria (EMBRAPA). Thus in 1990 joint work started on the rescue of local maize materials (Cordeiro, 1993; Machado, 1998). This work involved collection, character-ization and evaluation of local maize varieties. The collection of data on climate, soil and maize performance was carried out by PTA-network. These evaluation studies allowed the identification of the main problems that affect maize productivity in farmers' fields, notably waterlogging, nu-trient deficiency and low fertility. These problems affect not only small farmers' properties, but approximately 80 per cent of maize cultivation in Brazil. Another aspect of this work is the development of new varieties, and the introduction of genes to some varieties with high productive poten-tial but with some undesirable characteristics according to farmers, such as excessive height.

The rescue of local maize varieties is important to preserve diversity as well as to study its structure, assessing the extent of genetic erosion and the potential of local varieties for immediate or future use. For this purpose the EMBRAPA maize and sorghum programme evaluated the diversity and relationship with different existent races. For EMBRAPA this collabora-tive work was a great opportunity to balance its work with the demands of civil society, and to develop new methodologies and rethink how to apply science in order to provide for small farmers.

Participatory and integrated development of new varieties in Sol da Manhã

In the early 1980s new settlements formed in the rural area around Rio de Janeiro. Many of the settlers migrated from Minas Garais where soils had degraded and agricultural production was marginal. The conditions for farming in these settlements are dominated by stress: low soil organic matter, low nitrogen and pH, high aluminium and periods of heat and drought stress alternating with waterlogging. The farmers of one of these settlements, Sol da Manhã situated in Seropédica, Rio de Janeiro State, approached the National Agrobiology Research Center of EMBRAPA (EMBRAPA Agrobiology) in 1984 for support in the identification of maize varieties that could produce under these conditions. Farmers evalu-ated 20 improved varieties and advanced populations from the

EMBRAPA regional evaluation trials in 1986; local varieties from PTA-network were included in the evaluations in the following years. The best performing materials were the populations Nitrodent (ND) and Nitroflint (NF). These two populations were developed in Piracicaba in 1976 by Ernesto Paterniani, researcher-breeder at the University of São Paulo. They were each based on 36 populations from all over Latin America, and had 28 populations in common; they differed in the other eight contributing populations. Several years of recombination and selection under a range of conditions had resulted in the populations ND and NF. Their promising performance brought about their renaming by farmers as *Sol da Manhã ND* and *Sol de Manhã NF*, respectively. To pursue increasing adaptation of these two populations, the farmers and the breeder-researcher of EMBRAPA Agrobiology decided to work together in a collaborative selection scheme.

In the following 2 years, five farmers planted NF in their fields and carried out a mass selection. In order to combine genetic progress but avoid inbreeding over time, each of the farmers planted a minimum of 3000 plants, eliminated before flowering 600 plants which were not performing satisfactorily, marked 500 good-looking plants, and selected the cobs of these plants for harvest. From these 500 cobs the farmers selected on their kitchen table the 200 most regular and healthy-looking ones. 100 grains from the middle part of each ear were used for the selection plot next season, while the other grains were partly used for the planting of normal production and stored for safety. In the second year this selection procedure was repeated in the selection plot. In the third year, selected grains of each farmer were mixed into a pool. The reason for this was to avoid a negative effect of genetic narrowing in farmers' individual selections due to strong and variable stresses. In the evaluation of the following season (1989/90), the offspring of the pooled material performed better than most of the invidual farmers' selections. In the 1990/91 season, a half-sib selection was made from the pooled NF material in the EMBRAPA experimental station, which was evaluated in 1991/92 in the field of the farmers of Sol de Manhã and in EMBRAPA. After a recombination and a full-sib selection in 1992/93, the material was evaluated in 1993/94, again in farmers' fields and in the EMBRAPA station. In this phase, 60 of the 200 families were selected. With these 60 families an intensive research and testing programme was carried out to investigate the relation between low NO_3^- and NH_4^+ tolerance, and the activity of particular enzymes in the plants. The work also included root system evaluation (Machado, 1997). This research identified 20 families which had potential for tolerance to both low NO_3 and low NH_4, the two forms in which nitrogen is available to the plant (which form is most available depends on the intensity of the stress). With the 20 selected families, recombination and generation of S_1 families was carried out, followed again by evaluation and mass selection in farmers' fields and evaluation in the EMBRAPA station. In 1996 the result of this selection was evaluated in farmers' fields, and in 1997 seed was also mulitiplied by the EMBRAPA maize programme to produce basic seed.

The variety *Sol de Manhã NF* was officially released in 1998, after it had been settled in court that the variety would be registered in the public

201

domain – it was recognized that farmers' participation in the development of the material had been essential and did not allow for exclusive plant breeder rights or patenting by any individual organization. The good performance of the variety, including the fact that it is an open pollinating variety – meaning that the farmer is not forced to buy new seed for each planting – had captured the attention of the media. The 20 000 requests for seed which arrived at EMBRAPA clearly show the need for such adapted non-hybrid varieties. At present the EMBRAPA maize programme multiplies the basic seed and sells this to national seed companies who commercialize it. Since the Brazilian law allows for moderate royalties on materials registered in the public domain, it is now proposed that a 5 per cent charge on the seed of Sol da Manhã will be shared equally between the EMBRAPA maize programme, which multiplies the seed, and EMBRAPA Agrobiology and the farming community at Sol da Manhã who jointly developed the variety.

At present, EMBRAPA is developing the *Sol da Manhã ND* population with a similar process of selection and research for low-phosphorus conditions and potential for mycorrhizal phosphorus absorption, in combination with low nitrogen. The farmers in Sol da Manh continue with the maintenance and development of their own selection of their NF and ND varieties, still with some collaboration of the EMBRAPA breeder, but largely organizing and realizing the work on their own initiative. Since the maize work was effectively integrated with soil improvement, the stress to which the maize is subjected has been reduced and also benefits maize production.

The success of the work has also had an important impact on the activities of the PTA maize network in other communities and other parts of Brazil. While collection, evaluation and characterization continue in regional and national programmes of PTA, mass selection and crossing work to enhance the local varieties and develop improved non-hybrid varieties has been carried out since 1992 with approximately 30 of the best performing varieties to make available seed of improved, adapted, non-hybrid varieties for small farmers (Silva and Santos, 1998).

There are few activities in Brazil where public institutions work in partnership with the small farmer and the agricultural community. Such collaboration is essential for sustainable use and conservation of the agricultural genetic resources. In spite of recognition of the importance of these types of partnership, there is still great resistance against this kind of collaboration. The strong relationship between the public and private sector aiming at the development of products for the agribusiness market, the relationship of biotechnology and the regulation of breeders' rights and patent laws pose serious limitations for the development of collaborative relationships which have entirely different markets and objectives.

4.11. Participatory varietal selection and genetic diversity in high-potential rice areas in Nepal and India

John Witcombe, Krishna D. Joshi, Ram B. Rana and Daljit S. Virk

Introduction

In the developing world, most high-potential production systems are intensively cultivated irrigated areas. If the world is to feed its ever-increasing population then production from these systems will have to increase. One possible constraint is the high genetic uniformity of the crops grown in them. Lack of diversity is reported for high-potential rice and wheat production systems in Nepal and India (Witcombe, 1999). In this chapter we examine existing genetic diversity in high-potential rice systems in India and Nepal and review recent experimental evidence on how production, value of production and stability of production can be increased by increasing biodiversity.

Low biodiversity in irrigated *Chaite* rice systems in Nepal

Surveys of farmers growing February-sown (*Chaite*) rice showed low rice biodiversity in high-potential areas with irrigation in Nepal. The surveys were made in 1997 in nine villages of Chitwan and Nawalparasi districts. All households in these villages were interviewed and it was found that 657 households in the nine villages grew this crop. Each household told which varieties they grew (Figure 4.2).

Only a few varieties are grown, and rice biodiversity is very low. However, to put a quantitative value on the extent of diversity requires the coefficient of parentage of the varieties to be determined and weighted according to the proportion of the total area occupied by each of them. Witcombe et al. (1999) describe in detail how a weighted diversity can be estimated. Using coefficients of parentage determined by Dr G. McClaren of IRRI, the weighted diversity was 0.06 in East Chitwan, 0.02 in West Chitwan and 0.08 in Nawalparasi. In this example, where CH 45 predominates greatly in all three clusters, the diversity changes little when all the three regions are treated as one area (weighted diversity = 0.04).

Another aspect of diversity is its variation over time (temporal diversity). Chaite 4 was released in 1987 and CH 45 and Bagari are at least 35 years old. They have been grown consistently in the area over many years, indicating a low temporal diversity.

Biodiversity in relation to wealth status in India

Surveys on diversity for main (*kharif*)-season rice showed that in high-potential areas the wealth status of the farmer can be a factor which

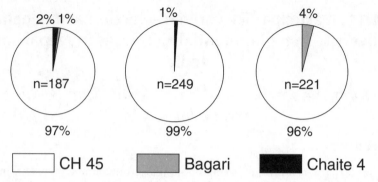

| CH 45 | Bagari | Chaite 4 |

Figure 4.2: *Proportion of area covered by different* Chaite *rice varieties, from a survey conducted in March 1997*

influences the rice diversity planted. The surveys were made in 1997 in three villages of Lunawada subdistrict, Gujarat-Kothamba, Thanasavli and Ladvel. It is a high-potential area as over 80 per cent of it is irrigated throughout the year by canal, tube wells and ponds. The average yield of rice is about 4t/ha. In each village farmers were classified into three wealth categories: upper, medium and lower, and in each village 20 farmers per category were interviewed.

Only a few old cultivars were grown in all wealth categories (Figure 4.3). The lower-category farmers grew fewer varieties and the highest proportion of GR11, the most widely grown variety overall. A hybrid (P6201) from the private sector was mostly grown by upper and medium wealth category farmers. Farmers of the lower wealth category also planted it, but possibly grew advanced generations of it.

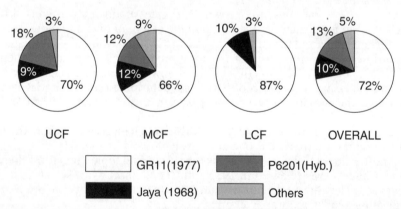

| GR11(1977) | P6201(Hyb.) |
| Jaya (1968) | Others |

Figure 4.3: *Proportion of area covered by* kharif *season rice varieties in three villages (Kothamba, Thanasavli and Ladvel) of Lunawada in 1997. UCF, upper; MCF, medium; and LCF, lower wealth category farmers. GR11 released in 1997; Jaya in 1968. Other varieties include IR8 (1966), IR36 (1981), Mahsuri (1971), Kasturi (1989) and GR4 (1981).*

The coefficients of parentage were calculated as described for *Chaite* rice in Nepal. They are approximates as the pedigrees have not been traced back for many generations, and those of the private-sector hybrids are not revealed (Witcombe et al., 1999). The weighted diversity over the three wealth classes and villages was 0.41.

Why is there low biodiversity, and can it be increased?

Low genetic diversity in crop varieties results from a policy of promoting only a few widely adapted recommended varieties. This is regarded as the most appropriate strategy because it is assumed that high-potential production systems are uniform.

However, high-potential areas are much more diverse than generally assumed, both physically and socio-economically, as illustrated for instance by the differences between wealth classes in Lunawada. Biodiversity can be increased in such high-potential production systems if, amongst existing cultivars, there are several that are superior to those currently grown and that can occupy niches within these systems. Nonetheless, any increase in biodiversity is dependent on a low degree of relatedness between the new cultivars and those that they partially replace.

This hypothesis was tested in Nepal and India using participatory varietal selection (PVS). Methods employed were the same as those described by Joshi and Witcombe (1996, 1998).

PVS in high-potential areas in Nepal and India

Six new varieties, none of which is officially recommended by the extension services, were offered to farmers in the survey area in Nepal. Data on yield were measured (Figure 4.4). Apart from yield, farmers' perceptions were recorded for many other traits, including plant height and crop duration. Kalinga III and NDR97 were preferred by farmers because they matured before the onset of the monsoon (i.e. before the second week of June), and all harvesting operations can be done during the dry season to produce a better quality grain. Although all four most preferred varieties were perceived to be shorter or about the same height as the local varieties, the shortness was never sufficient for farmers to reject the variety. Initial data show that Kalinga III and NDR97 are spreading through farmer-to-farmer exchange (Witcombe et al., 1999) Kalinga III appears to occupy a niche in the farming system areas where irrigation water is expensive, limited or unreliable.

In the survey area in India, 10 new cultivars were given to farmers, one variety per participating farmer. Participatory evaluation was done through farm walks and focus group discussions. Yield was measured in the trials from areas measured by project staff and total harvested yield measured by farmers (Witcombe et al., 1999). Earliness is a trait also much appreciated by farmers in this area, as it permits a more timely sowing of the following crop, usually wheat. Farmers are adopting all the three Pusa varieties. In all the new varieties farmers found that disease and insect pests were less than in GR11, emphasizing the benefits of temporal diversity.

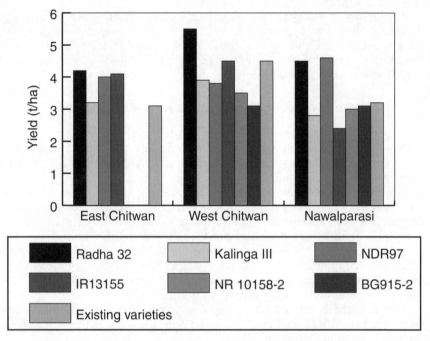

Figure 4.4: *Grain yield of six* Chaite *rice varieties across three clusters in comparison to existing varieties, Chitwan and Nawalparasi, Nepal, 1997*

Impact of participatory varietal selection (PVS) on biodiversity

Initially there were three varieties in East Chitwan and two in West Chitwan, Nepal, but after the PVS programme this increased to six and seven. In Nawalparasi the number of varieties increased from two to six. It is not yet possible to measure the impact of PVS on biodiversity by calculating weighted diversities before and after PVS. This is because the areas planted with the new varieties are not precisely known, and because the situation changes quickly from season to season. It is, however, interesting to make a preliminary estimate of the impact of Kalinga III. For example, if we assume that Kalinga III occupies 10 per cent of the area and largely replaces CH 45, then the overall coefficient of diversity greatly increases, from 0.06 to 0.22 (Table 4.4). Even if a 5 per cent adoption of Kalinga III is assumed, the diversity still increases to 0.13 per cent. The impact would not be as significant where the new and old varieties are genetically related. In Lunawada, for example, the new variety Pusa 44 has a coefficient of parentage of 0.25 with the existing variety GR11. This emphasizes the need to obtain new varieties from diverse sources, and in a second year of PVS such varieties have been added.

Table 4.4: Weighted coefficient of diversity in *Chaite* rice when taken across the three clusters and accounting for the introduction of Kalinga III (KIII)

W*	CH45 W = 0.88	Bagari W = 0.01	Chaite 4 W = 0.01	KIII W = 0.1
CH45 W = 0.88	1 × 0.77	0	0	0
Bagari W = 0.01	0	1 × 0.0001	0	0
Chaite 4 W = 0.01	0	0	1 × 0.0001	0.06 × 0.001†
KIII W = 0.1	0	0	0.06 × 0.001†	1 × 0.01

Weighted diversity = 1 −sum of cells in matrix = 1 −0.78 = 0.22.
* W = weight and equals the proportion of area occupied by the cultivar.
† Coefficient of parentage (COP): KIII and *Chaite* 4 have a COP of 0.06 (COP theoretically varies between 0 and 1; relatedness of cultivars to themselves is 1, other varieties are not related).

Conclusions

Participatory varietal selection has been at least as successful in these high-potential production systems in Nepal and India as when it is applied in marginal areas. This is because the recommendation domains of varieties for high-potential production systems are just as poorly defined by multi-locational trials as those for marginal areas. Varieties are recommended for too small an area, as evidenced by the adoption of cultivars introduced from outside the area. Any assumption that high-potential production systems are uniform is clearly incorrect because these systems proved far too diverse to be adequately served by a few widely adapted varieties.

The favourable impact on biodiversity at these initial stages of adoption is clear as the most widely grown variety loses its predominance. However, is this a transient phenomenon? There is convincing evidence that this will not be the case. For example, Kalinga III has clear niches that it will occupy, but it will never dominate. It will be grown where water is constrained in some ways. It will never occupy niches such as highly fertile, well irrigated fields. In the same way, NDR97 is liked for its earliness and for fertile, well irrigated conditions, but will not be adopted by farmers who wish to maximize yield with a longer-duration cultivar. In India, MTU 7029 is a niche variety for waterlogged conditions, and the grain quality of Pusa 834 and Pusa 33 is better than GR11. Farmers may choose to grow higher quality rice even if this quality is not always reflected in the market price.

An increase in overall production should result from the adoption of varieties for niches, as each niche becomes occupied by the variety best suited to it. An improved stability of production is also to be expected as an increased number of varieties are adopted that are better adapted to the diverse needs of the farming system. In the Nepal study, the quality of production may also have increased, as the earlier varieties will be less affected by rain at harvest time. In Lunawada, a greater diversity is now available in terms of grain quality. Market forces will determine the extent to which this diversity is maintained.

In both studies the farmers remarked on the reduction in pests and diseases. This is probably a function of temporal diversity as new varieties present a novel target to pests and diseases which have yet to adapt to the new hosts. However, overall vulnerability to pests and diseases should be reduced when a patchwork of genetically unrelated varieties is deployed.

The power of PVS has been demonstrated in marginal areas where it can have a big impact on the livelihoods of the rural poor. One of the major impacts of these methods in high-potential production systems will be on food security. The creation of new biodiversity by participatory plant breeding that has been successfully used for difficult environments (Sthapit et al., 1996) is another powerful method that can be employed in high-potential production systems. Along with biotechnology, we believe participatory approaches to crop improvement offer one of the greatest hopes of reliably feeding the world's ever-growing population.

Acknowledgement

This chapter is an output from project R6748 by the Natural Resources Systems Programme and the Plant Sciences Research Programme of the UK Department For International Development for the benefit of developing countries. The views expressed are not necessarily those of the DFID.

4.12. Scaling-up in participatory plant breeding

Margaret Smith and Eva Weltzien

Introduction

Efforts in participatory plant breeding (PPB) initiated by scientists have been motivated in most cases by the scientists' desire to bring the knowledge of genetics and experimental methods to bear on the problems faced by resource-poor farmers. These farmers often have not benefited from the 'improved varieties' developed through traditional plant breeding programmes. Deeper involvement of farmers in the formal plant breeding effort through PPB should improve the products' relevance and utility to those farmers, and also result in more diverse breeding products. In addition, it provides farmers with more influential roles in directing breeding programmes, altering the relationship of farmers and scientists. Thus PPB helps farmers to reap the benefits of genetics knowledge, and gain access to a broad range of germplasm and experimental methodology, without losing the essential aspects of genetic resource management that allow their farming systems to function effectively.

In this chapter, for the sake of simplicity we use the term 'scientist' to refer to plant breeders with formal scientific training, and 'farmer' to refer to agricultural producers who are also plant breeders, fully realizing that both carry out plant breeding and neither has a monopoly on the capacity to do research.

The scaling up of products and processes

Most experience to date with PPB has been on a small, local scale. For this approach really to benefit large numbers of farmers and scientists, however, scaling-up will be essential. One dilemma that is central to the challenge of scaling-up in PPB is that the improvement resulting from plant breeding is proportional to resources (primarily time and labour) invested in the breeding effort. For a 'traditional' centralized plant-breeding programme, a few scientists invest all of their time and that of various hired labourers, as well as considerable financial resources in developing varieties that will serve a broad target audience. The large potential area of use of these varieties justifies the resource investment (Duvick, 1996; Troyer, 1996). This traditional, centralized breeding approach has been very successful in cases where the environment is managed to make it relatively uniform over a large area, thus providing a large potential target area for individual varieties and justifying high resource investment per variety.

Participatory plant breeding approaches benefit from additional resources (relative to the traditional approach described above) in the form of farmers' time and labour. Furthermore, successful participatory breeding programmes will reduce resource waste resulting from the development of varieties that are never used, by establishing more appropriate breeding objectives, and by better targeting the varieties developed. For PPB the challenge of scaling-up will involve making efficient use of both farmers' and scientists' resources for variety development, testing and diffusion. Accomplishing this will require clearly defined roles and efficient forms of interaction between farmers and scientists. If this can be achieved, farmers' and breeders' combined resources should suffice to allow even those PPB efforts that target small, locally variable and continually evolving environments to achieve significant genetic improvement.

Scaling-up in PPB will ultimately involve both products and processes. The products that need to be scaled up include varieties developed, germplasm as a raw material for genetic improvement, and knowledge of genetics and experimental methods. The processes include the breeding methods and collaborative models by which breeding itself is done – in other words, the breeding programme. Although we touch on both products and programmes in the following discussion, the more difficult challenge will be to scale up PPB programmes themselves.

Scaling up PVS products

The vast majority of projects described as PPB are really participatory varietal selection (PVS) in Witcombe's terminology (Witcombe and Joshi, 1996a, b), where farmers are directly involved in evaluating the varieties produced by a breeding programme. Some PVS projects have been significantly scaled up, such as the variety evaluation projects organized by LI-BIRD in Nepal (Joshi et al., 1996). In one such project, over 1800 farmers received new rice varieties to evaluate. There may be significant benefits from making germplasm more broadly available so that farmers can evaluate it and make their own choices about its usefulness. The challenges to scaling-up PVS are largely logistical – how to produce and distribute seed efficiently and share knowledge about methods for comparing varieties. Harnessing the resources of national seed services and of governmental extension services, non-governmental agencies, and others involved in extension-type roles can help provide the resources needed for this logistical support. (It is worth noting that, in general, the resources devoted to PPB need not all come from scientists and farmers, as the preceding statement illustrates.)

Scaling up PPB products: germplasm and knowledge-sharing

Scaling-up evaluation of PPB varietal products could be done using these same approaches. Starting with local germplasm and finishing with genetically variable products are ways that scientists can increase the likelihood that varieties developed through PPB will be broadly useful. Local germplasm that is itself the product of farmers' management is likely to be buffered against a certain range of environmental variation. Furthermore, it is very likely to possess the traits that farmers regard as essential, thus providing a broadly acceptable starting point for breeding improvements. Emphasizing genetically variable products (multi-lines or mixtures rather than pure lines, open-pollinated varieties or synthetics rather than hybrids) increases the likelihood that products will be useful to farmers where environments or needs vary somewhat from those of the selection environment. The genetic variation inherent in such products allows individual farmer-users to tailor these varieties to their particular circumstances. A challenge to scaling-up use of the varietal products of PPB will be developing ways to respect farmers' and/or communities' intellectual property rights in their germplasm before it is widely distributed.

A second product involved in PPB that would be relatively amenable to scaling-up is germplasm as a raw material. Introduction, evaluation and intercrossing with new germplasm are inherent in farmers' approaches to genetic resource management. Mexican maize farmers knowingly allow crossing between their traditional varieties and introduced genetic materials, and frequently obtain new seed of both traditional and non-traditional varieties to incorporate into their genetic resource base (Louette, 1997; Rice et al., 1998). Scientists have ready access to a much broader range of germplasm than is accessible to most farmers, as well as having the means to evaluate that germplasm for important performance characteristics in a range of environments. Supporting farmers' interests by doing relevant evaluations and providing access to new germplasm is one way that farmers and scientists can jointly participate in plant breeding on a broad scale. Broadening this aspect of PPB will also be complicated by intellectual property rights issues revolving around germplasm access and exchange.

A third product involved in PPB that is readily amenable to scaling-up is knowledge – that of farmers and of scientists. A participatory maize-breeding effort in Honduras has included workshops where farmers and scientists exchange information (Smith and Gómez, 1996). During these workshops, scientists learn more about farmers' varietal needs and priorities, and farmers learn more about scientists' techniques for manipulating plant genetics. Other examples of knowledge sharing involve meetings among farmers and scientists in local agricultural research committees where results and implications of locally designed research are shared and discussed (Ospina et al., 1997). Such knowledge sharing can improve the scientists' focus on problems relevant to farmers, and can improve farmers' ability to place demands on the research system and to use available genetic resources and methods more effectively to carry out their own genetic resource management activities. Such knowledge-sharing activities can be scaled up by holding them in multiple communities. Working through existing farmers' organizations can increase the scale of this activity further.

Scaling up the process of collaboration

Scaling-up the process of plant breeding – actual PPB programmes – will be more difficult than scaling-up use of products. It is the nature of PPB, which relies on close farmer–scientist interaction in developing new varieties, for an actual breeding project to be quite local in scope. However, scientists working in locally variable regions can effectively scale up their efforts by building their programmes around decentralized breeding. A scientist could design her/his plant breeding effort to comprise several small participatory breeding projects in distinct environments. Such a programme would have the potential to develop varieties of use across a range of environments similar to those in which the projects are being conducted. The products of this scientist's work should then be of use beyond the immediate local areas where selection was done. Investment of time and labour from both the scientist and the collaborating farmers could result in greater output (greater improvement, more and/or more diverse products) from this type of breeding programme than might be expected from the same scientist managing a traditional, centralized breeding effort without farmer inputs.

Another model that could effectively scale up the breeding process is to turn the process over to farmers at an earlier stage than that at which a traditional breeding programme would move materials to on-farm testing. For example, early generation populations could be screened by scientists on-station for key traits that are not likely to be evident to farmers. Collaborating farmers could then select from among the remaining families those they believe are worth evaluating further on their own farms. From this point on, farmers would carry out the breeding process. This approach, which was used by Sperling and colleagues for beans in Rwanda (Sperling, 1996), seems more readily adaptable to naturally self-pollinated crops than to cross-pollinated crops. With self-pollinated species, continued inbreeding will lead to emergence of stable homozygous genotypes among which farmers can select as strongly as they choose. For cross-pollinated species, on the other hand, continued genetic recombination makes it less clear that significant progress can be made through purely farmer-managed selection. For the self-pollinated species, however, this approach allows a single scientist at a single research station to work with a very broad range of farmers in developing numerous products adapted to a potentially wide range of environments.

Scaling-up the process of PPB can also be accomplished by choosing collaborating farmers who can function as representatives of communities or farmer groups. Sperling (1996) combined this approach with that discussed above in her work on beans in Rwanda. Communities located in close proximity had different varietal preferences, re-emphasizing the role that PPB can play in addressing local varietal needs rather than seeking broad adaptation. Critical to the success of this technique is to identify appropriate local organizations and farmer representatives who will truly serve the needs of the groups they represent, while also being effective research partners. If strong local organizations exist, this seems an excellent way to ensure that PPB programmes reach beyond the individual collaborating farmers. Involving representatives of farmer groups should work equally well regardless of whether the breeding is done on-station and then shifted completely to farmers, as in Sperling's Rwanda work, or whether it is done simultaneously and jointly by scientists and farmers. In either case, effective farmer representatives can gather broad input to aid selection during breeding and ensure broad evaluation at desired points in the process.

Scaling up PPB and seed availability

Seed availability is an aspect of the breeding process that is usually addressed directly as an inherent part of the interaction with farmers in PPB projects. This is in contrast to the situation for traditional breeding programmes, where seed production and distribution are typically controlled by organizations that are not part of the breeding process and may be completely unconnected with breeders. Thus scaling-up of seed distribution may already exist in PPB projects, while it has often not been addressed at all in traditional breeding programmes. The upland rice variety Kalinga III (Witcombe and Joshi, 1996a,b), selected through a participatory variety selection project in six villages in India, provides an example where the variety has spread beyond the communities that initially tested it. This spread was facilitated through local institutions such as village-level 'news people' whose role was revived to include expertise on crop varieties. However, the spread of this variety is still within a relatively local region in India. National seed systems should have the capacity to provide much broader access to varieties, but this is not always the case. Where the national seed system is limited in its capacity or not well connected to breeders, PPB has an advantage over traditional breeding in scaling-up seed availability, simply by virtue of its direct connections with farmers.

A dilemma in scaling up PPB?

Finally, it must be recognized that although this discussion has focused on scaling-up and developing broadly usable products, the notions of 'scaling-up' and 'broad' adaptation are relative ones. Part of the reason that resource-poor farmers have typically not benefited from the 'improved varieties' developed through traditional plant breeding programmes is that these varieties have been developed through centralized breeding programmes that sacrificed local adaptation for very broad adaptation (Ceccarelli, 1989). This brings us back to the dilemma inherent in scaling-up PPB. If too broad a target area is the focus of a participatory breeding effort, scientists risk repeating this same pattern, with the primary difference being that farmers' time and labour has been contributed in addition to that of (better paid) scientists. Scaling-up in PPB will unavoidably be on a less 'broad' scale than is the case for the largest-scale traditional plant breeding programmes. Releasing genetically variable varieties for numerous, fairly focused target areas is probably essential to having an impact from PPB that goes beyond the participating farmers and their immediate neighbours. As noted above, this will involve complications related to farmers' intellectual property rights and national variety release policy in many cases. Careful forethought will be necessary and policy changes may be required to avoid problems in these areas.

Synthesis: Towards integrated plant breeding

Gary Atlin, Trygve Berg and Conny Almekinders

Forging partnerships between farmers and breeders

Effective breeding programmes have a clear focus on the needs of farmers and consumers. The papers in this section reveal participatory plant breeding (PPB) to be, above all else, a philosophy for ensuring that the needs of farmers and consumers are given primacy in the breeding process. This is particularly important in public-sector breeding programmes in developing countries, where professional plant breeders and programme administrators may be physically and socially remote from their clients. In developed countries (Smith, Chapter 4.5) and in the commercial sector in developing countries (van der Werff and van Donk, Chapter 4.4), market mechanisms ensure that commercial breeding programmes succeed or fail on the basis of how well they serve farmers. This finely tuned client orientation explains the success of the commercial seed sector in general. However, the scope for commercial enterprise involvement in most principal food crops in developing countries is still limited. Large breeding enterprises are not interested in small-scale farmers who are difficult to reach and have a very diverse and variable demand for seeds.

Currently only the public sector can address the needs of most farmers in developing countries. But although formal public-sector breeding programmes may be extremely effective in their ability to obtain a broad range of germplasm, create genetic variability, and separate genetic from environmental effects, they sometimes have difficulty in defining goals that result in useful end products. In the absence of market mechanisms, public-sector breeding goals have been set by scientist-breeders, who may have a limited understanding of the needs, values, culture and circumstances of the poorest of their clients (Song, Chapter 4.2). This has often resulted in the development of unsuitable varieties that were not adopted by farmers. For example, Song and Machado (Chapters 4.2 and 4.10) describe public-sector national maize-breeding programmes in China and Brazil, respectively, that had a near-exclusive focus on hybrid cultivar development for the commercial sector, but that did not attempt to address the needs of poor farmers faced with severe environmental and financial constraints. Song describes the efforts made by women farmers in the southwestern Chinese village of Wenteng to maintain and improve, without support of the formal sector, their stock of the introduced open-pollinated maize cultivar Tuxpeño I, a CIMMYT variety they valued for its stress tolerance and lodging resistance. She notes of the farmers that 'If they could have had help from scientists and more institutional support from the formal sector, they would have had greater impact . . .'

Participatory plant breeding and participatory varietal selection: models for institutionalizing farmer participation

PPB and PVS offer models for the provision of that support, and a framework for institutionalizing farmers' participation in the framing of objectives. Machado describes a participatory maize-breeding programme whose objectives were both to conserve local maize germplasm and to develop improved varieties in collaboration with farmers constrained by infertile soils and drought stress. In an intensive collaboration between farmers of the community Sol da Manhã and EMBRAPA scientists lasting 8 years, with selection both at the research station and in the community, stress-tolerant and highly productive cultivars were developed. Sthapit and

Subedi (Chapter 4.7) describe several cases wherein sets of rice lines, some selected by breeders from local landraces, were released for on-farm evaluation to hundreds of households in Nepal. A cold-tolerant genotype disseminated in this manner has been widely adopted. The common elements of these cases are the close collaboration between farmers and breeders in setting objectives and conducting evaluation. This collaboration can help ensure that farmers have access to useful germplasm that is adapted to their circumstances and that meets the quality requirements of the community.

The potential benefits of the farmer–breeder collaboration are difficult to overemphasize. In the PPB and PVS cases discussed in this section, farmers set goals and provide testing environments. They may also mass-select or rate cultivars. Breeders assemble germplasm, generate variable populations, inoculate with diseases and insects, and summarize information about genotype performance. Because of their familiarity with other regions and cropping systems, they may also bring new and useful traits to the attention of farmers.

Even when farmer input is solicited, it is important to ask 'Which farmers?'. Varietal mixtures in some crops are extremely complex, with diversity having a functional value for farmers (Weltzien, Chapter 4.8). Different farmers may have different requirements.

Participatory plant breeding and the conservation of crop genetic diversity

Seed systems, breeding programmes and public policy have complex effects on the genetic diversity deployed in farmers' fields. In the North, breeders' nurseries serve as the main repository of genetic diversity (Smith, Chapter 4.5). Market requirements, government policies and lack of intellectual property protection may greatly constrain the deployment of this genetic diversity in commercial cropping systems (Atlin, Chapter 4.3). Variety release policies and regulations can also constrain the availability of cultivars in the South. Witcombe et al. (Chapter 4.11) demonstrate that several rice-production niches in both productive and marginal areas in Nepal and India were not being served by restrictive release policies that favoured the dissemination of a few widely adapted cultivars. When given the opportunity to observe cultivars on their own farms through PVS programmes, farmers adopted cultivars for specific niches not targeted by formal-sector programmes. This increased the rice genetic diversity deployed on-farm in this region.

In the South, centralized breeding programmes have the potential to introduce valuable new cultivars into a region, but may lack knowledge about the desirable attributes of indigenous cultivars. Too often in the past such programmes have served as a one-way conduit, pouring exotic materials into a region. Increasingly, however, the CGIAR and national programmes are attempting to introgress useful genetic material into local germplasm, The back-crossing and selection needed to integrate desirable genes from exotic sources into local material require a long-term commitment of the breeder and public funding. Furthermore, fully to exploit the possibilities of blending local adaptation with valuable exotic characteristics, part of the selection and testing is best carried out under farmers' conditions. As Ngugi and Mugo (Chapter 4.1) point out, this is may not be as simple as it seems: it requires substantial financial resources and human capacity to accomplish the change. However, it is clear from several cases in this section that specialized commercial and public breeding have mobilized diverse genetic resources and introduced foreign genes into agricultural systems (Chapters 4.1, 4.4, 4.5). After introduction, farmers maintain and integrate these genes in the cultivated gene pool. New exotic genes may be added to the local gene pool in the form of new varieties which originate from other parts of the world, or of varieties that have been developed from a cross between local and exotic material.

The impact of successful PPB on conservation of local germplasm is hard to predict. All crop improvement involves selection of the better genotypes, and thus may result in reduction of genetic diversity within populations and the total or partial replacement of entire populations. Essentially, this effect will not change when more local germplasm is used. Cases exist where varieties introduced through PVS or PPB programmes have swept through large areas, at least partly supplanting local landraces (Sthapit and Subedi, Chapter 4.7). However, by incorporating farmers and their expertise about local varieties into the heart of the process, it seems likely that PPB will prove to be an effective brake on their loss.

Conclusions

Although the cases presented here differ in terms of culture, economic context and agricultural system, a common feature is discernible. Everywhere there are local communities with groups of farmers who are interested in exploring the collaboration with breeders for crop improvement. In some cases farmers are involved in selection of breeding lines (maize breeding in Brazil, Chapter 4.10; miscellaneous crops in Kenya, Chapter 4.1). But there are also examples of experimental involvement of farmers in the selection of parent materials and cross-breeding (potato in Bolivia, Gabriel et al., Chapter 4.9). Farmers are willing to share their knowledge and skills without restrictions. In some communities, seed-related knowledge and responsibilities are highly gender-specific. This emerges clearly in the case described by Weltzien dealing with pearl millet in Rajasthan, India, and by Song's study on local maize development. Farmers are also open to learn from partners from the scientific sector. Farmer involvement sometimes leads to teaching of biological concepts, such as reproduction biology, which may be experienced as a special pedagogical challenge (potato breeding in Bolivia, Chapter 4.9; Bertuso et al., Chapter 3.3)

By local testing using PVS, farmers can be exposed to and select from the whole range of released varieties. This usually results in adoption of more varieties and better matching of variety and local growing conditions, and is a potential tool in enhancing variety diversity in farmers' fields

(Sthapit and Subedi, Chapter 4.7 and Witcombe et al., Chapter 4.11). In-creased farmer involvement, sometimes emphasizing women's involve-ment, may be seen as a positive social output.

The cases of applied PPB described in this section are, to some extent, experimental. Both the social-institutional components (i.e. the participatory methods) and the technical components (i.e. the breeding technology) are subject to research. One aspect being explored is the opportunities offered by decentralization, i.e. selection in the target areas under farmers' conditions and management. Some breeders have expressed reservations about decentralization, arguing that farmers cannot handle the more complex selection schemes that are necessary to obtain the required genetic progress in high-variation and high-stress environments. Replicated, multi-location trials are the tools responsible for most of the genetic gains made by highly successful centralized breeding programmes. One of the most important research tasks for breeders in the development of PPB methodology will be to adapt this technology so that it can be decentralized and moved on to farms in developing countries.

Public breeding in developing countries is faced with complex objectives and serious limitations in available resources; relatively few breeders have to cover a wide variety of agro-ecological conditions, crops and types of farmers and needs. PPB and PVS offer models for integrating farmers into the breeding and variety dissemination process. This can improve the products of public breeding effort, multiply its reach, and potentially conserve local germplasm in use.

217

DIVERSITY, LOCAL AND FORMAL SEED SUPPLY

Introduction

Farmers have been relying on their own seeds since they began cultivating crops. Although formal seed-supply systems have been established since the 1950s in most developing countries the majority of farmers are still reproducing their own seed. Formal seed programmes have been designed and installed in order to improve the quality of seeds and planting materials and to diffuse improved and modern varieties to farmers. Since the 1950s a formal seed-supply sector has been established in most developing countries. The practices and functioning of farmers' and formal seed systems are quite distinct, and the two systems are poorly linked. It is widely recognized that the formal seed sector has not been successful in providing quality seed to farmers situated in agro-ecologically and socio-economically less-endowed regions. This section reflects on the functioning of local seed systems and their links with the formal seed supply. Efforts to improve seed supply to farmers by both formal and NGO sectors are presented. These experiences are strongly related to the conservation and utilization of crop genetic diversity.

For most farmers, on-farm seed production is a practice that is fully integrated in crop production. It represents a dynamic and complex system of seed supply, shaped by farmers' practices of seed handling, selection and exchange. This is the system described as the plant genetic resource system (see Figure 1, Introduction) but seen from the perspective of seed supply. Many local seed-supply systems harbour high levels of crop and varietal diversity. Examples of such local systems are described in this book, e.g. for sweet potato in Irian Jaya (Prain et al., Chapter 2.3), potato in the Andes (Sánchez and Cosío, Chapter 5.5) and cereals in Ethiopia (McGuire, Chapter 2.1 and Teekens, Chapter 5.6). Almekinders and Louette (Chapter 5.1) provide examples from Mesoamerica of such systems and farmers' ways of innovating them.

The formal seed sector is relatively young; it developed from specialized farmers' seed production at the beginning of the twentieth century in North America and Western Europe into commercial and public specialized organizations. In developing countries, public seed-production agencies have existed for only a few decades. These public seed agencies have been instrumental in generating the Green Revolution and improving seed supply in high-potential areas. For many reasons these agencies have not been successful in addressing the need for seeds and planting material of farmers in complex, diverse and risk-prone areas situated in the rest of the developing world. Cromwell and Almekinders (Chapter 5.2) elaborate on this role of the formal system: they discuss the dispute that has emerged over the impact of formal seed-sector activities and farmers' use of diversity. They explain that opinions on this point depend very much on the applied perspective. Richards (Chapter 5.3) shows how, in addition to formal seed agencies, relief interventions have a dramatic impact on farmers' options to employ genetic diversity, and reports a study that was carried out by local researchers in war-stricken regions of Sierra Leone.

Although seed produced on-farm is still preferred by many farmers as the source of next season's crop, some contributions in the present section argue that these local systems do not always provide seeds of the desired quality. Almekinders and Louette (Chapter 5.1) and Cromwell and Almekinders (Chapter 5.2) provide evidence that, in many cases, farmers lack sources of or access to new genetic diversity. Experiences of plant breeders becoming involved in participatory plant breeding also relate to this limitation (Chapters 4.8, 4.11 and 5.4).

Some authors of chapters in this section recognize that formal seed-sector interventions have not produced the desired outputs, and present other approaches, building upon local seed systems. Scheidegger and Prain (Chapter 5.4) report on the experiences of the Peruvian potato programme to improve the quality of potato tuber seed by taking local seed practices and exchange mechanisms into account. Sánchez and Cosío (Chapter 5.5) describe the seed system of native potato varieties in the Peruvian Andes. They consider ways to support the functioning of this system, aiming to increase farmers' seed security and augment access to preferred potato varieties. They argue that such interventions contribute to the maintenance of *in situ* conservation. Teekens (Chapter 5.6) documents the community seed banks in Tigray, Ethiopia. These seed banks were set up in a period of droughts and great political and social turmoil. They are based on traditional practices of seed selection and back-up saving of seeds, and aimed to strengthen the farmers' and community's capacity to maintain preferred varieties. Admasu and Struik (Chapter 5.7) address the propagation of local and modern enset varieties in Ethiopia, arguing that research can play a significant role in strengthening local management and reproduction of diversity in varieties of the locally important crop.

5.1. Examples of innovations in local seed systems in Mesoamerica

Conny Almekinders and Dominique Louette

Introduction

Interest in farmers' seed systems has increased in recent decades as it became clear that these systems are continuing to be the most important seed source for farmers, despite considerable large-scale efforts by the public sector to speed up agricultural development and improve seed quality through seed programmes. Farmers' or 'local' seed systems typically refer to an integrated complex of activities and practices of farmers dealing with on-farm seed production and seed exchange.

Farmers' practices of seed selection, handling, storage and seed exchange cannot be seen independently from crop development by farmers and their maintenance of diversity. Seed selection practices depend on the type of crop and variety, and differ for hybrid varieties or the segregating lines of self-pollinators. The type of variety depends on the crop, which can be a cross- or self-pollinator, or vegetatively propagated. Storage practices influence germination at the time of planting, but are also part of the human–environmental selection pressure: selection of healthy looking seeds favours emergence of the seed and is at the same time a form of selection for pest and disease resistance. Degenerated varieties and badly germinating seed are both reasons for farmers to replace seed from another source.

Local seed systems of bean and maize seeds in Rio Tinto, Honduras

Local seed systems are difficult to describe, as their character varies between crops and with the conditions and farmers (Almekinders et al., 1994). The seed system can vary for crops within any one farm (for example a cash crop versus one for home consumption), and may even be different within a crop where, for instance, local and modern varieties are managed differently. In general, farmers' seed production is more important for local varieties than for modern varieties, particularly in the case of cross-pollinating crops. This is well illustrated by the bean and maize seed systems in the community of Rio Tinto in Honduras.

In a survey in 1991, carried out by a research project on local seed supply systems and food security in developing countries (Wierema et al., 1993), Rio Tinto was selected as one of the survey sites where farmers were interviewed about the use of their varieties and seed of bean and maize crops. Similar surveys were organized for other sites in Honduras, Costa Rica and Nicaragua.

Of the 28 farmers interviewed in Rio Tinto, 91 per cent were growing one or two bean varieties: Vaina Blanca and/or Vaina Rojo. Both were local varieties and phenotypically differed only in pod colour, which can be the result of a single-gene difference. Although the national bean-breeding programme had released various varieties such as Catrachita, Danlí-46 and Dorado, only three farmers were growing a small plot with another variety apart from their plot with the Vaina Blanca or Vaina Rojo. Two of these were local varieties (frijol Negro and Chelito), and the third an improved variety (Juticalpa). Occasionally, farmers had tested small quantities of seed from elsewhere, but none of that seed apparently gave significant improvements over the use of their local varieties. They did not know about the extension service bringing in new varieties. They considered that their Vaina Blanca and Vaina Rojo were well adapted and tasted good.

In the case of maize the situation was quite different. Among the 28 farmers, eight different maize varieties were grown, most farmers planting one or two varieties. Some farmers grew local varieties only, others were growing a modern variety as well. Two varieties, Rocamex and Sintético Tuxpeño, were improved varieties of which seed had not been commercially available for many years. Other improved varieties planted by the farmers were: H-5, an open-pollinating variety, and a commercial hybrid which they called 'Dekalb' after the company producing the seed. They knew about the hybrid variety from advertisements over the radio, and farmers would travel to the nearest town to buy the seed in an agro-chemical store. The farmers who planted the 'Dekalb' hybrid all did so on land in the valley floor, i.e. the more fertile soils in the village. Farmers who had fields only on the hillsides planted predominantly Tusa Morada, recognizable by its reddish husk leaves. Tusa Morada was a much better variety for these poorer soils and poorer farmers, despite the disadvantage that it was a tall variety and vulnerable to lodging when strong winds hit the area.

At the bottom of the hillsides the varieties Tusa Morada and 'Dekalb' were growing close together. Farmers knew very well that in this part of the valley the maize varieties 'got married', and some farmers did pursue this cross-breeding. They liked the high yields of the 'Dekalb' hybrid but could not store the grain very well because the husk leaves did not cover the cob completely. This forced them to sell off the produce soon after harvest, when prices were lowest. On the other hand, second- or third-generation 'Dekalb' which had married the Tusa Morada would show better husk cover. And, although it would yield less than the pure hybrid seed on the more fertile fields of the valley bottom, it was better adapted to the poorer fields on the slopes, while having the advantage over Tusa Morada of shortness. Higher on the slopes Tusa Morada was yielding better than 'Dekalb'. Farmers kept Tusa Morada true to type by selecting for the red husk leaves and cobs with regular rows typical for this variety.

Seed-exchange practices in Mesoamerica

Diffusion and maintenance of diversity may be the most powerful character of the local seed systems. The mechanisms and channels by which seed lots are exchanged are usually strongly based on cultural traditions and relationships. For example, in the Andes a young married couple receives seed from the potato varieties their parents are growing, and labour for potato harvesting is often paid with native potato varieties. In other cultures, supplying your family, neighbours or other community members with seed when requested is a traditional social obligation; giving samples of seed of new varieties to friends and other relations is a normal practice, as well as the swapping of quality seed for consumption grain. There are also numerous examples of situations where traditional relationships developed between farmers in different growing areas to overcome problems of seed quality. In Nicaragua and Mexico, farmers were found to obtain their bean and maize seed for planting from farmers in an area where the rainy season was different from theirs in order to have fresh seed at planting (Almekinders et al., 1994; Louette et al., 1997). Similar examples of exchange relationships between villages and areas are known from other parts of the world and illustrate how farmers have developed solutions to problems in their seed systems.

The dynamics of the local seed systems are to a large extent defined by seed-exchange patterns. Seed exchange not only diffuses varieties and provides seed security, it also moves genes, which contributes to the dynamics of the gene pool. While the genetic heterogeneity of local landraces is generally considered a high value of the local systems, there are also situations in which local varieties have degenerated and the diversity of the gene pool has become limited. Seed flows may be particularly important for the local gene pool of a cross-fertilizer such as maize. A study of farmers' maize seed selection practices in Mexico indicates that the number of cobs that farmers use for the next year's seed could easily lead to inbreeding degeneration over time (Louette, 1999). The cross-pollination with varieties in adjacent fields and introduction of seed lots from outside the community may be important mechanisms to prevent such degeneration.

While farmers' own seed production is still the most important source of seed for farmers in developing countries, there is an important part of the seed that farmers do get from off-farm sources. The generally used estimation is that 80–90 per cent of all seed planted in developing countries comes from the informal seed sector, i.e. the farmer's own seed or other informal sources. The two studies in Mesoamerica reported here indicated that not more than 60 per cent of the bean seed was from the farmers'own production. In the case of a particular maize variety and planting season, only 57 per cent of the seed was from the farmer himself. However, the use of seed from the formal sector was on average lower than 10 per cent. Such relatively high levels of seed use from off-farm sources may be an indication of problems in the farmers' own on-farm seed supply, for instance with production stability, storage technology or genetic degeneration. They can, however, also be interpreted as indications of the flexibility and problem-solving capacity of the local system.

Conclusions

Studies have shown that local seed systems do have many valuable characteristics which have provided seed security to farmers over time. The systems are innovative and are acquiring materials and adapting technologies as they appear. The dynamics of seed systems described above also indicate that it is difficult to define the boundaries of the local systems. New varieties, both local and improved, but 'exotic' to the system are introduced by farmers themselves. These gene introductions may be essential for subsistence and development of these local seed systems, and without them there may be serious genetic degeneration.

5.2. The impact of seed-supply interventions on the use of crop genetic diversity

Elizabeth Cromwell and Conny Almekinders

Introduction

In many situations, seed supply from the formal sector (scientifically trained staff working in government, private or voluntary sector institutions) is intended to be instrumental in the distribution of the products of formal-sector breeding programmes, in the interests of agricultural development and national food security. On the one hand, the range of varieties supplied by the formal seed system reflects the generated genetic diversity of these breeding programmes; on the other hand the organization and functioning of formal-sector seed supply significantly determines the adoption of the products of formal-sector breeding programmes. This chapter reflects on the role of formal seed systems and the concerns associated with their effect on the use of crop genetic diversity by farmers.

Concerns related to conventional formal seed-sector interventions

As elaborated in earlier sections of this book, it is generally accepted that conventional formal-sector breeding programmes tend to generate a relatively small number of varieties, and varieties which are genetically homogeneous (composed of similar genotypes), compared with what is used by farmers in marginal, heterogeneous areas (Chapter 4.7).

Therefore, a major concern is that distributing seed from formal-sector breeding programmes has a negative effect on genetic diversity in local farming systems because a large proportion of the cropped area becomes planted to a limited number of modern varieties, and local varieties fall into disuse.

This is believed to be undesirable for a number of reasons. Some commentators argue that loss of genetic diversity in the farming system, whether the loss of particular genes or gene combinations of farmers' varieties, or because widespread 'monoculture' removes the niches in the farming system which are the natural habitat of other plants or animals, reduces ecosystem sustainability (e.g. Thrupp, 1998).

Other arguments relate to the narrower genetic base. This may increase the vulnerability of the cropping system to pest and disease attacks: more genetic uniformity can increase pest and disease pressure, thereby increasing the chance that variety resistances are broken by the pathogen.

Another concern is that formal-sector seed supply creates dependence on the purchase of expensive and potentially environmentally harmful external inputs such as chemical fertilizers, pesticides, etc. – because many modern varieties have been bred to be highly yield-responsive to applications of external inputs. Some critics suggest modern varieties yield well only if external inputs are applied, particularly in areas such as the heart of the Green Revolution in Asia, where modern rice varieties have now been grown continuously for a long period, and in areas such as substantial parts of dryland sub-Saharan Africa where environmental conditions are marginal for agriculture.

Another concern is that generally farmers cannot successfully maintain seed of modern varieties on-farm themselves, and so in order to continue to obtain the genetic and physiological benefits of using modern variety seed, farmers become tied into purchasing replacement seed on a regular basis: at least every few years in the case of self-pollinated crops, and each year for hybrid varieties. An implication is that seed is no longer recycled on-farm; this limits the evolution of the crop genetic base.

Critics imply that some commercial seed companies attempt to secure regular purchases of replacement seed by various tactics including deliberate promotion of hybrid varieties in preference to alternatives (e.g. composites and open-pollinated varieties in the case of maize); lobbying at international and national levels for legislation to prevent farmers using and trading seed that they have saved on-farm themselves; and investing in developments such as the Technology Protection System (the so-called 'terminator gene') which biologically prevents the germination of seeds from a harvested crop and thus the recycling of seed from one season to the next (Nap, Chapter 4.6).

Evidence from high-potential agriculture

What is the evidence for these concerns? In the higher potential agricultural areas, modern varieties now occupy a large proportion of the planted land: for example, about 90 per cent of rice land in Asia (FAO, 1994). Evidence indicates greater susceptibility to pest and disease attack in farming systems planted to monocultures of modern varieties (e.g. the infamous effects of *Helminthosporium* on the US maize crop in 1970, which wiped out half the harvest in the southern part of the country; or the current problems in wheat production in North America, see Mercer and Wainwright, Chapter 2.7). There is also evidence for environmental damage caused by chemicals used in the cultivation of modern varieties. For example, researchers in the Philippines have recently estimated that one-third (1.2 million ha) of the total cropped area has been severely degraded from the over-use of pesticides and chemical fertilizers (Basilio and Razon, Chapter 2.10).

However, supporters of the widespread distribution of modern varieties via formal-sector seed supply maintain that the most of these problems arise not from the reduction in genetic diversity in the local farming system *per se*, but from mistakes made in the ways modern varieties have been promoted: if modern varieties were replaced on a regular basis, resistance to pest and disease attack would be maintained; if chemicals were not over-subsidized, they would be applied more carefully and significant environmental damage would be reduced.

Furthermore, from another point of view, opinions on the use of genetic diversity can be quite different. Smith (Chapter 4.5) presents various arguments in support of the view that formal breeding has contributed considerably to the use of genetic diversity and the sustainability of agricultural production.

And some commentators argue that, in any case, reduction in genetic diversity is not necessarily associated with decreasing output or sustainability, nor are sustainability and productivity related to species diversity in natural ecosystems (Grime, 1979; Dover and Talbot, 1987; Wood, 1998).

Prospects for crop genetic diversity in marginal areas

Other commentators suggest that of greater immediate concern is the potential impact of formal-sector seed supply in the more marginal agricultural areas, many of which act as centres of diversity for many crops (beans in the Andes, sorghum in dryland west and southern Africa, etc). Diversity continues to exist in these areas because here farmers need a large number of varieties to fit the numerous agro-ecological niches on the land that they farm, and they rely on a broad genetic base in their farming system to enable them to cope with seasonal variations in rainfall and disease attacks (Hardon et al., Chapter 1.1) – their farming income is rarely sufficient to allow them to purchase external inputs such as irrigation equipment and agrochemicals to compensate for these variations.

It is sometimes suggested that the relative lack of penetration by formal-sector seed supply into marginal agricultural areas is a good thing, because this protects the local crop genetic resources base from erosion and 'contamination' by modern varieties. However, this is too simplistic a perspective, for various reasons. Firstly, there is a constant inflow and outflow of genetic material in all farming systems, whether 'modern' or 'traditional' – the result of natural processes as much as exchange and selection by farmers (Louette and Smale, 1996; see also McGuire, Chapter 2.1 and Almekinders and Louette, Chapter 5.1). Thus there is no reason to consider dynamics in the local crop genetic resource base as being intrinsically wrong, or wrong just because a 'modern' exotic variety is involved. Mutations, crossing and introgression can take place with 'old' as well as 'new' genes, and genetic diversity is subject to recombination and selection pressure as long as seed is recycled.

Secondly, there is growing evidence that farmers in 'traditional' farming systems, far from being faced with an abundance of crop germplasm from which to select, adapt and incorporate, more frequently feel they are lacking in suitable crop germplasm, and are actively searching for exogenous sources of material that they can incorporate into their farming system (Wood and Lenné, 1997; see also Chapter 2.1).

Lastly, following the work of Smale et al. (1995) and Bellon and Brush (1994) on maize in Malawi and Mexico, respectively, it is now well known that farmers rarely use new varieties to replace their existing crop genetic resources altogether, particularly in risky marginal areas; rather, they add

225

new material to their existing variety portfolio. So the likelihood that *a priori* formal-sector seed supply to farmers in marginal areas results in large-scale replacement of the existing local crop genetic resource base is remote.

Conclusions: seed policy and crop genetic diversity

So what is the overall verdict on the impact of formal-sector seed supply on crop genetic diversity, and what are the implications for future policy and practice in this area? Although there remains considerable debate about the precise level of and type of crop genetic diversity necessary for agro-ecosystem stability and sustainability, it is generally accepted that crop genetic diversity does play a valuable role and should be supported. There are various ways in which the formal sector can contribute to this role, and these are addressed in other chapters in this book. In relation to seed supply, these ways are strongly linked with plant-breeding strategies, the seed regulatory framework, and agricultural policies.

○ Formal-sector plant breeding – pursuing opportunities to adopt strategies and techniques that broaden the genetic base of the material farmers' receive. These include: breeding for specific adaptation; reducing reliance on simple single-gene traits; participatory varietal selection/plant breeding.
○ Regulatory framework – enabling the distribution of genetically heterogeneous product and quality farm-produced seed. This implies changes to national variety release procedures and seed certification systems (Chapter 6.4), and reduced restrictions at the international level to the extent that intellectual property protection is applied to seeds and varieties.
○ Agricultural policies – while recognizing the role of modern varieties in developing-country agriculture, governments need to be aware of the dangers of over-promoting them through policies of price support, input subsidies, and promotion of package deals designed to make these inputs economic to use for farmers where they would not otherwise be so.
○ Finally, for formal-sector seed programmes, supplying seed to marginal areas will always be relatively expensive and difficult. Since resource limitations will continue, formal seed supply may increasingly move to take advantage of local seed systems for producing and distributing seed. This has the added advantage of allowing some evolution of material on-farm. For the advantage to be realized, analysis of the strengths and weaknesses of local systems is needed, along with support for aspects that need improvement. This may include providing farmers with training in saving seed on-farm, and assistance with the development of low-cost seed stores and local gene bank technology, so that farmers can have access to local crop genetic resources necessary to maintain sustainable production without depending exclusively on national gene banks and the *ex situ* conservation system (Cromwell et al., 1992; Almekinders et al., 1994).

In this brief overview, we have seen that there is a case for increasing the range of genetic diversity in the material distributed by the formal-sector seed supply system. We have also indicated that technical and organizational changes can be made (and are already being made to a certain extent) to achieve this. Although these changes necessitate significant corresponding changes in technicians' and policy-makers' perspectives, we suggest this is a small price to pay compared with the long-term benefits of supporting crop genetic diversity in farmers' fields in terms of individual farm families' livelihoods, national food security, and ultimately global environmental security.

5.3. Seeds and relief in war and post-war reconstruction in Sierra Leone

Paul Richards with Malcolm Yusu, Catherine Longley, Harro Maat, Samual McKuwa and James Vincent

Introduction

Seeds are lost in conflict. Plant genetic resources may also be lost in post-war reconstruction. A significant amount of humanitarian assistance is provided in the form of seeds. Seed relief is often modernization 'by the back door', reflecting seed acquisition possibilities and the background of personnel. Humanitarian agencies have limited understanding of plant genetic conservation issues. There are no obvious reasons, other than lack of awareness, why humanitarian seed programmes could not be better designed to take into account plant genetic conservation consequences.

Following the 1996 Leipzig conference on global policy for management of plant genetic resources (FAO, 1996b), international agencies are under some obligation to consider the impact of war and humanitarian emergencies on seed systems and crop plant genetic resources (Richards and Ruivenkamp, 1998). This paper reports a study of the extent to which humanitarian agencies considered plant genetic resource management issues in relation to seed relief in Sierra Leone.

The Sierra Leone crisis

Sierra Leone has experienced insurgency by the Revolutionary United Front (RUF), a movement of socially excluded youth, affecting mainly the forested mineral-rich southern and eastern parts of the country, but later overspilling to all parts (Richards, 1998). Over 8 years of war, more than half a million Sierra Leoneans have sought refuge in neighbouring countries and an estimated 1.5 million (out of a total population of 4 million) have been internally displaced. Farming communities have been the main targets of RUF hit-and-run operations.

The advent of a democratic government (in early 1996) resulted in a peace agreement signed in Abidjan in November 1996. A coup followed in 1997, and not until February 1998 was the democratic government restored to power.

Driven back into the bush in 1998, the RUF hardcore vowed to continue its struggle, and resumed devastation of large areas of the rural north and east of Sierra Leone. Communities beginning to recover after the signing of the 1996 peace agreement were once again dislocated.

Crop plant genetic resources in Sierra Leone

Sierra Leone is the focus of the coastal West African Rice Zone (Richards, 1996a, b) where a number of distinct rice agro-ecosystems intersect: dryland, inland valley, riverine and coastal wetland systems. It is also home to a large number of cultivars of the African rice species *Oryza glaberrima*, some of which have hybridized with the now more widely cultivated Asian rice species *Oryza sativa* (Jusu, 1999). In-country rice genetic resource 'hot spots' are found in the south of the country and in the hills of the Liberia–Guinea–Sierra Leone borderlands. In this second area, fighting has been intense for the longest period.

The study

Although most expatriate aid-personnel were evacuated from Sierra Leone after the coup of May 25th 1997, some humanitarian agencies continued operations with local staff. Three in-country researchers made an assessment of these operations. The researchers travelled to most parts of the country where seed relief operations were being implemented, and visited refugee camps on the western border with Guinea. Intensive work with farmers was not possible, but humanitarian agency personnel were interviewed about the aims of the seed programme. We collected information from six of the distribution agencies – four international NGOs (ActionAid, Action contre la Faim, World Vision and Africare) and two smaller, national NGOs (ACORRD and CCSL). Personnel from the Ministry of Agriculture (MAFE) involved in 'upstream' seed activities (breeding, multiplication and testing) were also interviewed. Some farmers' group leaders were visited, and relevant reports and statistical information were collected. Operating conditions were hazardous, especially in the weeks leading up to the coup.

Seed relief in 1997–98

A grant to Sierra Leone of circa $800 000 from Swedish aid sources, administered by the FAO and European Union representations in Sierra Leone, was used to support displaced farmers – up to one-third of the total farming population – returning to war-affected chiefdoms. A major proportion of the grant was spent on tools and seeds, with emphasis on upland and wetland rice. About 4000t of rice seed were acquired for the 1997 planting season and distributed by 10 NGOs. Although the coup disrupted normal activities, the humanitarian agencies had delivered most of their seed by this time.

The impact of seed relief

The seed was acquired mainly in the less war-affected regions in the north and northwest of the country, long-established areas of surplus rice production. Most acquired varieties were 'modern' releases, mainly in the ROK series (releases from the national rice research station at Rokupr). Main upland varieties included ROK 3, 16 and 17, and main lowland types included salt-tolerant ROK 5, and ROK 22. ROK 3, 16 and 17 are pure-line selections from local and widely distributed landrace materials.

Seed delivered was equivalent to approximately 11 per cent of the total estimated seed rice requirement for Sierra Leone in a normal year, but may have been about 20–25 per cent of all rice planted in 1997 (many farmers still remained in the refugee camps). All other seed must have come from farmers' own local sources.

Undermined by war, the government institutions in Sierra Leone were still very weak in 1996–97 and private seed companies made up the shortfall. Some of these companies were set up by government employees to supplement irregularly paid salaries. Technical staff used their initiative to meet NGOs' anticipated seed rehabilitation needs by organizing farmers into supply co-operatives and placing advance orders. They used food aid granted by the World Food Programme to procure seed that farmers would otherwise have used for domestic consumption. Two Lebanese businesses entered the field as contractors to supply seed, buying from farmers in the boliland region, and in one case employing a former government seed specialist as technical adviser. Farmgate seed prices were approximately Le 10 000–12 000 per bushel (~ 25 Kg, 5–6 US$); the humanitarian agencies bought seed at Le 20 000 per bushel (~ 10 US$).

Genetic resource management issues

Humanitarian agency awareness of genetic resource management issues was the focus of our enquiry. Few of the managerial or field staff interviewed had given this aspect of their work much thought. Nearly all staff told us they had carried out 'needs assessments' with farmers' or refugees' groups to select the seeds to procure and distribute, but made clear they were constrained by what potential suppliers were 'programmed' to offer. Rokupr Rice Research Station and Seed Multiplication Project (SMP) are organized to supply mainly modern varieties (though, as indicated, some are selected variants of local landraces appropriate to difficult upland conditions in Sierra Leone).

Only one agency was carrying out serious on-farm evaluation of choices offered, but here it was made clear that rehabilitation offered an opportunity to introduce a better agriculture, based on modern fertilizer-responsive plant types and supported by training-and-visit extension methodology. It was not clear how the agency would have reacted if its on-farm trial results failed to confirm the superiority of modern fertilizer-responsive varieties in the tough conditions faced by returning farmers.

When pressed, several field agents reported that farmers often asked for locally adapted planting material, and that such material was recognized to be best in the difficult conditions. In Bo and Pujehun Districts, farmers' confidence in asking for adapted local seed types reflected long-term activities by the German aid-funded Bo-Pujehun Project, which promoted the use of the best locally adapted seed types during the mid-1980s.

In a few cases where it was possible to talk directly to farmers about seed supply (e.g. in refugee camps in Guinea) there were several complaints about delayed delivery, blamed on contractors employed by the UN High Commission for Refugees (UNHCR), and low seed quality. Low germination potential (below the standard minimum of about 80 per cent) was more of an immediate worry than the lack of potentially valuable locally adapted landrace material. One agency encouraged farmers not affected by the war to contribute material to community seed stores – a good idea in theory, but one which had led to a complete mixing of different seed types, with very unpredictable consequences when the material was redistributed to displaced farmers in the district. The quality of some of the commercial seed company material was also reported to be poor.

None of the agency staff interviewed mentioned the risks of genetic erosion in supplying large amounts of modern and relatively untried planting material. One agency, with considerable experience of seed supply in the south, did refer to the issue in an indirect way – noting that its seed ($\approx$ 20 per cent of local needs) supplemented rather than displaced local seed supply, thus freeing farmers to make better use of scarce amounts of local planting material. A second agency pointed out that it was policy to acquire seed material from the less war-affected north to reduce pressure on farmer-held local seed stocks in the south. Nevertheless, it remains a fact that no agency was explicitly monitoring availability of the rarer locally adapted varieties. One agency, however, presented us with a copy of a very interesting 'seed map' of the Bo area locating supplies of 50 different rice varieties, including 21 local types. The map legend classified the material into dryland and wetland types and provided basic information on seed characteristics; it did not distinguish any of the early weed-competitive upland African rice (*O. glaberrima*) or African rice × Asian rice (*O. sativa*) hybrid materials sought after by farmers as 'hunger-breaker' crops (Richards and Ruivenkamp, 1998; Jusu, 1999).

Some conclusions

The Swedish-funded FAO/EU/humanitarian agency seed distribution programme in Sierra Leone in 1997 was a well designed exercise that contributed significantly to the prevention of hunger in war-damaged rural districts under very difficult conditions. That it was also a step towards a *de facto* 'modernization' of the local rice seed landscape, with as yet unknown consequences for *in situ* plant genetic resource conservation, cannot be denied. Whether there will be significant consequences depends on how often it is repeated; replacement of 20 per cent of local seed stock (some of which would have been modern varieties – typically 5–10 per cent of all rices planted in many parts of the southeast) in one year is not by itself likely to produce irreversible population genetic effects. That agencies adopted a seed modernization approach appears to have been largely the result of circumstances. In most cases, modern varieties were used simply because they were available, and because field staff were recruited from government institutions and projects where these were the varieties of choice. Nevertheless, it is clear there is a gap between rhetoric and reality when it comes to needs assessment. Agencies believed farmers should be allowed to choose the varieties they preferred, but were simply not in a position to act on those choices. The patchiness of coverage also deserves comment. Some badly war-affected chiefdoms were too dangerous for any agency to contemplate operations, but in other areas the agency became 'mother and father' to the resettling farmers. In the northern part of Bo District, hitherto an area where farmer landraces of rice dominated, 91 per cent of all seed planted in 1997 came from agency sources. Country-wide, the impact of an unintended modernization of seeds may have been mild, but some local 'hot spots' appear to have been in danger of being over-whelmed by a combination of war and subsequent saturation with modern seeds.

Some recommendations

o Careful study of the specific consequences of seed relief schemes is needed, in areas where baseline data exist, to establish whether seed relief contributes to genetic erosion.
o To the extent that Sierra Leone is representative, humanitarian agencies are well practised at seed relief, but have not yet developed practical awareness of genetic resource conservation issues. Technologists and policy-makers from humanitarian and plant genetic resource conservation fields must meet to develop some good-practice approaches. Workshops will need to be convened to facilitate this agenda.
o The Sierra Leone case suggests that when humanitarian agencies take over from ministries and more conventional development projects, the change in institutional culture may not be as great as first imagined; this is because where the state is collapsing, many experienced technicians seek work in the NGO sector and carry their skills and attitudes with them. If plant genetic resource conservation issues are to be addressed in emergency assistance, the place to insert the relevant awareness is in the mainstream training of field-oriented development professionals.
o Where there is genetic erosion in war zones associated with humanitarian seed assistance, seed supply bottlenecks are a major cause;

contingency planning – regional back-up collection, seed multiplication and emergency seed transfer protocols – must be worked out in advance to support farmers' efforts to recover locally adapted landrace material.

5.4. Support to diversity in potato seed supply

Urs Scheidegger and Gordon Prain

Introduction

Many kinds of modern seed schemes tend to reduce on-farm genetic diversity of a crop: the seed industry, especially in developed countries, likes to work with only a few varieties per crop, and greater availability and quality of seed of the selected varieties tends to displace other varieties the farmers may be growing. In addition, the seed industry is usually closely linked with breeding programmes, permitting a rapid diffusion of new, high-performing varieties with wide adaptation, at the expense of local cultivars.

The example presented here of a potato seed programme in Peru shows that seed schemes may in fact enhance genetic diversity in production.

The Peruvian seed programme

Potato is the basic food crop and the major source of income for highland farmers in Peru. The rationale for embarking on a seed programme was the low yields (8t/ha) mentioned in the Peruvian statistics, especially for the heart of potato production, the Highlands. The hypothesis was that yield may be increased only if seed of better quality can be used. Thus in 1983 the Peruvian Institute for Agricultural Research (INIAA), the International Potato Center (CIP) and the Swiss Development Co-operation initiated a project to develop and implement new technologies for production of high-quality potato seed; to assess this seed on-farm; and to test strategies for large-scale distribution.

The programme established laboratories to eradicate pathogens from potato varieties via meristem-tip culture. The pathogen-free material was then multiplied *in vitro* and grown into tuberlets in greenhouses in five INIAA experimental stations throughout the highlands. This pre-basic seed underwent two field multiplications to yield annually about 1000t of basic seed.

The varieties in the programme were predominantly those that farmers were already planting: the basis for variety inclusion was surveys on farmers' variety use carried out between 1980 and 1986 in the important production areas (SEINPA, 1994). Of the 134 varieties found in farmers' fields, 20 modern and 16 native varieties as were identified as the most widespread or important, and were cleaned. Because of regional variation in variety use, the five INIAA stations had different responsibilities in subsequent multiplication and diffusion of the material.

Quality seed . . .

Good quality seed could be produced in this way, with total virus infection as checked by serological assays well below 2 per cent. On average, highland farmers could improve yields through the use of this basic seed (of their usual varieties) by just about 20 per cent on average. This was clearly below the expectations based on temperate climate experience, and appeared insufficient to justify farmers' investment in such expensive seed. It led the research team to ask under what circumstances the use of better quality seed might be profitable for small farmers.

. . . and how farmers use it

Despite the only moderate yield advantage, highland farmers showed a strong interest in the quality seed. In test sales, they readily bought this seed at two to three times the price of common seed, yet in quantities of only 10–20kg. Within two seasons of multiplication, they were usually able to plant their entire small plot of around 0.5ha with the renewed seed. And they counted on a further 5 years to go with the same seed stocks. Thus with only 20kg of basic seed they managed to improve the production on at least 2ha over a period of several years (Scheidegger et al., 1989). Economic analysis of the way farmers made use of the basic seed over time showed outstanding rates of return (over 5000 per cent). The quality seed had a great impact considering the small quantities that were channelled to traditional seed suppliers in the smallholder sector: within a few seasons each small lot of basic seed injected there had reached several small-scale farmers (10 on average) along the mechanisms of traditional seed flows.

The rationale for a seed programme

A diffusion strategy for quality seed was designed based around the three key elements of farmers' existing practices: seed renovation through obtaining small lots of seed of as good quality as possible; multiplication and use of that seed for several years; and obtaining seed via interzonal seed flows, usually originating in high-altitude, geographically closed locations.

Small quantities of basic seed (20kg) were sold by the seed programme to whoever was interested. Larger quantities (50–200kg) were sold or loaned to small farmers at the source of traditional seed flows. As there were already well developed personal relationships linking seed producers and users along these short-distance flows, the programme did not interfere any further in production, quality control or distribution of seed. Trusting in this kind of 'neighbourhood certification' proved to be effective and helped to avoid complicated regulations and structures for formal certification.

Detailed epidemiological studies done under the prevailing cropping systems found reinfection with virus to be slow, as compared with many other potato-production environments (Bertschinger, 1992), thereby providing the biological rationale for such a strategy of long-term use.

Multiplying and distributing seed of a wide range of varieties

The rationale for multiplying a wide range of varieties was twofold: (i) to meet the diverse needs of the farmers; and (ii) to avoid genetic erosion caused by favouring the (often modern) varieties that were most widespread due to better seed quality and availability, at the expense of the local varieties. The experience in the Peruvian seed programme shows that it is possible to work with a relatively wide range of varieties. Costs increased only moderately because:

o The programme concentrated on the initial part of the seed multiplication scheme (only the two early field multiplications), thus handling only limited volumes of seed and being able to adjust the offer quickly to demand.
o This operation was decentralized, with different stations handling different varieties and thus developing some specialization.
o Building on existing local seed systems made it possible to work without formal certification, thus avoiding the associated transaction costs (Thiele, 1999), which may be considerably increased by handling more varieties.

In addition, the surveys of farmers' variety use made researchers aware of (i) the large array of varieties used by farmers; (ii) the locally specific nomenclature of varieties (different names used for the same genotype on the one hand, and different genotypes referred to with the same name on the other); and (iii) farmer exploitation of genetic diversity to cope with the risk-prone and diverse environment. Therefore, even if the seed programme was not able to include all available varieties, it enhanced awareness among technicians of the value of diversity.

The fact that the demand for seed of a certain variety was not proportional to its importance in terms of area was a complicating factor for the programme. There was greater evident demand for seed of the few modern varieties grown by commercial producers in well endowed areas than there was for the many widely grown varieties (both modern and native) preferred by smallholders. This was because the commercial sector has higher replacement rates, and better contacts to the experimental stations. Careful balancing of production volumes was necessary to avoid unsaleable stocks or unsatisfied customers.

Impact on genetic diversity

The main objective of the programme was to improve farmers' livelihood through better quality potato seed. The positive impact of the programme

234

on diversity through a diverse supply of quality seed was an important spin-off. For two varieties notorious for their high virus infection levels, producers even claimed that they would be lost without the programme providing clean (renewed) seed. Unfortunately, due to civil unrest in the highlands some of the more interesting initiatives could not be followed through for longer-term effects, and therefore evidence for and quantification of the impact on genetic diversity is often lacking.

Combining seed supply with participatory breeding

Initially the programme concentrated on producing clean seed of the varieties most in use. Yet when the distribution strategy outlined above took shape, and it became clear that the quantities of seed to feed into the existing informal system needed to be only moderate, there was some scope for experimenting with new varieties. In collaboration with CIP and INIAA breeders, together with a group of farmers in the area, evaluation of advanced clones and some exotic native varieties was organized. Results showed that the highly diverse and complex cropping systems call for a high genetic diversity, and that the introduction of new varieties has the potential to enhance genetic diversity on-farm. However, most breeding programmes explicitly or implicitly go for wide adaptation varieties and hence in many cases contribute to the reduction in area or even the disappearance of some local varieties (Brush, 1992). In the Peruvian seed programme, joint evaluation of genetic material showed that farmers consider up to 39 different criteria to evaluate a new variety (Prain et al., 1991). And they were clearly not looking for the ideal variety, but rather for an ideal range of varieties which answer their diverse food systems needs. In a similar context of highly diverse smallholder production, Sperling et al. (1993) showed that Rwandan farmers successfully put to use large numbers of bean varieties with specific adaptation when they were given access to such material. In other words, when breeding programmes are not exclusively targeting wide adaptation they can contribute significantly to greater crop genetic diversity in production.

Changing attitudes of farmers

Several activities in the Peruvian programme are likely to have influenced farmers' attitudes towards their local germplasm, although evidence could not be collected systematically: through the interest of the formal system in native varieties (asking questions during the surveys, cleaning and producing the more widespread ones), these might have gained more prestige among farmers. The participatory breeding initiative is likely to have enhanced farmers' interest in germplasm *per se*, including their native varieties (local material was always included as checks in this study); this initiative, by explicitly recognizing farmers' germplasm expertise, might enhance their self-confidence in variety management, an important prerequisite for maintaining on-farm genetic diversity.

Vegetative propagation and conservation

While vegetative propagation is usually associated with a number of problems (bulky, perishable and expensive planting material that may carry diseases), the respective crops also offer certain advantages for linking development with conservation.

o True-to-type multiplication makes it easy for farmers to produce their own seed and makes it possible for formal seed programmes to build on existing farmers' seed systems (this is similar in self-pollinated crops).
o The slow multiplication rates reduce the risk of participatory breeding approaches (e.g. the risk of wide distribution of a variety with a disease susceptibility going unnoticed during the few seasons of testing).
o The bulky and perishable nature of planting material makes *ex situ* conservation cumbersome, thus enhancing the importance of on-farm maintenance.

While a positive impact on genetic diversity on-farm is expected from a well targeted seed programme, it is not the only element in conservation of genetic resources. Initial surveys and continuous monitoring of farmers' variety use, especially important because of the high costs of vegetative propagation, may enhance the quality of other conservation measures and will point out weaknesses in the overall system, allowing for well focused interventions such as targeted *ex situ* conservation.

Conclusions

The experience from the Peruvian potato seed programme shows that it is possible to combine development objectives (improving farmers' livelihoods) with conservation objectives. The first condition is that farmers must have a direct (short- to medium-term) benefit from the programme and its products. High and continued interest in the Peruvian programme shows that this was the case. The answer to the highly diverse, complex and risk-prone environment of the Andean highlands is diversity in production systems, including germplasm. Under such circumstances, appropriate options can be identified that at the same time increase productivity and genetic diversity.

5.5. Experiences with support to the community potato conservation system in Cusco, Peru

Isidoro Sánchez and Pompeyo Cosío

Introduction

In the Andes region of Peru there are more than 4500 small-farmer (*campesino*) communities, representing 29.9 per cent of the rural population of the country. Families from these communities live in extreme poverty and dedicate most of their time to agricultural activities. This chapter reports on the use and maintenance of potato genetic diversity in a number of small communities in the neighbourhood of Cusco, Peru. This use and maintenance by the communities represents a conservation system that is recognized and supported by NGOs operating in the area.

Communities and their agricultural production

Each family in these communities owns an average of 1ha of land for annual crops, and uses 2ha which belong to the community and are cultivated periodically. Each family's cultivated land is located in different agro-ecological zones or *pisos ecologicos*: the low valley, middle valley, and upper valley or mountainous region. Twenty small parcels per family, scattered over altitudes ranging from 3200 to 4200m a.s.l., is not uncommon. While facing large agro-ecological variation, this access to fields at different altitudes and with different conditions also represents a way of reducing risks, and provides farmers with opportunities to produce a diversity of crops and varieties (Goland, 1993). For instance, in the fields in the *microcuencas* Rio Huaccoto (3600m a.s.l) and Rio Tinki and Rio Lauramarca (4200m a.s.l.), seven different species of potato are found in farmers' fields. Various cultivars of each species have been grown, developed and maintained by the farmers throughout hundreds of years of cultivation.

Richness of potato species and varieties of the different *pisos ecologicos*

Each native cultivar and species has a particular microhabitat to which it is best adapted. In the higher zones (3800 and 4200m a.s.l.), farmers grow potato varieties which are bitter (due to glycoalkaloids in the tuber), with adaptation for colder zones and resistance to frosts. These bitter potatoes, such as the diploid varieties *Ruck'i, Mullu-winku, Q'anchalli, Mallk'u, Piñaza, K'eta* and *Pariña* (*Solanum juzepczukii*, diploid species, $2n = 2x = 22$) and the pentaploid varieties white-*Oqhoruri*, purple-*Oqhoruri*, *Waña, Shiri, Ugro-Shiri* and *China-mallk'u* (*Solanum curtilobum, $2n = 5x = 60$*), reach the upper extreme of climatic tolerance among all the crop species cultivated in the Andes. Along with these bitter species there are also cultivars of non-bitter or slightly bitter potatoes of the species *Solanum ajanhuiri* ($2n = 2x = 24$), with the predominant cultivar being Ajanhuiri. Non-bitter potatoes of other species are also cultivated in lower zones with warm weather; the more common are *Solanum stenotomum* and *Solanum tuberosum* subsp. *andigena*. Within each community the number of cultivars for the high zone varies from 34 to 170. In this zone potato is the sole cultivated crop, and after a potato crop a plot at this high altitude is left fallow for 5–8 years.

In the middle zone (3400–3800m a.s.l.), potatoes are grown with other species of Andean crops. Traditional potato cultivars of this zone are mainly the following: *S. stenotomum* ($2n = 2x = 24$), *Solanum goniocalyx* ($2n = 2x = 24$), *Solanum chaucha* ($2n = 3x = 36$) and *S. tuberosum* subsp. *andigena* ($2n = 4x = 48$). The list of cultivars among the nine study communities is large. A preliminary identification based on taxonomic morphology gives between 39, 8 and 29 representative cultivars for the first three cited species, and 163 for subsp. *andigena*. In this middle zone important commercial traditional cultivars are grown, such as *Wayru* and *Lomo* (both triploid), *Qompis*, *Yana Imilla*, *Sani Imilla* (tretraploid), and *Q'ello-waq'oto* (diploid). These varieties are in high demand at urban markets. In the same zone are improved tetraploid cultivars, generally hybrids of *andigena tuberosum*, with less dry matter content and high productivity.

In the low zone or valley (under 3200m a.s.l.), mostly *S. tuberosum* and *S. tuberosum* subsp *andigena* are cultivated in the form of improved potatoes and some traditional commercial varieties. Ninety per cent of production in this zone is taken to the markets.

Use and production of potato diversity

Particular varieties or species have different uses: some are for home consumption, exchanged with others, and used as food for those who participate in harvesting (Brush, 1991; Zimmerer, 1991b) Others, particularly the higher-yielding improved varieties, are specifically for marketing as they are considered watery and untasty. Within the group of potato varieties for home consumption, varieties differ in preparation and use. The bitter potatoes are 'processed' in the community as *chuño*, others are dried and stored after cooking as *papa seca*. The cultivation and use of potatoes represents a very rich agricultural system of plant genetic resource management and use which is integrated with the knowledge and cultural system of the people in the Andes (Zimmerer, 1991b)

In total, the communities in the Andes maintain an invaluable richness of potato genetic diversity. At the higher elevations, where native potato cultivars dominate, farmers grow the different varieties and species mostly as mixtures (Brush et al., 1981). The number of varieties in a field varies, but a farmer easily has 10–20 potato varieties mixed in one field. Also, the total number of potato varieties varies between farmers: Manuel Mamani in the Huaccoto *micro-cuenca* maintains eight varieties, while Bernando Turpo in the Tinka-Lauramarca *micro-cuenca* maintains 54. The varieties are difficult to distinguish from the plant characteristics, even for the farmers. Leaf form, plant habitat and flower colour do give indications, but farmers can recognize the varieties only from their tubers at planting and harvest times. Farmers say they grow the varieties in a mixture because 'one plant can help the other'. Mixing the different genotypes can help to reduce disease pressure. The extreme fluctuations in rainfall, hail and night frosts are other reasons to grow mixtures. In one year a particular group of varieties in the mixture may do well, while in the next year others do well. They also say it does not make sense to separate the varieties when only small plots are cultivated. And it is good to have a mix of boiled potatoes of different tastes and texture on the table for consumption.

Because of the variety richness, it may not be immediately observed at harvest that a particular variety is lost from the mixture. The representation of the variety may vary over years with the growing conditions. If conditions have been very unfavourable for a particular variety, its number of tubers in the mixture decreases, and the risk of its loss increases. It is often the women who observe the reduction or absence of certain types. They will then try to recover the missing varieties, mostly through exchange. The fiestas, *ferias* and family relations are very important for the purchase and exchange of varieties.

Conservation of potato diversity by NGOs

Realizing the importance of this potato diversity, and the threatened disappearance of many varieties which were less widely used, a group of NGOs participating in the Community Biodiversity Development and Conservation (CBDC) programme decided to collect samples of the different potato varieties. They maintain them as a collection on the field station of Arariwa, one of the NGOs, in the peasant communities in Urubamba. The objective was to be able to reintroduce varieties into communities when necessary. However it became very expensive to maintain the collection, especially because many of these varieties have their habitat at higher altitudes and produced few tubers in the NGO field station, and the disease pressure in Urubamba was a problem. In discussions on these problems, the NGO staff came to realize that maintaining the field collection involved problems similar to those the formal gene banks were confronting, including limited accessibility to the materials for farmers, and the risk that the collection could be wiped out or stolen. The conclusion from these discussions was that maintenance of diversity by farmers, who have more knowledge of the varieties than NGO staff, was a better option than a centralized field bank which is not managed by the farmers themselves. With this insight, it is recognized that the farmers' system of production, use and exchange represents a true *in situ* maintenance system of potato genetic diversity.

Reconsidering the local conservation system

In reaction to this conclusion, NGO staff have now returned the materials to the communities following discussions with farmers. Individual farmers have accepted the responsibility to maintain a collection of varieties as a community, in such a way that the responsibility for maintaining diversity is divided among the community members. Some farmers are maintaining 15 varieties, while others maintain up to 30. This interest of farmers in maintaining the diversity in the community is also an indication of increased awareness among farmers that their potato diversity represents an (agri-)cultural and economic value. The direct benefit for the farmers was access to seed tubers of varieties of which they did not have sufficient quantity. The NGO further supports the farmers in production and in covering some of the costs of inputs that ensure the harvest.

Returning the materials into the hands of farmers further allows the NGOs to focus on other types of support that also contribute to the maintenance of genetic diversity. For instance, activities that strengthen the exchange of seeds and tubers between farmers are important to facilitate the recuperation of lost diversity and the functioning of the seed system as a dynamic conservation system. Possibilities of providing clean seed tubers of native varieties through rapid multiplication are being explored, as well as the potential to use true potato seed for the propagation and improvement of native varieties through participatory plant breeding.

5.6. Local seed supply: the case of seed banks in Tigre, Ethiopia

Korstiaan Teekens

Introduction

The Abyssinian Centre is well known for its huge genetic resource base and its status as the centre of origin and diversity of several domestic plants (McGuire, Chapter 2.1, Tsegaye and Struik, Chapter 5.7). In Tigre, the northern province of Ethiopia, an interesting seed bank programme became operational in 1988, evolving from an emergency seed security service into a seed credit service supporting the on-farm conservation of local crop genetic resources.

Background

Tigre was affected by war for at least 17 years, until 1991. By then the Tigrean People's Liberation Front (TPLF), together with the Eritrean EPLF and other resistance movements organized in the Ethiopian People's Revolutionary Democratic Front (EPRDF), jointly won the struggle against the Stalinist dictatorship of Mengistu Haile Mariam. During the war certain parts of Tigre were isolated from the outside world by the regime in an attempt to trap the guerrilla army of the TPLF. In 1978 the TPLF established an NGO, the Relief Society of Tigre (REST), to give support to the population of Tigre, operating by unofficial border crossings from the Sudan.

In 1984–85 the conflict, together with the occurrence of drought, caused a serious famine. The famine resulted in discussions within the farming communities on how to secure the supply of local seed, and how to prevent exploitation of drought victims by seed- and money-lenders. It was recognized that some farmers, who were known for their expertise in seed selection, had better yields than others while working under the same soil and climatic conditions (Berg, 1992). As a result of these discussions the *baitos* or TPLF village committees initiated the establishment of community seed banks, in response to demand from farmers to secure seed supply and actively share the benefits from favourable practices and the local knowledge system in seed selection.

Initially the seed stores were local granaries at selected farmers' homesteads in 42 *kushets* or villages in Central Tigre. The selected farmers were, in most cases, those who were known to be good seed selectors. REST provided them with training in the basic administration skills and they managed the seed security programme.

The prevailing farming system in Central Tigre can be characterized as a smallholder mixed farming system in which mainly seed crops are cultivated.

Recent development

After the war, REST reorganized the seed bank programme as part of the shift from relief to economic development and the implementation of the Integrated Agricultural Development Programme (IADP). Over the past 8 years REST has become the leading actor in rural development in Tigre by involving the governmental Bureau of Agriculture and Natural Resource Development (BoANRD) and several other NGOs in the implementation of the IADP in Central Tigre. The community seed bank programme developed into an influential seed security programme, mainly with financial support of the Norwegian Development Fund. It can now be considered as the major alternative formal seed supply system alongside the Sasakawa Global 2000 programme, implemented by BoANRD and supported by Japan, which promotes modern varieties and an agro-input package. In 1995 central seed bank stores were constructed in each of the 10 *woreda*s or subdistricts covered by the IADP. In 1996 all local granaries used as community seed banks, in a radius of 30km around the newly constructed stores, were closed down. In several remote villages they are still in use.

The local organization of reorganized seed banks

Seed technicians were trained by REST and employed at each of the 10 central seed banks. They are responsible for storage management and the registration of all transactions. The seed technicians are supervised by IADP field officers who are in charge of the implementation of the programme at *woreda* level. The purchase of the seed is managed by the seed bank committees. These committees are organized at the level of both *woreda* and *tabia* (cluster of villages, around 2000 inhabitants; a *worede* is composed of 10–20 *tabias*).

The *woreda* seed bank committee provides the *tabia* seed bank committees with training and is responsible for the transfer of financial resources from REST to the *tabia* seed bank committees. The *woreda* seed bank committee is chaired by a representative of the *woreda* Economic Development Affairs, a government institution. The secretary is a BoANRD representative. The REST–IADP *woreda* co-ordinator and two knowledgeable farmers are members of the comittee. The *tabia* seed bank committees are responsible for the actual purchase of seed for the seed bank. Field assessment, seed purchase, transportation of seed to local granaries or central stores, selection of beneficiaries, distribution of seed and collection of loans are the major tasks of the *tabia* committee. The chairman of the *tabia* committee is a representative of the *tabia* Economic Development Affairs. The secretary is a BoANRD extension agent and members are two knowledgeable farmers and a BoANRD field worker.

The community's ownership of the seed banks is accomplished by its local representation on the seed bank committees. The chairpersons and farmer members of the committees are involved in the overall implementation, monitoring and evaluation of the programme. The BoANRD is the major external actor giving technical advice, and monitoring and evaluating the programme. REST's input is limited to the execution of the programme, giving periodical training for the proper functioning of the central seed banks and releasing money to the seed bank committees.

Purchase, storage and distribution

Each harvest season the *tabia* seed bank committees assess crop performance in the area. The owners of fields in which very high-performing crops are found are requested to sell the harvest to the seed bank. The local seasonal market price determines the price that is paid to the supplying farmers. The crop is harvested, threshed and sacked by the farmer and brought to the seed bank by local transport. In the seed bank the seed is registered, mechanically cleaned, labelled and stacked. The sacks are arranged in stacks by *tabia* of origin, and within each stack by crop type. During storage the room is fumigated at least once. The seed is regularly checked for the presence of storage pests and diseases, and further treatments can be applied.

At sowing time the seed is offered as a credit to poor farmers who face seed shortage due to crop failure in the preceding season or severe storage losses. The beneficiaries are selected at *tabia* level by the seed bank committees consulting the local BoANRD fieldworkers. The seed purchased from a specific *tabia* is also distributed to farmers within the *tabia*. The beneficiaries are expected to arrange transport themselves.

The rate of interest is fixed at 15 per cent per year. The loans are collected as soon as the beneficiaries have harvested their crop. Loans are repaid in cash, generally 6 months after seed distribution, meaning the beneficiaries pay on average 7.5 per cent interest over the value of the seed. In case a farmer cannot repay the loan because of crop failure due to natural calamities, the *tabia* committee can postpone repayment to the next season.

Mostly the demand for seed bank seed exceeds the supply. Many farmers who do not face the problem of seed shortage themselves are still very much interested in the seed bank services due to the good quality seed that is offered at a relatively low price. The improved storage conditions and the quality control only partially explain the success of the seed bank programme. The main reason why farmers have confidence in the programme is that local varieties are involved and local knowledge is employed in seed selection.

Strengthening the seed bank system

In order to support the seed bank system, REST aims for further development and adoption of favourable seed selection practices by farmers. With this objective, a study was carried out to obtain insight into the local knowledge and seed selection systems in the area. A major secondary objective of the study was to seek confirmation of the assumption that the rural community of Tigre contributes to the maintenance of the region's crop genetic resources.

Sixty farmers were involved in a small survey in two *woreda*s, Hahaile and Ade Ahferom, comprising 10 and 14 *tabias*, respectively. The farmers were questioned on several seed-related subjects such as selection criteria applied, number of varieties, storage, the exchange of seed and experience in seed selection. Respondents were both selected and randomly chosen farmers, and both individual and group interviews were conducted. The questionnaire was semi-structured but was mainly straightforward.

The seed selection system

From the survey it was learned that most farmers in the study area practise pre-harvest selection in their cereal crops. Farmers have a holistic approach in observing their crops, and a complex of selection criteria are used at the same time. Thoughout the growing season the farmers store all their observations in their memory in order to select the favoured plant type. Selection practices vary widely among farmers.

Many farmers use a 2-year seed-selection cycle in teff, wheat and barley. Some farmers multiply the selected seed separately for more than 1 year when starting amounts are very small. Mass selection is most common, but some farmers explained a selection process resembling a 'line selection', based on the selection of one or more ears. Farmers who pay a lot of attention to selection may select the other way around, taking the most fertile plots for the multiplication of selected seeds and giving the crop special attention.

All farmers interviewed stated that their spouses participate in seed selection. Ten farmers admitted that their spouses play an important role in selecting because the females are experts in selecting on food-processing quality. Several farmers explained that their young children are also involved in seed selection, in order to transfer the applied knowledge and experience to future generations. All farmers exchange seed with other farmers. They explained that special meetings are organized to discuss 'seed matters', to negotiate and to exchange seed. Also on regular gatherings, on holidays or at village meetings, discussions on crop performance and seed selection take place.

Most farmers explained that they have a strong culture respecting everything inherited from their parents, including their crops and varieties. Introduced modern varieties are used only in addition to the local varieties, and will not replace them.

A large number of local landrace varieties are cultivated by the respondents. The 60 farmers involved in the study listed seven varieties of local teff, 22 of wheat, 10 of barley, seven of maize, 14 of sorghum and four of finger millet. The high number of wheat varieties may indicate its ritual importance: farmers offer their best wheat heads to the local church. All varieties mentioned by the farmers were found to be included in the seed banks.

The survey also took an inventory of farmers' selection criteria to help understand variety needs (Teekens, 1997). Farmers are very critical of introduced modern varieties and screen them on their specific requirements. Two modern wheat varieties (Bulk and Enkoi) were introduced to the region in the 1970s. These varieties are early-maturing and rust-resistant. However, they were not appreciated by the farmers because the straw production and straw quality are too low. According to the farmers, the rust-resistance collapsed within a few years.

Conclusion

It is of vital importance that farmers' knowledge, experience and demands are seriously considered in designing support to local seed systems and in breeding programmes. Participatory plant breeding appears to be the only appropriate method of supporting local crop development in the region. The community seed bank programme with farmer-experts in seed selection can play a key role in both seed security and the development of an effective collaborative plant breeding programme in Tigre. At present the Ethiopian Biodiversity Institute, famous for its role in the development of *in situ* conservation (Worede and Mekbib, 1993) has taken up the idea of seed banking. The Ethiopian Biodiversity Institute is implementing and supporting six seed banks in different parts of Ethiopia, because securing seed supply of the diversity of varieties is a strategy to support the use and thereby the *in situ* maintenance of landraces.

5.7. Research supporting the genetic diversity of enset in southern Ethiopia

Admasu Tsegaye and Paul Struik

Introduction

Enset is a (mainly) vegetatively propagated multi-use crop grown in the highlands of southern and southwestern Ethiopia, primarily for the starch in the pseudostem and the corm. The crop has a wide genetic diversity which is recognized and exploited by the different ethnic groups in the region. This genetic diversity is now considered a valuable resource. A better understanding of the factors leading to the loss of existing variation and the generation of new variation in this crop is needed to support the use of diversity by farmers and their families. This chapter presents some results from preliminary studies by national researchers that contribute to increased understanding.

Ensete ventricosum is a vegetatively propagated, banana-like plant (herbaceous monocot) that is grown for the starch in its pseudostem and corm in the highlands of south and southwestern Ethiopia. It is a regionally dominant staple crop covering approximately 168 000ha and is the main source of food for about 7–10 million people (CSA, 1997a). The crop has been grossly neglected by national and international research insititutes, despite its decisive contribution to the survival of the people in the highlands of south and southwestern Ethiopia during the droughts of the past decades in East Africa which caused hunger and death elsewhere in the region.

Recently, the importance of the crop has been recognized and survey studies have been carried out to determine its use and distribution. Studies on its agronomy, crop physiology, multiplication and genetic diversity have been initiated. Enset is an example of a minor crop with a large importance in a small region, with little information on its genetic diversity but with a wealth of indigenous knowledge on the crop. Moreover, it is typically a women's crop. Women know how to discriminate between types, and how to grow, nurture and process it. Some concern is also justified: population pressure, devastating diseases (such as bacterial wilt), and recurrent drought have taken their toll on the genetic diversity. On the other hand, improved transport has resulted in increased exchange of diversity among tribes and regions. Some of these aspects are discussed here, and the role of national research in increasing knowledge of the crop is addressed.

The crop and cropping system

Enset is a herbaceous monocot that looks like a banana and grows 4–11m high. Enset plants are normally grown from suckers obtained from a buried corm. These suckers are transplanted several times before they are planted in the place of production for a few years. In some areas the different generations of transplants are separated in the field; in other areas they are mixed. Enset accumulates starch in the pseudostem, corm and mature stalk of the inflorescence before flowering. An enset plant needs up to 2–10 years to flower; the number of years varies with the agro-ecological conditions (temperature), frequency of transplanting, type of clone, spacing and crop husbandry. Although the enset plant can be harvested at any stage of development, to obtain high quality and yield quantity it must be harvested soon after producing an inflorescence and before fruit setting. Later harvesting can even result in a reduced amount of starch in the pseudostem and corm. An enset plant needs at least 3 years to reach a harvestable stage; the age at which it is harvested depends on the food situation of the farmer's household, but normally varies from 3 to 7 years.

Every household in enset-growing regions has enset. The average farm size in most enset-growing regions is 0.5–1.5ha, with 10–50 per cent of its area covered by enset. Rich households have more land than poor, and also grow more enset plants. In most enset-growing areas young enset plants are placed very close together, often so close as to make it difficult to walk through some parts of the plantation. As there is a shortage of land in most enset-growing areas, this system of production enables farmers to use the available space more efficiently. In other enset-growing regions, young enset plants are intercropped with annual crops (such as maize, beans, cabbage, taro and potatoes), and older enset plants with perennials (such as avocado, coffee and citrus). The enset crop is grown closest to the house so that the enset field can easily be fertilized with cow dung and house refuse.

Diversity in enset

Enset-growing areas are inhabited by the Gurage, Kembata, Wolaita, Sidama, Gedio, Gamo, Keficho, Goffa, Dawro, Oromo and related ethnic groups. Ethnic groups show considerable variations with respect to tradition, culture and language. As enset is cultivated by several tribes in an extensive area of land, the cultural practices of enset growing such as cycles of transplanting, propagation, leaf pruning and processing methods vary from place to place. Enset may also be grown for other purposes: it produces fibre, provides construction and packaging material, and is believed to have medicinal value. Particular varieties may excel for one or more of these uses. Since one variety can never fulfil all the criteria and needs, farmers tend to grow five to seven different enset types on their farm. As a result of the different growing conditions and different uses, there is much genetic diversity.

Although it is not common, farmers in some parts of enset-growing regions use seeds to produce seedlings. Reproduction by seeds requires 1–2 additional years, and no part of the plant can be used for other purposes. Therefore only rich farmers who do not have a shortage of food can afford this source of planting material; other farmers are known occasionally to collect seed or suckers from wild ensets which are still found in some river valleys in southwestern Ethiopia. This wild planting material represents a source of new genetic variation. The enset is thought to be principally self-fertilizing, but out-crossing is likely to take place as well. Little is known about the genetic variation present in the wild populations and how this contributes to the genetic diversity in cultivated enset.

The fact that enset can be grown from seeds and is also vegetatively propagated means that the genetic variation in the crop is generated and lost in different ways from crops that are multiplied only by seed. In this sense, enset is very similar to potato which is also occasionally multiplied via botanical seed. Propagation through seed provides interesting mechanisms for recombination of genes. If particular seedlings or suckers from wild plants have very favourable characteristics, farmers can easily select them and maintain them through vegetative propagation. It is not well understood how vegetative propagation relates to the risk of losing genetic diversity. Can farmers who lose the few plants of a particular enset type due to bacterial wilt or other problems easily regain the genotypes? And how does this compare to the risk of loss of genetic diversity in maize crops?

Harvesting and processing enset for starch

The starch from the scraped leaf sheaths of the pseudostem together with the grated corm is fermented in a pit (fermentation silo) in the soil with a lining of enset leaves. The pit is often circular, up to 1.5m deep, with a diameter up to 1m. For proper storage and fermentation, every 2–3 weeks the pit is opened and rearranged. The result of this process is a product that can be stored for several years. After 2–3 months' fermentation the starch can be used for preparing meals. The fermented starch is used for the production of *kocho*, the major local staple food. The corm can also be cooked fresh to produce *amicho*. Finally, *bulla* may be obtained by squeezing the mixture of grated corm and scraped leaf sheaths of the pseudostem and allowing the resultant starch to concentrate into a white powder. This is considered to be the best product, and is obtained in large quantities only when harvesting mature enset plants.

Poor families will have to harvest the plant a few years after planting, whereas rich families can afford to let them grow much longer, thus gaining in yield and quality. In all instances they must be harvested before flowering. In this way the enset plants can serve as a food bank: they can be harvested for (almost) immediate use when needed in periods with short food supplies, or saved for further growth when adequate supplies of food can be obtained from the other crops. Since the storage of the consumable product is also very flexible, the crop gives a very versatile food supply. Rich households may thus have secured food supplies for up to 7 years. Poor families may have reserves that last only 2 years or – in periods of food shortage – may already be consuming the plants in the early stages of bulking of starch.

Factors influencing enset genetic diversity

Rapid rural appraisal studies in Hadyia have clearly indicated that there is a difference in enset diversity among rich, medium and poor households.

Rich households maintain more landraces in their fields than poor households. Rich farmers have more land, more enset plants and more animal manure to fertilize them, so they can afford to plant some landraces for very specific purposes (such as for medicinal or even ornamental purposes). It also appeared that having more types of enset gives prestige to the household. Conservation may profit from an increased supply of inputs and improved processing techniques, since this will make the poor households less dependent on the highest-yielding types and will allow them to grow types for specific purposes.

Recent studies on enset diversity and the factors influencing it have already indicated that diversity is still great. Some farmers in the region suggested that diversity increases because of improvements in road transport, which facilitate travel and exchange of enset materials. Yet types may have been lost due to biotic or abiotic stresses, forcing poor farmers to stick to types that are most resistant. The increase in population density is also a threat to the diversity of the crop, both because the habitats of the wild enset are destroyed, and because land shortage will stimulate planting of monocultures of the highest-yielding types.

Women play a crucial role in the conservation of the current diversity. They are able to identify the different types, and they know the specific characteristics of these types better than men. This is probably due to the fact that they fertilize, grow and process the plant.

Efforts to conserve enset genetic diversity must take these findings into consideration. Conservation of the present diversity through utilization may be enhanced by involving governmental, non-governmental and farmers' organizations.

National research on genetic diversity in enset

The people of Ethiopia are becoming increasingly aware of the richness of the crop genetic diversity in their country, including enset. Many research projects are being undertaken to identify, document, classify, evaluate and preserve this diversity. This is necessary as systematic, documented knowledge on genetic diversity and the factors affecting it is scarce.

The Awassa College of Agriculture, situated near different enset regions and with an internationally trained staff with a keen interest in locally relevant research, is one of the organizations working on the biodiversity of enset. The College has already carried out surveys using participatory approaches to describe indigenous knowledge of the crop. It has developed and perfected a methodology for using this knowledge to identify and evaluate the current diversity and the trends therein, despite problems with the many languages in the area resulting in myriad vernacular names for landraces. It has also described the current crop husbandry and its variations from tribe to tribe and from one agro-ecological zone to another, and has a good overview of the methods of multiplication currently applied. Researchers from the College have already collected a wide variety of genetic material from different enset-growing regions, and have access to more material. This material will be grown in the experimental site of the College for further identification, classification, evaluation, study and conservation. In this research the College collaborates with researchers from the Ethiopian Agricultural Research Organisation and the Ethiopian Biodiversity Institute.

More research is needed, for instance in relation to the occurrence of pests and diseases (bacteria, nematodes and viruses). The possibilities for adapting simple, rapid multiplication techniques to local conditions (tissue culture) will be explored and these may become relevant technologies to provide farmers with a diversity of disease-free planting material. Thus the combination of insights into factors reducing the available genetic diversity in enset for farmers and the development of simple and adapted tissue-culture techniques may offer important support to the use and maintenance of enset genetic diversity.

Owing to its exposure to and contacts within the international scientific world, the Awassa College of Agriculture is able to establish co-operation with centres of excellence elsewhere in the world to make use of the most modern techniques to further analyse the present diversity. For example, several scientists from the Awassa College of Agriculture and other institutions are carrying out enset research within the framework of a PhD programme at Wageningen University and Research Centre in the Netherlands. Researchers in Awassa thus have early exposure to new approaches in plant genetic resource management and access to information and techniques (such as gene mapping) not yet available in their home country. Such exposure strengthens the academic environment in Awassa and enriches it with new knowledge, insight, research ideas and challenges.

In this way a knowledge chain is established, starting with the indigenous knowledge of farmers, made available and deepened by the expertise of local scientists, and further advanced by expertise and knowledge from elsewhere in the world. The knowledge and skills of the young university staff immediately serve the trainees at the Awassa Agricultural College, who will serve the country as future extensionists, agricultural teachers and administrators, and thereby this knowledge and these skills are disseminated with great speed.

Synthesis: Towards integrated seed supply

Conny Almekinders and Jaap Hardon

Introduction

As described in Hardon et al. (Chapter 1.1), farmers' seed production is an integral part of the total farm household system. This is also clear from the cases presented in this and other sections. Analysis of the seed production practices of farmers in Mesoamerica (Almekinders and Louette, Chapter 5.1), Ethiopia (McGuire, Chapter 2.1), China (Song, Chapter 4.2) and elsewhere indicate that seed for the next cropping season generally is not a random sample from the harvested crop, but results from different forms of selection by farmers (often women) and thus represents a dynamic system of continuous crop development. Farmers are continuously looking for new varieties: they mix different types of materials resulting in recombination of genetic diversity and select seeds on the basis of desired ideotypes, seed health and appearance, and hence are involved in breeding activities.

Pressure on the local seed system

Other contributions in this book illustrate the resilience and robustness of farmers' seed systems in coping with difficult circumstances and still providing the seed needed for planting. A particularly dramatic socio-political situation is described by Richards (Chapter 5.3), in which the formal system completely collapsed. The potato seed systems in the Andes (Sánchez and Cosío, Chapter 5.5) and the bean seed system described by Catalán and Pérez (Chapter 2.4) are examples of how farmers' seed systems are at the same time dynamic conservation systems. The nature and extent of conservation is still poorly understood, but is touched upon in many other contributions in this book.

Changing conditions exert tremendous pressures on the functioning of these local seed systems. Migration from rural areas to the cities in search of a better future is one important factor disrupting local seed systems. Urban migration changes the labour situation on farms, which affects cropping systems and often leads to abandonment of particular varieties, leading to a reduction of diversity in farmers' fields (Zimmerer, 1991a). Catalán and Peréz (Chapter 2.4) describe how the migration of families also disrupts the functioning of the local seed-exchange system.

New approaches building on local systems

A better understanding of the local seed systems has contributed to understanding why the formal seed systems have, so far, not been very successful in many developing countries (Cromwell and Almekinders, Chapter 5.2). This increased understanding has also generated new opportunities for both public and NGO sectors to improve farmers' seed supplies by building on the strengths of these local systems. The experiences of the Peruvian Potato Programme show that approaches can be worked out by which the formal system does address the need for quality seed and diversity. The ongoing project in Ethiopia on local enset diversity and related propagation practices and limitations (Admasu and Struik, Chapter 5.7) also follows this approach. The first step of the study is to understand the use of diversity by farmers and to identify limitations. The study is expected to provide building blocks for the design of interventions to improve enset production and at the same time maintain diversity. The important role of farmers' seed systems for seed security is illustrated by the examples of Peru and Sierra Leone, where terrorism and civil unrest led to a total breakdown of the formal seed system.

Attempts to strengthen local seed systems tend to stimulate attention to the conservation of local materials. A clear example is provided by seed banking in Tigre (Teekens, Chapter 5.6). Initially these activities were started to secure seed availability, but it was soon realized that 'good' seed was closely linked to varietal nature and required the maintenance of diverse materials. For this reason, the Ethiopian Biodiversity Institute (the former gene bank, recently renamed the Institute of Biodiversity Conservation and Research) is supporting the establishment and operation of various local seed banks in the country. This is a form of combining improved local seed supply with *in situ* conservation, and includes training farmers in managing genetic diversity.

Improving and supporting local seed supply

While farmers generally appreciate the need for good seeds, and farmer-produced seed is generally of reasonable quality, a better understanding of such systems often indicates opportunities for further improvement on local knowledge and practices. This is illustrated, for instance, in the case of the native potato varieties planted by farmers in the Andes (Scheidegger and Prain, Chapter 5.4). In general, however, little information is available on the quality of farmers' seed and how this relates to the crop performance. Such information is badly needed in order to identify possibilities for improving seed production practices. Proper selection of plants in the field prior to harvesting, in addition to selection from harvested seed, can provide opportunities for improving seed quality. Seed storage is another area in which much improvement may be possible. Seed certification agencies could play an important role in such support. Considering that farmers' seed production is an important, if not the major, supplier of seeds to farmers, these agencies could assist extension services and NGOs in analysing and monitoring seed quality in the local seed system and identifying the need for support and training.

Building on the local system provides multiple opportunities to support farmers in the production of good quality seed. The expertise on seed production and seed quality that is available in the formal system is, in adapted form, relevant for the training of key farmers and NGO staff and trainers. Trained farmers and NGO staff can be catalysts for their communities and, in time, may form the beginning of local seed industries.

Trained farmers may specialize in seed production and become suppliers of seed for other farmers. These farmers may, individually or collectively, produce seed on contract for NGOs or commercial firms, or they can develop into small private enterprises. Small enterprise development may be stimulated by the government's seed policy and incentives, for example by providing credit facilities (normally not available for this type of small agricultural enterprise) and supported by training in the basics of small enterprise management.

Attention to seed production of local varieties is definitely required to support farmers in obtaining better access to and improving their use of diversity. The multiplication and distribution of promising advanced materials from breeding programmes can make an important contribution to improving access to diversity, further developed and tested in participatory forms of plant breeding (e.g. Chapters 4.8 and 4.11).

Re-orientation of seed programme activities

Seed production activities can serve the reintroduction of materials from the collections held by gene banks, in order to introduce small quantities of fresh, good quality seed into the local system on a regular basis. This is an approach that is pursued by the PROINPA genetic resources programme in Bolivia, which maintains an important collection of native potatoes on-station in Toralapa (F. Torrez, pers. comm.). From surveys it is clear that farmers' seed of these varieties often has high levels of virus infection, and clean seed is difficult for farmers to find. However, as a genetic resource programme they are not equipped and do not have the financial resources to produce clean seed, and the potato seed programmes in Bolivia are not used to the multiplication and diffusion of small quantities of seed of a large number of varieties. As a consequence, nothing happens and an opportunity is missed.

Conclusion

A basic message from many of the contributors to this section is that improvement of seed supply to farmers should not only consider the formal seed system, but should also recognize farmers' seed systems as the main suppliers of seed to farmers. This has important consequences for development strategies and the most appropriate policy environment. Central to such new approaches are farmers' participatory testing of new materials, and the supply of materials covering a much wider range of environments than is done by modern improved varieties. This suggests functional roles for gene banks and improved exchange between communities. These developments are totally contrary to the increased centralization that tends to take place in the commercial seed industry. Contributions in this section suggest that new developments are taking place, but that much more needs to be done before a real impact is seen.

POLICY FRAMEWORK AND GENETIC DIVERSITY

Introduction

The institutional and policy framework regulating and directing crop improvement, seed supply and the conservation and use of genetic resources has been in a state of dynamic transformation and change for almost a century. Before that time, in fact since agriculture began, it was farmers who domesticated and gradually modified and improved crops, adapting them to a wide diversity of environments far beyond their original habitats, and to human requirements far beyond their original phenotypes. Early in the 20th century, with the rediscovery of the laws of Mendel, scientific plant breeding developed as a practical application of genetics. This happened simultaneously with the first production of artificial fertilizers, and the industrial revolution transforming production processes, giving rise to the industrial complex as the dominant force in economic development. In industrial countries modern agriculture transformed the rural landscape. The autonomous local farmer was replaced by the rural entrepreneur, relying on a supply industry to provide him with seeds and other inputs to grow crops that were sent to an anonymous market for processing and distribution to consumers. The vital importance of good seed for farmers, and the impossibility of ascertaining its quality and identity from its physical appearance, led to a seed regulatory framework to protect the interests of farmers. Parallel to this form of 'consumer protection', the interests of commercial plant breeders needed protection to stimulate private investment in crop improvement and seed production. This was realized through plant breeders' rights legislation specifically adapted to the requirements of agriculture.

Both systems functioned apparently satisfactorily for many years as countries started to adopt and harmonize these regulations, based on their own needs and in the wake of the gradual industrialization of their agriculture. In this section, contributors discuss the evolution of this regulatory framework as its functionality is becoming stretched. On the one hand, biotechnology has opened the way for applying industrial patents to plants and animals, providing far more restrictive protection, customary for industry but which is in conflict with the common norms and values of agriculture. The so-called Green Revolution of the 1960s and 1970s saw a dramatic increase in the adoption of modern high-input practices accompanied by the high-yielding modern varieties. Initially generally acclaimed as a major achievement in development, soon some negative aspects became apparent. These included loss of genetic diversity through replacement of original landraces, and questions raised about legal ownership protecting modern varieties while farmers' varieties remained freely available. The establishment at the FAO of the Commission on Plant Genetic Resources in 1983 opened up the debate on a global level. The strategic importance of genetic diversity in local landraces and wild relatives of crops was realized, and its management, access and use became an issue of international debate, culminating in the UN Convention on Biological Diversity of 1992.

The increased importance of policy questions relating to ownership of genetic resources; the national sovereign rights of states over those resources; conditions of access to the material and benefit sharing; and new developments in biotechnology (especially genetic engineering and marker technology) with a strong focus on property rights questions; increased attention to natural resource rights, indigenous knowledge and the rights of farmers, provide for an extremely complex set of issues. All this takes place at a time when, through the World Trade Organization (WTO) and the negotiations on Trade Related Intellectual Property Rights Systems (TRIPS), nations are obliged to adopt regulatory systems satisfying global requirements.

This section provides views and insights from a range of perspectives on present national and international developments.

6.1. International policies related to the management and use of genetic diversity

Susan Bragdon

Background

Agriculture and biological diversity are often perceived as being in an adversarial relationship. The reasons for this perception are not unjustified. The predominant patterns of agricultural production have eroded biodiversity in agroecosystems, including diversity in plant genetic resources, livestock, insects and soil systems. Yet humanity depends on the agriculture/agrobiodiversity relationship being expressed positively. Biological diversity is fundamental to agricultural production and food security, and is a critical component of environmental conservation. Furthermore, the loss of diversity increases vulnerability to climatic and other stresses, increases the risks to farmers, and undermines the stability of agriculture. Practices that integrate the maintenance of biological diversity with agricultural practices have multiple ecological and socio-economic benefits, one of the most important being helping to ensure food security (Thrupp, 1996). Agrobiodiversity is the centrepiece of the transition to sustainable agriculture.

The projected growth in the world's population over the coming decades means that major increases in agricultural production during this period will be required to keep pace with human needs. The FAO estimates that food requirements in developing countries will double over the next 50 years (FAO, 1996a). Strategic deployment of genetic resources through the conservation and sustainable use of the broadest possible range of agricultural biodiversity is among the most promising approaches for achieving food security (Arnold, 1986; Wilkes, 1987; Frankel, 1988). Yet these resources are disappearing at an alarming rate (Ehrlich and Wilson, 1991). Population pressure, coupled with changes in land-use patterns, has resulted in the loss of millions of hectares of some of the most diverse natural ecosystems in the world. In agriculture, diversity is lost as farmers replace their local crop varieties with new, genetically uniform ones (FAO, 1996b). At the close of the 20th century there is heightened global concern and political recognition of the need to safeguard biodiversity and to promote its sustainable use for development.

At the same time, major advances in conservation science and technology, particularly in molecular genetics and information management, are changing the scene dramatically by increasing our capacity to conserve and make more effective use of genetic resources. However, the rapid rate at which these technologies are advancing and being employed is outpacing the ability of societies – and the law – to understand, analyse and devise appropriate measures for managing their complex implications.

The actors have also changed. Until recently, efforts to conserve and develop genetic resources had to a large extent been undertaken by public-sector institutions. Over the past decade, however, the involvement of private companies in genetic resources research and development has significantly increased. Privatization of agricultural research, catalysed by technological advances which facilitate the realization of the economic value of genetic resources, has resulted in growing conflict over the rights and responsibilities with respect to these resources. Today, humankind is faced with complex questions of what kinds of access and entitlement regimes should be placed over genetic resources in terms of both both sovereign rights and private rights, such as intellectual property rights. Intellectual property decisions have major implications for national food security, agricultural and rural development, and environmental conservation. It is in this context that basic questions of ethics and equity arise.

Four international fora

The genetic resources policy environment has changed significantly because of developments in international and national law and policy since the early 1980s. The following fora have a significant impact on international and national agrobiodiversity policies:

○ FAO Undertaking on Plant Genetic Resources (IUPGR)
○ Convention on Biological Diversity (CBD)

- International Union for the Protection of New Varieties of Plants (UPOV)
- Trade Related Aspects of Intellectual Property Rights (TRIPS), an element of the negotiations of the World Trade Organization (WTO).

The resulting policies dramatically change farmers' and community's access, control and ownership of agrobiodiversity. These changes often conflict with and undermine indigenous and traditional patterns and indigenous resource rights which have developed over centuries. At the same time, they have created a policy environment in which the status of conservation organizations (gene banks), their collections, and the division of labour and responsibilities are modified to a more rigid configuration at national and international levels. Because of the high impact on policy frameworks guiding crop-development organizations, these trends have direct repercussions on the opportunities of these organizations for the development of alternative and more integrated strategies for crop conservation and development.

FAO International Undertaking on Plant Genetic Resources

The IUPGR is a non-binding intergovernmental agreement to promote the conservation, exchange and utilization of plant genetic resources. In the FAO resolution by which the IUPGR was adopted in 1983, member states recognized that 'plant genetic resources are a heritage of mankind to be preserved, and to be freely available for use, for the benefit of present and future generations'. At present, more than 160 countries are IUPGR signatories. The body overseeing IUPGR is the FAO Commission on Genetic Resources for Food and Agriculture (with 157 member countries). Since the mid-1990s the Commission has been engaged in a negotiation process to revise the IUPGR to bring it into harmony with the CBD, perhaps eventually becoming a protocol to that treaty.

The IUPGR and Commission were conceived in controversy during FAO meetings between 1981 and 1983. In this controversy, governments of developed and developing countries became engaged in a debate on a number of issues: the ownership and control of plant germplasm; gene bank safety; management of genetic resource flows by the International Board for Plant Resources (IBPGR, forerunner to IPGRI); and national germplasm embargoes. In years following the adoption of IUPGR, it was recognized to be incomplete and to contain ambiguities requiring clarification. During the 10 years after its adoption, three interpretative resolutions were adopted in attempts to clarify concepts and terms in the IUPGR.

Three outstanding issues dominate current IUPGR negotiations: scope and access, benefit sharing, and farmers' rights. Questions remain as to the scope of what the IUPGR will cover and how access will be regulated. Some governments prefer to confine the scope of the IUPGR to a relatively small number of critical food crops, while others wish to have all plant germplasm associated with food and agriculture incorporated into the IUPGR. There is still a long way to go. In general, developing countries have approached 'scope and access' defensively. They are concerned that they are being asked to donate their germplasm freely while industrialized countries privatize the same material through intellectual property regimes.

The debate over benefit-sharing is dominant in the negotiations and closely associated to the issue of scope and access. Both issues are also addressed in the CBD. Some industrialized countries believe that developed countries are adequately compensated for their germplasm merely by having access to the information and breeding created by open international exchange. Some developing countries consider this a 'trickle-down' approach, which does not adequately recognize the contribution of farming communities and national governments. Others have suggested that benefit-sharing might best be achieved through the full implementation of the FAO Global Pan of Action (GPA). The GPA aims to create a global and multilateral system for the conservation and sustainable utilization of plant genetic resources.

Convention on Biological Diversity (CBD)

The CBD is one of the two legally binding agreements signed in Rio de Janeiro at the Earth Summit in 1992. It has 170 countries as parties. The CBD can be classified into categories corresponding to its three objectives.

○ Conservation of biodiversity – conservationists were concerned that international laws for the protection of wildlife were a patchwork covering only selected issues, areas and species. A more general agreement was required that would embrace a broader concept of nature and its value, and protect elements not covered by existing laws.
○ Sustainable use – there was a move to incorporate the goal of sustainable use of biological resources into conservation policies, recognizing the need of local people living amidst biodiversity for sustainable development, and to mobilize support for conservation by providing local benefits.
○ Fair and equitable sharing the benefits – obligations should be included in the treaty with respect to exchanging and sharing benefits from plant genetic resources for use in agriculture. However, some key issues with respect to agrobiodiversity (the status of pre-CBD *ex situ* collections, and farmers' rights) were left outstanding.

The CBD establishes a range of general, flexible obligations that emphasize national action within national jurisdiction for conservation and sustainable use. The CBD establishes a framework of general principles for structuring the international exchange of genetic resources, based on the national sovereignty of each country over genetic resources originating within its jurisdiction. Within its framework, the CBD explicitly emphasizes the implementation of both *in situ* and *ex situ* conservation of biodiversity.

The CBD can be considered an ambitious attempt to integrate previously distinct policy goals. Since the CBD was formulated 1993, its implementation has proceeded slowly. Tension remains about the CBD's three objectives. Different governments select different priorities from among the broad array of possible initiatives within the scope of the CBD.

International Union for the Protection of New Varieties of Plants (UPOV)

UPOV is an intergovernmental organization based in Geneva, Switzerland. It is based on the International Convention for the Protection of New Varieties of Plants, as revised since its signature in Paris in 1961. Up to 1997, UPOV had 32 members; most are industrialized countries. UPOV encourages the adoption of *sui generis* laws for protecting new plant varieties by creating its own distinct system outside patent law. There are four versions of UPOV. All require that a plant variety be new, distinct, homogeneous (uniform) and stable in order to be eligible for protection. The criterion of uniformity excludes the possibility of protecting landraces and farmers' varieties due to their dynamic and often heterogeneous nature. A trend is emerging in UPOV to strengthen the rights granted. The growth of biotechnology and the possibility of formal patents created pressure on UPOV, which in 1991 shifted its direction to:

o extend the rights of rights-holders beyond reproductive material, to harvested material and products obtained through illegal use of propagating material
o allow members the legal option for patent or UPOV-style protection
o extend coverage to all plant genera and species.

Extending the rights of holders to harvested materials has significant implications for the rights of farmers to save seed for replanting. Rather than assuring this right, UPOV 1991 gives members the option of allowing farmers to save seed for their own use. Without positive action by the UPOV member, the right of farmers is lost.

In addition, the authorization of the rights-holder is required for the use of varietal material which has essentially been derived from protected varieties. The uses for which permission must be sought include production or reproduction, conditioning for the purpose of propagation, offering for sale, selling or other marketing, exporting or importing, and stocking for any of these purposes.

Agreement on Trade-Related Aspects of Intellectual Property Rights (TRIPS)

The TRIPS Agreement is one of the agreements of the WTO adopted in 1994. It came into force in 1995, simultaneously with the inauguration of the WTO. The TRIPS and other WTO agreements are binding on the 131 member countries.

The TRIPS Agreement is innovative from both a trade and intellectual property perspective. From the trade perspective, TRIPS embodies the relatively novel and counter-intuitive notion that trade restrictions, such as embargoes on 'counterfeit' goods that imitate copyrighted or trademarked products, are necessary to promote trade liberalization. Intellectual property had previously been seen as a domestic policy to be tailored to fit a country's level of development and technological goals, not as a matter of trade policy. The TRIPS Agreement expands the scope of international trade rules into previously unaffected aspects of domestic production and marketing.

TRIPS indicates that members may exclude from patentability 'plants and animals other than micro-organisms, and essentially biological processes for the production of plants or animals other than non-biological and micro-biological processes. However, members shall provide the protection of plant varieties either by patents or by an effective *sui generis* system or by any combination thereof.'

This language narrows the scope of exclusions previously maintained in many countries. A number of countries must now modify laws excluding living things from patenting; their laws will have to be revised to provide for patenting of micro-organisms. The requirement of intellectual property protection for plant varieties, in the form of either patents or a *sui generis* system, will also necessitate legislative changes by a number of WTO members. These changes may have a direct impact on the development of conservation strategies addressing local management of genetic resources.

The TRIPS Agreement requires parties to provide protection for plant varieties, either by patents or by an effective *sui generis* system, or by any combination thereof. The article does not specifically mention UPOV, despite it being the most significant instrument for *sui generis* plant variety protection. This omission in TRIPS was intended to allow the parties a degree of flexibility in designing a system for plant variety protection.

Policy trends and local crop development

TRIPS and UPOV require their parties to establish certain standards for rigid intellectual property systems over plant genetic resources that could potentially conflict with the functions of genetic resources in traditional and agricultural systems. Historically, PRGFA had been exchanged among farmers and between communities, crossing huge distances and country borders. The IUPGR was built on the principle of genetic resources as part of the common heritage of mankind. This position suggests shared ownership and a common and public responsibility for its conservation.

Local crop development systems have not (yet) been wiped out by the industrial approach. In many particularly marginal and poor regions of the world, farmers have maintained their innovative and adaptive capacity, responding to changing ecological and social conditions. Such situations are dominant in what may be considered a periphery in the non-industrialized world. One of the principal factors contributing to the growing interest in farmers' management of genetic diversity as a conservation strategy is that farmers in this periphery have hardly benefited from the advances in agricultural research and development. Through *in situ* or on-farm activities of the institutional sector, farmers' management of genetic diversity may be strengthened (a clear development objective), resulting in enhanced utilization of germplasm by farmers.

Farmers' rights

The term 'farmers' rights' emerged in 1989 in the context of the IUPGR, as a political effort to respond to the perceived imbalance created by the growing use and expansion of plant breeders' rights and intellectual property rights over genetic resources. In an annexe to the IUPGR, countries agreed that farmers' rights would be recognized through an international fund. In the IUPGR debates, the term 'farmers rights' is used as either a political or a legal concept. Those viewing it as a legal concept made proposals defining the rights as an alternative form of intellectual property right covering, for example, the products of farmers' selection and breeding. Those viewing it as a political concept made proposals to establish a fund to finance plant genetic resources conservation and development work. The question boils down to whether the international community is being asked to establish and recognize rights (legal concept), or whether it is being asked to recognize the contribution of farmers and farm communities and assume responsibility for this recognition (political concept).

The CBD's emphasis on national sovereignty and action and its bilateral orientation towards access and benefit-sharing reinforced the legalistic approach to the farmers' rights debate. How farmers' rights will be operated is of critical importance to the conservation and use of plant genetic resources, particularly with respect to the implementation of *in situ* conservation of agrobiodiversity on-farm. The interest in *in situ* conservation on-farm has been supported in an indirect manner by the international debate on the ownership and legal status of plant genetic resources. The construction of 'farmers' rights' was strongly rooted in finding new balances between the local and higher levels of resource ownership. Farmers' rights are a response to the development of intellectual property rights over plant genetic resources. When linked to sustainable utilization, *in situ* conservation opens up opportunities for more equitable sharing of the benefits of agrobiodiversity, as indicated by the CBD.

In response to this shift in international and national policies, the role of farmers and communities in the development and conservation of genetic resources has been put on the plant genetic resources agenda. The interest in *in situ* conservation on-farm is partially enforced by this response. Various mechanisms of sharing benefits are proposed to acknowledge the farmers and communities who originally developed and nurtured these resources. This issue has not come to any consensus or implementation at the international level because of the difficulties in implementation and the consequences it would have on access to genetic resources. Real action

260

with farmers' rights has taken place at the national level, particularly in India where farmers' rights and plant breeders' rights have been integrated in the country's framework for variety legislation. However, the discussion on farmers' rights has placed the issue of ownership, access and control of genetic resources by farmers on the agenda of any programme dealing with *in situ* conservation on-farm. In this sense the debate has resulted not in direct international mechanisms, but rather in enhanced awareness of the issue of local ownership.

Conclusion

The past decade has seen significant changes in the global policy and legal environment governing the exchange and use of genetic resources. These developments have direct implications for any government, institution or individual with an interest in genetic resources because they determine the policy context in which it operates. The coming into force of the CBD, for example, has prompted the CGIAR – whose centres are primarily technical entities – carefully to examine its global trusteeship responsibility as a holder of the largest international collection of genetic resources, and to explore ways of responding to the needs of its national partners as they struggle to cope with rapid technological advances and increased privatization of agricultural research.

The fact that there is continued debate regarding international exchange of genetic resources, and particularly the role of intellectual property rights in agricultural research and development, is indicative of the complexity of the issues involved. Periodic review of the rapidly evolving national and international policies and laws will be essential in order to assess existing gaps in their coverage and improve their implementation. Specific issues which will need to be addressed include the effectiveness of measures being devised by countries for regulating access to genetic resources pursuant to the CBD, and the implications of the TRIPS Agreement on the use and exchange of agrobiodiversity. It is expected that the outcome of current IUPGR negotiations will result in clearer intergovernmental direction on all these issues, and hence the basis for a more conducive multilateral system for the exchange of plant genetic resources for food and agriculture. Lasting solutions to these major policy questions can come about only through the active participation of all concerned.

6.2. The agricultural treadmill and plant genetic resources

Niels Röling

After World War II agriculture developed very rapidly in response to the disruption of the global food system and the ensuing high food prices. This was made possible partly by the emergence of large-scale, science-based, uniform farming systems, especially in the mid-west of the USA. An example of the technologies that rapidly spread among farmers is hybrid maize. It is no coincidence that the 'diffusion of innovations' was invented in Iowa by observing the spread of hybrid maize among farmers (Ryan and Gross, 1943). This research perspective has had a tremendous impact on the design of research and extension systems (Rogers, 1995). The same can be said of a related and even more powerful perspective, the 'agricultural treadmill' of Cochrane (1958) in relation to another mid-western state, Minnesota. The agricultural treadmill is a concisely formulated narrative that has shaped, and to a large extent still shapes, the 'social contract' of agriculture, and provides a rationale as to why the public sector should fund agricultural research, extension and education and otherwise subsidize or support agricultural development.

The treadmill mechanism

Agriculture is characterized by a large number of small firms all producing the same commodity. Single firms can affect the price of the product, so all try to produce as much as possible against the going price. An innovator who is able to apply a new technology that enables him/her to produce the commodity more efficiently captures a pioneer profit. As more farmers begin to adopt the new technology (the 'diffusion of innovations'), the total quantity of product increases – consumers do not eat more when more is produced. This causes downward pressure on the price of the product. Farmers who have not adopted the technologies see their incomes drop. In the 'tail', those who cannot or will not adopt drop out, and their resources are absorbed by those who make the pioneer profit. This process results in 'scale enlargement' of the production units.

The economic benefits and policy implications of this development are the following:

o a relatively small investment in research and extension is all that is needed to ensure a continuous stream of efficiency-enhancing innovations;
o inefficient farmers are automatically squeezed out (typically 2 per cent per annum) – this process has resulted in a reduction in the proportion of farmers in the working population in industrial societies from 50 per cent to 5 per cent;

- labour is freed for development in other sectors;
- the benefits from efficiency gains are passed on to consumers and agri-business in terms of lower food prices, allowing wages to remain low and/or income to be spent on other products;
- this improves competitive advantage relative to other countries;
- an added benefit for the policy-makers is that the politically important farmers are the ones who (hope to) catch the pioneer profits – they love the treadmill, and support policies based on it.

Treadmill and social contract: losing ground

The treadmill continues to work at the global level as a result of cheap transport of agricultural products around the globe. Hence farmers with the lowest production costs can drive out farmers with higher production costs everywhere. But this state of affairs not only reflects a Ricardian relative advantage of some production areas over others, it also reflects the advantages of having stepped on to the treadmill earlier, and of having increased the efficiency of agriculture with the help of public research, extension, education and land development. In a free global market, agricultural industries that have benefited from the treadmill can prevent a similar development of agricultural industries elsewhere. One could argue that in areas that are late in stepping on to the treadmill, the global treadmill and the availability of imported cheap food prevent population growth being translated into higher food prices, and hence prevent the Boserupian scenario of investment in agriculture. This leads to a Malthusian scenario in which farmers are forced to exhaust their resources for short-term survival (Koning, 1999).

Thus the continued operation of the agricultural treadmill can be said to have two important consequences.

- Agriculture in industrial countries that has been on the treadmill since World War II has now reached a point where so few farmers are left that they no longer can counteract the price squeeze by being ahead of the pack. The remaining farmers are experiencing continuous income pressure. The resultant search for ways to reduce costs leads to unsustainable forms of farming. In industrial countries, the relentless extraction of wealth from agriculture and natural resources needs to be compensated with a reverse flow to agriculture. Lack of understanding of the treadmill mechanism has so far prevented political support for such a reverse flow.
- Countries that still have to jump on the treadmill are prevented from doing so by competition from farmers and agricultural industries with a labour productivity perhaps 30 times as high as theirs, thus easily offsetting the higher costs of labour in the North. Lack of understanding of the treadmill, and lack of resources and power to create an autonomous economy, leave these countries little choice but to continue to beggar their farmers.

In both situations, public investment in agriculture, for example in research and extension, is not politically attractive. The beneficiaries are large multinational seed and chemical companies that have developed the inputs farmers need in order to produce as efficiently as possible. New roles for the public sector have hardly been developed. Even where governments are beginning to realize that agriculture is multi-functional and is not just serving to produce cheap food, they have not been able to translate these insights into new forms of rural income support. The same goes for situations where economies with large numbers of small farmers are expected to adapt in a very short period to competition with economies with 'treadmilled' agriculture. Examples are Poland and Turkey, as they prepare themselves for membership of the European Union. But in the present era of globalization, 'peasant' areas in developing countries of Africa, Asia and Latin America face the same transition.

For the time being, there is no generally agreed alternative basis for agricultural policy to the agricultural treadmill.

Future implications

Countries are faced with dilemmas: accepting free trade rules for agriculture means accepting that food will be imported from areas where it can be produced most cheaply. This might not be a good idea, given the uncertainties with respect to the vulnerability of large-scale uniform agriculture, the non-sustainability of the provision of cheap energy, the questionable availability of water, and our capacity to respond to global climate change. So far, an acceptable basis for supporting agriculture has not been developed and, save for subsidies in one form or another, most policies are still based on the treadmill. It is unclear and unpredictable into what kind of situation the treadmill is leading us: it is not likely to be a situation in which ecology has much of a chance. Alternative narratives are not readily available.

Plant genetic resources

Plant breeding is one of the main technological bases of the agricultural treadmill. Accompanying the introduction of chemical fertilizers, the 'new' seeds (e.g. hybrid maize in Iowa, modern rice and wheat in the Green Revolution) have been the basis for sharp increases in food production in Asia and Latin America. Hence they have contributed to the rapid but consistent decrease of global food prices during the past 30 years. The treadmill is the main mechanism which governs the adoption of these modern varieties, and hence has provided the conditions for the rapid loss of genetic diversity in recent years.

Even if they have done so in the past, one cannot expect farmers who have become exposed to treadmill processes to maintain diversity, except as a hobby or for producing favoured festive or old-fashioned foods. Unless a different, ecological, basis for a new social contract for agriculture is developed, it is unlikely that public funds will be made available for farmers' conservation of genetic diversity.

There is a strong relationship between (i) crop genetic diversity and (ii) the resilience of our food systems in the face of climate change, collapse as a result of breakdown of the 'immune system' of agriculture, soil destruction, water depletion, etc. Promoting the widespread understanding of this relationship can help bring about a new social contract for agriculture.

6.3. The decrease in agrobiodiversity in the Netherlands: new challenges and approaches beyond *in situ* and *ex situ*

Joost Jongerden and Guido Ruivenkamp

Introduction

Ex situ *and* in situ *polarities, and beyond*
Small things can trigger big issues. Seeds do. Ever since the 1950s conferences have been organized on conserving and using seeds, and hence the genetic diversity they contain. Breeders and conservationists widely acknowledge the practical value of genetic diversity and the need for conservation of old varieties, landraces and wild relatives of the important food crops. Both have varying interests in the conservation of this genetic diversity *in situ* and *ex situ*, and these interests vary with the roles that formal breeding and conservation play in the plant genetic resource system (see Begemann et al., Chapter 3.1). However interesting the pros and cons of different conservationist strategies might be, the final issue for breeders and conservationists is the employment of this genetic diversity in agriculture in general, and in sustainable agricultural in particular. What does that mean for agricultural systems using high input levels as in the Netherlands? In answering these questions, we argue that it is necessary to analyse and understand the developments that have resulted in the present situation of an agriculture with a narrow genetic basis. We present empirical data to illustrate the impact of modernization of agricultural production on the use of genetic diversity in the Netherlands.

Modernization of agriculture

Post-World War II agricultural development in the Netherlands was characterized by the reduction of environmental variation through the use of high levels of inputs, allowing mechanization and standardizing production methods. Uniform crop growth and development was a condition for mechanization of cultivation practices. This required a uniform environment and a genetically uniform plant population.

High input levels increased yields per hectare. However, this was not sufficient to increase labour income out of farming; mechanization was the important factor that contributed to higher farm incomes and labour productivity. For investments in mechanization to be profitable, farmers needed to work larger fields and larger farms. Agricultural policy favoured the mechanization of agriculture, and the increase in scales of operation with increased land and labour productivity could keep food prices low.

The increase in scale of Dutch agriculture may be seen from the average size of Dutch farms: 7.4ha in 1950, and 16.0ha in 1990 (Table 6.1). While the use of capital strongly increased, at the same time the use of labour per farm increased, as well as production per hectare and per labourer. Production volume per farm increased by a factor of 10. These data indicate the intensification of production. As a result of this modernization, between 1950 and 1990 the number of farms in the Netherlands reduced by 60 per cent, from 315 000 to 125 000. The use of labour in the agricultural sector reduced by approximately the same percentage.

Table 6.1: Structural developments in agriculture in the Netherlands, 1950–90

Parameter	Unit	1950	1960	1970	1980	1990
Number of farms	× 1000	315	284	185	145	125
Labour	× 1000 AJE*	550	437	297	260	226
Total area agricultural land	× 1000 ha	2328	2317	2143	2020	2006
Volume capital	Index	97	100	125	173	190
Volume factor input	Index	123	100	71	63	57
Volume non-factor input	Index	53	100	160	240	255
Volume gross production	Index	71	100	145	219	295
Labour intensity	AJE/farm	1.75	1.54	1.61	1.79	1.81
Farm size	ha/farm	7.4	8.2	11.6	13.9	16.0
Production volume per farm	Index	64	100	222	426	660
Volume capital per farm	Index	84	100	190	339	430
Production volume per ha	Index	71	100	153	251	340
Volume non-factor input per ha	Index	53	100	170	275	295

* AJE = labour-year unit. Source: Landbouw-Economisch Bericht, LEI-DLO, 1993.

These figures are informative for two reasons. Firstly, because they characterize the transformation of Dutch farms since the 1950s: the intensification and increase of scale (although they do not show an important third characteristic of the transformation, i.e. the specialization of farms). Secondly, because they show the fivefold increase of capital and inputs of goods and services per farm. This second aspect illustrates the increasing relationship between farms on the one hand, and industry, banking etc. on the other. Modern agriculture can no longer be considered as a sector in itself, but is increasingly integrated into the agro-industrial production chain which consists of four links: (i) companies which supply inputs such as varieties, chemicals, credits, information; (ii) agricultural production at the farm level; (iii) the processing industry; (iv) distribution to consumers. This organization of the chain is no different from other industrial production chains. Activities related to the employment of genetic diversity, such as conservation and crop breeding, also have to take account of this production chain.

Genetic diversity and agriculture

In the context of agro-industrial production chains, a capital- and input-intensive production regime evolved. As described above, the higher input levels were part of a larger set of factors that changed agricultural production. More uniform growing environments and more uniform crops changed the nature of agriculture by facilitating a production regime which could be tailored to a large extent to the conditions of mechanization and the market. High (chemical) input/high (product) output breeding developed simultaneously with this modernization. The result has been a narrowing circle of genetic diversity. We can describe this narrowing as a process characterized by four aspects.

The first aspect is outlined in Table 6.2, which shows the replacement of landraces by breeders' varieties. This illlustrates the early transition in the Netherlands from a farmer-based variety system (landraces) to a breeder-based system.

In the process of early modernization almost all Dutch wheat landraces were lost before they could be conserved. The replacement of landraces by breeders' varieties does not necessarily imply a loss of diversity in agriculture; it is also a replacement of diversity by other diversity. But this leads to the second aspect of the process: the domination of the total area planted by a small number of breeders' varieties (Table 6.3). At first glance, little changed in this phase except the replacement of the few dominating varieties by other dominating ones. However, although their relative share of the total area planted was a little smaller, the total area planted with the dominating varieties increased considerably (Jongerden and Ruivenkamp, 1996). In 1950 the number one wheat variety, Alba, was cultivated on 36 000ha, while in 1989 the number one wheat variety, Obelisk, was cultivated on 79 000 hectares. This is the third aspect of the process.

The fourth aspect of the narrowing circle lies in the genetic diversity employed by modern breeders in developing new varieties. Breeders tend to take the proven high-yielding varieties as 'input' to their breeding programmes. For example, the variety Wilhelmina was a major gene donor to the next generation of top varieties, Juliana, Alba and Manella (Maat, 1998). The same is suggested for barley (Jongerden and Ruivenkamp, 1996).

Who loses diversity?

If diversity is lost, one has to ask whose diversity is lost? 'Modern plant breeding, the applied science of genetics, aims to develop new, widely adaptable varieties which satisfy a narrow set of breeding objectives' (Hardon and De Boef, 1993). These varieties with a narrow set of breeding objectives are used in an agriculture which also has a narrow set of

Table 6.2: Area planted with farmers' varieties in different regions of The Netherlands in 1931 and 1935 (percentage of total area of each crop)

	Rey		Summer barley		Winter wheat		Oats	
	1931	1935	1931	1935	1931	1935	1931	1935
Groningen								
Noord	15	1	5	3	–	–	1	2
Oldambt	2	1	5	2	–	–	6	9
Veenkoloniën	2	1	5	3	–	–	25	20
Friesland								
Klei	5	5	5	10	–	–	N	3
Zand	5	5	20	20	–	–	3	25
Drenthe								
Veen	2	1	5	2	–	–	78	50
Zand	2	4	25	19	–	–	65	65
Overijssel								
Veen	2	2	–	5	–	–	50	20
Zand	25	5	–	–	–	–	5	15
Ijsselstreek	10	5	10	7	–	–	–	–
Gelderland								
Veluwe	10	5	25	10	–	–	15	12
Graafschap	5	5	20	13	–	–	4	5
Betuwse Lijm	15	3	20	6	43	10	2	N
Utrecht								
Klei	4	1	19	5	16	12	–	–
Zand	4	1	15	2	20	–	10	20
Noord Holland	10	4	5	5	–	–	1	N
Zuid-Holland	5	5	5	5	–	–	–	N
Zeeland								
Eilanden	5	1	4	3	–	–	–	–
Zeeuws-Vlaanderen	17	15	5	4	–	–	N	–
Brabant								
Zeeklei	10	5	9	6	–	–	3	N
Rivierklei	8	3	7	8	–	–	2	3
Zand	22	7	13	4	–	–	15	11
Limburg								
Noord	7	2	8	5	–	–	5	8
Zuid	7	6	10	9	–	–	N	N

N = unknown, probably negligible
Source: Variety List Agricultural Crops, 1932–36.

Table 6.3: Breeders' varieties of wheat cultivated in The Netherlands and their relative shares

Year	Top 3 share (per cent)	Distribution of the top 3 (per cent)	Major variety	Institute/company
1931	75	67–4–4	Wilhelmina	IvP
1939	67	52–9–6	Juliana	IvP
1950	83	49–26–8	Alba	
1960	63	29–22–12	Felix	Saatsucht Langdorfler (D)
1970	84	65–13–6	Manella	Cebeco Handelsraad
1980	83	37–36–10	Okapi	Mansholt, Geertsema, Van der Have
1989	79	61–2–6	Obelisk	Zelder

production objectives, namely bulk production (van der Ploeg and Ettema, 1990; Jongerden and Ruivenkamp, 1996). The narrowing circle of genetic diversity shows two parallel tendencies: (i) to tailor different varieties from a small gene pool, for (ii) an agricultural production system narrow in scope. From the perspective of the dominant agricultural system, varieties are performing well. Both high-input farmers and breeders are quite satisfied. However, from the perspective of organic agriculture these modern varieties are performing unsatisfactorily for four groups of characteristics: they (i) lack the ability to compete with weeds; (ii) are not adapted to lower levels of nutrition and poorer soil conditions; (iii) lack resistance against disease epidemics; and (iv) lack good food quality characteristics. Thus farmers aiming at sustainable, organic, low-input agriculture are confronted with the loss of useful genetic diversity, and see only more varieties for fewer production systems.

Conclusion

An important conclusion is that the loss of genetic diversity in agriculture is experienced as a lack of varieties for different production systems. Varieties are bred for high-input/high-production agriculture, but not for low-input production systems. Low-input farmers in the Netherlands have to select their varieties from a variety-pool which is developed, tested and released for high-input conditions, whereas low-input conditions require more and different diversity (see Wiskerke, Chapter 2.8). Therefore a strategy must be developed to target the employment of genetic diversity in these agricultural production systems. In such a strategy, breeding activities must be well linked to the production chain in order to identify the specific conditions and characters that must be met by crops for those production systems and consumption preferences. Depending on these requirements (in terms of characteristics, resources needed for breeding, and size of target group of farmers), breeding for low-input conditions may or may not need different organization than breeding for high-input systems.

6.4. Seed legislation and the use of local genetic resources

Niels Louwaars and Robert Tripp

Introduction

Seed supply by the formal seed system is commonly regulated at the national level through a seed law prescribing institutions, procedures and quality standards. Such seed laws have evolved in Europe and North America in order to protect farmers from planting bad seed and varieties, and to protect quality seed producers from their less serious competitors. During the Green Revolution in the 1960s and 1970s, a dominant agricultural development strategy was based on plant breeding for yield potential. Seed production was seen as the necessary vehicle for technology transfer and implementation. This led in the 1970s to the development in many countries of seed rules and regulations similar to those in industrial countries, in order to support the development of a formal seed industry for their main food crops.

The major common features of most seed laws include the establishment of a National Seed Council, a variety registration and release procedure, and a seed quality control procedure. In a growing number of countries plant variety protection, an intellectual property rights system specially designed for the protection of plant varieties, is included in the seed laws.

Seed laws regulate the seed chain from variety registration to the procurement of seed by farmers. They are not designed to regulate plant breeding nor the use of specific types of germplasm therein. There is, however, no doubt that seed regulations indirectly have a broad effect on breeding strategies.

This chapter investigates the effects of seed regulatory frameworks on plant breeding and genetic resource management, through their influence on the operation of local seed systems. The common features of these regulations will be described. The subsequent analysis of the effects of these regulations is based on personal experiences in a number of countries and on findings from a workshop on seed policies and regulation organized in London in 1996 by the Overseas Development Institute, in collaboration with CPRO-DLO Wageningen and the Centre for Arid Zone Studies, Bangor (Tripp, 1997).

Objectives and operational aspects of seed laws

Most seed laws are primarily designed to promote seed quality and to protect farmers from planting substandard quality seed. In many countries governments want to promote private investment in plant breeding and seed production through economic and legal measures, including adaptation of seed legislation and by introducing intellectual property rights protection.

Seed quality

Regulation of seed quality usually leads to seed certification procedures guaranteeing varietal identity and uniformity. Seed quality, usually measured in terms of viability, purity and seed health, either has to satisfy fixed minimum standards or is regulated through a 'trueness to labelling' requirement. To be able to certify the varietal identity of a seed lot, the variety has to be clearly identifiable from other varieties, and stable over different generations. This can be properly achieved only if varieties exhibit a high level of uniformity. This immediately excludes landraces from certification, as almost by definition they are neither uniform nor stable.

The allowable number of off-type plants in a seed production field is commonly extremely low. In order to arrive at such homogeneous seed crops, the seed law prescribes a so-called generation system. This means that any certified seed lot can be traced back to a highly selected breeder's seed lot (pre-basic seed) and limits the number of generations that any seed class may be reproduced in the system. The breeder's seed class is produced through very intensive selection on identity and uniformity.

Variety release
The second quality focus relates to the value of the varieties that are allowed on the seed market. Many countries operate an extensive system of 'value for cultivation and use' (VCU) tests through multi-locational trials where newly developed varieties are tested for their adaptation to agro-ecological conditions and processing quality. This system aims to select and recommend only the best varieties. A proposed variety also has to be described in such a way that the certification system is able to distinguish the variety from other varieties in the seed production and marketing chain. In countries where plant variety protection (PVP) is part of the seed legislative system, varietal description for PVP and for seed certification generally follow an identical procedure.

Options
Most seed laws formulated in developing countries in the 1970s and 1980s resemble the regulation of field crop seeds in Europe in the 1960s. There are, however, markedly different options. Currently different provisions apply to different crops in Europe. Seed certification may be voluntary or obligatory. The scope of the laws may also differ. In many countries of the Commonwealth of Independent States (former USSR), all seed planted by farmers has to be certified (farm-saving is not allowed). In most countries all 'marketed' seed has to conform with standards determined by law, i.e. all seed, except farm-saved (and locally bartered) seed. More recently, laws are developed that regulate marketed seed of a limited number of 'notified' crops only. These are usually the major crops for food and industry. In some countries special provisions are included to promote the use of landraces, e.g. the draft seed act of Eritrea (N.L., personal observation).

The implementation of seed regulations is commonly the task of independent variety testing and seed certification authorities. In many developing countries variety testing is done by the (public) breeders themselves, after which a Variety Release Committee, considering the results, decides on the actual approval. Seed certification is occasionally done by a separate unit of the (public) seed multiplication programme, but in most cases by an independent service under the ministry of agriculture. In some countries seed quality control is executed by private associations or by seed producers themselves.

Analysis: seed certification

Seed certification and quality control are potentially very important services to farmers who rely on buying seed in the market. Seed quality cannot be established visually, hence a seed buyer depends either on the good faith of the supplier (brand name or personal relationship with the seller), or a dependable certification label. A major disadvantage of a formal seed certification system is that it tends to promote uniformity and increases cost, especially where inefficiencies of public institutions are reflected in the seed price.

Problems arise when authorities responsible for regulating the seed sector lose sight of its primary objective – to provide a form of protection to seed producers and seed users. In many instances regulating and certification becomes an objective in itself. There is a tendency for authorities to use seed regulation to promote formal seed production and the use of uniform 'modern' varieties, and to discourage the production of seed on-farm. It should be realized, however, that in most countries on-farm produced seed provides over 95 per cent of the seed requirement for most crops. It is a robust and extremely reliable system, it maintains important sources of genetic diversity and, from all evidence, it produces seed of acceptable quality under an efficient system of social control (Almekinders et al., 1994; H. van Amstel, pers. comm., H. Smolders, pers. comm.).

Legalistic interpretation of seed laws, bureaucratic institutional attitudes of responsible authorities, and a 'blue-print' approach to establishing seed certification units by copying procedures followed in the industrial countries, are widespread. Hence while seed certification is essentially meant to protect the interests of farmers, in practice it may lead to conflicts with farmers' organizations and NGOs. For example, under a strict interpretation of the law, selling seed of a landrace may be illegal (non-uniform and non-released variety), as is the distribution of seed in a participatory plant breeding programme before official release.

The organization and implementation of seed certification should be based on clear objectives derived from a thorough analysis of the total seed system (institutional, commercial, farmer). Rather than discouraging farmers' seed production, seed certification agencies could become constructively involved in improving the quality of on-farm produced seed in various ways. They could collect information on aspects of seed quality in the local seed system, on the loss of identity of modern varieties in various generations of on-farm multiplication, on patterns and rates of distribution of new varieties entering the farmer system, etc. Also, these agencies could actively support initiatives by public and non-governmental organizations that aim at improving the quality of seed beyond the formal sector. Essentially it means that authorities recognize the farmers' seed system as a valuable asset rather than an old-fashioned system that should be replaced with the assistance of the law. It is exactly this local seed system which nurtures agrobiodiversity and which is the basis of any *in situ* strategy for plant genetic resource management.

Analysis: variety release

In Europe and North America, modern plant breeding was introduced simultaneously with the increased use of chemical fertilizers and subsequently of chemical control of pests and diseases. Hence it was part and parcel of a process transforming agriculture to use external inputs. This transformation meant that while previously landraces were adapted to particular environments, now environments could to some extent be adapted to the requirements of particular crops and varieties. This, combined with already fairly homogeneous environments over large major agricultural areas (the plains of northwestern Europe, the US mid-west) led to the selection of new varieties adapted to extensive geographic regions. These conditions facilitated the testing of varieties at a limited set of sites under standardized practices and standardized uses.

In principle, an objective test of a variety prior to its release in the market is an important service to farmers and will guard against some protection malpractices. However, as in seed certification, formal and compulsory testing may have some serious drawbacks (Louwaars, 1998).

○ Plant breeders, dependent on formal release of their varieties, may gear their breeding programmes mainly to satisfying VCU release procedures, possibly at the expense of solving agricultural problems. Formal release then becomes the yardstick by which the success of breeders is measured, not the value of the varieties for farmers.
○ Release procedures often include certain standards of uniformity to facilitate distinctiveness. This does not encourage breeding for diversity.
○ The statistical analysis of multi-locational testing favours broad adaptability. This is a reasonable objective where the range of target environments is limited, as in high external-input agriculture in Europe and North America. However, in most tropical and subtropical regions the differences between environments and users are substantially wider. Also, in many countries in the South, on-farm yields are much lower than yields achieved on official VCU testing sites (Virk et al., 1996). Hence VCU test results have little meaning to farmers. Evidence suggests (Ceccarelli, 1989) that in widely different environments breeding for specific adaption is a serious option, requiring a totally different approach to VCU testing.
○ VCU testing is usually biased to standard criteria directly related to yield. Farmers, especially in more marginal areas, often place more emphasis on yield security (which is difficult to measure and is related to disease and pest resistances/tolerances); on product quality (cooking time, taste); on secondary products such as straw, and others (Louwaars and van Marrewijk, 1996).

Consideration should be given to these aspects in deciding on procedures for release of varieties. One option to improve on satisfying farmers' criteria is on-farm testing. However, the inclusion of farmers' opinions in bureaucratic procedures has proven difficult.

Another option is to make VCU testing optional, i.e. to provide for a formal recommendation to varieties that have been tested, but also to allow the production of quality seed of other varieties. This would increase the diversity in the seed market and would need a formal release system to prove its value.

Concluding remarks

Farmers' interests and food security, certainly in many developing countries with large numbers of smallholders and highly diverse cropping systems, would benefit from a more diversified seed supply system. In such a diverse seed system, formal and informal, public and private components need to be recognized as partners in development, as opposed to current policies which tend to classify only formal – and preferably private – seed production as 'modern'. National seed policies have an important task in guiding the improvement of such a diverse seed system in terms of seed quality and the availability of appropriate seed types to farmers. In the current concentration of private seed production in the hands of few global players, governments have to take national interests into account. Total reliance on foreign sources of major food crop seeds and varieties for national food production would seem unwise.

In order to support diverse seed systems, seed regulations should be carefully geared to support these components, with their widely differing structures. The main aspects are as follows.

○ Rules for seed certification and quality control should provide for farmer protection where necessary, while avoiding undue blockages to local seed systems. This could be implemented by regulating marketed seed of selected crops only, or by making certification voluntary rather than compulsory. Voluntary systems can be proposed only when there is sufficient competition in the market and where customers have sufficient information (farmers are literate, seed labels are checked regularly). Seed quality-control institutions can act as valuable partners in non-formal initiatives to improve seed quality and seed security only when the seed law allows them.
○ Variety release procedures should concentrate on providing information on value for cultivation and use, rather than reducing to the minimum the number of varieties that farmers can choose from. This means that the results of well designed variety trials are scrutinized by a Variety Review Committee rather than a Variety Release Committee. This committee must take farmers' opinions into account and it has to be sensitive to localized agronomic conditions and consumer preferences. This way there will be no legal hindrance to participatory plant breeding, the upgrading of diverse landraces and other methods of breeding for diversity.
○ Legal mechanisms to reward breeders, such as intellectual property rights, should carefully balance their primary objective, i.e. promotion of commercial plant breeding, with other objectives of the national seed policy, i.e. to promote the use of the best varieties by remote and resource-poor farmers; to promote breeding for diversity; to promote both formal and local seed production initiatives, etc.

Agriculture in many developing countries is much more diverse than in most parts of Europe and North America. A single seed system, whether formal, informal, public or private, cannot cater for the diverse needs of these farmers. Adapted legislation and implementation systems are necessary to develop these different methods for seed supply, in order to obtain the highest seed security.

6.5. On-farm conservation: a matter of global concern or local survival?

Robin Pistorius and Jeroen van Wijk

Introduction

In the growing international political debate, there is some agreement between formal- and informal-sector representatives about the importance of conserving landraces on-farm for both local and global interests. This disregards the deeper problem of the marginalization of local farming systems. Therefore on-farm conservation projects should be framed in broader political programmes to ease the pressure on local farming systems by the increasingly dominant industrialized agricultural production systems. Conservation targets should strengthen rural development programmes, not serve as the prime motivation of conservationist interventions.

The crucial role of local farming systems in the maintenance of genetic diversity is now generally recognized in political and academic circles, and has led to a re-validation of the role of local farming systems in biodiversity conservation at the global level. On-farm (*in situ*) conservation and crop management have even become one of the flagships in the international debate on sustainable development. In most international fora (currently notably the Conference of Parties of the CBD, and the FAO Commission on Plant Genetic Resources for Food and Agriculture) it is agreed that the real advantage of on-farm conservation lies in its ability to meet both local needs (local food security) and global needs (demands of genetic information in the crop improvement industry).

The idea that local and global conservation strategies are compatible or even mutually enforcing should be treated with the utmost care, however. Firstly, it suggests that the use of landraces and wild relatives in non-industrialized farming systems matches global agro-ecological interests, and *vice versa*. Secondly, it neglects the hard reality of the intense rivalry between the agro-industry that has the capacity to exploit landraces and wild relatives in advanced breeding and genetic engineering programmes, and the non-industrialized farming systems where such plants are collected.

Global versus local conservation

On-farm conservation programmes embody a dangerous projection of modern Western conservation strategies on local farming systems. For non-industrialized farming systems the use of genetically diverse crops is not an objective in itself, but an integrated and essential element of their farming system in order to cope with a variable and often adverse production environment in an effort to achieve yield security. Spreading risks by planting different varieties should, however, not be considered as a 'conservation strategy' analogous to the strategies developed in countries of the Organization for Economic Co-operation and Development (OECD) by agricultural or environmental institutes over the past century. Such an equation disregards the fact that the on-farm use of landraces fully depends on practical, *ad hoc* considerations of individual farmers. The most important consideration is that a plot, when planted with genetically different landraces, runs a smaller risk of being wiped out completely. This age-old farming practice implies that as soon as a landrace does not contribute further to this risk-spreading strategy, it is likely to be abandoned. Abandoning landraces on the basis of direct usefulness, however, is very much against the philosophy of the long-term, globally oriented conservation strategies as developed in OECD countries.

The marriage between global conservation strategies and rural agricultural development essentially concerns the deeper-rooted dilemma between conservation and development. We may visualize this dilemma by posing the following question: should local farming systems that are not useful for global conservation purposes be excluded from on-farm conservation programmes? Those who respond in the affirmative can be accused of a rather instrumental vision of the role of local farmers in international conservation objectives: farmers are only welcome in on-farm conservation programmes if they 'serve the global cause'. Those who do not agree may be accused of polluting the global conservation strategy by involving farmers who do not really contribute to the maintenance of biological diversity.

The idea that non-industrialized farming systems are considered the best mechanism to safeguard genetic diversity in landraces worldwide evades the question whether such conservation strategy matches the short-term interests of small farmers. The emphasis is on the short term because farming in developing countries is a matter of a constant adaptation to changing environmental circumstances, a process in which one landrace is easily replaced by another. That small farmers use or abandon landraces according to their direct interests raises questions as to their interest in long-term global collection efforts. Industrialized countries, on the other hand, do have a long-term interest in conserving landraces. This interest is likely to grow if the seed industry in OECD countries accelerates its efforts to explore new markets in developing countries.

Industrialized versus non-industrialized agriculture

Creating links between local and global conservation strategies denies the intense pressure on the non-industrialized farming systems that sustain agrobiodiversity. Developing countries increasingly use seed of technologically advanced, high-yielding plant varieties, for various reasons. Firstly, the population is growing quickly, while in some countries income increases induce dietary shifts toward wheat and meat consumption. Especially in regions where arable land can no longer expand, such as in Asia, the growing food requirements necessitate a boost in agricultural productivity for which new varieties are required. Secondly, governments of many developing countries are increasingly inclined to organize their agricultural production on the basis of competitive advantage and open up their agricultural markets to foreign producers.

Both developments have profound implications for national and local seed markets. Domestic seed firms increasingly meet competition from foreign producers, most of which are based in OECD countries. Imported varieties (notably of grain crops and potatoes) often diminish the use of landraces for region-specific varieties of traditional crops. The increasingly open world food market boosts the use of modern, imported varieties. The import of commercial varieties from OECD countries has become conditional for producing export commodities that meet industrial processing requirements and the quickly changing consumer preferences in OECD markets.

The influx of foreign varieties into national and local seed markets is not only due to the increasingly open food market. In many developing countries, the existence of farmers who are still growing traditional varieties is often seen as a sign of backwardness of the country's agricultural sector. Often a combination of seed laws and additional policies, notably fiscal incentives and credit facilities, stimulate the adoption of modern varieties among traditional farmers (Sthapit and Subedi, Chapter 4.7). Until recently, many governments stimulating the production and import of varieties considered the replacement or disappearance of genetically diverse landraces as an (inevitable) side-effect of a necessary switch to an industrialized agricultural production strategy. Governments of currently industrialized countries took a similar stance over the past 100 years.

Whether small farmers will continue to use (and indirectly conserve) landraces depends on the acceptance of non-industrialized farming systems as a viable alternative for the increasingly dominant industrialized system. The current discussion about on-farm conservation strategies should therefore be broadened by discussion of the rivalry between the highly industrialized, (bio-)technology driven, globally organized production strategy on the one hand, and the non-industrialized, traditional, locally organized production strategy on the other.

Clashes between the two production strategies are most intense in developing countries where the social costs involved in the combination of a more liberal economic policy and agro-industrialization often cannot be adequately compensated (Pistorius and Van Wijk, 1999). Along with this political controversy over the production strategy comes disagreement over the (economic) value of seed, the products they yield, the optimal organization of agricultural production, as well as the optimal relationship between agricultural production and the social, natural, and cultural environments. Not surprisingly, many farmers in developing countries oppose not only the new varieties, but also the associated regulation that determines the rules for reproduction and dissemination of seed. This regulation, however, is one of the cornerstones of industrialized agriculture.

Putting on-farm conservation in perspective

The broad support for compatible local and global conservation strategies contrasts sharply with limited attention to the fundamental cause of the disappearance of agrobiodiversity, i.e. the disappearance of local farming systems themselves. Conservation targets should strengthen rural development programmes in order to re-establish the closed circle of conservation, local breeding and agricultural production, rather than serving as the prime motivation of interventions inspired by conservationist principles. Although genetic diversity generated by on-farm conservation may sometimes match long-term global conservation strategies, it would be wrong to conclude that local crop management can easily be integrated into international conservation programmes.

Conservationist interventions should recognize farmers' rationality in the use or abandonment of landraces. This rationality used to be determined by local or national market conditions. The decision of a growing number of governments in developing countries to open up their agricultural market to international competition now also allows cheap food and new varieties to enter even the remotest rural areas. How can farmers who have to compete with cheap foreign imports rely on landraces? How can farmers defend their informal seed exchange system when it is increasingly curtailed by new intellectual property regulation? Political decisions, such as import and export levies for agricultural products, intellectual property protection on new varieties, organization of the dissemination of seed, and support for marginalized farmers, have a large but still little recognized impact on landrace conservation.

Policies that attempt to implement on-farm conservation should rest on unambiguous objectives for the recognition of non-industrialized farming systems as a viable alternative to industrialized agriculture. As long as the intense pressure of industrialized agriculture on non-industrialized agriculture is not recognized, on-farm conservation remains a weak concept in the light of current developments in international agriculture.

6.6. Intellectual property rights: patents or *sui generis* systems?

Niels Louwaars and Jan Engels

Introduction

Planting material is an essential resource for farming. Farmers' selection and seed production has been an integral part of crop domestication and adaptation of crops to different cultivation techniques and uses. Modern plant breeding has built on this farmer selection in terms of both methods and materials. Planting material has traditionally been regarded as a highly valued communal or public resource.

The development of modern plant breeding is supported in a number of countries by public investment, or through prizes for outstanding varieties decided upon in national or regional seed fairs or payment from a national fund, and in some countries through intellectual property rights such as plant variety protection. More recently, plant materials have been included in the patent system in some countries. This trend of individual rights over plants and plant varieties results in gradual limitations in the freedom for farmers to acquire and use particular forms of plant genetic resources.

The spread of intellectual property rights is facilitated by the Agreement on Trade Related Aspects of Intellectual Property Rights (TRIPS). It prescribes that members of the World Trade Organization (WTO) provide for patent protection of all inventions. Members may, however, exclude from patentability:

> Plants and animals other than micro-organisms, and essentially biological processes for the production of plants or animals other than non-biological and micro-biological processes. However, members shall provide for the protection of plant varieties either by patents or by an effective *sui generis* system or a combination thereof.

A *sui generis* system is a system 'of its own kind', i.e. in WTO's terms an intellectual property right other than a patent. The different plant variety protection systems that are currently operational in member countries of the Union Internationale pour la Protection des Obtentions Végétales (UPOV) may be considered *sui generis*, but systems other than UPOV may be designed as long as they correspond with the TRIPS requirements.

Many countries that never had property rights protection systems for plants are now in the process of designing one. Intellectual property rights systems, even though primarily designed to regulate the formal system, do affect local seed systems, and through disturbing the dynamics of these local seed systems they may affect the *in situ* management of agrobiodiversity.

Intellectual property rights

Intellectual property rights are applied in several countries to protect the interests of inventors, with the aim of supporting investments in innovative research. Plant varieties are excluded from patentability in most countries for ethical reasons (patenting life forms is considered unethical); technical reasons (self-replicating nature, inherent heterogeneity of the subject matter, lack of 'inventive step' in conventional breeding); and economic reasons (food policy). In a number of countries, plant varieties are protected by plant variety protection (PVP) systems.

Patents provide for very strong protection to the patent-holder against the commercialization of the invention by others, i.e. producing/using the protected subject matter and all aspects of marketing. A patent-holder may licence the right to others, i.e. to allow the production of prescribed quantities for prescribed markets, commonly in return for the payment of a royalty. An exemption to the patent rights provides for the liberty for anyone to research the invention. In case this research results in a product that can be commercialized, the patent-holder has to consent to this use, i.e. he/she may grant a licence on mutually agreed terms. Standard patent protection, when applied to plants, limits the freedom of users (farmers) and competing inventors (breeders), and may lead to monopolistic situations. This means that specific genetic diversity or even complete gene pools of a given species may be locked up by patent holders, rendering them inaccessible for further breeding by others.

The PVP systems that have evolved from the first UPOV Convention in 1961 provide for a level of protection that is adapted to agricultural practice in the UPOV member states (initially only Western European countries). This is characterized by the use of uniform varieties in high external-input production systems. Important characteristics of UPOV's PVP compared with patents are the protection requirements for distinctiveness, uniformity, stability and novelty that are related to the mode of reproduction of the variety, along with a strong breeders' exemption and a farmers' privilege.

The breeders' exemption allows any protected variety available to be used in further breeding. The only restriction is that the rights on a new variety that is essentially derived from another variety, i.e. developed through minor modification of the genome, become dependent on the rights of the owner of the original variety (UPOV 1991).

The farmers' privilege provides for different levels of farm-saving (UPOV 1991) and non-commercial trade (UPOV 1978, as interpreted in the USA) of seed of protected varieties without the consent of the rights-holder, and without payment of royalties. This provision is optional to individual member states in UPOV 1991, but is limited in scope. A glossary of terms is given in Box 6.1.

Policy issues in relation to plant variety protection

Policy-makers in countries that have ratified the World Trade Agreement have to determine what kind of protection should be granted to plant varieties in accordance with Article 27(3)b of TRIPS. It is advisable to ensure a balance between the interests of different players in the agricultural sector, ranging from subsistence farmers to commercial seed companies and exporters of agricultural products. In addition, compliance with TRIPS should be arranged in such a way that there is no conflict with other international agreements.

The export sector may be served best by full protection of the varieties of these export crops, which complies with the protection levels in the importing countries, and the countries of origin of the planting material. This improves access to the newest varieties that fetch the best prices in international markets.

Near-subsistence farmers might, however, be served best by the absence of any intellectual property rights that restrict the availability of seed of any variety that may suit their farming conditions. Patents or full PVP probably have this effect, as they restrict the farmer-to-farmer diffusion of seed. *Sui generis* intellectual property rights that do not have such negative side-effects are possible. Options include, for example, limiting the scope of protection to certified seed only, or specifically prescribing amounts that can freely move from farmer to farmer, leaving the local seed system untouched. This can be done through well chosen definitions of 'seed' and through a wide interpretation of the farmers' privilege. This option, however, results in minimal rewards for breeders and thus calls for public investments in (participatory) breeding for such conditions.

Alternative options that have been discussed in agrobiodiversity circles include the relaxation of the requirements for protection, for example with regard to novelty and uniformity. This would allow for the protection of 'improved landraces', putting farmer-breeders on equal footing with their large-scale commercial counterparts. However, protection is useful only in a market where farmers are able to pay for seed, and are willing to pay a mark-up on the seed price for the breeder. Relaxing the uniformity requirement seems positive for farmer-breeders but also opens ways to monopolize gene pools.

Diverse development objectives are common within the same countries. These can be accommodated in a *sui generis* system providing full protection for export crops such as flowers, based on UPOV 1991 without a farmers' privilege, and a very liberal privilege for small-farmer food crops. This can be done by introducing lists of crops for which particular regimes apply. For crops that are grown both by commercial and subsistence farmers, an extended privilege can be granted to the latter class, for example based on cropped area or maximum output – only farmers with more than 10ha paying royalties.

Policy issues in relation to biotechnology patents

A fairly recent phenomenon is the patenting of genes and biotechnological methods in a limited number of countries. If biotechnology patents are applied to their full extent, varieties that contain such patented genes should be freely available for further breeding under the PVP, but are in effect fully blocked for further use by the patent. A plant containing more than one patented gene requires the consent of all patent holders both for commercialization and for further breeding. There is a risk that biotech companies can obtain strategic control over particular germplasm. The European directive on biotechnology patents, however, includes a strong compulsory licensing clause to reduce possible monopolistic tendencies. Secondly, under the patent farmers may not be allowed to multiply seed on-farm even when the patented gene was introduced through natural introgression into a local variety. Of course, such rights will be enforced only when the cost of exercising the right is less than the benefits.

A doomsday scenario is, however:

○ a beneficial gene is introduced into a landrace
○ both natural and farmer selection operate in favour of the gene
○ after a number of generations the patent-holder can claim full control over the landrace.

Policy-makers have to realize these dangers and design sufficient 'escape routes' in their intellectual property rights laws.

Opportunities

Article 27.3b of TRIPS offers two interpretations that can avoid negative influences by patents on local seed systems.

The first option can be summarized as follows:

o when a country chooses not to patent plants under Article 27.3, also parts of plants such as genes cannot be patented, or
o when plants are not patentable, it means that patents on parts of plants may not lead to the *de facto* extension of the patent to (or beyond) the plant.

This means that exemptions similar to those in the PVP system enter patent legislation for biotech-innovations, i.e. a farmers' privilege and a breeders' exemption. The latter can be arranged either with the consent of the patent holder or with an automatic compulsory licence system.

The second broad option is to apply the patent system strictly, i.e. have a strict analysis of the basic requirements of existing patent systems – innovative step, novelty, and the scope of protection.

o Innovative step/non-obviousness – conventional breeding is by definition not innovative, as crossing parents and selection of new varieties uses methods that are known by all breeders. The choice of particular parents is in almost all cases quite obvious. Furthermore, a variety can be described in such a way that another person skilled in the art can develop the same variety using the same parents and the same selection method. Conventional varieties thus cannot be protected by patents.
o Novelty – a natural gene may not be patented even if the gene is new in a particular genetic background (i.e. was taken from another species). This restricts the patent system to man-made DNA sequences that do not exist in a functional manner in nature. This avoids the majority of patent applications on genes becoming effective.
o When a 'new' gene is inserted into a plant, a patent may be granted on that gene in that plant. When the same gene is then transferred to other varieties through natural means it may not be necessary to extend the protection to these varieties, since the patent-holder has no any influence on the (natural) crossing. This avoids process patents on transformation methods extending to all (indirect) products, and in this way avoids monopolistic effects. Transferring the gene to another species (e.g. *Bacillus thuringiensis*) is in fact a quite obvious step and thus not innovative. This interpretation further avoids broad claims such as the one on 'all genetically modified cotton' granted in the USA.

The above measures do not support the transfer of technology from technology-rich countries to countries that do apply this rather liberal interpretation of patents. It is, however, debatable whether such softening rules have a negative effect on national biotechnology research investments. History has shown that countries that have a weak position in a particular field of technology can benefit from the absence of patents. This allows the national industry freely to use technologies that are protected in other countries for the home market, and thus reduce the technology gap over time. Clearly this goes against the spirit of TRIPS, but developing countries may consider this option.

Other interests

The spread of intellectual property rights coincides with global trends towards the use of legal instruments in support of the conservation and sustainable use of plant genetic resources and the recognition of farmers' rights and national sovereignty over these resources. The Convention on Biological Diversity, the International Undertaking on Plant Genetic Resources (non-legally binding), and the international debates on traditional resource rights all deal with access to and sharing of benefits arising from the use of plant material. Even though intellectual property rights on plant varieties deal with similar mechanisms, the objectives (to promote breeding) are so different from those in this group of agreements (to conserve and recognize farmers' contribution to plant genetic resources) that combining them in one legal framework is not likely to yield a workable system. Attempts in various Asian countries have not yet yielded operational systems that combine farmers' and breeder's rights.

It is, however, possible to introduce appropriate linkages between farmers' and breeder's rights in a *sui generis* system for the protection of plant varieties. This can be done by introducing an obligation for the breeder applying for protection of a variety to declare the origin of the materials used in breeding, and to present evidence that these materials were acquired legally and used in accordance with existing rules (prior informed consent). The UPOV system does not allow for such specific additional requirements. These obligations can, however, be covered by the 'eligibility clause' within a UPOV-compatible law.

The diversity of conditions among and within countries, and the diversity of development options, make it impossible to design one model law for *sui generis* protection of plant varieties in the South. There are, however, significant advantages to high levels of international harmonization for both the seed industry and the authorities. This applies to both laws and implementation systems. The WTO could use the expertise of organizations such as IPGRI, Plant Research International and others to assist new member states in this manner.

6.7. Institutional transformation to support diversity

Janice Jiggins and Helle Munk Ravnborg

Introduction

The dominant transformation processes in agriculture today are those that reduce diversity. National and international agencies have supported such transformation processes in order to secure reliable planting materials and seeds, increase yield, reduce harvest fluctuations, and reach industrial efficiencies of scale enlargement and standardization. These processes involve a range of public and private institutions, principally those engaged in policy formulation, design and implementation of incentive structures, input supply, agricultural research, extension, processing and marketing.

Until recently in the majority of countries, and still today in many developing countries, these institutions have sought to exercise centralized authority. They have done so in order to control and prescribe what farmers should do, so as to satisfy national policy goals. Reduction of diversity, it could be argued, was a necessary condition for centralized and hierarchical research and extension services, incentive structures, etc., to function. There are few cases in which institutions have been designed flexibly to support and adapt according to the actual, multi-faceted diversity of farming contexts, farmers' goals and the spatial and temporal dynamics of ecosystems.

Institutions appear to have operated on the basis of assumptions such as '700 000 farming families are all busy preparing their maize fields in the second week of November and are all applying between five and 15 bags of fertilizers when planting', as if farms are – or could become – uniform units of production operating within the simplicities of industrial decision-making (a goal perhaps attained in the US mid-west). Yet even in the large areas of South and South-East Asia, there is evidence for considerable local variation in irrigated rice or wheat within the apparent homogeneity and stability of the production environment. In more typical dryland farming situations, where farmers may cultivate a dozen or more different crops and many more varieties within complex schemes of staggered planting and intercropping, it would be more accurate to use the metaphors of a 'dance' or 'performance' to describe the evolution of decision-making in the dynamics of socio-economic and biophysical contexts.

If the goal is to maintain and even enhance diversity within agriculture, then the challenge is to design institutions that support local innovation and evolution. This would entail the repatriation of responsibility and accountability to context. Several preconditions and design criteria could be listed.

Preconditions:

○ a will to change – enough people are fed up with the system as it operates today, and they pool efforts to redefine and realize common interest in preserving the quality of natural resources and human communities on which all farming depends;
○ a willingness to devolve control from central institutions to other scales and levels of interaction.

Design criteria:

○ a process- and problem-oriented management style within institutions which allows flexibility and promotes communication;

○ institutional mechanisms which promote horizontal communication within and among all groups of stakeholders (Ravnborg, 1996).

The local agricultural research committees promoted by the Hillsides Programme of Centro Internacional de Agricultura Tropical (CIAT) offer as an example an experiment which moves toward satisfying these criteria. Its structure promotes farmer experimentation, local innovation, horizontal communication and evolution of local institutional capacity (Ashby and Sperling, 1995). Yet the process itself is determined and designed from the outside by researchers and implemented by extension agents, following a predetermined and very strict scheme. It does not base its point of departure in farmers' own ways of assessing opportunities or formulating problems, or seeking solutions. More interesting examples of horizontal communication and local institutional capacity are to be found among indigenous groups in the Colombian Amazon, who have their own systems for learning how to become crop farmers, hunters, etc. (Kronik, 1998). Central events are parties or dances to which people are invited from the surrounding area. If it is a party for cassava, hosted by the person who is in the process of becoming a good crop farmer, guests will bring examples of their own cassava varieties. They pose to the farmer riddles or questions about the cassava in order to 'test' the farmer's learning and capacity to innovate through systematic enquiry, observation and experimentation. It is a system with no outside judge and focuses on learning rather than education.

Scope for new institutional initiatives; constraints and threats

There may be increasing scope to recognize and build on informal institutions of learning and innovation, and to transform centralized agencies into institutions better adapted to the local context. With growing acceptance of economic liberalization and globalization policies, public-sector agricultural and food agencies are being privatized and/or commercialized, leading to a much more pluralistic institutional scene in agriculture. At the same time, the role of governments in defining the public interest is becoming more inclusive, with other stakeholders, based in civil society rather than the public sector, having a voice in shaping policy. And central governments, with greater or lesser energy, are devolving some of their powers and capacities to local governments and local agencies. On the face of it, these trends offer considerably more potential for farmers' organizations, local conservation interests and community institutions to guide and participate in the conservation of diversity in agriculture in ways that suit the context.

However, some important distinctions and reservations should be noted. Agriculture in industrial countries has become such a small employment sector that it can no longer be the main wellspring of livelihoods and welfare in rural areas, nor the main voice in the conservation of diversity.

The institutional web of stakeholders in conserving diversity thus is necessarily somewhat disconnected from intimate management of the resources themselves. This poses tricky issues in terms of adaptive management. In the South, the problem is somewhat different. Many families are still dependent on resource management for their welfare and livelihood, but may lack technical options or the institutional resources to raise yield and incomes in ways which conserve diversity.

However, the same political and economic forces which are opening up the institutional space at local levels have led already to extreme concentration at higher levels of interaction. Agricultural commodity trading and processing globally are dominated by a handful of multi-nationals; companies dealing in veterinary products, pharmaceuticals, seed supply and agrochemicals play an increasing role in the transformation of agricultural diversity; and agricultural policy is formed increasingly within institutions such as the World Trade Organization. One of the less tangible but crucial issues that arise is the extent to which individual and community knowledge of biodiversity is being abstracted and hoarded (under patent and genome scripts) in the private commercial sector and, increasingly, in universities whose research is funded by commercial interests. Institutional memory of how to manage adaptively at the local level is lost in the process.

Adaptive management: theory into practice

At a theoretical level, one might observe that institutions serve society by capturing tested experience and embedding this in action. In this sense, institutions serve to increase stability. In agriculture they increasingly do so not by merely moderating, but by eliminating in the short term the influence of natural variation (rainfall, pests, fertility, soil quality, seed diversity, etc.). The consequence is that farmers become vulnerable to institutional and policy failure. In different ways this in effect transfers instability to individual farmers and farm sectors in both the North (e.g. beef farmers during the UK's BSE crisis; wheat disease in Minnesota – see Mercer and Wainwright, Chapter 2.7), and the South (e.g. small-scale farmers caught in a price squeeze under structural adjustment; all farmers – especially women – who are not well served by extension, credit and marketing services). Farmers become more vulnerable to institutional malfunction or breakdown, increasing their exposure to the loss of ecological resilience that a loss of diversity implies.

Studies of the social–ecological practices and institutional mechanisms that farmers have evolved in order to maintain resilience describe over 14 practices based on ecological knowledge (e.g. related to management of landscape patchiness, habitat protection, species protection, temporal restrictions, succession management, resource rotation within and across ecosystems, seed exchange, etc.), and a hugely diverse range and mix of social arrangements governing the generation, accumulation and transmission of knowledge, institutional structures and dynamics, internalization of resource management behaviour, and the evolution of worldviews and values

(Becker et al., 1995; Berkes et al., 1997). Only some of these are likely to survive unchanged in the present competitive environment.

Diversity is not always upheld at the individual farmer level, but rather at the 'community' level, and certainly not always as part of a deliberate strategy. As an example, a recent study in Honduras (Escolán et al., 1998) found that although Honduras has a long tradition of growing maize and beans, and thus presumably hundreds of local varieties, most farmers interviewed in three watersheds in different parts of Honduras claimed to cultivate only one variety (81 per cent for maize and 77 per cent for beans out of 440 and 347 households, respectively). However, the variety was not necessarily the same for all households in a watershed nor the same for each household for each year, but it was most frequently a local variety, chosen for reasons of higher and more stable yields, better pest resistance and lower costs. Commercial seeds are physically available but apparently not attractive. Thus at the same time there is a situation of (i) limited diversity in agricultural practice at the household level (one variety per household per year); (ii) many local varieties available to call into use which are used as needed or desired; and (iii) availability of a few commercial varieties which, however, remain largely unused. This means that in this case of bean and maize varieties farmers (knowingly and co-ordinated or not) manage diversity collectively rather than individually. In such cases there is scope for institutional interventions that support farmers in preserving or enhancing the existing diversity.

6.8. Consuming diversity: a long way to go?

Joost Jongerden

Introduction

How is agricultural production, and hence agrobiodiversity, linked with consumers' issues in the Netherlands? This linkage is usually regarded as more apparent then real. In this chapter I argue that in the modern agricultural production system in the Netherlands, the characteristics and quality of food products are not necessary connected with the characteristics and quality of agricultural production; in fact they are disconnected from each other. In a modern production system as in the Netherlands, the production of diversity takes place at the level not of the agricultural production process, but of food processing, markets and distribution. Hence uniformity at the farm level and diversity at the consumer's level exist in parallel and are not contradictory to each other. But it could be different.

Re-organization of food production

The industrialization of society has not left agriculture unaffected. The industrial logic in agricultural production is described by three typical characteristics. Firstly, agriculture is organized as a production chain which consists of a supplying industry, farming; a processing industry; and distribution to consumers (Jongerden and Ruivenkamp, Chapter 6.3). Changes in agriculture cannot be understood without taking the relationships in that chain into consideration. Secondly, the chain implies specialization (activities such as selecting new varieties and processing food are carried out by specialized actors and are thereby externalized from the farm) and standardization (agriculture becomes heavily dependent on technology, which dictates the employment of production resources). Thirdly, agriculture produces commodities, which implies that market and price relations have become dominant for the production process.

The industrialization of the production process has had a great impact on the technology used in agriculture and on the use of genetic diversity as part of that technology.

> During recent decades a seemingly irresistible process has washed over Europe's countryside. Farming and green space have been thoroughly reshuffled. The modernization process has affected the remotest corners of the continent. Whilst markets and the supply of agricultural technologies became increasingly interwoven and standardized, farming itself was deliberately restructured to fit new economic and technological conditions (van der Ploeg and van Dijk, 1995).

The Dutch used the term *productivisme* to refer to that process of modernization. Key concepts were increasing production per hectare/animal and per labour unit; standardization; specialization; and increase of scale (Chapter 6.3). The increase of scale takes place not only at the farm level (the level of production), but also at the level of input supply and markets. Today agricultural production is intensively interwoven in markets on a world scale. It is now quite common that vegetables, fruits and arable farming products travel thousands of kilometres before meeting their consumers. The Dutch Alternative Consumers' Union *Alternatieve Konsumenten Bond* raised this issue in a book entitled *How Many Kilometres did you Eat Today?* (Absil et al., 1997**).** The trend is that food products are more and more being assembled from agricultural components such as carbohydrates, oils and proteins; these components – rather than the products – become the new globetrotters. The components for a tin of tomato soup come from from Italy, USA, Germany, the Netherlands, Japan, Belgium, South America, UK and China; the globalization of a cup of soup.

These interwoven markets have internationalized food and drink. French cheese which in the past was sold in the Netherlands only in specialized shops is now a standard product which can be purchased from any supermarket. So consumption alternatives have increased through the creation of a global market. Not only the internationalization of agricultural production and distribution, but also the development of food-processing technology have contributed to this increase in product diversity. Modern food processing is based on fractionating agricultural products into components and assembling them as new food products. The globalization of markets and the development of technology have re-arranged space (markets) and time (seasons) in such a way that, if one can afford it, it is possible to purchase any product at any time.

Food and farmers

Some speak about the internalization of food cultures and the coming of a global kitchen. But the suggestion that food and taste became more indistinct is a false one. Although food cultures are not so much tied to a particular area, local and regional, social-economic and cultural differences all still play an important role. If the integration of new food products in a specific food culture takes place, this is almost never a simple introduction. Often the taste and character of the original dish is changed. Dutch paella is very different from the Spanish original, and pasta in the Netherlands is eaten as a main dish whereas it is a starter in the Italian kitchen (Jobse van Putten, 1995).

For the consumer there is no uniformity; on the contrary, at the level of consumption one can distinguish a great diversity of products. But the paradox of modern agricultural and food production is that diversity at the level of consumption goes hand-in-hand with uniformity at the level of production. This is mainly due to the kind of interactions involved in agricultural production: farmers, food processors, retailers and consumers. In short, for food processors and retailers their point of departure is the food-product that is sold on the supermarket shelves. Communication with consumers about foods and drinks principally refers to the end product – it is about the quality and quantity of ingredients and components, the fats, carbonates, sugars, vitamins, additives, etc. Communications are strongly based on the (de)construction of marketing strategies which strongly link with cultural and social lifestyles (youth, health food, etc.). In communicating about food the actual production process is of minor importance, although fair-trade organizations and organic agriculture argue against this. It may also be incorrect to refer to the character of the agricultural production process, for example its regionality: Gouda cheese was historically produced in the area near the city of Gouda, but today Gouda is a brand name without any direct connection to that location.

What does this logic of food production means for farmers? In modern food production the characteristics of desirable food products originate not at farm level but at industry level, therefore the agricultural production process has become of less importance for the production of food products. At the farm level the emphasis is not on quality, but on quantity. This is the message from the industry to farmers, as some members of a regional agricultural initiative experienced when they were told by an agro-industrial co-operative that 'Farmers do not have to bother about the production of quality. The job of farmers is to produce as cheaply as possible, that of the co-operative to sell as expensively as possible; by means of profit-sharing farmers will also benefit from that'.

In the 'productivist' agricultural production system now found in the Netherlands, in general bulk is produced (large quantities of agricultural materials with low surplus value) which is processed into a wide range of different food products. This would not be a problem if this production system were not so vulnerable, both in ecological terms (pollution of the environment, lack of diversity at farm level making it ecologically vulnerable) and in economic terms (low prices for agricultural products, high debts for farmers).

New perspectives

During the 1970s the productivist system of agriculture was opposed by many farmers. Different NGOs emerged in the agricultural landscape, some with a regional and sectoral orientation, others with national ambitions, and on many occasions established by farmers and/or students from the Agricultural University in Wageningen who sometimes would become farmers after graduation. Those NGOs questioned the dairy and arable farming policies (sectoral), the industrialization of agriculture, environment and payment issues (national), North–South relations (international), and raised the issues of the hidden and often unrecognized role of women farmers and farmers' wives (gender) and of research and technology (science). But debates and awareness-raising alone are not enough for a dynamic of change. Moreover, the farmers who kept the NGOs alive were also looking for new perspectives for their own farms and labour. Some of them made a choice for organic farming, and in the 1980s we saw the first steps towards a new production system which is referred to as 'quality production', 'regional production' or 'diversity agriculture'. Those initiatives are characterized by van der Ploeg and van Dijk (1995).

The case of the *Zeeuwse Vlegel* and diversity

An example of such a new production system is that of the *Zeeuwse Vlegel*, an initiative of arable farmers in the southern Netherlands (see Wiskerke, Chapter 2.8). The initiative has its roots in the wheat-study clubs that flourished in the 1980s where farmers discussed the use of varieties, fertilizers and pesticides, and compared farm results. A group of young farmers and members of the environmentalist *Zeeuwse Milieu Organisatie* agreed that time was lost in arguing, and that the way forward would be to develop a common perspective. In 1988 they formulated their plan to produce environmentally sound wheat, processing and marketing it as a special bread, and at the same time establishing closer contacts between producers and consumers (Anon., 1996). Environmentally sound wheat production allowed the use of herbicides before sowing, but not any other use of agrochemicals. On the consumer–producer relationship, one of the *Zeeuwse Vlegel* farmers commented that 'among consumers awareness

291

about food is far away; among farmers actually as well. All think in kilograms and in money. Producers are alienated from what they produce and consumers are alienated from what they consume' (Jongerden and Ruivenkamp, 1996). The *Zeeuwse Vlegel* today also makes cookies and produces barley for beer.

Quality and diversity

The text 'Here your *Zeeuwse Vlegel* is growing' is posted on large signs in the fields planted with wheat for *Zeeuwse Vlegel* bread. This way a direct link is made between production at the farm level and the bread one can buy at the baker. What the passer-by does not see is that on the 70ha of *Zeeuwse Vlegel* wheat production eight different varieties are planted (Table 6.4). This situation contrasts with the common Dutch wheat agriculture where two or three varieties dominate (Chapter 6.3). The choice of eight varieties is part of the production strategy: the *Zeeuwse Vlegel* does not use chemicals, so in order to suppress pathogen growth a diversity of varieties are employed. The second reason is economic: the *Zeeuwse Vlegel* cannot produce a surplus to compensate for possible yield losses as this will lower the economic return. All wheat has to be of good quality, as the price of *Zeeuwse Vlegel* wheat is related to the fact that the wheat is processed into bread. Last but not least, the diversity of varieties is grown in order to make an excellent blend of flour for baking bread. So diversity at the level of agricultural production is created by producing quality at both farmer and consumer levels. The *Zeeuwse Vlegel* farmers have been able to find varieties that match their requirements, but with difficulty (Chapter 2.8).

Table 6.4: Varieties grown by the *Zeeuwse Vlegel*

Variety	Area (ha)	Area (per cent)
Winter wheat	41.70	58.3
Renan	17.77	24.8
Torfrida	14.45	20.2
Florin	9.32	13.0
Ramses	0.6	0.8
Summer wheat	29.85	41.7
Anemos	3.25	4.5
Cadenza	2.2	3.1
Arcade	18.6	26.0
Sunnan*	5.7	8.0
	71.55	100.0

Source: Anon., 1996.
* On farm-produced seed.

New institutional relations

In order to end consumers' alienation and to link the production and consumption of diversity, new institutional relationships are needed. This involves research institutes, actors from the agro-industrial production chain, and environmental and consumers' organizations. Apart from 'pushing' institutions and breeders to work for high quality in consumers' as well as ecological terms, 'pulling' incentives are also needed: getting the market and hence the consumers interested. Consumers' organizations should be instrumental in increasing consumers' involvement; however, so far experiences with Dutch consumers' organizations are not very promising. One of the *Zeeuwse Vlegel* farmers commented: 'Consumers' organizations are not involved at all; it is a problem we have been struggling with for some years already' (Jongerden and Ruivenkamp, 1996).

There are two consumers' organizations in the Netherlands: the large, mainstream *Consumentenbond* (CB, Consumers' Association) and the smaller *Alternatieve Konsumenten Bond* (AKB, Alternative Consumers' Union). Both organizations have a particular position in consumers' issues.

The main orientation of the AKB is on organic agriculture. As the *Zeeuwse Vlegel* is a strange kind of hybrid between organic and regular agriculture, it is out of the scope of the AKB. However, AKB considers regional production, with its short production chain, sustainable and productive use of local resources and regional production of surplus value as an important impetus for renewal of the countryside. But this is advocated more in terms of policy than in practical initiatives.

The mainstream CB has a position which reflects the 'productivist' agriculture and food production system. The CB tests food and drink among other items. It does so from a component and price perspective, and does not pay attention to production processes. The CB is not particularly interested in trying to restore relations between sustainable agriculture and high-quality food consumption. As one of the CB co-ordinators comments: 'We see that our magazine, in which we compare consumer products, is highly appreciated when we assess mass consumption goods. Articles about products for specific consumer groups have a low appreciation. Every now and then we write about those regional initiatives. But, in general, these initiatives have to make use of regional media'.

Regional initiatives are not regional because of bordering walls, but because of their relation to resources. This encompasses both regional/ local and national and international agendas. 'The potential of 'local design', using specific, endogenous, local resources, and the capacity to link this approach to an extended network that includes state agencies, is crucial for success' (de Bruin, 1995).

Coalitions and support are crucial for making new approaches work. It is typical that in the newly emerging networks, organized consumers are still missing from discussions of new sustainable relations to local resources at the farm level and the production of food. The least consumers' organizations can do is expose regional initiatives. The CB, with its strong tradition of comparative research into consumer products, could include new test criteria such as environmentally and economically sound production methods, something they embark on extremely cautiously and slowly. They seem to follow the interests of consumers rather than taking the inititiave to make changes. The consumers' organizations could also be instrumental in the development of a consumers' hallmark for goods that are produced in an ecologically and economically sound manner. Such a hallmark could be independent, but also part of a (yet to come) federal hallmark that will integrate different existing hallmarks. In this way the link between food products and agricultural production processes could become more real than apparent.

6.9. Supporting the utilization and development of traditional leafy vegetables in Africa

James Chweya and Conny Almekinders

Introduction

The indigenous leafy vegetables can be placed in the category of minor and under-utilized crops, and represent an important genetic resource with an unknown potential for development. Their decreased use in the traditional diet is associated with a pressure on at least a part of this group of plants as a genetic resource. Understanding the reasons for this decreased utilization could contribute to the design of support for the utilization and development of this plant genetic resource.

The traditional use of indigenous leafy vegetables in East Africa

Traditionally, the leafy vegetables have an important place in the African rural diet (Keller et al., 1969). Cat's whiskers (*Cleome gynandra*), nightshade species (*Solanum* ssp.), jute (*Corchorus olitorius*), *Amaranthus* ssp. and *Launaea cornuta* are among the important species in this group in Kenya (Chweya, 1994; Maundu et al., 1999). The vernacular names vary from country to country, and very often from region to region.

The leafy vegetables are cultivated, semi-cultivated and collected from natural, spontaneously growing populations. The cultivated ones are mostly grown as vegetables near the homestead, but also include the leaves of pumpkins (*Cucurbita* spp.), cowpea (*Vigna unguiculata*) and cassava (*Manihot esculenta*). The semi-cultivated and wild ones – sometimes also weedy species – are mostly collected from, and only to some extent nurtured in, their natural habitats such as the humid tropical forests or natural grasslands, or as weeds in the field, the vegetation around fields, water courses and roads. They are often collected in the rainy season when the crops are still not mature and food supplies in the household stores are low.

For this reason, for many households they are an important food source during this 'hunger gap'.

Most cultivated indigenous vegetable species and varieties in Africa are well adapted to low-input agricultural production. They are valued by the farmers – in Africa usually women – for their freedom from diseases and low requirements for inputs. They fill particular niches in the agro-ecosystem, and may have insect-repellent properties that could be useful in more intensive production systems. Apart from their culinary values, leafy vegetables are appreciated for their medicinal properties. Some vegetables are known to give strength to the blood and increase the production of mothers' milk, others are recommended to cure stomach aches, anaemia and dry skin and to remove worms (Maundu et al., 1999). Their yield and nutritional value compare well with the most commonly used exotic vegetables such as lettuce and cabbage (Table 6.5). The leafy vegetables in general, both exotic and indigenous ones, are an important source of vitamins and nutrients in the African diet, and are a necessary complement to the staple food.

Table 6.5: Fresh yield and content of proteins, vitamin A and C, calcium and iron of four indigenous leafy vegetables and two exotic ones that are important in Kenya

Species	Yield (t/ha)	Protein (g)*	Vitamin A mg β carotene	Vitamin C (mg)†	Ca (mg)†	Fe (mg)†
Gynandropsis gynandra	10	5.4–7.7	6.7–18.9	127–177	434	11
Solanum nigram	30	3.2–4.6	2.7–7.9	37–141	215	4
Corchorus olitorius	7	4.5–5.5	3.9–5.4	170–204	270	8
Amaranthus spp.	45	4.0–4.3	5.3–8.7	92–159	800	4
Latuca sativa	10	0.8–1.6	0.2–7.8	3.33	17	0.5–4.0
Brassica olearea var. apitata	26	1.4–3.3	Tr.–4.8	20–220	30–204	1–2

* g per 100 g fresh weight of the edible parts.
† mg per 100 g fresh weight of the edible parts
Source: adapted from Chweya (1994) and Imungi (1989 cited byn Chweya, 1994).

Decreasing importance of indigenous leafy vegetables

The traditional importance of indigenous leafy vegetables has been strongly affected in Africa over the past decades as a result of modern development. This contrasts with the situation in Asia, where the indigenous leafy vegetables continue to be important and are also included in the activities of the commercial breeding and seed companies (Grubben and Almekinders, 1997; see also van der Werff and van Donk, Chapter 4.4).

Although there is evidence that the use and production of some traditional leafy vegetable species is increasing and their value to users higher than estimated (Chweya and Eyzaguirre, 1999), the overall importance of this category of plants is probably still in decline. There are various reasons. Firstly, the introduction and promotion of 'exotic' vegetables for production and consumption has had a negative effect on the status of traditional vegetables. 'European' vegetables were efficiently produced on commercial farms, providing a stable supply to urban markets. The consumption of tomato and cabbage was more fashionable and associated with being part of modern society. Eating the traditional vegetables was considered backward and represented poverty. Also, urban markets offer exotic vegetables in abundance, while the indigenous ones are hard to find. The indigenous leafy vegetables are more difficult to keep fresh after harvest, during transport and at the market place than tomatoes and cabbages. People wanting to eat traditional leafy vegetables often grow and collect these around their own homestead, hence there is a degree of self-sufficiency for these vegetables. For commercial producers the exotic vegetables are more attractive, and infrastructure and entrepreneurial activities for traditional vegetables are absent.

For the semi-domesticated and wild species there is another threat. The increasing population pressure increases both the intensity of collection of these plants and the destruction of the habitats in which they occur. An extreme example is, for instance, the wild-growing *Cleome*, *Solanum*, *Asystacia* and *Crotalaria* in the Kakamega forest (M. Opole, pers. comm.), which is the last remnant of the tropical rainforest in western Kenya. New settlers have built homesteads and converted woodlands into arable land. This has minimized the forest area and resulted in the over-exploitation of the remaining forest for wood, grazing and plant collection, leading to a reduction in the population of the various edible plant species. Even the proclamation of this forest as a nature reserve and fencing it off have not been able to stop this process.

With decreased utilization of traditional plant species, knowledge related to their use and preparation is also disappearing. It is been suggested that often the erosion of knowledge on the use of species as vegetable, medicine or otherwise precedes their genetic erosion. In the absence of systematic and comprehensive information on the genetic diversity in the group of indigenous leafy vegetables, the actual rate of loss of genetic diversity is difficult to assess. A survey among the Tharaka in central Kenya indicated that 20 species and varieties had either disappeared or were no longer being used (Maundu et al., 1999)

Supporting the utilization of indigenous vegetables

Activities which support the use of indigenous vegetables and other underutilized crops can be seen from two perspectives. Firstly, they are aiming at developing a resource that can contribute to food security and household income. Secondly, the promotion of these vegetables will contribute to their continued growing, nurturing and consumption, whereby they are maintained or conserved *in situ* as a genetic resource in agro-ecosystems.

The genetic diversity and diversity in agronomic and culinary characters present within the species of this group of plants is largely unknown, or perhaps rather has not been systematically documented. Since they are considered economically and socially unimportant, there has been little attention or funding for collecting, maintaining and researching these species. However, the value of genetic diversity is evident as it determines the potential for developing these species to domesticate them and increase their productivity.

Different areas of activities are distinguished that can contribute to strengthening and improving utilization of the indigenous vegetables:

○ awareness-raising
○ plant genetic resource collection, breeding and agronomic research
○ development of market and processing opportunities.

Awareness-raising

The increasing importance of cultural identity in a rapidly globalizing world is leading to a revived interest in cultural–ethnic traditions and associated knowledge, in both developed and developing countries. This includes an interest in preparation and consumption of traditional food crops and dishes. In Nairobi, Kenya, supermarkets (where the better-off people buy their food) are becoming interested in adding indigenous vegetables to their stock. Many of their customers have migrated to the town in the last generation and still remember the use of these vegetables from earlier days. Promotion seems to be very effective in raising awareness on the value of these vegetables in relation to nutrition, culture and biodiversity conservation. As a result, the status of these vegetables is slowly changing and their consumption is becoming a statement of care for culture and environment, rather than generating contempt. There is a momentum which offers opportunities for developing the utilization of indigenous crops, including the indigenous leafy vegetables. The preparation of leaflets, articles in newspapers or magazines, and presentation on radio programmes and television may be very effective ways to increase the appeal of the indigenous vegetables – as well as for other under-utilized plant genetic resources such as medicinal plants. Apart from promotion and awareness-raising aimed at changing the status of these vegetables, this also re-introduces knowledge on the use and preparation of these plants. This information is often collected by NGOs from older women in local rural communities.

Leafy vegetables are important from a nutritional point of view. Activities and promotion campaigns should address this point, and will contribute to these vegetables regaining their traditional position in the diet, and thereby to their use and maintenance.

Plant genetic resource collection, breeding and agronomic research

Since very little work has been done on most of the indigenous crops, there is much to be gained from systematic documentation, collection, evaluation and breeding/selection activities (Chweya, 1994). For the African continent, exchange, evaluation and selection of materials could provide useful information on the diversity available and the potential for improvement. High-performing materials of *C. olitorius* from West Africa, Egypt and the Middle East could provide interesting materials for farmers in Kenya, Tanzania or Zambia. Moreover, evaluation of the performance of the various species under different growing conditions would add to agronomic and physiological knowledge on these species. However, such an exchange and evaluation requires co-ordination of researchers and development workers at a supra-national level. A network for such activities does not exist at present. Agronomic research on indigenous vegetables is also needed; so far there are few data on the adaptation of these plants to low-input conditions and their disease control. Especially if species are to be increasingly cultivated and produced with more intensive production technology (fertilizers, monoculture), there may be clear limitations for the commercial production of these species. Information on nutrient use efficiency and fertilizer responses would also contribute to a better understanding of the potential of the various indigenous leafy vegetables species. Work on seed-related aspects (flowering, seed set, seed production and supply) needs to be considered for a number of these species, but many of them set abundant seed, and farm-saved seed and informal seed supplies do exist in most situations. If these species increase in importance, it can be expected that an informal seed sector will automatically develop as well. If interesting varieties can be developed and significant improved seed quality of improved cultivars can be produced, there may be scope for commercialization through more formal channels.

Development of market and processing possibilities

An important problem for the commercialization of indigenous leafy vegetables is the short period over which they can be kept fresh. The production of indigenous leafy vegetables as a cash income-generating crop would be of interest for the rural communities in the neighbourhood of larger cities. However, transport and time between harvesting and sale pose serious limitations for the communities in more remote regions which are most in need of new income-generating opportunities. Adapted technologies for dehydration and deep freezing need to be developed to overcome this limitation and develop the vegetables as an appealing product for a wider urban-consumer public. Seasonality of production is a problem in processing, which requires year-round supply. The seasonality of production also conflicts with the year-round demand for consumption (Lapido, 1997). Other identified market limitations are the small size of production per farmer and the spread of farmers over a wide area; a lack of uniformity in quality of the product; and a lack of market information to farmers (Lapido, 1997). Organization of producers and support for technical production and marketing may eliminate some of these limitations.

Conclusions

Promotion, breeding and agronomic research, and the development of market-oriented processing, are needed to increase the use of traditional leafy vegetables. This will have a positive effect on the nutritional diet of the African people in rural and urban areas. The leafy vegetables may be an interesting source of income generation, especially as they are well adapted to low-input conditions and require less cash input from producers. Their use will also contribute to the *in-situ* conservation of genetic diversity. However, the implementation of supporting work and co-ordination of the work between formal and informal organizations requires considerable input and financial means, while its impact cannot be expected in the short term. So far the main effort in relation to indigenous crops has gone into ethnobotanical studies (Schippers, 1997). Providing the input for developing the potential of indigenous leafy vegetables and other under-utilized crops requires long-term commitment. Since the prospects for indigenous vegetable production and marketing do not seem to give much scope for large commercial involvement in the short run, the support for such activities by national agricultural research services and NGOs has to come from donors interested in development assistance and genetic resource conservation, and from a shift in the priorities of national research and development. But these actors also want an impact in the short term, which may explain their weak interest shown so far in supporting the exploration of the potential of under-utilized plant species in general, and indigenous leafy vegetables in particular. For these reasons, the communities themselves are the most important actors in the development and conservation of this group of plants. They do, however, need support, and grassroot organizations are best placed to provide, co-ordinate and channel that support.

6.10. Policies of the Netherlands on international co-operation and Agenda 21

Henri Jorritsma

Introduction

Agenda 21 and the 1992 Convention on Biological Diversity (CBD) represented important new impulses in policies of the Directorate General of International Co-operation (DGIS) of the Netherlands Ministry of Foreign Affairs. Initially, the CBD was exclusively concerned with natural biodiversity, and ignored biodiversity managed, used and maintained as part of agriculture. However, through Agenda 21 and negotiations to link the earlier 1982 FAO International Undertaking on the Conservation and Sustainable Utilization of Plant Genetic Resources for Food and Agriculture (the FAO Undertaking) to the CBD, steps have been taken, strongly supported by the Netherlands, to rectify this apparent imbalance. The key to providing appropriate balances, however, rests with national policies, since the CBD is a binding Convention only to its signatories, while both Agenda 21 and the FAO Undertaking only represent agreed intentions open to individual country interpretation and adherence.

Natural and agricultural biodiversity

The central policy objective of international co-operation of the Netherlands is to contribute to the alleviation of poverty. The conservation and sustainable use of biological diversity is considered of critical importance for meeting food, health and other needs of a growing world population, for which access to and sharing of both biological diversity and relevant technology are essential. However, having said that, identification and implementation of appropriate programme support appears to offer problems.

The traditional approaches to nature conservation have been to exclude human exploitation and maintain a natural environment in parks and protected areas. The same approach led to the initial exclusion of representation from the agricultural sector in negotiations leading up to the CBD. Agriculture was seen as the main threat to nature and natural biodiversity. While in a sense that may be true, people need to eat and secure livelihoods. It is now recognized that nature has traditionally been a major source of livelihood to people, and that management regimes by many communities have not only been sustainable, but have even contributed to biological diversity. The present policies and programme support the Netherlands attempt to achieve proper balances in nature management, combining conservation with sustainable use.

In agriculture, the situation has been relatively clearer. The importance of maintaining agrobiodiversity is evident, since it represents the basic raw material for continued improvement and adaptation of crops and domesticated animals. Initially, the emphasis in conservation of agrobiodiversity was to satisfy the expected needs of modern plant and animal breeding as part of the modern (industrial) agricultural complex in *ex situ* gene banks. However, increasingly the importance is recognized of maintaining locally adapted genetic diversity in crops in the more marginal areas, often with resource-poor, small-scale farmers. For both environmental and economic reasons, modern high-input agriculture does not seem to be a viable option. This is referred to as *in situ* conservation through use. For agrobiodiversity there is therefore a range of technological and economic alternatives open to support, depending on the respective target groups and objectives.

Target groups and objectives

Ultimately the Netherlands' international co-operation wishes to have an impact on the poor, including poor farmers and their families. However, to achieve that objective support is considered necessary at a number of different levels. At the international and national levels, the aim is to contribute to a policy environment that is favourable to sustainable management and conservation of agrobiodiversity. In this context, DGIS helped to facilitate the 1996 FAO Conference on Genetic Resources in Leipzig and the adopted Global Plan of Action (GPA; FAO, 1996e). Subsequently it contributed to financing a number of regional workshops to broaden support for the GPA and translate it into regional and national programmes for action. At the institutional and technical levels, DGIS continues to be a major contributor to the programme of the International Plant Genetic Resources Institute (IPGRI) and to other CGIAR institutes. Support to national programmes primarily depends on requests from national governments, most of which so far seem to have other priorities. Finally, at the level of small farmers DGIS provides support to a number of NGOs active in raising awareness (Genetic Resources Action International, GRAIN; Rural Advancement Foundation International, RAFI, and others) and in actual on-farm programmes (Community Biodiversity Development and Conservation, CBDC).

Problems in implementation

Biodiversity issues are high on the agenda of DGIS, and on those of many other donors. There is considerable diplomatic dialogue on biodiversity, related to claims of ownership and access. Despite this, implementation of the GPA at the national and regional levels is slow. A major bottleneck is a lack of suitable project proposals. The impression is that the international dialogue is more about principle than about practice and, with a few exceptions, has not yet resulted in appropriate institutional structures at the national level necessary for actual programme and project support. This ambiguity is also apparent in the Netherlands (and many other developed countries) where the CBD and agreements on Agenda 21 have yet to affect national programmes. A possible problem is that biodiversity issues transcend the mandates of different ministries and remain isolated from the actual practice of conservation. As a result, the partners for DGIS so far have been mainly NGOs, strengthening the voices of farmers and civic society and re-orienting policy environments.

Initiating change

Under the present circumstances, the role of DGIS is primarily in contributing to policy change at international and national levels. DGIS favours international co-operation and regulatory frameworks that provide broad access to genetic diversity while safeguarding national interests and those of farmers still maintaining and using important genetic resources as part of their agricultural systems. The main emphasis is on countries that favour and actively combine sustainable management of natural resources with poverty alleviation. Capacity-building through training of professionals and policy-makers at all levels, i.e community, national NGO and government organization, is the principal means through which DGIS addresses these objectives. In addition, national and international awareness-raising activities are supported to contribute to generating a more enabling environment. DGIS is closely following and involved in discussions around the creation of a special fund, additional to the Green environment fund, focusing specifically on agrobiodiversity.

6.11. Agricultural biodiversity: a perspective of Dutch policy-makers

Peter Vermeij, Marcel Vernooij and Mario Nagtzaam

Motives

The Netherlands is highly industrialized, but is also one of the world's largest exporters of agricultural products. In addition, it is one of the most densely populated countries in the world. The pressure on land is consequently very high for human needs such as housing, enterprises and recreation. In such a situation, maintaining and ensuring sustainable use of biodiversity provides an enormous challenge.

Dutch agricultural policy is based on the concept of sustainable agriculture, which starts from the awareness that natural resources are limited and therefore have to be used sparingly in order to conserve them for future generations. Biodiversity has for a long time been closely interwoven with many aspects of Dutch society, and is important to various economic sectors such as agriculture and horticulture, livestock farming, forestry, fisheries, recreation and tourism. Therefore, in addition to ethical, aesthetic, social and ecological interests, the Netherlands has an economic interest in the maintenance and sustainable utilization of biodiversity.

There is a great deal of public support for the conservation of biodiversity in the Netherlands, particularly in the form of nature conservation and environmental protection: more than 15 per cent of the adult population are members of a nature conservation organization.

The motivation for conserving agricultural biodiversity also has a strong international dimension. The Netherlands is a flat river delta with open ecological borders to neighbouring countries. Our ecosystems are generally a natural continuation of ecosystems abroad. Our rivers and wetlands and the Dutch agro-ecosystems are crucial links in migration routes of numerous bird species. Moreover, various sectors of the Dutch agricultural economy, from seed production to livestock farming, directly or indirectly affect and depend on access to biodiversity, both at home and abroad.

Agricultural biodiversity: points of departure

Agrobiodiversity is defined by the Convention on Biological Diversity (CBD) and includes '. . . the genetic diversity among all living organisms associated with cultivating crops and rearing animals and the ecological complexes of which they are part'. The point of departure is therefore the total agricultural ecosystem, similar to the ecosystem themes of marine biodiversity and biodiversity of forests.

An ecosystem approach to agrobiodiversity implies that three coherent subsets can be distinguished:

○ genetic resources – the diversity of crops, fish and non-domesticated wild resources of food
○ biological production factors – non-harvested species/communities of species supportive to agricultural production, including soil micro-organisms and pollinators
○ natural elements – non-harvested species/communities of species or sub-ecosystems in the wider environment that are an integral part of the agricultural ecosystem or support agricultural production.

Overall agrobiodiversity and its components are viewed in the context of two issues crucial for both national and international policies:

○ sustainability – how to develop a sustainable (economically, socially and ecologically) agriculture for the long term
○ food security – how to secure enough food for a growing world population.

Sustainability is a major concern for agriculture in the Netherlands. Over the past decades impressive productivity gains have been achieved by high inputs providing maximum control of the environment. However, in the process, chemical pollution of soil and both ground and surface water have become major environmental problems. Reducing chemical pollution and restoring soil and water ecosystems are primary policy objectives of the Netherlands government, providing a sustainable natural resource base for its agriculture and fisheries and improving the environmental quality for its citizens.

The successful development and implementation of policies aiming at the sustainable use of agricultural biodiversity largely depends on the degree of public awareness and understanding of its basic importance for society. This is in line with article 13 of the CBD: 'contracting parties shall promote and encourage understanding of the importance of, and the measures required for, the conservation of biological diversity'.

The conservation and sustainable use of agricultural biodiversity is considered to be an integral part of the policy for sustainable agriculture and rural development. In relation to the genetic resources within the agro-industrial system itself, the government is aiming for the *in situ* and *ex situ* conservation and sustainable use of varieties of plants, animals and micro-organisms with an actual or potential value for agriculture and Dutch society. Conserving genetic resources *ex situ* is aimed at partnerships with agriculture businesses, as they have great stakes in it: for example, in securing flexibility to react to changing consumer demands.

Contributing to global food security clearly takes place in an international context. Agrobiodiversity in modern industrial agriculture is primarily seen as raw material for plant breeding. The Netherlands maintains an internationally oriented gene bank and supports international efforts to promote open access and exchange of genetic resources, while recognizing the interests and rights of original developers and custodians.

Traditional farming systems, specifically in centres of diversity of crops, are a major source of genetic diversity for modern agricultural systems. They have so far received little attention and few benefits in return. The Netherlands supports conservation and equity in use and benefits of agricultural biodiversity, and supports the efforts of the international community to make progress in talks on the revision of the International Undertaking for Plant Genetic Resources. Efficient, effective and transparent solutions have to be developed by the international community for the conservation, sustainable use of, and access to genetic resources and the sharing of benefits arising out of these resources.

Animal genetic resources are considered of equal importance to plant resources. Therefore the further development by FAO of a global strategy for the management of farm animal genetic resources conservation *in situ* of rare breeds of productive livestock is imperative.

Strategic action plan for biodiversity

The strategy for addressing the responsibilities accepted by the Netherlands government in signing the CBD is formulated in the Strategic Action Plan for Biodiversity, adopted by Parliament in 1995. It introduced a number of new policy themes specifically geared to the conservation and sustainable use of biodiversity, which have to be integrated through specific actions into existing policy frameworks for agriculture, among other fields. Policy themes within the Plan are:

○ putting policies into practice for areas outside the National Ecological Network, in particular focusing on management of biodiversity on agricultural land
○ widening the concept of biodiversity
○ strengthening the capacity of Dutch institutions to provide the knowledge required for conserving biodiversity (in 1998 an interdepartmental research programme started on biodiversity, in addition to regular funding systems)
○ raising political and administrative awareness, both nationally and internationally.

The implementation of the Plan was evaluated in 1998. The major conclusions were:

○ the actions formulated in the Plan had, in general, started, especially concerning research programmes
○ existing policy frameworks are probably inadequate to prevent a further decline in biodiversity in The Netherlands
○ objectives of the CBD needed to be more integrated into policies for economic development, fisheries, and agriculture
○ interest groups, stakeholders and other organizations in society are insufficiently incorporated in efforts to implement the CBD
○ communication between government and society needs to be improved to clarify the issues and objectives of the CBD and promote public interest in the conservation and use of biodiversity.

Following the evaluation, the government decided to prepare a governmental policy document for submission to Parliament at the end of 1999. This document should clarify:

○ the significance and opportunities of biodiversity for Dutch society
○ the aims for conservation and sustainable use of biodiversity
○ the way interest groups and society may or should be involved in conservation and sustainable use of biodiversity.

International policy

After a review of the foreign policy of the Netherlands, the importance of multilateral approaches to development co-operation was reaffirmed, centred around the following directions:

○ strengthening the Dutch role in multilateral organizations (FAO, CBD)
○ a more thematic approach in regional programmes
○ policy development through an integrated approach
○ proactive and future-oriented thinking.

The Netherlands has a prominent position in plant breeding, the seeds industry, biotechnology and livestock breeding. It is considered unlikely that any country is or will be self-sufficient in genetic diversity now or in the future. Hence there exists mutual interdependence between countries. This is, beside ethical, social and ecological interests, another reason for supporting international programmes concerned with the conservation and sustainable use of agricultural biodiversity.

In its support of the internationalization of conservation of genetic resources, the Netherlands government welcomes the co-operation between FAO and CBD. Close interaction should be expanded and strengthened with other organizations concerned with different aspects of genetic resources conservation such as IPGRI, CGIAR, the World Bank, GEF, IUCN, UNEP and other national and regional organizations. A good basis is provided by rhe FAO Global Plan of Action for the Conservation and Sustainable Use of Genetic Resources.

The Netherlands has decided to intensify its bilateral co-operation with a number of countries in the field of biodiversity. A co-operation agreement for sustainable development has been signed with the so-called BBC countries (Buthan, Benin and Costa Rica).

Conclusion

The Netherlands Ministry of Agriculture, Nature Management and Fisheries considers the conservation of agrobiodiversity important and is committed to promoting awareness and influencing processes that lead to international co-operation.

At the national level, a Strategic Action Plan forms the basis for the formulation of a co-ordinated policy on the conservation of biological diversity to be presented to the Netherlands' Parliament at the end of 1999.

Effective co-operation between different stakeholders is stimulated, involving the government, research institutions and universities, private industry, civil organizations and others.

The position, interest and commitment regarding agricultural biodiversity is substantial. It is aimed at putting pressure on the ongoing processes and achieving high political involvement in this major ecological, economic and social issue.

Nationally the preparation stage is completed with formulating the Strategic Action Plan. Now the next phase has begun, of formulating a co-ordinated policy on this theme in a new policy document presented to the Dutch Parliament at the end of 1999.

Internationally multilateral and bilateral approaches are favoured. This is manifested in the search for closer and more effective co-operation between government, private organizations and business and research communities.

6.12. Advocacy and lobbying in South-East Asia: experiences of SEARICE

Neth Daño and Rene Salazar

Introduction

Over the past decade SEARICE has gained substantial lessons from its experience in policy advocacy and lobbying in issues related to community-based conservation and development of plant genetic resources. The experiences cover activities directed at both national governments and international institutions. Our activities have been based on interactions with different stakeholders. Analyses of the approaches, tactics and strategies adopted are discussed, and lessons derived from these experiences are analysed.

One of the guiding principles of SEARICE is to ensure a synergy between policy advocacy and lobbying initiatives, and experiences and activities at the community level. SEARICE sees itself essentially as an intermediary serving community interests. Issues identified and experienced at the community level are brought to the attention and lobbied for at appropriate levels of government or society, while in turn relevant policies and issues are raised with communities. A major objective is empowerment of people and communities to protect their interests and determine their own fate (Bertuso et al., Chapter 3.3 and Montecinos and Salazar, Chapter 3.5).

Policy advocacy and lobbying in the Philippines: tactical bedfellows

Since its establishment in 1982, much of SEARICE's initial development interventions focused on community organization. As SEARICE gained experiences in community-based conservation and development of plant genetic resources, it became clear that effective action was needed to influence policies at the national level. As a result, SEARICE became involved in policy discussions at the national and international levels and communicated these back to the communities for consultation and information.

Policy advocacy was initially concentrated in the Philippines. One reason was that in the Philippines NGOs were given reasonable opportunities to function in democratic processes and were in fact encouraged to take part in various aspects of economic development. SEARICE policy and advocacy activities covered a range of issues related to plant genetic resources conservation and use at the community level, and included campaigns on biosafety, bioprospecting, chemical pesticides and others. Depending on the issues and circumstances surrounding these issues, relationships between SEARICE and the Philippine government ranged from directly confrontational to collaborative.

Two cases are presented to illustrate SEARICE activities. The first describes how SEARICE confronted the International Rice Research Institute (IRRI) on developments in biotechnology and the introduction of genetically modified organisms (GMOs). The second case describes how SEARICE changed its tactics from confronting government agencies on issues of genetic resources to becoming involved in policy formulation and representation of the Philippines in international dialogue and negotiations.

Case 1: SEARICE versus IRRI

SEARICE as a movement has its origin in opposing high-input technologies as championed by the IRRI, branding IRRI as the 'enemy promoting the evils of the Green Revolution'. In 1989 SEARICE and a number of local NGOs and academics launched a campaign against IRRI to oppose the field release of transgenic organisms. The initial campaign led to a Senate investigation and the drafting of National Biosafety Guidelines.

Encouraged by the Senate's responsiveness to civil society demands, in 1992 SEARICE led a group of Philippine NGOs to enter directly into dialogue with IRRI on broader aspects of agricultural research and the perceived negative impacts of the so-called Green Revolution technology on the lives of small farmers and the sustainability of the production environment. This approach was heavily criticized by the more militant NGOs. However, it led to some mutual understanding between IRRI and part of the NGO movement, and extended to discussions at the South-East Asian regional level. A consensus document was formulated serving as a guiding principle and 'rule of engagement' in contacts between the parties. However, the dialogue broke down in 1994 when IRRI, without consulting its NGO partners, initiated an on-farm conservation programme. The NGOs viewed this as a breach of trust and a denial of the past dialogue process.

During the same period, the implementation of National Biosafety Guidelines ran into problems. Applications for laboratory and greenhouse research piled up at the National Committee on Biosafety. It soon became apparent that there were loopholes in the guidelines and that there were serious doubts about the government's capacity to implement the guidelines. This led in 1995 to a new, more confrontational campaign specifically targeted at IRRI as a major player in the development of GMOs. This campaign was supported by a broad range of NGOs and farmers' organizations, and spilled over to other countries in the region. A Congressional hearing on IRRI's research followed, and the intensity of the debate provided proof of widespread concern and a confrontation of civil society organizations with the government's science and technology agenda. SEARICE intensified the campaign to popularize the issues around GMOs and reach out to a wider audience, joined by some 20 NGOs and other organizations from different parts of the country. The collaborating groups decided to institutionalize their co-operation with the formation of the NGOs Opposed to Genetically Modified Organisms (NO GMO) in December 1998, with SEARICE serving as the focal organization.

So far SEARICE's main activities had been concerned with strengthening community organizations. However through the NO GMO campaign, SEARICE became involved with more activist approaches such as rallies, pickets and challenging the authorities. A SEARICE-led picket of Monsanto headquarters in Manila and a similar picket of an FAO regional meeting on The Global Plan of Action for Food and Agriculture, specifically targeting the Terminator-gene technology, gained widespread publicity and stimulated the Philippine Senate to debate a Resolution and a Bill on concerns involving the introduction and release of GMOs in the country. The apparent success of these 'extra-legal' activities encouraged SEARICE to adopt them in complementary strengthening of community organizations, media exposure and legislative activities in order to maximize impact.

Case 2: tactical co-operation between civil society and the state

SEARICE has its roots in concerns about genetic resources and sustainability. This is an area where government agencies are also actively involved. In 1993 the government established the Philippine Council for Sustainable Development (PCSD) as a forum for the government, NGOs and the business sector to discuss and influence policy directions affecting sustainable development, consistent with the government's commitment to UN Agenda 21. SEARICE, taking a constructive attitude and giving this development the benefit of the doubt, joined PCSD. SEARICE even became co-chair of the Sub-Committee on Biological Diversity. The Council drafted a progressive Philippine Agenda 21 in 1997, which developed into a powerful advocacy tool for civil society organizations in the country, despite questions on the government's capacity and commitment to implement its provisions.

Through the PCSD, NGOs were able to influence official positions of the Philippine government in international negotiations, in drafting a national biodiversity action plan and generally in shaping overall government policies. This required debate and give-and-take with often-opposing views of business representatives and frequently divergent positions of various government agencies. However, in general it was felt that the tactic of 'changing from within' had merits. SEARICE representatives became official members of Philippine government delegations to meetings of the Conferences of Parties to the Convention on Biological Diversity (CBD) and meetings of the FAO Commission on Genetic Resources, and headed the delegation in two recent rounds of re-negotiation of the FAO Undertaking on which it convened a national consultation in 1997.

The decision to institutionalize co-operation with the government and join delegations created some controversy in NGO circles, and doubts were articulated about SEARICE's ability to remain independent and critical. On the other hand, it was argued that in the face of increasing influence and power of multi-national corporations controlling the seed industry and application of biotechnology, the commonalities in the positions of the government and civil society organizations are magnified and mutually strengthened. New alliances are needed with the state to face common enemies.

Lessons learnt and reflections

It is clear that SEARICE has gone through a process of evolution over the past 10 years: from being an organization primarily focused on strengthening and organizing farmers to help them protect their own interests, SEARICE is now also concerned with broader aspects of developments in

309

agriculture that affect the livelihoods of rural communities and society as a whole. Fighting on different grounds required new tactics and new alliances, and brought new adversaries but also new opportunities to support the interests of what remained the primary target group: small farmers. The main lesson learned is that society constitutes a very complex web of interacting interests and contradictions which leaves little room for dogmas and narrow-mindedness and preconceived positions. SEARICE has become a more pragmatic organization. A major challenge is to combine this with clear overall basic principles.

6.13. Plant genetic resources in Europe: an NGO perspective

Patrick Mulvany

Introduction

Europe is a region full of diversity. At a 1998 meeting of plant genetic resource specialists from 44 European countries, 35 national mother tongue languages were spoken. This linguistic diversity has been reflected in the diversity of its plant genetic resources. However, in the past century these resources have been severely eroded, albeit from a comparatively low starting point, as the dominance of industrial agriculture has replaced most local varieties with varieties characterized by genetic uniformity. Europe is relatively gene poor, especially in its northern countries (FAO, 1996b), although southern Europe does have some significant centres of diversity, particularly for vegetable crops. Europe is historically heterogeneous in culture, ecology and agriculture, and this diversity needs to be reflected and recognized by European agricultural and horticultural policymakers.

In response to the creation of a uniform genetic landscape, European NGOs became actively involved in PGR issues supporting the sustainable use and conservation of PGR. For more than two decades, NGOs have translated their concern into practical activities. The Henry Doubleday Research Association (HDRA) in the UK, Arche Noah in Austria, Pro Specie Rara in Switzerland, to name but three, have paved the way for practical seed saving and distribution of plant genetic resources. Other organizations, such as the alternative plant breeders HERA in Germany, are breeding new varieties for organic farming. Various NGOs are concentrating on policy issues, playing important advocacy and information roles. Genetic Resources Action International (GRAIN) is the most prominent NGO operating at a policy level in Europe.

310

NGO activity areas

NGOs' major contributions to supporting conservation and utilization of plant genetic resources in Europe have been made through a range of activities. In this chapter we describe the following activity areas: conservation and sustainable use, advocacy and public information, research, networking and formal–informal sector collaboration.

Conservation and sustainable use

In many European countries, NGOs and small private organizations provide unique access for the public to old de-listed and niche varieties, especially for organic growers. The public may borrow or purchase a diversity of seeds, bulk up varieties, source and exchange materials, and support the local *ex situ* conservation of varieties. The three text boxes in this chapter present illustrations of the role that NGOs are playing in developing practical, 'informal' conservation and utilization programmes (Austria; Box 6.2); conserving and supporting the utilization of old or forgotten varieties (HDRA, UK; Box 6.3); and rescuing varieties in threatening situations (Croatia; Box 6.4).

Advocacy

NGOs have greater freedom of expression than the formal sector in the area of advocacy. Through collaboration on advocacy and public information campaigns, the latent synergy of formal- and informal-sector collaboration is best realized. Both sectors aim, in principle, to contribute to a more diverse and sustainable agricultural production with a plurality of suppliers, producers and retailers. Within both sectors, specialists are aware of major threats to plant genetic resources, opportunities for plant genetic resource conservation and sustainable use, and mechanisms for fair and equitable sharing of benefits from the use of plant genetic resources. However, this awareness is not reflected in the policies of the European Union (EU), its member states and other European countries. The formal sector may be constrained from advocating changes supportive of (or publicizing threats to) diversity by national and political mandates that favour modern biotechnology and the privatization of genetic resources. NGOs are also often constrained by a lack of human and financial resources to advocate successfully and increase public awareness. However, it is hoped that increased awareness by policy-makers of plant genetic resource issues, fuelled by public opinion, may facilitate changes in policy which will help to ensure a real diversity of agricultural products and real choices to consumers. A joint approach bringing together both the informal and formal sectors could be more effective in creating regulatory frameworks that defend and support the use of diversity.

The Seeds Action Network, led by the International Coalition for Development (ICDA, then GRAIN), played a pioneering role in arguing successfully for an EU genetic resource conservation programme. This

Unexpected growth of the Austrian organic farming sector and a consequent seed shortage has led to farmers breeding their own varieties adapted to organic farming practices and specific climatic conditions, in response to consumer demands. Major constraints on marketing and selling seeds of these 'newly bred old varieties' are existing seed laws. Negotiations have been held for more than a year involving government representatives, breeders, NGOs and organic farmers, but legally binding agreements are hard to achieve. As with other conservation topics, the Austrian media have been quite intense in their support and have awakened interest in diversity among farmers and consumers.

Awareness of old or forgotten varieties has grown among farmers in the past decade, and NGOs have been helping with the reproduction and distribution of these varieties. The NGO *Arche Noah* (Noah's Ark) is involved in the reproduction and dissemination of a range of varieties of vegetables and potatoes. Öko-Kreis Waldviertol and various local organizations have been successful in satisfying the demand for old fruit varieties. Many varieties and species have also become commercially available. Groups of organic farmers have started breeding, distributing and marketing organic grain varieties. Austrian organic farmers have become especially interested in einkorn and emmer wheat, as the baking quality of these wheat varieties is good and these species are resistant to a range of diseases occurring in bread wheat. In other European countries, these wheat species have been called 'obsolete' and are pushed to the back of the gene bank shelves. In Austria, organic breeders are requesting these materials from official gene banks; work with these gene banks to produce new varieties; and develop new varieties. It is paradoxical that it is not possible to sell seeds of these wheat species, even though they possess a market potential equal to bread wheat varieties. Narrow EU guidelines for seed laws and regulations currently restrict reproduction and marketing of varieties of these wheat species.

programme aimed to accommodate the concerns of both formal and informal plant genetic resource actors. The resulting Council Regulation (EC) No 1467/94 had the objective to co-ordinate and promote, at Community level, work undertaken in the Member States on the conservation, characterization, collection and utilization of genetic resources in agriculture. However, questions have been raised by NGOs as to its effectiveness in dealing with the substantive issues of threats to European plant genetic resources.

Public information

Since Leipzig (FAO, 1996b), awareness of plant genetic resource issues has increased among European NGOs. The NGOs are the principal proponents of positive messages and have been effective in using the media to

Box 6.3: Henry Doubleday Research Association, UK

The Henry Doubleday Research Association (HDRA) first took an interest in the issue of vanishing varieties in the 1970s. At that time the major concern of the Director, Lawrence Hills, was to warn people of the dangers of losing biodiversity. He made an attempt to collect rare varieties and set up vegetable sanctuaries as a means to save these varieties threatened with extinction. In 1991, HDRA raised the debate on access to and trading of old varieties. It played a major role in translating this complex debate to farmers, gardeners and consumers using accessible and popular language. HDRA started providing access to historical varieties through the Heritage Seed Library (HSL). HSL currently attracts an active membership of over 9000 people, increasing yearly by about 1000. Its members support the project with their subscriptions. In return, they receive six packages of seed from its annual catalogue, which features over 100 varieties of vegetables selected from a total collection of more than 800 accessions. In addition HDRA gives members a forum for swapping varieties through a separate section of the catalogue.

Currently HSL is working on improving all aspects of its work, particularly in relation to obtaining good data on varietal characteristics and developing proper storage methods for the collection. HSL has just launched a new Environmental Action-funded campaign to collect family heirlooms nationally, 'The Seed Search'. This project hopes to reach out to gene banks and collections in former British colonies. The hope is to encounter old European varieties that were once taken by colonial administrators and emigrants to repatriate these heirlooms and add them to the collection.

The work of HSL would be impossible without volunteers. The largest body of these are its Seed Guardians who raise significant quantities of seed for redistribution to members through the catalogue. Currently HSL has some 250 Seed Guardians, typical of whom are Jenny and Jeremy Garth of Cheshire.

Jeremy is a retired geologist and his wife Jenny is a tax inspector. Both keen vegetable growers, they garden in 2.5 allotments and in their home garden. They joined HSL in 1993 and 2 years later volunteered as Seed Guardians. They now look after eight HSL varieties, including the medieval 'Martock bean'. Jeremy and Jenny have no special equipment for generating these seeds. All they need to keep these varieties alive are their traditional skills in gardening. What initially attracted them to HSL was the possibility of finding varieties with a better flavour. They looked for varieties that were originally bred for small-scale production and gardeners rather than for the mass market and agribusiness. Other aspects of varietal conservation soon fascinated them: history, diversity of form and appearance of the crops, and political and social issues. By becoming Seed Guardians they have found a practical way of contributing to a more interesting, more diverse and more sustainable world.

Box 6.4: A Croatian story

After the war in Croatia and subsequently in Bosnia, humanitarian groups collected money and goods for distribution to the needy in war-torn areas. One campaign of the major Austrian charity *Nachbar in Not* (Neighbour in Need) was called *Saatgut für den Frieden* (Seeds for Peace). Austrians are very generous in emergency situations and understood the campaign as traditional neighbourly help. A large amount of money was spent on sending seeds of field crops, and also garden vegetables, to the war-torn areas. The selected varieties included commercial varieties from West Europe. Through this well-meant charitable campaign, more genetic diversity was lost than through all the vicissitudes of war. Gardeners abandoned their old varieties, which were still available in other areas, and planted 'new, improved' varieties in colourful seed packages. The following year, seeds saved from hybrid seed did not do well and the seeds of commercial open-pollinated varieties were regrown, displacing traditional varieties.

A Croatian woman who lives in Austria, Bozica Papes-Mokos, recognized the acute dangers posed by this development and mobilized the help of an Austrian NGO, *Arche Noah* (Noah's Ark) to organize a collecting mission to the areas not too badly touched by war. A small note in the members' newsletter was enough to raise modest financial resources for this undertaking. In the course of 2 weeks, four women visited three separate areas in Croatia and gathered more than 200 different local varieties. One of the women represented the German gene bank in Gatersleben. The seed samples were divided into four portions: one for the Croatian genebank, one for the Croatian NGO, one for *Arche Noah*, and one for the Gatersleben genebank. In subsequent years each of these institutions reproduced the material and tried to channel it back to Croatia. One of the possibilities for seed distribution appeared to be the annual Seed Exchange Market in Zagreb. The seed fair is in its fourth year (1998); it attracts growers from areas well outside the capital. Members of the Seed Savers Exchange in the USA have donated material originally from Croatia to the project. Croatian emigrants originally took the varieties to the USA. It is interesting to note that many varieties that were once common in Austria but are now extinct could be found in Croatia. As a consequence of Austrian involvement in the rehabilitation project, these varieties were also re-introduced to Austria. This collecting mission is an example of successful collaboration between formal and informal sectors. However, this initiative could not have been taken without the swift appraisal of the situation and call for help by a person within the country.

achieve this. An example of one activity was the Celebration of Plant Diversity – the Braunschweig Seed Fair – held in June 1998. This fair informed visitors of the importance of plant genetic resources and the inherent dangers of genetic modification, including the 'Terminator

to natural resource management and integrated crop management, while considering the effects of genetic diversity within and between crops, on crop rotation, and so on. Good experimental results have been obtained in a number of crops with breeding for more natural partial but durable forms of resistance, frequently based on polygenic systems as an alternative to single-gene, absolute forms of resistance (which often break down due to adaptive mutations in the disease organisms). While these developments may be encouraging and have considerable appeal to consumers, developments in the seed industry seem to go in the opposite direction. Multinational seed companies, when given a choice between a biotechnological solution or one realized by cross-breeding, will opt for the former because they gain more exclusive control of the new variety. Biotechnological gene transfer is by nature at the level of single genes. Biotechnologists (see Nap, Chapter 4.6) essentially see existing varieties as basic frames to which they expect to be able to attach any desired new gene at will. While nature may be more robust and recalcitrant than biotechnologists give it credit for, it does illustrate an extreme form of reductionist thinking. Combined with present seed laws that insist on high levels of uniformity of varieties, it should be clear that the legal framework, including intellectual property rights systems, discourages increased use of genetic diversity in farmers fields. It also discourages population breeding and broadening the genetic basis of varieties, and by negating the importance of genetic diversity it will contribute to genetic erosion through institutional neglect.

Conclusion

The present institutional, legal and policy framework is not in harmony with the needs of agriculture for sustainability, and certainly does not encourage a broader use of agrobiodiversity in farmers' fields in order to cope with environmental diversity and, in the longer term, possible environmental change. Unless one believes that free market economies and shareholder interests will ultimately benefit society as a whole and will get things right, there is a need to generate a fundamental discussion about the whole legal, policy and institutional framework that regulates plant breeding and biotechnology. The following questions should be considered.

○ Does the present application of intellectual property rights in biotechnology encourage and reward research, or are patents primarily providing the means for concentration of control of the seed industry in large industrial complexes at the expense of small local companies?
○ Does the present application of intellectual property rights in living organisms encourage the appropriate use of biodiversity, including through cross-breeding, or does it impose a bias toward solving problems with biotechnology?
○ How far does the present seed legislation encourage or discourage genetic diversity in the field?
○ What are the effects of seed legislation on the farmers' seed system relative to the formal institutional/commercial system?

These are fundamental questions that concern the place of agriculture in society. Should crucial decisions on the use of agrobiodiversity be made in the boardrooms of a few multinational companies, or should legal and institutional frameworks provide better protection of a common good, and encourage a more diversified crop improvement with closer links to farmers? The future of agriculture and food production may well depend on finding the right answers.

ENCOURAGING DIVERSITY: A SYNTHESIS OF CROP CONSERVATION AND DEVELOPMENT

7.1. Discouraging or encouraging diversity

Conny Almekinders and Walter de Boef

Introduction

The objective of this book is to develop a concept for local management of plant genetic resources that contributes to its conservation as well as to the development of farmers' livelihoods. In this final section we draw some general lessons and conclusions. We reflect on the previous sections in the book and discuss them in relation to each other.

This chapter starts by recapturing the central focus of the book: farmers' livelihood systems. Farmers are the central actors in the *in situ* use and management of crop genetic diversity (Section 2). The importance of genetic diversity in their livelihood systems is offset against the trends in global policy and the institutional environment described in the various contributions in Section 6. In Chapter 7.2 we discuss farmers' needs and global trends from an ecological perspective, and in Chapter 7.3 we analyse the experiences and perspectives presented in the case studies and place them in the context of local versus global interests. With this analysis we arrive at a synthesis between crop conservation and development. Finally, we look at the emerging picture of a plant genetic resource system, and compare it with the local/institutional system as described in the Introduction. Based on this comparison, we discuss the need for a paradigm shift in plant genetic resource management. We elaborate our argument that an institutional re-orientation is needed to enhance the capacity to flexibly and dynamically support farmers' management of plant genetic resources in the context of their livelihood systems.

Our perspective is that of professionals in the institutional system, looking for opportunities to converge the objectives of crop conservation with the general need for agricultural development.

Livelihood system, indigenous knowledge and cosmovision

Cases in this book provide illustrations of farming systems that are more than just production systems. In their synthesis of the cases in Section 2, Prain and Hagmann conclude that farmers use crop genetic diversity as a part of their livelihood system. Therefore *in situ* and on-farm conservation not only address farmers' management of genetic diversity, but also support rural people's livelihoods. This includes the maintenance and functioning of their indigenous knowledge and cultural identity.

In general, diversity matches farmers' specific needs in specific situations; it is dynamic as it varies from household to household and from place to place, and changes over time, and it serves several purposes. It is used as insurance and provides farmers with options to respond to change. Farmers thus manage and utilize plant genetic resource in a dynamic manner.

Access to genetic diversity, in particular to the diversity that is adapted to their farming conditions, is an important attribute and condition for farmers' plant genetic resource systems. Access and exchange contribute to the dynamic and adapted nature of farmers' management. They are also ways that the local plant genetic resources system interacts with the institutional system.

Farmers' access to plant genetic resource in marginal and high potential areas

The options for farmers to utilize genetic diversity have been diminished. The cases in Section 2 demonstrate that farmers both in the North and the South express an interest in and a need for improved genetic diversity. This is not only the case in the marginal production areas where, at least in general terms, much diversity is still present. Various cases in the book, for example from the Philippines (Basilio and Razon, Chapter 2.10), Nepal and India (Witcombe et al., Chapter 4.11), the Netherlands (Wiskerke, Chapter 2.8) and the USA (Mercer and Wainwright, Chapter 2.7) demonstrate that farmers in high-potential areas also need diversity. Farmers in both low- and high-potential environments need diversity to cope with pests, diseases and changed market conditions. Prain and Hagmann (Section 2, Synthesis) and Witcombe et al. (Chapter 4.11) indicate that these needs for diversity have generally been underestimated. However, the kind of genetic diversity needed has changed from the diversity that farmers used 50 or more years ago.

Encouraging learning in plant genetic resource management organizations

In Chapter 7.2 we elaborate how farmers and farmers' groups have become engaged in alternative approaches to managing plant genetic resource at the local level. With these initiatives they aim to reverse the treadmill of agricultural development (Röling, Chapter 6.2) that leads to a reduction of genetic diversity in agro-ecosystems. Enhancing the use of plant genetic resources, they also aim to restore resilience in agro-ecosystems.

Cases in the various chapters of this book illustrate how actors in the institutional system have identified opportunities to respond to farmers' need for diversity. These opportunities are taken up by a range of stakeholders: conservationists, public and commercial breeders and seed producers, NGOs, and farmers themselves.

In Chapter 7.3 the common goals of efforts by the actors involved in conservation, plant breeding and seed supply are discussed. Even though the activities as implemented by these actors appear different, they contribute to a similar target: all aim to strengthen the local plant genetic resources system and stimulate the utilization of plant genetic resources by farmers. They unify plant genetic resource conservation, utilization and development perspectives under headings of encouraging diversity and supporting farmers' management.

We realize that the cases in this book are not mainstream; they are relatively isolated cases of innovative farmers and professionals. However, these experiences illustrate the opportunities for plant genetic resource organizations, i.e. institutions involved in crop genetic conservation, development and seed supply, to become more responsive to local management dynamics by taking a learning perspective.

The need to arrive at a new framework for the implementation of such activities is elaborated in Chapter 7.4. With this chapter on adaptive plant genetic resource management we advocate the development of an alternative framework that can accommodate the integrated, innovative and learning approaches as developed by the various actors described in this book. We consider learning organizations, institutions that can contribute more effectively to the 'adaptive' management of genetic resources. This learning perspective is the next step in the synthesis between crop conservation and development.

7.2. Reversing the treadmill and restoring agro-ecosystem resilience

Walter de Boef, Conny Almekinders and Niels Röling

An ecological perspective to agricultural development

With agricultural development, farming has increasingly used mechanization, mineral fertilizers and improved varieties to suppress ecological processes. The inputs are used to optimize production and to suppress ecological variations caused by biotic and abiotic stress factors (see also Almekinders and Struik, Chapter 1.3). Pesticides and resistant varieties accomplish independence from weed, insect, fungal and bacterial life. Application of chemical fertilizers has reduced the interactions between crop root systems and organic soil life. Crops are made genetically uniform to facilitate mechanization. Uniformity of crop produce is also required for the marketing and processing of agricultural products. Yearly seed purchases of varieties eliminate natural selection and adaptation to environmental conditions. Applications of biotechnology, such as linking varieties to the use of herbicides, are another example of a further industrialization and alienation of agriculture from ecological processes. Crop production has become a 'throughput' system of inputs; outputs are economically maximized by regulating and controlling water and nutrient availability (abiotic factors) and by diminishing interactions with other growth-regulating organisms (biotic factors).

The suppression of ecological processes has made 'modern' agricultural systems 'brittle' or vulnerable to environmental disturbances. In ecological terms this is referred to as reduced resilience of agro-ecosystems to respond to ecological dynamics. Various cases in the book provide examples of less-resilient agro-ecosystems; they show that with reduced deployment of crop genetic diversity, production systems have become fragile and have lost their capacity to respond to natural and unavoidable ecological variations. Taking this ecological perspective, these less-resilient agro-ecosystems become 'systems waiting for an accident to happen', as illustrated by Mercer and Wainwright (Chapter 2.7). A small change in the environment may cause agro-ecosystems to collapse; various cases – often related to the occurrence of pests and diseases or slight variations in the climate – illustrate such ecological crises in agriculture. They also demonstrate the limited capacity to respond of the institutional system involved in plant genetic resource management and agricultural research. The system has not anticipated such events by developing alternative scenarios to avoid these 'environmental accidents'. The current organization of plant genetic resource management and agricultural research is primarily and increasingly driven by economic feedbacks, while ecological feedbacks are eliminated, ignored, or translated into economic terms. However, frequent 'environmental crises' in high-input and intensive crop and animal production systems demonstrate that we are unable to completely restrain ecological dynamics. Our technological and scientific responses to these ecological variations appear inadequate. And, in many cases, if responses developed by public and private agricultural research become available, farmers and consumers no longer accept them. This point becomes increasingly important for agriculture and food production. Civil resistance to the use of pesticides, antibiotics and genetically modified organisms may no longer be ignored by policy-makers, companies and other organizations involved in agricultural research and plant genetic resource management.

Treadmill and an economic imperative on plant genetic resource management

Instead of management within ecological boundaries, agricultural production is increasingly defined by the economic organization of the world. This economic organization and its impact on the management of genetic diversity are described in various chapters in Section 6 (e.g. Chapters 6.5 and 6.13). Agriculture is first and foremost driven by an increasingly globalized market of supplies and research products in the hands of a few agro-industrial conglomerates. Agricultural products are delivered to the food processing industry and to a market of consumers who are not prepared to pay more than a minimum price (Wiskerke, Chapter 2.8; Jongerden, Chapter 6.8). In Europe and North America, but also in many developing countries, farmers have over the past 30 years not received a penny more in absolute terms for their agricultural products (such as cereals), even though the prices for some products paid by consumers have increased. This imbalance has pushed for a more and more intensive mode of production with high ecological and social, and indirect economic costs to farmers and society.

In Section 6 we learnt that variety and seed legislation primarily conforms to the economic organization of agricultural research and plant genetic resource management, rather than an organization within ecological boundaries (Louwaars and Tripp, Chapter 6.4). Guided and enforced by the treadmill of agricultural development (Röling, Chapter 6.2), farmers and farms, like crop production, have become 'throughput systems'. As these systems are subject to external (economic) forces, they have become links in an industrial chain of agricultural production (Jongerden and Ruivenkamp, Chapter 6.3). Several cases illustrate how some farmers and other stakeholders involved in plant genetic resource management are resisting the forces of this treadmill; these cases report on efforts that aim to restore the link between farming and ecological processes, and to encourage and restore the use of genetic diversity.

Treadmill in high-potential and marginal production environments

In Chapter 6.2 Röling indicates that resistance to the forces that keep the treadmill of agricultural development going is essential to develop a more sustainable agricultural production. The treadmill is associated with increasing genetic uniformity, particularly in high-potential areas. Ecological variations in these agricultural systems in terms of biotic and abiotic stress factors are dealt with by agrochemicals, only to be replaced by pollution problems. Socio-economic variations need to be accommodated in more profitable production and organization of the agricultural sector. In this manner, rural livelihoods have become vulnerable to both ecological and socio-economic dynamics. Instruments in farmers' hands enabling them to respond or adapt at the individual level have been reduced. Agricultural research, extension and education systems have all been tailored to promote the treadmill of agricultural development, resulting from the industrialization of farming and the globally organized economy for products of the primary sector. In addition, these trends are enforced by a concentration of research efforts on high-potential areas and high-input agricultural production systems.

In marginal areas, the treadmill and the trends in research described above have had less impact, because standard procedures for technology development tailored for high-potential areas have proven to be of limited use for the constraints and complexities encountered in these environments. Public policies for research and development, but also continuing low prices for primary agricultural products that are associated with the treadmill, have further marginalized farmers in these areas. Public research and extension do not cater for the needs of these farmers, nor do these farmers benefit from research and technology development in the private sector. However, in many cases farmers' local varieties and technologies have become inadequate to encounter current ecological and socio-economic problems. New strains of pests and diseases emerge, to which local varieties are not resistant or tolerant. To make a living and earn sufficient family income, farmers need to respond to market demands that drive them to abandon landraces and use a limited set of 'modern' varieties. Although farmers experiment to find solutions, they are often restricted in their access to germplasm and scientific knowledge in their dynamic local system of innovation and plant genetic resource management. Modern technologies (including varieties) originally appropriate in high-potential areas and high-input regimes are often not suitable to meet production constraints in these sub-optimal production environments. The current organization of agricultural research has been shown to be limited in its capacity to deliver varieties and technologies adapted to the diversity of production systems in these environments. Many of the experiences and methods for participatory and decentralized plant breeding, as elaborated in Section 4, have been initiated by breeders in public research organizations with a mandate to develop varieties of crops cultivated in these marginal production environments. The withdrawal of the public sector from agricultural research in many countries, and global developments with respect to the 'appropriation' of germplasm and products of private research in plant breeding and biotechnology further reduce farmers' access to adequate research results.   '

Farmers seeking alternatives

Contributions in various sections provide examples of farmers who oppose the trends leading to a reduction of genetic diversity in farming. The ever-ongoing treadmill and recurrent ecological problems in agriculture bring farmers into a position where they have little space to manoeuvre. They are left with few possibilities to respond to environmental crises and changing market forces. They have made high capital investments, become dependent on an input-supply market, and specialized in one mode of production. This ecologically, socially and economically insecure situation is encountered among farmers in industrialized countries, but also among farmers in high-potential areas of developing countries. The problems experienced by rice farmers in the Philippines (Basilio and Razon, Chapter 2.10; Bertuso et al., Chapter 3.3) and cereal farmers in North America and Europe (Mercer and Wainwright, Chapter 2.7; Wiskerke, Chapter 2.8; Scott, Chapter 2.9) are examples of the situation faced by many farmers in the world of today.

This book focuses on crop genetic diversity. We have not included examples of crises associated with the intensification of animal production and the reduction of genetic diversity in livestock. The succession of crisis situations in animal production in the late 1990s in Europe (BSE, swine fever) demonstrates that the path of intensification and reduction of diversity has led to alarmingly vulnerable production systems, threatening entire agricultural sectors. In a few decades the treadmill has pushed farmers to extreme intensification, disconnecting production from natural resources and land, and reducing genetic diversity in animal production to an extreme. In response to the tremendous costs to society of responding to ecological crises, governments have started to support ecological agriculture and high-quality production, and to support farmers to develop alternative strategies for production. Moreover, the confidence of European consumers in animal production has been reduced dramatically.

The treadmill and resistance against it should be placed in 'global versus local' and 'economy versus ecology' perspectives. Farmers start to seek local solutions to reverse the treadmill and restore agro-ecological resilience. Various cases demonstrate how farmers' groups, NGOs and people working for research organizations develop alternative models to agricultural production and associated plant genetic resource management, sometimes parallel to, but outside mainstream agriculture. The cases of Brazil (Machado, Chapter 4.10), the Philippines (Bertuso et al., Chapter 3.3), Canada (Pittenger, Chapter 3.4) and the Netherlands (Wiskerke, Chapter 2.8) illustrate how farmers regain an interest in using diversity as means of restoring resilience. They move into alternative markets and increasingly use diversity to survive as farmers in times of environmental crises.

Several chapters provide examples of alternative approaches as developed by farmer groups. Farmers form groups in response to these trends, and start autonomous processes of innovation and revised plant genetic resource management at the local level. The cases of maize breeding in China (Song, Chapter 4.2) and cereal farming in Canada (Scott, Chapter 2.9) demonstrate that farmers are actively developing alternatives to standard recommendations and 'high external-input' solutions. The case of maize breeding in China describes how female farmers developed their varieties in the absence of any viable alternative. Farmers in the Philippines, Canada and the Netherlands look for alternatives in order to reintroduce or maintain genetic diversity as part of a strategy to keep their system ecologically balanced and to make these alternatives socioeconomically viable. This diversity of local alternatives to modern agricultural development counteracts the strategy founded on transfer of technology and supported by the agricultural treadmill.

Challenges and lessons

The question remains as to how the experiences and lessons of local efforts can be translated in a manner that will restore the ecological balance in agriculture as a whole. Many of the innovative cases in this book deal with conservation, plant breeding and seed supply in an integrated manner, and demonstrate local and adaptive strategies for plant genetic resource management. Many cases illustrate how these strategies encourage instead of reducing diversity in farming, and how they are built upon farmers' initiatives and capacities in plant genetic resource management. Many of the experiences illustrated in this book emphasize the function of biodiversity in agriculture on three levels: genetic; crop (species); and agro-ecosystem diversity. The most convincing arguments with respect to the value and function of diversity in agriculture are articulated by ecologists who refer to biodiversity as an 'ecological service'. This current and future service or value of biodiversity is directly associated to agro-ecosystem resilience: the capacity to respond, now and in the future, to the continuous and unavoidable natural (and socio-economic) dynamics that we meet when we practice agriculture. Another challenge ahead is how the alternative strategies described can reverse processes initiated and caused by the agricultural treadmill. It can reverse trends such as the increasing appropriation of genetic diversity which places crop genetic diversity as an ecological service into the hands of few private crop development conglomerates.

We conclude from the cases and experiences described here that new global–local and economic–ecological balances need to be found in plant genetic resource management. These balances also refer to the division of responsibilities among stakeholders operating in public, private and civil domains of plant genetic resource management. In many cases, alternatives could be developed when stakeholders were encouraged to join platforms that aim to find solutions for environmental or social problems. These platforms often brought together stakeholders in democratic fora where they could engage in joint learning, thus enhancing their individual, but above all joint, capacity to develop solutions. The current linear and disciplinary configuration of the institutional plant genetic resource system, with separate organizations in charge of conservation, plant breeding and seed supply, is a barrier for these stakeholders to work directly with farmers' groups on these platforms. In Chapter 7.3 we elaborate how the various organizations in the institutional plant genetic resource system may become more integrated in their plant genetic resource management once they start to support the local system and enhance the use of genetic diversity in farming. In Chapter 7.4, adaptive management is explored as a normative perspective for the development of a framework that accommodates learning.

7.3. Synthesis between crop conservation and development

Conny Almekinders, Walter de Boef and Jan Engels

Introduction

In the current chapter we analyse the cases in this book from the perspective of conservation, plant breeding and seed supply (principally sections

institutional frameworks that support farmers' management are suggested by various authors in Section 6 (Jongerden and Ruivenkamp, Chapter 6.3; Louwaars and Engels, Chapter 6.6). Examples of this type of activity include those that raise awareness of consumers and policy-makers (Jongerden, Chapter 6.8; Vermeij et al., Chapter 6.11). National NGOs and policy-makers can aim to influence the global framework and national policy-makers in other countries, for example through participation in international fora (Daño and Salazar, Chapter 6.12; Jorritsma, Chapter 6.10). In Chapter 7.4 we discuss the institutional aspects that will enable researchers and development-oriented actors to support *in situ* conservation more effectively.

The mismatch between plant genetic resource management strategies and local needs

Conventional plant breeding and seed-supply systems typically apply a fixed set of research methodologies, transfer standard messages and technologies, and disseminate seeds of relatively few improved, genetically homogeneous varieties to farmers who are treated as a homogenous group of clients. However, many cases in this book demonstrate a mismatch between the strategies of the institutional plant breeding system and the actual requirements of farmers. Song (Chapter 4.2), in her case study of maize breeding in China, illustrates the mismatch between plant breeding strategies and varieties developed by the formal system, and farmers' needs. The successes with participatory pearl millet breeding at the local level in Rajasthan, India find their explanation in the experience that standard technologies, varieties and extension messages of a centralized research system have not been adopted by farmers because they do not suit the farmers' demands (Weltzien, Chapter 4.8). Cromwell and Almekinders (Chapter 5.2) elaborate the mismatch between institutional and local seed-supply systems. Rather than concluding that improved technologies and varieties are of no use, they argue that there may be a missing link, i.e. the step of adaptation of technologies, varieties and dissemination strategies to the diversity of farmers' requirements, conditions and capacities in plant genetic resource management. Ngugi and Mugo (Chapter 4.1) illustrate the need for adaptation of technology for maize breeding in Kenya; the genetic materials that national breeders obtain from international programmes do contain characteristics that may be valuable to farmers in the low-potential area. However, these materials need to be adapted to the local setting, i.e. crossed with locally adapted and preferred varieties. They refer to the need of farmers to maintain and exchange seed of varieties in the local plant genetic resource system. In the case of maize this means producing open-pollinated varieties instead of hybrids, thus supporting the conclusion of Song (Chapter 4.2).

Participatory plant breeding: increasing access and utilization

Farmers have limited possibilities to access exotic genetic materials that can significantly contribute to improved crop production. The book contains many examples of breeding activities in which NGOs and national and international research organizations address farmers' needs for more and improved diversity, and increase farmers' access to new or exotic materials.

Seeds generally move rapidly through the traditional exchange systems. The movement of specific characteristics or genes appears much more restricted. Sthapit and Subedi (Chapter 4.7) provide an example of how local varieties in high-altitude agriculture in Nepal were genetically improved with exotic cold resistance and grain characteristics. It required support from a breeder (in this case from an NGO) to identify the exotic material and to make the crosses with the local varieties. As in many of the cases in Section 4, farmers' access to exotic and enhanced germplasm is increased through participatory breeding approaches.

The cases described demonstrate a wide variation in the type of farmers' involvement in plant breeding activities. Sthapit and Subedi (Chapter 4.7), Weltzien (Chapter 4.8) and Witcombe et al. (Chapter 4.11) illustrate how some breeders in the international and national research systems and NGOs in India and Nepal work together with relatively small local groups of farmers. They introduce promising materials from elsewhere, and tap into farmers' knowledge and capacity in selection, building upon farmers' seed-exchange systems in disseminating advanced materials and improved varieties. In this manner, farmers indicate to breeders which varieties they consider to be best adapted to their local conditions; at the same time breeders obtain a better understanding of farmers' selection criteria. The breeders' role is one that importantly facilitates the transfer of improved germplasm and supports farmers in selection by providing technical skills, for example in the design of experimental trials and teaching some basic statistics. The experience of PROINPA in Bolivia of participatory potato selection shows a different type of farmer–breeder interaction. Gabriel et al. (Chapter 4.9) describe how farmers' involvement initially supported breeders in identifying suitable materials, and how the farmers' role in the evaluation of materials developed over the following growing seasons. Machado (Chapter 4.10) supplied farmers in Brazil with maize populations that were developed in a breeding programme and which included genes from both local and exotic materials. Farmers were involved in the selection of plants from these maize populations. Variation exists in the type of interaction and in the timing of farmers' participation in the breeding process. These two aspects depend on the objectives of the breeders, the reproduction system of the crop, and the farmers' experience, knowledge and interest in selection and crop development.

Several cases in Section 4 demonstrate how the genetic diversity used by farmers increases through participatory plant breeding. Sthapit and Subedi (Chapter 4.7) show how their approach contributed to the use of more rice varieties in the mountainous part of Nepal. Witcombe et al. (Chapter 4.11) illustrate how in high-potential areas the supply of diversity through participatory varietal selection has contributed to increased deployment of genetic diversity by farmers. This supports the hypothesis that farmers always, for one reason or another, like to employ and experiment with genetic diversity.

Strengthening local seed supply

As with plant breeding, modern seed technologies can support the local plant genetic resource system by building on local knowledge and capacity. In particular, enhancing local seed exchange and the quality of farm-produced seed and planting material can be relevant.

Seed programmes conventionally focus on the diffusion of quality seed of improved varieties released by breeding programmes. This implies that seed programmes usually aim to launch relatively large volumes of seed of a few improved varieties. They may, however, be at least as effective with relatively small seed volumes. The experience of Scheidegger and Prain (Chapter 5.5) suggests that when seed programmes insert the right materials into the right place in the local system, farmers can successfully reproduce and disseminate these materials.

Other activities to improve farm-produced seed address seed processing and storage. In some cases these activities target individual farmers, but more often farmers' groups or communities. These activities are particularly effective when referring to local varieties, as for these varieties the only seed source is the farm-produced seed. Teekens (Chapter 5.6) describes the establishment of community seed banks supported by an NGO as a means to enhance seed security in Tigre, Ethiopia. Local seed security is the first objective. However, increased seed security also contributes to the maintenance of local varieties, as it implies that quality seeds of desired varieties are readily available to farmers, for instance after total crop failure. Two cases describe how players in the institutional seed-supply system provide farmers in the local system with healthy material. Scheidegger and Prain (Chapter 5.4) describe such a mechanism for the distribution of seed potatoes in Peru. Tsegaye and Struik (Chapter 5.7) illustrate a similar effort for another vegetatively propagated crop, enset, in Ethiopia. Both cases illustrate that disease contamination is an important problem in local multiplication of vegetatively propagated crops. Through supporting local reproduction or providing healthy and viable reproductive material of local varieties, farmers are at the same time supported in maintaining valuable local varieties.

Divergent perspectives with converging agendas

Encouraging the utilization of genetic diversity in livelihood systems is a strategic means of arrive at the goal of *in situ* conservation. Participatory breeding and improved local seed supply can be considered powerful tools to implement *in situ* conservation. Bertuso et al. (Chapter 3.3) describe the shift from community conservation to farmer breeding for CONSERVE, an NGO project in the Philippines. Similarly, the importance of participatory plant breeding and supporting local seed supply are emphasized in two international programmes aiming at the construction of *in situ* conservation: the IPGRI *in situ* Project (Jarvis and Ndungú-Skilton, Chapter 3.6) and the Community Biodiversity Development and Conservation (CBDC) Programme (Montecinos and Salazar, Chapter 3.5). Community seed banks, seed fairs and introduction of genetic materials are emphasized by various authors (e.g. Teekens, Chapter 5.6; Sánchez and Cosío, Chapter 5.5; Sthapit and Subedi, Chapter 4.7) as activities that contribute to dynamic plant genetic resource management by farmers. The activities aiming at crop development and seed security, implemented by development-oriented actors in the plant genetic resource system, are the same as the activities on the agenda of the *in situ* conservationists. This means that even though perspectives vary from supporting local plant genetic resource conservation to breeding or seed supply, the agendas merge and provide a common basis for activities to encourage genetic diversity in farmers' hands.

Encouraging diversity

A picture emerges in which innovative approaches aiming at *in situ* conservation do not essentially differ from those aiming at development through participatory plant breeding and supporting local seed supply. *In situ* conservationists are involved in seed supply when they support community seed banks, and are involved in crop development when using methods of participatory plant varietal selection to re-introduce local materials. Through these activities they enhance farmers' access to and use of plant genetic resource diversity. Similarly, plant breeders and seed people are supporting activities which directly contribute to farmers' management of genetic diversity. Although having a different institutional perspective, the common target is support to the local plant genetic resource system in a context of a livelihood system. Figure 7.2 illustrates these new perspectives as new and more intense interactions between the institutional and local plant genetic resource systems. Each of the perspectives and approaches presented in this book arrives in one way or another at the central objective: the enhancement of farmers' management and use of genetic diversity.

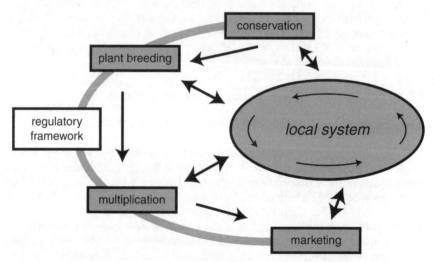

Figure 7.2: *Interactions between the institutional and local plant genetic resource systems in a conventional setting*

7.4. Adaptive plant genetic resource management

Walter de Boef, Conny Almekinders, Jan Engels and Niels Röling

Upscaling and institutional re-orientation

This book brings together a range of experiences of professionals who recognize the need for enhanced use and maintenance of genetic diversity; they also emphasize plant genetic resource management in the context of farmers' livelihood systems. These professionals describe opportunities of linking and collaborating with farmers. By building on farmers' knowledge and capacities, participatory approaches enable agricultural researchers to better target their activities to address farmers' location-specific plant genetic resource needs. They thus create opportunities for professionals to operate in a diversity of settings, and pave the way for enhanced use of genetic diversity by farmers and their communities. The implementation of participatory approaches that support farmers' plant genetic resource management has a number of institutional implications. Opportunities for scaling-up individual efforts and 'mainstreaming' practices and programmes by plant genetic resource organizations depend on enabling policies and an conducive institutional environment. In the current chapter we explore ways to link such efforts in an alternative paradigm and learning perspective that we refer to as adaptive plant genetic resource management.

Towards decentralized and learning organizations

The institutional plant genetic resource system is generally designed and structured for implementing standard measures and uniformly applicable solutions. Recognition of the importance of agro-ecosystem resilience (Chapter 7.2) and the important role of genetic diversity in this ecological concept requires another perspective and organization of the institutional plant genetic resource system. Even though the case studies provide ground-breaking experiences in this direction, they describe relatively isolated examples of farmers' collaboration in projects of usually individual professionals in agricultural research organizations, universities and NGOs. The implementation of similar activities and processes in other places is not likely to be a linear process of multiplication of efforts. Upscaling asks for flexibility that allows proper adaptation to varying prevailing conditions in a process in which farmers and plant genetic resource researchers continuously interact and learn together. This asks for recognition not only of the importance of genetic diversity, but also of the fact that joint learning enhances plant genetic resource organizations' capacity to support farmers in their efforts to cope with and respond adequately to agro-ecological and socio-economic changes.

Integrated approach to plant genetic resource management

The use of integrated, dynamic approaches asks for a flexible and adaptable institutional setting. Activities that support farmers' plant genetic resource systems in an integrated manner cross disciplinary boundaries, involve several organizations and require a re-think of institutional and professional mandates. Activities that support local seed-supply systems are relevant for *in situ* conservation; participatory breeding activities have elements of strengthening local seed-supply systems; and the re-introduction of local germplasm stored in gene banks is often implemented via participatory varietal selection. In other words, support to local plant genetic resource management involves a wide range of aspects and actors, and despite the divergent perspectives of the various actors, at the local level their agendas merge in addressing the needs of a farming community.

Support to farmers' plant genetic resource systems is the means to arriving at the goal of *in situ* conservation. This support must relate to the broader context of farmers' livelihood systems. Taking such a comprehensive support and livelihood perspective, other factors such as health and nutritional issues, market factors, political and cultural issues cannot be ignored (Hardon-Baars, Chapter 1.6; Prain and Hagmann, synthesis, Section 2). In the case of support to farmers' plant genetic resource management, this holistic approach is further emphasized by the strong relationship between variety development and dissemination and local seed-supply systems. These aspects are integrated into very location-specific agro-ecosystems, socio-economic and cultural settings. This relationship is one of the basic components for a synthesis between crop conservation and development, and thus forms a logical and common basis for various plant genetic resource organizations such as gene banks, plant breeding programmes and seed agencies to support the local plant genetic resource system.

Dynamic agendas

As a consequence of changing farmers' needs, the involvement and interest of other stakeholders in the management of crop genetic diversity are also changing. For example, the focus of activities of *in situ* conservation may shift as the threat to genetic diversity increases or decreases. Areas that were losing crop genetic diversity may suddenly show an increase in farmers' use of diversity as a road opens up the area and facilitates access to other regions. Such a change was described by Admasu and Struik (Chapter 5.7) for the diversity of enset in Ethiopia. However, in other situations the opening of roads may lead to replacement of a diversity of landraces by improved varieties. NGOs and conservationists may both be interested in community seed banking to support seed security and increase farmers' germplasm access. In another situation, NGOs may want to support small enterprise development in order to improve local seed security. They may also consider farmers' political empowerment and capacity development a priority over conservation. Participatory varietal selection and plant breeding are means

Salazar (Chapter 3.5) describe the CBDC Programme, in which various stakeholders share in a global network their concerns with the community management of plant genetic resources. In this programme, platforms for plant genetic resource management and innovation are established at regional, national and local levels. Jarvis and Ndungú-Skilton (Chapter 3.6) describe the IPGRI *in situ* Project which links research activities strengthening the scientific basis of *in situ* conservation with the establishment of more adaptive national and local platforms for plant genetic resource management. In these global projects, participating organizations share a common concern, and consequently engage themselves in joint action. At the global level, partners in both the CBDC Programme and IPGRI *in situ* Project form platforms that aim to translate lessons learnt at local and national levels to the global level of plant genetic resource management. A challenge is to link the local and individual lessons in these global programmes and the individual experiences reported upon here, and translate these into a guiding and enabling framework and paradigm for plant genetic resource management.

Building new social contracts for plant genetic resource management

Intellectual property rights issues are enforced at a global level; several papers in Section 6 draw an alarming picture of the global dimensions of plant genetic resource management that restrict or otherwise affect adaptive opportunities for plant genetic resource management at national and local levels. Like farmers, plant genetic resource organizations are also subject to a treadmill that is being driven partly by this trend of 'appropriation' and 'globalization' of plant genetic resources. Accordingly, global issues have an impact on national and local agendas, and in turn negatively affect opportunities for these organizations to support the local plant genetic resource system. The resulting global policy framework appears to restrict opportunities to encourage farmers' use and management of plant genetic resources. An example of such a restriction is the limitations imposed by variety and seed regulations on farmers' seed production and exchange of varieties. A serious bottleneck to sustainable plant genetic resource management may not be the capacity of public organizations to deal with these dynamics of plant genetic resources and farmers' management, but their capacity to deal with the structures of their often rather bureaucratic, rigid institutional and regulatory frameworks (Pimbert, 1999). Consequently, plant genetic resource organizations' adaptive activities may be in conflict with global and institutional trends to which they are subjected. As public institutions, plant genetic resource organizations have a direct responsibility towards civil society; they should be socially and also politically accountable to the public or civil society for their actions. This counts for local, regional, national and international plant genetic resource organizations that operate in the public domain. NGOs play an important role in monitoring these public organizations. Processes of institutional change are difficult and

345

require considerable time, but if successful they will strengthen the social contract between farmers and other stakeholders in civil society and public plant genetic resource organizations. This social contract covers organizations that are, for example, responsible for conservation (gene banks), plant breeding and seed supply. The ongoing discussion on genetically modified organisms demonstrates that this social contract also applies to the relation between consumers and farmers, with both public and private organizations involved in agro-genetic research. Adaptive management as learning perspective may support both public and private plant genetic resource organizations to review, renew or revise their social contract with civil society. It is a perspective that visualizes and analyses links between plant genetic resource organizations and the society that they are supposed to serve.

Encouraging diversity

This book has brought together a diversity of perspectives and experiences which illustrate the encouragement of diversity in farmers' plant genetic resource management. When we began, we expected that conservation and development perspectives would often represent conflicting interests. However, from the case studies in this book we have learnt that the perspectives, while different, are not in conflict. Many of the contributors started their activities from a conservation, breeding or development perspective and objective. Over time they learnt that at the local level their agendas may have merged or coincided with other stakeholders' agendas in their relation to farmers' livelihood systems.

Another important lesson is that the majority of local activities related to plant genetic resource management are built on partnerships between farmers and professionals. Collectively, groups of farmers and professionals have started to develop new approaches and have established often informal platforms for plant genetic resource management which link conservation, breeding and seed supply in one integrated framework. Because of the learning nature of these platforms, they have the potential to create capacity at both local and national levels to respond to changes encountered in ecology and society.

The book brings together and reveals common ground among a diversity of experiences in the North and South, and in marginal and high-potential production areas. Farmers across the world experience similar risks and uncertainties; genetic diversity is used by farmers as a means to respond to and manage these dynamics. In the current chapter we have introduced adaptive management as a learning perspective and emerging paradigm for the development of an integrated approach to plant genetic resource management. We are aware that we only open a door to adaptive management, and do not further elaborate the framework and the paradigm. This step appeared most opportune following the synthesis in Chapter 7.3 and the questions that emerged with respect to the enabling and guiding institutional framework as reflected upon in Chapter 7.2. We see as the next step in the process the elaboration of the paradigm and the implementation of an enabling framework of adaptive plant genetic resource management at local, national, regional and global levels. Adaptive management has the potential to guide these processes of up-scaling the book's impressive volume of individual experiences and methods of strengthening local plant genetic resource management.

This brings us back to our discussion on the relationship between crop conservation and development. This relationship was, and remains, an important aspect of the debate regarding the development and implementation of the *in situ* conservation strategy as supported by the CBD, Agenda 21 and FAO's Global Plan of Action. Adaptive plant genetic resource management emerges as a potential forceful perspective in this debate, as it breaks barriers between farmers, farmers' groups, consumers, plant genetic resource researchers and conservationists, plant breeders, development workers, activists and policy-makers. It creates dynamic learning environments in which policies are implemented and continuously revised and guided by farmers' and other involved organisations' practices. A challenge for groups of professionals is to realize and accept that working in variable, dynamic and unpredictable environments requires constant and, above all, joint learning on platforms in which stakeholders are brought together and share responsibility for plant genetic resource management. Using an adaptive management perspective, experiences shared in this book help to transform the institutional and policy framework into one that facilitates and supports the use of crop genetic diversity in agriculture, and thereby contributes to an agriculture that is more ecologically sound.

With this book, above all we have learnt that *in situ* conservation cannot only be the outcome of conservation activity. *In situ* conservation of genetic diversity is the result of a process that aims to keep desirable genetic diversity in farmers' fields as a component of a sustainable livelihood system. *In situ* conservation becomes an output of joint efforts of a range of stakeholders that support farmers' management and utilization of plant genetic resources. When farmers' utilization of plant genetic resources is given a central position, *in situ* conservation becomes a management rather than a conservation strategy.

References

Absil, P., Idema, M., Wijn, M. and Beekman, P. (1997) *How Many Kilometres did you Eat Today?* Consumentenwijzer over voedsel en transport. AKB, Amsterdam.

Almekinders, C., Starren, M., Visser B. and de Boef, W. (1997) International workshop. 'Towards a synthesis between crop conservation and development'. Baarlo, The Netherlands, 30 June – 2 July 1997. Compilation of workshop information, posters and summaries of position. Wageningen, CPRO-DLO, Centre for Genetic Resources, The Netherlands.

Almekinders, C.J.M. and Louwaars, N.P. (1999) *Farmers' seed production: New approaches and practices*. Intermediate Technology Publications, London.

Almekinders, C.J.M., Louwaars, N.P. and De Bruijn, G.H. (1994) Local seed systems and their importance for an improved seed supply in developing countries. *Euphytica* **78**: 207–216.

Almekinders, C.J.M., Fresco, L.O. and Struik, P.C. (1995) The need to study and manage variation in agro-ecosystems. *Netherlands Journal of Agricultural Science* **43**: 127–142.

Anon. (1996) Annual Report, 1996. *Zeeuwse Vlegel*, the Netherlands.

Arnold, M.H. (1986) Plant gene conservation. *Nature* **319**: 615.

Arriola, P.E. and Ellstrand, N.C. (1996) Crop-to-weed gene flow in the genus *Sorghum* (Poaceae): spontaneous interspecific hybridization between johnsongrass, *Sorghum halepense* and crop sorghum, *S. bicolor*. *American Journal of Botany* **83**: 1153–1159.

Ashby, J.A. (1990) *Evaluating Technology with Farmers: A Handbook*. Cali, CIAT.

Ashby, J. and Sperling, L. (1995) Institutionalizing participatory, client-driven research and technology development in agriculture. *Development and Change* **26**: 753–770.

Baker, R. (1984) Some of the open-pollinated varieties that contributed most to modern hybrid corn. In: *Proceedings of the 20th Annual Illinois Corn Breeders' School*, Champaign, Illinois, pp. 1–9.

Barbault, R. (1993) *Ecologie Générale. Structure et Fonctionnement de la Biosphère*, 2e édition. Masson, Paris.

Bastidas, G. (1991) *Agricultores Genetistas*. Paper prepared for the XV Reunión de la Asociación Latinoamericana de la Papa, 8–14 septiembre 1991, Lima, Peru.

BDP (1997) *Geschäftsbericht 1997*. Bundesverband Deutscher Pflanzenzüchter e.V., Bonn.

Becker, C.D., Dustin C. and Ostrom, E. (1995) Human ecology and resource sustainability: the importance of institutional diversity. *Annual Review of Ecology and Systematics* **26**: 113–133.

Bellon, M.R. (1996) The dynamics of crop infraspecific diversity: a conceptual framework at the farmer level. *Economic Botany* **50**: 26–39.

Bellon, M.R. and Brush, S.B. (1994) Keepers of maize in Chiapas. *Economic Botany* **48**: 196–209.

Bellon, M.R., Pham, J.L. and Jackson, M.T. (1997) Genetic conservation: a role of rice. In Maxted, N., Ford-Lloyd, B.V. and Hawkes, J.G. (eds) *Plant Genetic Conservation. The in-situ approach*. Chapman & Hall, London, pp. 263–285.

Bengtsson, B. and Thornstrom, C.-G. (1998) *Biodiversity and Future Genetic Policy. A Study of Sweden*. Environmentally Sustainable Development Agricultural Research and Development Group, Special Report No. 5. World Bank, Washington, D.C./SIDA, Stockholm.

Berg, T. (1992) Indigenous knowledge and plant breeding in Tigray, Ethiopia. *Forum for Development Studies* **1**: 13–22.

Berg, T. (1996) The compatibility of grassroots breeding and modern farming. In: Eyzaguirre, P. and Iwanaga, M. (eds) *Participatory Plant Breeding*, Proceedings of a Workshop on Participatory Plant Breeding, 26–29 July 1995, Wageningen, The Netherlands. IDRC/FAO/CGN/IPGRI, Rome, pp. 31–26.

Berg, T., Bjornstad, A., Fowler, C. and Skroppa, T. (1991) *Technology Options and the Gene Struggle*. Occasional Paper No. 8. NorAgric, Oslo.

Berkes, F., Colding, J. and Folke, C. (1997) *Rediscovery of Traditional Ecological Knowledge and Adaptive Management*. Beijer Discussion Paper Series No. 109. Beijer International Insitute of Ecological Economics, Royal Swedish Academy of Sciences, Stockholm.

Bertschinger, L. (1992) Modelling of potato virus pathosystems by means of quantitative epidemiology: an exemplary case based on virus degeneration studies in Peru. Dissertation No. 9759. ETH, Zurich.

Boef, W. de, Hardon, J. and Louwaars, N.P. (1997) 'Integrated organisation of institutional crop development as a system to maintain and stimulate the utilisation of agro-biodiversity at the farm level'. Paper presented at the International Meeting 'Managing Plant Genetic Resources in the African Savannah', Bamako Mali, 24–28 February 1997.

Borlaug, N.E. and Downwell, C.R. (1994) Feeding a human population that increasingly crowds fragile plants. Keynote Lecture, *15th World Congress of Soil Science*, 10 July, 1994, Acapulco, Mexico.

Boster, J.S. (1984) Inferring decision making from preferences and behavior: an analysis of Aguaruna Jivaro selection. *Human Ecology* **12**: 343–357.

Bretting, P.K. and Duvick, D.N. (1997) Dynamic conservation of plant genetic resources. *Advances in Agronomy* **61**: 1–51.

Bretting, P.K. and Widrlechner, M.P. (1995) Genetic markers and plant genetic resources. *Plant Breeding Reviews* **13**: 11–86.

Brush, S.B. (1991) A farmer-based apporach to conserving crop germplasm. *Economic Botany* **45**: 153–165.

Brush, S.B. (1992) Reconsidering the green revolution: diversity and stability in cradle areas of crop domestication. *Human Ecology* **20**: No. 2.

Brush, S.B. (1993) *In situ* conservation of landraces in centers of crop diversity. Paper prepared for the *Symposium on Global Implications of Germplasm Conservation and Utilization*, 85th Annual Meeting of the American Society of Agronomy, Cincinnati, Ohio. Department of Applied Behavioral Sciences, University of California, Davis, CA.

Brush, S.B. (1995) *In situ* conservation of landraces in centers of crop diversity. *Crop Science* **35**: 346–354.

Brush, S.B., Carney, H.J. and Huaman, Z. (1981) Dynamics of Andean potato agriculture. *Economic Botany* **35**: 70–88.

Campilan, D. (1998) Dynamics of household food security in rural Philippines. Paper presented at the *FAO Technical Consultation on Rural Household Food Security*, Bangkok, Thailand, 15–19 September 1998.

Campilan, D.M. (1999) *Introducing a Livelihood Systems Framework in Participatory Agricultural Research*. CIP/UPWARD, Los Baños, Philippines.

Canadian Food Inspection Agency (1998) List of varieties which are registered in Canada. Variety Registration Office, Canadian Food Inspection Agency, www.cfia-acia.agr.ca/english/plant/variety/

Carrasco, E., Estrada, N., Gabriel, J., Alfaro, G., Larondelle, Y., García, W. and Quiroga, O. (1997) Seis cultivares potenciales de papa con resistencia al tizón tardío (*Phytophthora infestans*) en Bolivia. *Revista Latinoamericana de la Papa* **9/10**: 106–122.

Ceccarelli, S. (1989) Wide adaptation: how wide? *Euphytica* **40**: 197–205.

Ceccarelli, S., Grando, S. and Booth, R.H. (1996) International breeding programmes and resources and resource-poor farmers: crop improvement in difficult environments. In: Eyzaguirre, P. and Iwanaga, M. (eds) *Participatory Plant Breeding*, Proceedings of a Workshop on Participatory Plant Breeding, 26–29 July 1995, Wageningen, The Netherlands. IDRC/FAO/CGN/IPGRI, Rome, pp. 99–116.

Christinck, A. and vom Brocke, K. (1998) Evaluating pearl millet cutivars with farmers. In: *Participatory Plant Improvement*. Proceedings of a Workshop on Farmer Participatory Methods in Research and Development for the Semi-Arid Tropics, ICRISAT, Patancheru, India, 27–28 October 1998. M.S. Swaminathan Research Foundation, Chennai, India, pp. 9–16.

Christinck, A., vom Brocke, K., Kshirsagar, K.G., Weltzien R.E. and Bramel-Cox, P.J. (1999) Testing participatory methods for collecting germplasm with farmers in Rajasthan, India. *Plant Genetic Resources Newsletter.*

Chweya, J. (1994) Potential for agronomic improvement of indigenous plant germplasm in African agriculture – a case study of indigenous vegetables in Kenya. In Putter, A. (ed.) *Safeguarding the Genetic Basis of Africa's Traditional Crops.* CTA, The Netherlands/IPGRI, Rome.

Chweya, J. and Eyzaguirre, P.B. (eds) (1999) *The Biodiversity of Traditional Leafy Vegetables.* IPGRI, Rome.

Cochrane, W.W. (1958) *Farm Prices, Myth and Reality.* University of Minnesota Press, Minneapolis.

Cooper, D., Vellvé, R. and Hobbelink, H. (eds) (1992) *Growing Diversity. Genetic Resources and Local Food Security.* IT Publications, London.

Cordeiro, A. (1993) Rediscovering local varieties of maize: challenging seed policy in Brazil. In: de Boef, W., Amanor, K., Wellard, K. and Bebbington, A. (eds) *Cultivating Knowledge. Genetic Diversity, Farmer Experimentation and Crop Research.* IT Publications, London, pp. 139–162.

Cromwell, E. (1996) *Governments, Farmers and Seeds in a Changing Africa.* CAB International, Wallingford, UK.

Cromwell, E., Friis-Hansen E. and Turner, M. (1992) The Seed Sector in Developing Countries: A Framework for Performance Analysis. ODI Working Paper No. 65. Overseas Development Institute, London.

CSA (1997a) *Enset Sample Survey Results.* Central Statistical Authority, Addis Ababa, Ethiopia.

CSA (1997b) *Estimate of Improved Seed, Irrigation, Pesticide and Fertiliser Applied Area and their Percentage Distribution by Crop for the Main Season, Private Peasant Holdings 1995–1996 (Ethiopian Calendar 1988).* Central Statistical Authority, Federal Democratic Republic of Ethiopia, Addis Ababa.

Cummings, R. (1978) Agricultural change in Vietnam's floating rice region. *Human Organization* **37**: 235–245.

Darwin, C. (1859) *The Origin of Species by Means of Natural Selection or The Preservation of Favoured Races in the Struggle for Life.* Penguin, Harmondsworth, UK (1985 edn).

De Bruin, R. (1995) Local cooperatives as carriers of endogenous development. In: van der Ploeg, J.D. and van Dijk, G. (eds) *Beyond Modernisation, the Impact of Endogenous Rural Development.* Van Gorcum, Assen, The Netherlands.

De Franco, M. and Godoy, R. (1993) Potato-led growth: the macroeconomic effects of technological innovation in Bolivian agriculture. *Journal of Development Studies* **29**: 561–587.

De Steenhuysen Piters, B. (1995) Diversity in agro-ecosystems. PhD thesis, Wageningen Agricultural University, Wageningen, The Netherlands.

Dennis, J.V. (1987) Farmer management of rice diversity in Northern Thailand. PhD thesis, Cornell University, USA.

Devos, K.M. and Gale, M.D. (1997) Comparative genetics in the grasses. *Plant Molecular Biology* **35**: 3–15.

Dhamotharan, M., Weltzien R.E., Whitaker, M.L., Rattunde, H.F.W., Anders, M.M., Tyagi, L.C., Manga, V.K. and Vyas, K.L. (1997) *Seed Management Strategies of Farmers in Western Rajasthan in their Social and Environmental Contexts.* Results from a workshop using new communication techniques for a dialogue between farmers and scientists, 5–8 February 1996, Digadi Village, Jodhpur District, Rajasthan, India. ICRISAT, Patancheru, India/University of Hohenheim, Stuttgart, Germany.

Dover, M. and Talbot, L.M. (1987) *To Feed the Earth: Agro-ecology for Sustainable Development.* World Resource Institute, Washington, D.C.

Duvick, D.N. (1984) Genetic diversity in major farm crops on the farm and in reserve. *Economic Botany* **38**: 161–178.

Duvick, D.N. (1996) Plant breeding, an evolutionary concept. *Crop Science* **36**: 539–548.

Ehrlich, P.R. and Wilson, E.O. (1991) Biodiversity studies: science and policy. *Science* **253**: 758–772.

Elings, A., White, J.W. and Edmeades, G.O. (1997) Options for breeding for greater maize yields in the tropics. *European Journal of Agronomy* **7**: 119–132.

Escolán, R.M., Méndez, M.A., Mendoza, F. and Ravnborg, H.M. (1998) *Development of a Regional Poverty Profile for Three Honduran Watersheds: Río Saco in Atlántida, Tascalapa in Yoro and Cuscateca in El Paraíso.* CIAT, Tegucigalpa, Honduras (in Spanish).

Eyzaguirre, P. and Iwanaga, M. (1996) Farmers' contribution to maintaining genetic diversity in crops and its role within the total genetic resources system. In: Eyzaguirre, P. and Iwanaga, M. (eds) *Participatory Plant Breeding*, Proceedings of a Workshop on Participatory Plant Breeding, 26–29 July 1995, Wageningen, The Netherlands. IDRC/FAO/CGN/IPGRI, Rome, pp. 9–18.

Fakir, S. (ed.) (1996a) *Genetic Resource Conservation.* Workshop Proceedings, 19–20 March 1996. Land and Agricultural Policy Centre, Johannesburg, South Africa.

Fakir, S. (1996b) *Genetic Resource Conservation and Economic Use in South Africa: A Review of the Current Policy Situation.* Land and Agricultural Policy Centre, Johannesburg, South Africa.

FAO (1983) International Undertaking on Plant Genetic Resources for Food and Agriculture. FAO, Rome.

FAO (1994) *FAO Seed Review 1989–90.* Food and Agriculture Organisation of the United Nations, Rome.

FAO (1995) *Dimensions of Need: An Atlas of Food and Agriculture.* FAO, Rome.

FAO (1996a) *Food Requirements and Population Growth.* The World Food Summit, Technical Background Document No. 4. Food and Agriculture Organisation of the United Nations, Rome.

FAO (1996b) *State of the World's Plant Genetic Resources for Food and Agriculture. International Technical Conference on Plant Genetic Resources*, Leipzig, Germany, 17–23 June 1996. Food and Agriculture Organisation of the United Nations, Rome.

FAO (1996c) Germany: Country Report. In: *State of the World's Plant Genetic Resources for Food and Agriculture. International Technical Conference on Plant Genetic Resources*, Leipzig, Germany, 17–23 June 1996. Food and Agriculture Organisation of the United Nations, Rome.

FAO (1996d) Cuba: Country Report. In: *State of the World's Plant Genetic Resources for Food and Agriculture. International Technical Conference on Plant Genetic Resources*, Leipzig, Germany, 17–23 June 1996. Food and Agriculture Organisation of the United Nations, Rome.

FAO (1996e) *The Global Plan of Action for the Conservation and Sustainable Utilization of Plant Genetic Resources for Food and Agriculture.* Food and Agriculture Organisation of the United Nations, Rome.

FAO (1998) *Technical Consultation on Intra-household Dynamics and Rural Household Food Security.* Women in Development Programme, FAO Regional Office for Asia and the Pacific, Bangkok.

FAO/IPGRI (1994) *Genebank Standards.* Food and Agriculture Organisation of the United Nations, Rome/International Plant Genetic Resources Institute, Rome.

Fowler, C. and Mooney, P. (1990) *Shattering.* University of Arizona Press, Tucson.

Frankel, O. (1988) Genetic resources: evolutionary and social responsibility. In: Kloppenburg, J.R. (ed.) *Seeds and Sovereignty: The Use and Control of Plant Genetic Resources.* Duke University Press, Durham NC and London, pp. 19–46.

Frey, K.J. (1998) *National Plant Breeding Study III: National Plan for Genepool Enrichment of US Crops.* Special Report No. 101. Iowa Agriculture and Home Economics Experiment Station, Iowa State University, Ames, IA.

Friis-Hansen, E. (1996) The role of local plant genetic resource management in participatory breeding. In: Eyzaguire, P.B. and Iwanaga, M. (eds) *Participatory Plant Breeding*, Proceedings of a Workshop on Participatory Plant Breeding, 26–29 July 1995, Wageningen, The Netherlands. IDRC/FAO/CGN/IPGRI, Rome, pp. 66–76.

Friis-Hansen, E. (1999a) Genetic erosion of plant genetic resources: causes and effects. *Danish Journal of Geography* 1999: 61–69.

Friis-Hansen, E. (1999b) *The Socio-Economic Dynamics of Farmers' Management of Local Plant Genetic Resources – A Framework for Analysis with Examples from a Tanzanian Case Study.* Working Paper No. 99.3. Centre for Development Research, Copenhagen.

Friis-Hansen, E. and Sthapit, B. (eds) (1999) *Participatory Approaches to Conservation and Use of Plant Genetic Resources.* IPGRI Technical Bulletin No. 3. International Plant Genetic Resources Institute, Rome.

GAO (1997) *Information on the Condition of the National Plant Germplasm System.* GAO-RCED-98-20. US General Accounting Office, Washington, D.C.

Gerhart, J. (1975) *The Diffusion of Hybrid Maize in Western Kenya.* CIMMYT, Mexico City.

Goland, C. (1993) Agricultural risk management through diversity: field scattering in Cuyo Cuyo, Peru. *Culture and Agriculture* **45/46**: 8–13.

Gonese, C. (1999a) The three worlds. *Compas Newsletter for Endogenous Development* **1**: 20–22.

Gonese, C. (1999b) Culture and cosmovisions of traditional institutions in Zimbabwe. In: Haverkort, B. and Hiemstra, W. (eds) *Food for Thought: Ancient Visions and New Experiments of Rural People.* Zed Books, London.

Graham, R.D. and Welch, R.M. (1998) *Breeding for Stable Food Crops with High Micronutrient Density. Agricultural Strategies for Micronutrients.* Working Paper No. 3. IFPRI, Washington D.C.

Grime, J.P. (1979) *Plant Strategies and Vegetation Processes.* Wiley, Chichester, UK.

Grubben, G. and Almekinders C.J.M. (1997) Developing the potential of local vegetables, using experiences from Africa and South-East Asia. In: Schippers, R. and Budd, L. (eds) *Workshop on African Indigenous Vegetables*, Limbe, Cameroon, January 13–18 1997. IPGRI, Rome/NRI, Chatham, UK, pp. 12–18.

Gunderson, L.H., Holling, C.S. and Light, S.S. (eds.) (1995) *Barriers and Bridges to Renewal of Ecosystems and Institutions.* Columbia University Press, New York.

Hammer, K., 1998: Agrabiodiversität und pflanzengenetische Ressourcen – Herausforderung und Lösungsansatz. *Schriften zu Genetischen Ressourcen* **10**: 98S.

Hammer, K., Esquivel, M. and Knupffer, H. (eds) (1992) *Origin, Evolution and Diversity of Cuban Cultivated Plants.* Vols I and II. Institute für Genetik und Kulturpflanzenforschung, Gatersleben, Germany.

Hammer, K., Esquivel, M. and Knupffer, H. (eds) (1994) *Origin, Evolution and Diversity of Cuban Cultivated Plants.* Vol. III. Institute für Genetik und Kulturpflanzenforschung, Gatersleben, Germany, pp. 455–824.

Hardon, J. and de Boef, W. (1993) Linking farmers and breeders in local crop development. In: de Boef, W., Amanor, K., Wellard, K. and Bebbington, A. (eds) *Cultivating Knowledge. Genetic Diversity, Farmer Experimentation and Crop Research.* IT Publications, London, pp. 64–71.

Hardon, J.J. (1995) The Global Context: Breeding and Crop Genetic Diversity. In: Eyzaguirre, P. and Iwanaga, M. (eds) *Participatory Plant Breeding*, Proceedings of a Workshop on Participatory Plant Breeding, 26–29 July 1995, Wageningen, The Netherlands. IDRC/FAO/CGN/IPGRI, Rome, pp. 1–15.

Hardon-Baars, A.J. (1996) *User/Use-Oriented Approaches to Technology Assessment and Innovation: Some Lessons from Marketing Research.* Into Action Research: Partnerships in Asian Rootcrop Research and Development. UP-WARD, Los Baños, Laguna, Philippines.

Hardon-Baars, A.J. (1997) *Users' Perspectives. Literature Review on the Development of a Concept.* UPWARD Working Paper No. 4. UPWARD, Los Baños, Laguna, Philippines.

Harlan, J.R. (1992) *Crops and Man*, 2nd edn. American Society of Agronomy, Madison, WI.

Harrison, M. (1970) Maize improvement in East Africa. In: Leakey, C.L.A. (ed.) *Crop Improvement in East Africa.* CAB International, Wallingford, UK.

Hassan, R.M., Njoroge, K., Mugo, N., Otsyula, R. and Laboso, A. (1998) Adoption patterns and performance of improved Maize in Kenya. In: Hassan, R.M (ed.) *Maize Technology Development and Transfer. A GIS Application for Research Planning in Kenya.* CAB International, Wallingford, UK.

Hawkes, J.G. (1985) *Plant Genetic Resources. The Impact of the International Agricultural Research Centres.* Study Paper No. 3. CGIAR, Washington, D.C.

Hedrick, U.P., Tapley, W.T., Enzie, D. and Eseltine, P. van (1928–1937, two volumes). *The Vegetables of New York.* Albany, New York.

Heider, K.G. (1979) *Grand Valley Dani: Peaceful Warriors.* Holt, Rinehart & Winston, New York.

Holbert, J.R., Flint, W.P., Bigger, J.H. and Duncan, G.H. (1934) Resistance and susceptibility of corn strains to second brood chinch bugs. In: *Symposium Commemorating Six Decades of the Modern Era in Botanical Science*, 15–16 November 1934, Department of Botany, Iowa State College, Ames, IA.

Holling, C.S. (1986) Resilience of ecosystems, local surprise and global change. In: Clark, W.C. and Munn, R.E. (eds) *Sustainable Development of the Biosphere.* Cambridge University Press, Cambridge, pp. 292–317.

Howard-Borjas, P. (1998) *Gender, Biodiversity and Plant Genetic Resources Management: An Annotated Bibliography.* Wageningen Agricultural University, Wageningen, The Netherlands.

Howard-Borjas, P. (1999) Some implications of gender relations for plant genetic resources management. *Biotechnology and Development Monitor*, **37** (March) 2–5.

353

Hufny, M. (1998) The international regime of genetic resources: an analysis of North–South issues. Paper presented to 2nd International Conference of the European Society for Ecological Economics, March 4–7 1998, University of Geneva. GIDS/IUED, Geneva.

Jackson, P., Robertson, M., Cooper, M. and Hammer, G. (1996) The role of physiological understanding in plant breeding from a breeding perspective. *Field Crops Research* **49**: 11–37.

Jarvis, D.I. and Hodgkin, T. (eds) (1998) *Strengthening the Scientific Basis of* In Situ *Conservation of Agricultural Biodiversity On-Farm*. Proceedings of a workshop to develop tools and procedures for *in situ* conservation on-farm, 25–29 August 1997, Rome. International Plant Genetic Resources Institute, Rome.

Jarvis, D. and Hodgkin, T. (1999) Farmer decision making and genetic diversity: linking multi-disciplinary research to implementation on-farm. In: Brush, S. (ed.) *Genes in the Field: Issues in Conserving Crop Diversity On-Farm*. International Plant Genetic Resources Institute, Rome.

Jarvis, D., Hodgkin, T., Eyzaguirre, P., Ayad, G., Sthapit, B. and Guarino, L. (1998) Farmer selection, natural selection and crop genetic diversity: the need for a basic data set. In: Jarvis, D.I. and Hodgkin, T. (eds) *Strengthening the Scientific Basis of In Situ Conservation of Agricultural Biodiversity On-Farm*. Proceedings of a workshop to develop tools and procedures for *in situ* conservation on-farm, 25–29 August 1997, Rome. International Plant Genetic Resources Institute, Rome, pp. 5–19.

Jarvis, D.I., de Boef, W.S., Engels, J.M.M. and Hodgkin, T. (2000) An international and scientific effort: constructing *in situ* conservation on-farm. In: de Boef, W.S. (ed.) *Tales of the Unpredictable. Farmers, Institutions and Adaptive Management of Agro-biodiversity*. Wageningen Agricultural University, Wageningen, The Netherlands.

Jongerden, J. and Ruivenkamp, G. (1996) *Patterns of Diversity, a Reconnaissance Study on the Decreasing Agro-Biodiversity in The Netherlands and on the Initiatives to Stimulate Agro-Biodiversity inside and outside the Agro-Industrial Production Chains*. Wetenschapswinkel and Werkgroep Technologie en Agrarische Ontwikkeling, Wageningen, The Netherlands (in Dutch).

Joshi, A. and Witcombe, J.R. (1996) Farmer participatory crop improvement. II. Farmer participatory varietal selection in India. *Experimental Agriculture* **32**: 461–477.

Joshi, A. and Witcombe, J.R. (1998) Farmer participatory approaches for varietal improvement. In: Witcombe, J.R., Virk, D.S. and Farrington, J. (eds) *Seeds of Choice: Making the Most of New Varieties for Small Farmers*. CAZS/ODI. Oxford IBH, New Delhi/IT Publications, London.

Joshi, K.D., Rana, R.B., Subedi, M., Kadayat, K.B. et al. (1996) Addressing diversity through farmer participatory variety testing and dissemination approach: a case study of *chaite* rice in the western hills of Nepal. In: Sperling, L. and Loevinsohn, M. (eds) *Using Diversity. Enhancing and Maintaining Genetic Resources On-Farm*. Proceedings of a workshop, 19–21 June 1996, New Delhi, India. IDRC, New Delhi, pp. 158–175.

Joshi, K.D., Subedi, M., Kadayat, K.B., Rana, R.B. and Sthapit, B.R. (1997) Enhancing on-farm varietal diversity through participatory variety selection: a case study of *Chaite* rice in Nepal. *Experimental Agriculture* **33**: 1–10.

Joshi, K.D., Sthapit, B.R. and Rana, R.B. (1998) *The Monitoring of Varietal Spread of PPB Products in the High Altitudes of Nepal*. Technical Report Series. LIBIRD, Pokhara, Nepal.

Jusu, M.S. (1999) Management of genetic variability in rice (*Oryza sativa* and *O. glaberrima*) by breeders and by Temne, Susu and Limba farmers, in Sierra Leone. PhD thesis, Wageningen Agricultural University, Wageningen, The Netherlands.

KARI (1994) *Strategic Plan for Cereals in Kenya (1993–2013).* Kenya Agricultural Research Institute, Nairobi, Kenya.

Karp, A., Kresovich, S., Bhat, K.V., Ayad, W.G. and Hodgkin T. (1997) *Molecular Tools in Plant Genetic Resources Conservation: A Guide to the Technologies.* IPGRI Technical Bulletin No. 2. International Plant Genetic Resources Institute, Rome.

Keller, W.E., Muskat, E. and Valder, E. (1969) Some observations regarding economy, diet and nutrition status of Kikuyu farmers in Kenya. In: Kraut, H. and Crane, H.D. (eds) *Investigation into Health and Nutrition in East Africa.* Weltforum Verlag, Munchen, Germany.

Kelly, T.G., Parthararathy Rao, P., Weltzien R.E. and Purchit, M.L. (1996) Adoption of improved cultivars of pearl millet in an arid environment: straw yield and quality considerations in western Rajasthan. *Experimental Agriculture* **32**: 161–171.

Keystone Centre (1991) Keystone International Dialogue Series on Plant Genetic Resources. Oslo Plenary Session. Final consensus report: global initiative for the security and sustainable use of plant genetic resources. Washington D.C., Genetic Resources Communication Systems, Inc.

Klug, A. (1998) Introductory remarks. In: Waterlow, J.C., Armstrong, D.G., Fowden, L. and Riley, R. (eds) *Feeding a World Population of more than Eight Billion People.* Oxford University Press, New York, pp. xiii–xv.

Koning, N. (1999) Hunger defeated? Reflections on the long-term dynamics of food security and agricultural growth. Paper for the *Congress of the European Association for Evolutionary Political Economy*, Prague, November 4–6 1999. http.\\eacpe.tuwien.ac.at/papersgg/konig.doc

Kronik, J. (1998) *Dance of the Fruits of the Earth.* Video (18 min). Centre for Development Research, Copenhagen.

Lapido, D.O. (1997) Marketing and post-harvest constraints of traditional vegetables in sub-Saharan Africa. In: Schippers, R. and Budd, L. *Workshop on African Indigenous Vegetables*, Limbe, Cameroon, January 13–18 1997. IPGRI, Rome/NRI, Chatham, UK, pp. 58–62.

Lehmann, C.O. (1990) Hundert Jahre Sammlung und Nutzung von Landsorten – zur Erinnerung an Emanuel Ritter von Proskowetz und Franz Schindler. In: Dambroth, M. and Lehmann, C.O. (eds) *Gemeinsames Kolloquium 'Sicherung und Nutzbarmachung pflanzengenetischer Ressourcen'.* FAL, Braunschweig, Germany, pp. 10–22.

LI-BIRD (1998) *Project Briefs.* LI-BIRD, Pokhara, Nepal.

Lin, J.Y. (1998) *How did China Feed Itself in the Past? How will China Feed Itself in the Future?* CIMMYT Economics Programme, Second Distinguished Economist Lecture. CIMMYT, Mexico.

Loomis, R.S. and Amthor J.S. (1996) Limits to yield revisited. In: Reynolds, M.P., Rajaram, S. and McNab, A. (eds) *Increasing Yield Potential in Wheat: Breaking the Barriers.* CIMMYT, Mexico, pp. 76–89.

Loomis, R.S. and Connor, D.J. (1992) *Crop Ecology: Productivity and Management in Agricultural Systems.* Cambridge University Press, Cambridge, UK.

Lopez-Pereira, M.A. and Morris, M.L. (1994) *Impacts of International Maize Breeding Research in the Developing World; 1966–1990.* CIMMYT, Mexico.

Louette, D. (1994) Gestion traditionnelle de variétés de maïs dans la Réserve de la Biosphère Sierra de Manatlan (RBSM, états de Jalisco et Colima, Mexique) et conservation *in situ* des ressources génétiques de plantes cultivées. Thesis, l'Ecole Nationale Supérieure Agronomique de Montpellier, France.

Louette, D. (1997) Seed exchange among farmers and gene flow among maize varieties in traditional agricultural systems. In: *Gene Flow among Maize Land-*

355

races, Improved Maize Varieties and Teosinte: Implications for Transgenic Maize (Proceedings), El Batán, Mexico. CIMMYT, Mexico, pp. 56–66.

Louette, D. (1999) Traditional management of seed and genetic diversity: what is a landrace? In: Brush, S.B. (ed.) Genes in the Field: In Situ Conservation Of Crop Genetic Resources. Lewis, New York.

Louette, D. and Smale, M. (1996) Genetic Diversity and Maize Seed Management in a Traditional Mexican Community: Implications for In Situ Conservation Of Maize. NRG Paper 96–03. CIMMYT, Mexico.

Louette, D., Charrier, A. and Berthaud, J. (1997) In situ conservation of maize in Mexico: diversity and maize seed management in a traditional community. Economic Botany 51: 20–38.

Louwaars, N.P. (1998) Breeding for field resistance in crops: regulatory aspects. Biotechnology and Development Monitor 33: 6–8.

Louwaars, N.P. and van Marrewijk, G.A.M. (1996) Seed Supply Systems in Developing Countries. CTA, Wageningen, The Netherlands.

Maat, H. (1998) The breeding of wheat in the Netherlands. In: NEHA Jaarboek 1998. NEHA, Amsterdam, The Netherlands (in Dutch).

Machado, A.T. (1997) Perspectiva do Melhoramento Genético em Milho (Zea mays L.) Visando na Utilizaço de Nitrogênio. PhD thesis, UFRJ, Rio de Janeiro, Brazil.

Machado, A.T. (1998) Resgate e caracterizaço de variedades locais de milho. In: Soares, A.C., Machado, A.T., Silva, B.M. and von der Weid, J.M. (eds) Milho Crioulo. Conservaço Uso da Biodiversidade. AS–PTA, Rio de Janeiro, Brazil, pp. 82–92.

Magnifico, F.A. (1996) Community-based resource management: CONSERVE (Philippines) experience. In: Sperling, L. and Loevinsohn, M. (eds) Using Diversity. Enhancing and Maintaining Genetic Resources On-Farm. Proceedings of a workshop, 19–21 June 1996, New Delhi, India. IDRC, New Delhi, pp. 289–301.

Mann, C. (1997) Reseeding the green revolution. Science 277: 1038–1043.

Matson, P.A., Parton, W.J., Power, A.G. and Swift, M.J. (1997) Agricultural intensification and ecosystem properties. Science 277: 504–509.

Maundu, P.M., Njiro, E.I., Chweya, J.A., Imungi, J.K. and Seme, E.N. (1999) Kenya. In: Chweya, J.A. and Eyzaguirre, P.B. (eds) The Biodiversity of Traditional Leafy Vegetables. International Plant Genetic Resources Institute, Rome, pp. 52–84.

Maxted, N., Ford-Lloyd, B.V. and Hawkes, J.G. (1997a) Complementary conservation strategies. In: Maxted, N., Ford-Lloyd, B.V. and Hawkes, J.G. (eds) Plant Genetic Conservation. The In Situ Approach. Chapman & Hall, London, pp. 15–39.

Maxted, N., Ford-Lloyd, B.V. and Hawkes, J.G. (eds) (1997b) Plant Genetic Conservation. The In Situ Approach. Chapman & Hall, London.

Mayet, M. (1997) Overview of the Legal Environment Pertaining to the Conservation and Sustainable Use of Agricultural Resources. WP 67. LAPC, Johannesburg, South Africa.

Melnyck, M., Scoones, I., Hinchcliffe, F. and Pimbert, M. (1995) La cosecha escondida. Alimentos silvestres y sistemas agrícolas. Biodiversidad 5: 17–21.

Mendoza, T.C., Briones, A.A. and Briones, A. M. (1989) Green revolution and its impact on ecosystem and traditional culture. Seminar on Environmental, Social and Cultural Impacts of Development Projects, November 20–24 1989, Cortona, Italy.

MISA (1999) Red River Valley. Draft Working Paper, July, 1999. Minnesota Institute of Sustainable Agriculture, St. Paul, University of Minnesota, Minnesota.

Montecinos, C. (1995) Creando puentes entre agricultores y no agricultores. Biodiversidad 6: 8–9.

Mooney, P. (1996) The Parts of Life: Agricultural Biodiversity, Indigenous Knowledge and the Role of the Third System. Development Dialogue. (Special Issue) 1–2.

Morgan, D.L. and Krueger, R.A. (1998) *The Focus Group Kit.* Sage, London.

Moss, H. (1996) *The Application of Intellectual Property Protection to Biodiversity and Agriculture in South Africa. Consequences, Concerns and Opportunities.* WP 36. LAPC, Johannesburg, South Africa.

Mugo, S.N. and Njoroge, K. (1997) Alleviating the effects of drought on maize production in the moisture stress areas of Kenya through escape and tolerance. In: Edmeades, G.O., Banziger, M., Mickelson, H.R. and Pena-Valdivia, C.B. (eds) *Developing Drought- and Low N-Tolerant Maize.* CIMMYT, Mexico.

Muhammed, L., Scott, F. and Steeghs, H. (1985) *Seed Availability, Distribution and Use in Machakos District.* Ministry of Agriculture, National Dryland Farming Research Center, Katumani, Kenya. Unpublished report.

Müller, K.-J. (1998) Nutzung genetischer Ressourcen in der Züchtung für den ökologischen Landbau. *Schriften zu Genetischen Ressourcen* 8, 176–185.

Murphy, P.J. and Witcombe, J.R. (1982) Variation in Himalayan barley and the concept of centres of diversity. In: *Barley Genetics IV.* Proceedings of the IV International Barley Genetics Symposium, Edinburgh, 1981. Edinburgh University Press, UK, pp. 26–36.

Njoroge, K., Kanampiu, N., Otsyula, R., Muthamia, Z., Gathuri, C. and Chivatsi, W. (1992) The high-altitude maize breeding program. In: *Proceedings of a Workshop on Review of the National Maize Program.* Kenya Agricultural Research Institute/International Service for National Agricultural Research, Nairobi, Kenya, pp. 20–31.

Ospina, B., Smith, L. and Bellotti, A. (1997) Adaptation of farmer participatory research methods for developing integrated crop management in cassava-based systems in northeast Brazil. In: *CIAT's Experience with Systems Research and Future Directions (Proceedings).* CIAT, Cali, Colombia.

Pandey, S. (1996) Socioeconomic context and priorities for strategic research on Asian upland rice ecosystems. In: Piggin, C. *et al.* (eds) *Upland Rice Research in Partnership.* Proceedings of the Upland Rice Consortium Workshop, January 4–13 1996, Padang, Indonesia. International Rice Research Institute, Los Baños, Philippines, pp. 103–124.

Patch, L.H., Still, G.W., App, B.A. and Crooks, C.A. (1941) Comparative injury by the European Corn Borer to open-pollinated and hybrid field corn. *Journal of Agriculture Research* 63: 355–368.

Pedersen, J.F., Toy, J.J. and Johnson, B. (1998) Natural outcrossing of sorghum and sudangrass in the Central Great Plains. *Crop Science* 38: 937–939.

Perrino, P. (1994) Plant genetic resource activities in Italy. In: Begemann, F. and Hammer, K. (eds) *Integration of Conservation Strategies of Plant Genetic Resources in Europe.* ZADI/IPK, Gatersleben, Germany, pp. 34–45.

Pham, J.L., Sebastian, L.S., Sanchez, P., Calibo, M., Quilloy, S., Bellon, M.R., Francisco, S.R., Erasga, D., Abrigo, G. and Loresto, G.C. (1998) On-farm diversity of rice varieties: collecting and analysis of genetic data in the Philippines. In: Jarvis, D.I. and Hodgkin, T. (eds) *Strengthening the Scientific Basis of In Situ Conservation of Agricultural Biodiversity On-Farm.* Proceedings of a workshop to develop tools and procedures for *in situ* conservation on-farm, 25–29 August 1997, Rome, Italy. International Plant Genetic Resources Institute, Rome, p. 34.

Pimbert, M. (1999) *Sustaining the Multiple Functions of Agricultural Biodiversity.* Gatekeeper Series No. 88. International Institute for Economics and Development, London.

Pistorius, R.J. and Van Wijk, J.C.A.C. (1999) *The Exploitation of Plant Genetic Information: Political Strategies in Crop Development.* CAB International, Wallingford, UK.

357

Prain, G., Uribe, F. and Scheidegger, U. (1991) Small farmers in agricultural research: farmer participation in potato germplasm evaluation. In: Haverkort, B., van der Kamp, J. and Waters-Bayer A. (eds) *Joining Farmers' Experiments: Experiences in Participatory Technology Development*. Intermediate Technology Publications, London, pp. 235–250.

Qualset, C.O., Damania, A.B., Zanatta, A.C.A. and Brush, S.B. (1997) Locally based crop plant conservation. In: Maxted, N., Ford-Lloyd, B.V. and Hawkes, J.G. (eds) *Plant Genetic Conservation. The* In-Situ *Approach*. Chapman & Hall, London, pp. 160–175.

RAFI (1989) *Community Seed Bank Kit*. Rural Advancement Foundation International, Pittsboro, USA.

RAFI (1999) *Human Nature. Agricultural Biodiversity and Farmer-based Food Security*. Rural Advancement Foundation International, Pittsboro, USA.

Ravnborg, H.M. (1996) *Agricultural Research and the Peasants. The Tanzanian Agricultural Knowledge and Information System*. Centre for Development Research, Copenhagen.

Rice, E., Smale M. and Blanco, J.-L. (1998) Farmers' use of improved seed selection practices in Mexican maize: evidence and issues from the Sierra de Santa Marta. *World Development* **26**: 1625–1640.

Richards, P. (1996a) Agrarian Creolization: the ethnobiology, history, culture and politics of West African rice. In: Ellen, R. and Fukui, K. (eds) *Redefining Nature: Ecology, Culture and Domestication*. Berg, Oxford, UK.

Richards, P. (1996b) Culture and community values in the selection and maintenance of African rice. In: Brush, S. and Stabinsky, D. (eds) *Intellectual Property And Indigenous Knowledge*. Island Press, Covelo, California.

Richards, P. (1998) *Fighting for the Rain Forest: War, Youth and Resources in Sierra Leone*. James Currey, Oxford, UK (1998 edn).

Richards, P. and Ruivenkamp, G. (1998) *Seeds and Survival: Plant Genetic Resource Management in Conflict and Post-war Recovery*. International Plant Genetic Resources Institute, Rome.

Rogers, E.M. (1995) *Diffusion of Innovations*, 4th edn. Free Press, New York.

Röling, N.G. and Wagemakers, M.A.E. (eds) (1998) *Facilitating Sustainable Agriculture. Participatory Learning and Adaptive Management in Times of Environmental Uncertainty*. Cambridge University Press, Cambridge.

Roset, P. and Benjamin, M. (eds) (1993) *Two Steps Back, One Step Forward. Cuba's Nationwide Experiment with Organic Agriculture*. Global Exchange, San Francisco.

Ryan, B. and Gross, N. (1943) The diffusion of hybrid seed corn in two Iowa communities. *Rural Sociology* **8**: 15–24.

Salazar, R. (1992) Community plant genetic resources management: experiences in Southeast Asia. In: Cooper, D., Vellvé, R. and Hobbelink, H. (eds) *Growing Diversity. Genetic Resources and Local Food Security*. IT Publications, London, pp. 17–29.

Scheidegger, U., Prain, G., Ezeta, F. and Vittorelli, C. (1989) *Linking Formal R&D to Indigenous Systems: A User Oriented Potato Seed Programme for Peru*. Agricultural Administration (Research and Extension) Network Paper 10. Overseas Development Institute, London.

Schippers, R. (1997) Domestication of indigenous vegetables for sub-Saharan Africa: a strategy paper. In: Schippers, R. and Budd, L. (eds) *Workshop on African Indigenous Vegetables*, Limbe, Cameroon, January 13–18 1997. IPGRI, Rome/NRI, Chatham, UK, pp. 125–135.

Schmidt, G.W. (1995) *In-situ*-Erhaltung pflanzengenetischer Ressourcen im ökologischen Landbau. *Schriften zu Genetischen Ressourcen* **1**: 116–135.

Schneider, J. and Yaku, A. (1996) Conservation for development. The relevance of indigenous rootcrop knowledge in Irian Jaya. In: Prain, G. (ed.) *Into Action Research: Partnership in Asian Rootcrop Research and Development.* UPWARD, Los Baños, Philippines, pp. 3–9.

Schneider, J., Widyastuti, C.A. and Schmiediche, P. (1997) *Preservation of Sweet-potato Biodiversity in Indonesia. Final Report.* Centro Internacional de la Papa – East, South-East Asia, and the Pacific, Bogor, Indonesia.

Scoones, I. and Thompson, J. (1994) Knowledge, power and agriculture – towards a theoretical understanding. In: Scoones, I. and Thompson, J. (eds). *Beyond Farmer First. Rural People's Knowledge, Agricultural Research and Extension Practice.* IT Publications, London, pp. 16–32.

Seeds of Diversity, Heritage Seed Programme. How to save your own vegetables. P.O. Box 36, Station Q, Toronto, Ontario, Canada, M4T 2L7, p. 33.

SEINPA (1994) *La Experiencia del SEINPA: Presente y Futuro de las Semillas de Papa en el Perú.* Proyecto de apoyo a la producción de semilla e investigación para mejorar la productividad de la papa en el Perú (SEINPA), Lima, Peru.

Silva, B.M. and Santos, J.M. (1998) O melhoramento ao alcance dos agricultores. In: Soares, A.C., Machado, A.T., Silva, J.M. and von der Weid, J.M. (eds) *Milho Crioulo. Conservaço uso da Biodiversidade.* AS–PTA, Rio de Janeiro, pp. 63–67.

Simmonds, N.W. (1993) Introgression and incorporation. Strategies for the use of crop genetic resources. *Biology Review* **68**: 539–562.

Sinclair, T.R. (1998) Historical changes in harvest index and crop nitrogen accumulation. *Crop Science* **38**, 638–43.

Smale, M. and Bellon, M.R. (1999) A conceptual framework for valuing on-farm genetic resources. In: Wood, D. and Lenné, J.M. (eds) *Agrobiodiversity: Characterization, Utilization and Management.* CABI Publishing, Wallingford, UK.

Smale, M., Heisey, P.W. and Leathers, H.D. (1995) Maize of the ancestors and modern varieties: the microeconomics of high-yielding variety adoption in Malawi. *Economic Development and Cultural Change* **43**: 351–368.

Smith, M.E. and Gómez, F. (1996) *Farmer Participation in Maize Breeding. Annual Report.* Cornell International Institute for Food, Agriculture and Development (CIIFAD), Cornell, Ithaca, NY.

Softing, G.B., Hindar, K., Walloe, L., Wijkman, A. and Benneh, G. (eds) (1998) *The Brundtland Commission's Report – 10 Years.* International Research Conference, Oslo, 3–4 October 1997. Division for Environment and Development, Research Council of Norway, Oslo.

Song, Y. (1998) New seed in old China. Impact of CIMMYT's collaborative programme on maize breeding in south-western China. PhD thesis, Wageningen Agricultural University, Wageningen, The Netherlands.

Sperling, L. (1996) Results, methods and institutional issues in participatory selection: the case of beans in Rwanda. In: Eyzaguirre, P. and Iwanaga, M. (eds) *Participatory Plant Breeding*, Proceedings of a Workshop on Participatory Plant Breeding, 26–29 July 1995, Wageningen, The Netherlands. IDRC/FAO/CGN/IPGRI, Rome, pp. 44–56.

Sperling, L. and Loevinsohn, M.E. (eds) (1996) *Using Diversity. Enhancing and Maintaining Genetic Resources On-Farm.* Proceedings of a workshop, 19–21 June 1996, New Delhi, India. IDRC, New Delhi.

Sperling L., Loevinsohn, M.E. and Ntabomvura, B. (1993) Rethinking the farmer's role in plant breeding: local bean experts and on-station selection in Rwanda. *Experimental Agriculture* **29**: 509–519.

Sperling, L., Scheidegger, U. and Buruchara, R. (1996) *Designing Seed Systems with Small Farmers: Principles derived from Bean Research in the Great Lakes Region in Africa.* Agricultural Administration (Research and Extension) Network Paper 60. Overseas Development Institute, London.

Stemler, A.B.L., Harlan, J.R. and de Wet, J.M.J. (1977) The sorghums of Ethiopia. *Economic Botany* **31**: 446–460.

Sthapit, B.R. (1991) Screening for cold tolerance in Nepal. *International Rice Research Newsletter* **16**: 12.

Sthapit, B.R. (1992) Chilling injury of rice crop in Nepal: a review. *Journal of the Institute of Agricultural and Animal Science* **13**: 1–32.

Sthapit, B.R, Pradhanang, P.M. and Witcombe, J.R. (1995) Inheritance and selection of field resistance to sheath brown rot disease in rice. *Plant Disease* **79**: 1140–1144.

Sthapit, B.R., Joshi, K.D. and Witcombe, J.R. (1996) Farmer participatory crop improvement. III. Farmer participatory plant breeding in Nepal. *Experimental Agriculture* **32**: 479–496.

Subedi, K.D., Sthapit, B.R., Joshi, K.D., Floyd, C.N., Pandey, R.R. and Rana, R.B. (1992) Indigenous *ghaiya* (upland rice) culture in the western hills of Nepal: contribution of farmers' knowledge in rainfed farming. In: *Proceedings of the International Symposium and Second National Meeting on Sustainable Agriculture: Importance and Contribution of Traditional Agriculture*. CEICADAR, Mexico, pp. 52–58.

Swaminathan, M.S. (1997) *Gender Dimensions in Biodiversity Management*. Report for FAO Regional Office for Asia and the Pacific, Bangkok, Thailand.

Tanksley, S.D. and McCouch, S.R. (1997) Seed banks and molecular maps: unlocking genetic potential from the wild. *Science* **277**: 1063–1066.

Teekens, K. (1997) *Farmers' Knowledge in Seed Selection. A Case Study in Ade Ahferon and Hahaile, Trigre, Ethiopia*. Larenstein International Agricultural College, Deventer, The Netherlands, pp. 27–30.

Teshome, A., Baum, B.R., Fahrig, L., Torrance, J.K., Arnason, J.T. and Lambert, J.D. (1997) Sorghum [*Sorghum bicolor* (L.) Moench.] landrace variation and classification in North Shewa and South Welo, Ethiopia. *Euphytica* **97**: 255–263.

Thiele, G. (1999) Informal seed systems in the Andes: why are they important and what should we do with them? *World Development* **27**: 83–99.

Thiele, G., Gardner, G., Torrez, R. and Gabriel, J. (1997) Farmer involvement in selecting new varieties: potatoes in Bolivia. *Experimental Agriculture* **33**: 1–16.

Thrupp, L.A. (ed.) (1996) *New Partnerships for Sustainable Agriculture*. World Resources Institute, Washington, D.C.

Thrupp, L.A. (1998) *Cultivating Diversity. Agrobiodiversity and Food Security*. World Resources Institute, Washington, D.C.

Tripp, R. (1996) Biodiversity and modern crop varieties: sharpening the debate. *Agriculture and Human Values* **13**: 48–63.

Tripp, R. (1997) *New Seed and Old Laws: Regulatory Reform and the Diversification of National Seed Systems*. Intermediate Technology Publications, London.

Troyer, A.F. (1996) Breeding widely adapted, popular maize hybrids. *Euphytica* **92**: 163–174.

Valdivia, R., Choquehuanca, V., Reinoso, J. and Holle, M. (1998) Identification of the dynamics of biodiversity in microcentres of Andean tubers in the Circumlacustrine Highlands, Puno, Peru. In: Jarvis, D.I. and Hodgkin, T. (eds) (1998) *Strengthening the Scientific Basis of* In Situ *Conservation of Agricultural Biodiversity On-Farm*. Proceedings of a workshop to develop tools and procedures for *in situ* conservation on-farm, 25–29 August 1997, Rome. International Plant Genetic Resources Institute, Rome, p. 19.

van Beuningen, L.T and Busch, R.H. (1997a) Genetic diversity among North American spring wheat cultivars: I. Analysis of the coefficient of parentage matrix. *Crop Science* **37**: 570–579.

van Beuningen, L.T and Busch, R.H. (1997b) Genetic diversity among North American spring wheat cultivars: II. Ancestor contributions to gene pools of different eras and regions. *Crop Science* **37**: 580–85.

van der Ploeg, J. (1994) Animal production as a socio-economic system: hetero-geneity, producers and perspectives. In: Huisman, E.A. *et al.* (eds) *Biological Basis of Sustainable Animal Production.* Publication No. 67. European Associa-tion for Animal Production, Wageningen, The Netherlands, pp. 29–37.

van der Ploeg, J.D. and Ettema, M. (1990) *Between Quality and Bulk, Agricultural Food Production and Health.* Van Gorcum, Assen, The Netherlands (in Dutch).

van der Ploeg, J.D. and van Dijk, G. (1995) *Beyond Modernisation, the Impact of Endogenous Rural Development.* Van Gorcum, Assen, The Netherlands.

van Putten, J. (1995) Eenvoudig maar voedzaam, cultuurgescheidenis van de dage-lijke maaltijd. SUN, Nijmegen, The Netherlands.

Vavilov, N.I. (1951) *The Origin, Variation, Immunity and Breeding of Cultivated Plants.* Roland Press, New York, USA.

Virk, D.S., Packwood, A.J. and Witcombe, J.R. (1996) *Varietal Testing, Popularisa-tion and Research and Management.* Centre for Arid Zone Studies, Bangor, UK.

Walters, C. and Engels, J.M.M. (1998) The effects of storing seeds under extremely dry conditions. *Seed Science Research* **8** (suppl): 3–8.

Weltzien R.E., Whitaker, M.L. and Anders, M.M. (1996) Farmer participation in pearl millet breeding for marginal environments. In: Eyzaguirre, P. and Iwanaga, M. (eds) *Participatory Plant Breeding*, Proceedings of a Workshop on Participa-tory Plant Breeding, 26–29 July 1995, Wageningen, The Netherlands. IDRC/FAO/CGN/IPGRI, Rome, pp. 128–143.

Weltzien R.E.,Whitaker, M.L., Rattunde, H.F.W., Dhamotharan, M. and Anders, M.M. (1998) Participatory Approaches in Pearl Millet Breeding. In: Witcombe, J.R., Virk, D.S. and Farrington, J. (eds) *Seeds of Choice. Making the Most of New Varieties for Small Farmers.* Oxford/IBH Publishing, New Delhi, pp. 143–170.

Wierema, H., Almekinders, C., Keune, L. and Vermeer, R. (1993) La Producción Campesina en Centroamérica: los Systemas Locales de Semilla. IVO, Tilburg, The Netherlands.

Wilkes, H.G. (1987) Plant genetic resources: why privatize a public good? *Bioscience* **37**: 215.

Wiskerke, J.S.C. (1995) Arable farmers: a new interpretation of sustainable baking wheat cultivation. In: Van der Ploeg, J.D. and Van Dijk, G. (eds) *Beyond Mod-ernization: The Impact of Endogenous Rural Development.* Van Gorcum, Assen, The Netherlands, pp. 233–255.

Wiskerke, J.S.C. (1997) *Zeeuwse akkerbouw tussen verandering en continuïteit: een sociologische studie naar diversiteit in landbouwbeoefening, technologieontwikkel-ing en plattelandsvernieuwing.* Circle for Rural European Studies, Wageningen, The Netherlands.

Witcombe, J.R. (1999) Do farmer-participatory methods apply more to high poten-tial areas than marginal ones? *Outlook on Agriculture* **29**: 57–59.

Witcombe, J.R. and Joshi, A. (1996a) The impact of farmer participatory research on biodiversity of crops. In: Sperling, L. and Loevinsohn, M. (eds) *Using Diver-sity. Enhancing and Maintaining Genetic Resources On-Farm.* Proceedings of a workshop, 19–21 June 1996, New Delhi, India. IDRC, New Delhi, pp. 87–101.

Witcombe, J. and Joshi, A. (1996b) Farmer participatory approaches for varietal breeding and selection and linkages to the formal seed sector. In: Eyzaguirre, P. and Iwanaga, M. (eds) *Participatory Plant Breeding*, Proceedings of a Workshop on Participatory Plant Breeding, 26–29 July 1995, Wageningen, The Netherlands. IDRC/FAO/CGN/IPGRI, Rome, pp. 57–65.

Witcombe, J.R., Joshi, A., Joshi, K.D. and Sthapit, B.R. (1996) Farmer participa-tory crop improvement. I: Varietal selection and breeding methods and their impact on biodiversity. *Experimental Agriculture* **32**: 445–460.

Witcombe, J.R., Virk, D.S. and Farrington, J. (1998) *Seeds of Choice. Making the Most of New Varieties for Small Farmers.* Oxford/IBH Publishing, New Delhi/London.

Witcombe, J.R., Petre, R., Jones, S. and Joshi, A. (1999) Farmer participatory crop improvement. IV: The spread and impact of a rice variety identified by participatory varietal selection. *Experimental Agriculture*, p. 471–87.

Wood, D. (1996) The benign effects of some agricultural specialization on the environment. *Economic Economics* **19**: 107–111.

Wood, D. (1998) Ecological principles in agriculture. *Food Policy* **23**, 371–381.

Wood, D. and Lenné, J. (1997) The conservation of agrobiodiversity on-farm: questioning the emerging paradigm. *Biodiversity & Conservation* **6**: 109–129.

Worede, M. (1997) Ethiopian *in situ* conservation. In: Maxted, N., Ford-Lloyd, B.V. and Hawkes, J.G. (eds) *Plant Genetic Conservation. The* in situ *Approach*. Chapman & Hall, London, pp. 290–301.

Worede, M. and Mekbib, H. (1993) Linking genetic resource conservation to farmers in Ethiopia. In: de Boef, W., Amanor, K., Wellard, K. and Bebbington, A. (eds) *Cultivating Knowledge. Genetic Diversity, Farmer Experimentation and Crop Research*. Intermediate Technology Publications, London, pp. 78–84.

Yadav, O.P. and Weltzien R.E. (1998) *New Pearl Millet Populations for Western Rajasthan*. Integrated Systems Project Report No. 10. ICRISAT, Patancheru, India.

Yuliantiningsih, C. (1995) Peranan tenaga kerja wanita dalam kegiatan usahatani ubi jalar dan penyebaran berbagai jenis ubi jalar di desa Waga-Waga Kecamatan Kurulu dan desa Woogi Kecamatan Assologoima Kabupatan Jayawijaya. (The role of female labour in sweet potato cultivation and in the diffusion of sweet potato cultivars in the villages of Waga-Waga, Kurulu District, and Woogi, Assologoima District, Jayawijaya Regency). MSc. Thesis. Agricultural Faculty. Manokwari, Irian Jaya, Cenderawasih University.

Zimmerer, K. (1991a) Labour shortages and crop diversity in the Southern Peruvian Sierra. *Geographical Review* **81**: 414–432.

Zimmerer, K.S. (1991b) The regional biogeography of native potato cultivars in highland Peru. *Journal of Biogeography* **18**: 165–178.